A CRITICAL HISTORY

OF THE

DOCTRINE OF A FUTURE LIFE

OTHER WORKS BY THE SAME AUTHOR.

THE APOCALYPSE OF BARUCH.—Translated from the Syriac: Chapters I.-LXXVII. from the Sixth Century MS. in the Ambrosian Library of Milan, and Chapters LXXVIII.-LXXXVII.—**THE EPISTLE OF BARUCH.**—From a New and Critical Text based on Ten MSS. and published herewith. Edited, with Introduction, Notes, and Indices. 7s. 6d. net.

THE ASSUMPTION OF MOSES.—Translated from the Latin Sixth Century MS., the unemended Text of which is published herewith, together with the Text in its restored and critically emended form. Edited, with Introduction, Notes, and Indices. 7s. 6d.

LONDON: A. & C. BLACK.

THE BOOK OF ENOCH.—Translated from Dillmann's Ethiopic Text (emended and revised in accordance with hitherto uncollated Ethiopic MSS. and with the Gizeh and other Greek and Latin Fragments), with Introduction, Notes, and Indices. 8vo, 16s.

THE ETHIOPIC VERSION OF THE HEBREW BOOK OF JUBILEES.—Edited from Four MSS. and critically revised, emended, and restored in accordance with the Hebrew, Syriac, Greek, and Latin Fragments of this Book. 4to, 12s. 6d.

THE BOOK OF THE SECRETS OF ENOCH.—Translated from the Slavonic by W. R. MORFILL, M.A., and edited, with Introduction, Notes, and Indices, by R. H. CHARLES, M.A. 8vo, 7s. 6d.

OXFORD: THE CLARENDON PRESS.

A Critical History

OF THE

Doctrine of a Future Life

In Israel, in Judaism, and in Christianity

OR

HEBREW, JEWISH, AND CHRISTIAN ESCHATOLOGY FROM PRE-PROPHETIC TIMES TILL THE CLOSE OF THE NEW TESTAMENT CANON

BEING THE JOWETT LECTURES FOR 1898-99

BY

R. H. CHARLES, D.D.
PROFESSOR OF BIBLICAL GREEK, TRINITY COLLEGE, DUBLIN

LONDON
ADAM AND CHARLES BLACK
1899

PREFACE

The present work is the result of studies begun over twelve years ago, and pursued unremittingly for the past ten. This long period of preparation is partly to be explained by the fact that some of the most important books in the history of the development of Jewish eschatology had to be studied afresh and re-edited before their evidence was available for such a work as the present. After a severe and prolonged examination of the Apocalyptic and Apocryphal literature of Judaism, I proceeded to carry my investigations backward into the Old Testament and forward into the New, and in both cases, I hope, with fresh and fruitful results. I am painfully aware, however, of the unsatisfactory treatment of some of the books in the New Testament, such as the Apocalypse, and of the need of a deeper and fuller treatment of the Messianic hope of the Nation in the Old Testament.

It seemed good, however, not to delay publication further, and accordingly I gladly accepted the invitation of the Jowett Committee to give a course of lectures on the subject of these studies.

Throughout this work I have been obliged repeatedly to abandon the beaten track in dealing with the eschatology both of the Old and of the New Testament. This has been due in part to the method pursued; for it became clear to me many years ago that, in order to apprehend the evidence of a passage dealing with the religious hopes of Israel, it was necessary to study it not only in its textual but also in its historical context.

All scholars with any pretension to thoroughness have already recognised the duty of studying a passage in its textual context; but very few have seen that it is just as necessary to study it in its historical context, that is, in its rightful place in the development of religious thought. Thus two writings may be composed within the same decade: yet one may be reactionary in character, and belong to a bygone period of development, while the other may be spiritual and progressive, and in the van of the religious thought of the time. In such cases it is the part of the historian to allow the definitive passages in both writings their full weight, and not to force them into unnatural conformity by spiritualising some or materialising others.

It is only by such a scientific method of investigation that we can hope to arrive at any valid conclusions on such subjects as Universalism, Conditional Immortality, or Eternal Damnation. Such conclusions are not to be gathered so much from isolated statements in the New Testament books, which may vary in accordance with the spiritual endowments of the writer, as from the consummation to which the eschatological development of the past undoubtedly points, and, above all, from that consummation foreshadowed and implied in the great fundamental truths proclaimed by Christ and variously unfolded in Apostolic teaching.

As in nature, so in religion, God reveals Himself in the course of slow evolution.

A learned book on the same subject as the present work has recently been published by Principal Salmond. Since, however, our method and treatment have taken different lines, I have refrained throughout from referring to the work of this well-known scholar.

In order to make this book easy to consult, I have provided it with an elaborate index. This index consists of an alphabetical list of names and subjects: but it is more; for under each subject-heading an analytical treatment is attempted, from which the reader can gather the historical development of the particular conception through the course of nearly a thousand years.

Finally, I wish to express my thanks to Messrs. A. & C. Black, the publishers of the *Encyclopædia Biblica*, and to its editors, Drs. Cheyne and Black, for permitting me to use my article on Eschatology in that work as the basis of the present work.

I would also gratefully acknowledge the many helpful suggestions which I owe to Dr. Cheyne, as well as Dr. Black's revision of the proofs, notwithstanding the multitudinous claims on his time and energies.

17 BRADMORE ROAD, OXFORD,
September 1899.

CONTENTS

CHAPTER VII

CHAPTER VIII

CHAPTER IX

CHAPTER X

CHAPTER XI

CHAPTER I

ESCHATOLOGY OF THE INDIVIDUAL IN THE OLD TESTAMENT PRIOR TO THE ORIGIN OF THE BELIEF IN IMMORTALITY.

Scope of this work.

THE purpose of this work is to deal with Hebrew, Jewish, and Christian eschatology, or the teaching of the Old Testament, of Judaism, and of the New Testament on the final condition of man and of the world. It is but too generally assumed that we are already fully acquainted with this subject; but such an assumption is by no means justified. We have yet much to learn, and the work of patient research is still far from fruitless in this field.

So far as this work bears on Old Testament eschatology, the writer is under infinite obligations to Old Testament scholars,[1] but notwithstanding the fulness of their labours, he has not unfrequently been compelled in the special subject of these lectures to take new departures and pursue paths

[1] Particularly to Cheyne, Stade, Robertson Smith, Schwally, Smend, Nowack, and a host of others.

CHAP. I.

of his own. The necessity for such new departures, alike in the Old Testament and the New Testament, arose in connection with his attempt to grasp the whole course of eschatological development from the time of Moses to the close of the New Testament. The nature of such new departures will appear in the sequel.

Doctrine of the conception of God must to some extent be studied concurrently with Hebrew eschatology.

From the period of Moses, the religious and political founder of Israel, to the time of Christ, we can with some degree of certainty determine the religious views of that nation on the after-world. But the facts are often so isolated, the sources so often defective and reset in later environments, that, if we confine our attention to ideas of the after-life alone, it is possible to give only a disjointed statement of beliefs and expectations with large lacunæ and unintelligible changes, and lacking that coherence and orderly development without which the mind cannot be satisfied.

Now we find that we can impart some degree of coherence and intelligibleness to the subject by considering the development of the conception of God in Israel. On this conception hinges ultimately every other religious conception of the nation. Obviously, however, only the salient points in this development can be dealt with; but these will be sufficient for our present purpose.

Illustration.

Let me give an illustration of the necessity of treating the conception of God in connection with that of the after-world. How comes it that in the second century B.C. the conception of the after-world is mainly moral and retributive, whereas from the fourth century back to Moses' time it is non-moral, being in fact a piece of pure Semitic heathenism. This change of conception is mainly due to monotheism, which, partially apprehended by the great prophets of the eighth century, and more fully by those of the sixth, was at last carried to its logical results. No part of the Universe created by God, religious men felt and religious men reasoned, could be withdrawn from His influence. Hence in due course the rejection of the heathen Semitic view of Sheol for one that was moral and retributive. Till, however, monotheism was the accepted belief of the nation, this transformation of Sheol was impossible.

Old Testament not to be explained as a natural development.

Before I enter on the subject I may premise that, though I have to deal so to speak with the anatomy of Old Testament religious thought, I do not pretend or hold it possible to explain it as a merely natural development. All true growth in religion, whether in the past or the present, springs from the communion of man with the immediate living God, wherein man learns the will of God, and becomes thereby an organ of God, a personalised conscience, a revealer of divine truth for men less inspired than himself. The truth thus revealed through a man possesses a divine authority for men. In the Old Testament we have a catena of such revelations. At the Exodus God took Israel, Semitic heathens as they were for the most part, and taught them in the measure of their

CHAP. I.

capacity: revealed Himself at the outset to them as their God, the God of their nation, and claimed Israel as His people. He did not then make Himself known as the Creator and Moral Ruler of the world, for in the childhood of Israel's religious history these ideas would have been impossible of comprehension. Yahwè was Israel's God, and Israel was the people of Yahwè. Yahwè was a righteous God, and required righteousness in His people. From this stage the divine education of Israel is carried forward, till in Jeremiah and the Second Isaiah God becomes known to Israel as the Sole Supreme all-loving Creator and God of all mankind.

In the following chapters our investigations will be guided by the results of Old Testament criticism. Since, however, some of these results are still provisional, the same provisional character will attach to some of our conclusions.

The divine name to be pronounced Yahwè, and not Jehovah.

We shall throughout these studies revert to the original pronunciation of the divine name Yahwè. Owing to their dread of misusing this name (Exod. xx. 7; Lev. xxiv. 11) the Jews avoided pronouncing it with its legitimate vowels, and supplied its vocalisation from Adonai; or where this word had appeared immediately before, with the vocalisation of Elohim.

From an ignorance of these facts the false pronunciation Jehovah was introduced through a sixteenth-century scholar, Petrus Galatinus, in his work, *De Arcanis Catholicæ Veritatis*, 1518 (see

Marti, *Gesch. d. Isr. Rel.* p. 60). The true pronunciation is attested by Clement of Alexandria ('Ιαουέ) and Theodoret ('Ιαβέ), not to speak of authorities of an earlier date.

I. Preprophetic Yahwism.

I. *Preprophetic Yahwism.*—We shall make no attempt to trace the various stages through which Yahwism passed before it became monotheistic, but consider it broadly as divided into two periods, namely, (i.) Preprophetic Yahwism, from Moses to the eighth century; and (ii.) Prophetic Yahwism. Our attention will be mainly confined to the former, for the possibility of understanding Early Hebrew eschatology is conditioned by our prior comprehension of the limited scope of preprophetic Yahwism. From whatever source the worship of Yahwè[1] was ultimately derived, it was probably through Moses that Yahwè became the God of Israel, that is, the national God. Now a nation originates not merely through the increase and extension of the tribe, but through the federation of tribes descended from the same or from different ancestors, and worshipping independent tribal gods. Such a federation may arise from a common danger or from common interests. Should the community of interest and action thus established be of lasting duration, a

[1] Full information on the development of Yahwism from different standpoints will be found in Marti, *Geschichte der israelitischen Religion*, 1897; Kuenen, *The Religion of Israel* (translated from the Dutch); Montefiore, *Lectures on the Origin and Growth of Religion*, 1892; König, *Die Hauptprobleme d. altisrael. Religionsgeschichte*, 1884; Smend, *Alttestamentliche Religionsgeschichte*, 1893; Valeton in Chantepie de la Saussaye's *Religionsgeschichte*,[2] i. 242-325, 1897. Davidson, Art. "God" in Hastings' *Bible Dictionary*, ii. 199-205.

CHAP. I.

nation is the result. The incorporation of different tribes into a nation is a sign that the tribal consciousness has vailed to the consciousness of the larger community, and that in this process the tribal gods have been forced into a subordinate relation to the new god of the nation.

This god had often no doubt been the god of the chief tribe in the confederacy. Wellhausen thinks that Yahwè was originally the God of the tribe of Joseph, on the ground that the ark was placed in the territory of Joseph; and that Joshua—the oldest historical name compounded with Yahwè—belonged to the tribe of Joseph. But there are overwhelming difficulties in the way of this theory. Into these, however, it does not concern us to enter here. The origin of Yahwism is still buried in mystery.

Was this divine name known before the time of Moses?

It is a moot question whether God was known under the name of Yahwè before the time of Moses. On the one side it has been argued by Smend (*Alttestamentliche Religionsgesch.* pp. 17, 18) and others that Moses would have appealed in vain to the tribes in Egypt if he had come to them in the name of a hitherto unknown god. This, moreover, was the view of the Yahwist (Gen. iv. 26, "Then began men to call on the name of Yahwè"). On the other hand, in the Elohist in Exod. iii. 11-14, and the Priests' Code in Exod. vi. 2, 3, it is stated that the name Yahwè was first revealed to Moses. The latter passage runs as follows: "And God spake unto Moses, and said unto him: I am Yahwè, and I appeared unto Abraham, unto Isaac, and unto

Jacob as El Shaddai, but by my name Yahwè was I not known unto them." The latter view is strongly supported by the evidence of proper names. Thus the first proper name undoubtedly compounded with Yahwè is that of Joshua.[1] But as this question does not closely affect our subject we may pass on to more important issues, only adding that the higher teaching of Moses must have had points of affinity with pre-existing beliefs within his people or tribe.

Whatever the ultimate derivation of Yahwism may have been, its character in Israel was unique.

Whatever Yahwè may have been conceived in His essential nature,[2] whether as God of the thunderstorm or the like, this question fell early into the background, and all stress was laid upon the nature of His activities within the nation. Hence the character of His religion is therefore not metaphysical and dogmatic, but ethical and experiential. The very name, moreover, being so indefinite in content and free from associations which could limit its development, presented a framework within which the unhampered growth of piety was possible. This fact is of especial importance for the development of monotheism. The ultimate derivation of Yahwism could thus affect only the external form: its true content and character within Israel were unique.

Faith in Yahwè the motive force in the founding of the nation.

Moses, as we have above remarked, was the

1 See Buchanan Gray's *Hebrew Proper Names*, 190, 191, 257, 258. Possibly it appears in *Jochebed*, Exod. vi. 20.

2 On the various derivations of this divine name, see Smend, *Alttestamentliche Religionsgeschichte*, p. 21; Marti, *Geschichte der israelitischen Religion*, pp. 61, 62; Davidson in Hastings' *Bible Dictionary*, ii. 199.

true founder of the nation and of Yahwism. Through his personal communion with God he reanimated an enslaved race that was perishing under Egyptian oppression. His certainty that the living God was his inspirer and stay was the impelling force in his action, and in this certainty he carried with him the bulk of the people. There was, however, no absolute break with the past. The traditions and spiritual limitations that Israel had in the past in common with their Semitic kindred reappear in the early forms of Yahwism. The name Yahwè formed the point of departure, and the mainstay of the religious movement thus initiated, in which Israel became a nation. It was not Israel that had chosen Yahwè to be their God, but Yahwè that had chosen Israel to be His people, and revealed Himself to Moses as the living God. This faith was the motive force in the formation of the nation.

Religion and history of Israel interwoven from the beginning.

As the national God, Yahwè was the invisible Head of the nation. As such, He inspired and controlled its action and shaped its destinies. Thus the religion and history of Israel were interwoven from the beginning, and the unfailing inspirations of the former so influenced the march of the latter that Israel's spiritual development is absolutely unique in the world: for despite frequent halts and retrogressions, its advance was steadily from strength to strength and truth unto truth, till at last it was consummated in the final revelation of the personality of the Christ.

That the first revelation of Yahwè's intervention on behalf of Israel is connected with the deliverance from Egypt is full of significance. His religion is thus characterised from the outset as a religion of redemption: "I am Yahwè thy God, which brought thee out of the land of Egypt, out of the house of bondage" (Exod. xx. 2). Herein Israel found the stay of its faith, the ground of its trust, and pledge of salvation in the dawn of evil days.

Yahwism a religion of redemption.

As the Head of the nation, Yahwè was pre-eminently its Leader in battle and War-god. It is in this character that He mainly appears in the earlier days. His presence was nowhere felt so strongly and really as in the battlefield. He is, as the Hebrew poet declares, "A man of war" (Exod. xv. 3), and His people are called Israel, that is, "soldiers of God."[1] The first altar erected in His name by Moses is named "Yahwè nissi," that is, "Yahwè is my banner" (Exod. xvii. 15). Religious and national enthusiasm were in preprophetic times almost synonymous. Israel's enemies were Yahwè's enemies (1 Sam. xxx. 26); Israel's wars were the wars of Yahwè (Num. xxi. 14; 1 Sam. xviii. 17). He is the God of the armies of Israel (1 Sam. xvii. 26, 36, 45).

Yahwè as the War-god of Israel.

These considerations supply us with the original sense of the divine name "Yahwè of Hosts." That this meant at the outset the Lord of the hosts of Israel is clear from 1 Sam. xvii. 45, where David

Yahwè of Hosts.

[1] So Gesenius, Ewald, Kautzsch. Dillmann and E. Meyer take it to mean "God contends," Buchanan Gray (*op. cit.* 218) "let God contend."

declares that he goes forth to meet Goliath "in the name of Yahwè of Hosts, the God of the armies of Israel." With the later significations[1] of this phrase we have at present no concern.

Ark originally sanctuary of Yahwè the War-god.

The ark was originally regarded in Israel as the actual sanctuary of Yahwè the War-god.[2] As such it was borne into the field and represented Yahwè's presence (1 Sam. iv. 3-11, v. 6; 2 Sam. vi. 1-12). In this connection we can apprehend the significance of the ancient prayers when the ark set forward and when it rested: "Rise up, Yahwè, and let thine enemies be scattered, and let them that hate thee flee before thee": and, "Return, O Yahwè, unto the thousands of the thousands of Israel" (Num. x. 35, 36). But it was not merely that the interests of Israel were Yahwè's interests: the interests of Yahwè were likewise those of Israel. Thus the tribes of Israel mustered to the help of Yahwè (Judg. v. 23): in His honour was the war cry raised, "A sword for Yahwè and for Gideon" (Judg. vii. 18, 20).

Yahwè the God of justice and purity.

But Yahwè was not only the God of war: He was also the God of justice and right. On Israel's

[1] In later times He was conceived not as the God of the hosts of Israel but of all powers, whether human, stellar, or angelic. This later development is due probably to Amos. See p. 86; Marti, *Gesch.* 139-141; Driver on Joel and Amos, 231, 232.

[2] A later view of the ark as the receptacle for the two tables of stone is found in Deut. x. 1-3; Exod. xxv. 10-22. That the ark originally contained *a* stone, *i.e.* a Bethel or "house of God" (Gen. xxviii. 18, xxxv. 14), is generally accepted. This fact would point to the ark as a constituent of Semitic heathenism before its adoption into the service of Yahwism. In any case the ark lost its significance on the advent of monotheism. See Benzinger, *Hebräische Archäologie*, 367-370; Marti, *Gesch.* 67-69; Nowack, *Hebräische Archäologie*, ii. 3-7.

deliverance from Egypt naturally followed their internal organisation. This was carried out under the name of Yahwè, who was recognised as the central authority of justice. His sanctuary was the depository of law, and the priests were the interpreters of His will. The teaching or torah of the priests had at once a legal and a moral character. In the course of many centuries this teaching came to assume a stereotyped form in the written Law or Pentateuch. But besides being the God of justice, Yahwè was essentially the God of purity. Whilst the worship of other Semitic deities was characterised by various forms of licentiousness, none such was ever connected with the uncorrupted worship of Yahwè. Though conceived as a person, He had no other deity, and particularly no goddess beside or beneath Him. These important ethical elements in Yahwè's character, which required justice and purity in His people, lie at the base of primitive Yahwism, and contain the promise and potency of the later monotheism.

Sovereignty of Yahwè originally conceived as conterminous with His own land and people.

Having now recognised two of the chief characteristics of Yahwè, namely His warlike and His ethical character, in accordance with which He moulded the outer and inner histories of Israel, we have next to touch on the views held by Israel regarding the gods of the neighbouring nations, which were in some degree applicable also to Yahwè. In these preprophetic times the actual existence of such independent deities outside Israel

CHAP. I.

was fully acknowledged. Each nation had its own god. Milcom was the god of Ammon, Ashtoreth of the Zidonians, and Chemosh of Moab (Num. xxi. 29; 1 Kings xi. 33; Jer. xlviii. 46). According to the beliefs of the time, it was these gods that had given their respective peoples their territories, just as Yahwè had given Canaan to Israel. Thus in Judg. xi. 24 Jephthah sends the following message to the Ammonites[1]: "Wilt not thou possess that which Chemosh thy god giveth thee to possess? So whomsoever Yahwè our God hath dispossessed before us, them will we possess." Not only was the power of the national deity conceived to be paramount within his own land, but all who were resident in his country were regarded as in duty bound to worship him. Thus David complains to Saul that he had been driven forth from his own land and forced to forsake the worship of Yahwè for the service of other gods (1 Sam. xxvi. 19): "If it be Yahwè that hath stirred thee up against me, let him accept an offering; but if it be the children of men, cursed be they before Yahwè; for they have driven me out this day, that I should have no share in the inheritance of Yahwè, saying, Go serve other gods." Thus the sovereignty and interest of the national deities were popularly held to be conterminous with the bounds of their own lands.

[1] There is clearly a mistake in the text here; for Milcom and not Chemosh was the god of the Ammonites: see 1 Kings xi. 7, 33; 2 Kings xxiii. 13; Jer. xlviii. 7, 13, 46; Num. xxi. 29, and the Mesha Inscription, where Chemosh is always spoken of as the god of Moab.

Again, just as Israel explained its national reverses through the anger of Yahwè with His people, so likewise did Moab, as we learn from the Moabite Stone; for there the subjection of Moab to Israel is represented as due to the wrath of Chemosh with his people. When, however, this wrath was appeased, Chemosh restored to Moab its lost provinces through the agency of Mesha. The Moabites no doubt regarded the might of their god as superior to that of Yahwè.[1]

Certain unethical traits in the early conceptions of Yahwè.

We shall point out two further analogies between Yahwè and the neighbouring Semitic deities. The first of these is that certain unethical and unintelligible moods appear in Yahwè just as we might expect in a national god; for the national god is a personification of the genius of a people, the embodiment of its virtues and its vices on an heroic scale. Thus the anger of Yahwè is at times unintelligible. It was, for example, kindled against Uzzah to his destruction when he stepped forward to prevent the ark from falling at the threshing-floor of Nacon (2 Sam. vi. 6, 7), and likewise against the men of Beth Shemesh for gazing too curiously upon it (1 Sam. vi. 19). David can imagine that Saul's undeserved enmity may be due to the motiveless incitement of Yahwè (1 Sam. xxvi. 19), and the early historian in 2 Sam. xxiv. 1 finds no difficulty in attributing to Him an apparently unreasonable wrath; for he represents Yahwè as causing David

[1] See the description of the Moabite Stone in Driver's *Notes on the Hebrew Text of the Books of Samuel*, pp. lxxxv.-xciv.

CHAP. I.

to number the people, and then as punishing the people for the sin which He had prompted. It is noteworthy that when the chronicler some centuries later was recounting the same event he assigns this action not to Yahwè but to Satan (1 Chron. xxi. 1): "And Satan stood up against Israel, and moved David to number Israel." Thus the anger of Yahwè in preprophetic times was not necessarily conceived as due to sin in Israel: it might spring from other causes. But this imperfect conception of the divine wrath is not recognised by the prophets. To them Yahwè's wrath is never unaccountable; for it is always ethically conditional and kindled by the sin of the nation.

Interests of Yahwè and of Israel originally identified.

The next analogy between the conception of Yahwè and that of the gods of the heathen nations is that as a national god His interests were absolutely identified with those of His nation. Though He might become temporally estranged, He could never forsake His people. To imagine such a possibility would have been the act not merely of a blasphemer but of a madman. This was the *popular* view in Israel in the eighth century, and even later.

Accordingly, the reverses that Israel sustained at the hands of the neighbouring nations were to the unthinking masses so many proofs that Yahwè had temporarily forsaken His land, but to the prophetic vision they were the discipline wherewith Yahwè was educating His people. In the case of a purely heathen religion outward disasters involved the people and their god in the same humiliation, and ultimately in the same destruction, but in the very catastrophes that proved fatal to the gods of the heathen Yahwè vindicated His true sovereignty over the earth.

These limitations and defects are heathen survivals in the domain of Yahwism, and as such were attacked and destroyed by the prophets.

We have now considered the chief defects that clung to the conception of Yahwè in preprophetic times. These shortcomings mark nearly all the period when Israel was passing from a monolatrous to a true monotheistic belief. They are clearly to be regarded as heathen survivals in the domain of Yahwism, that is, in the people's conception of Yahwè. They form the ground of Yahwè's great controversy with Israel. In this controversy Yahwè manifests in ever clearer form His will and purpose, which are directed to the spiritual enfranchisement of His people. While the heathen gods always remained on the same moral level as their worshippers, and so were powerless to deepen and develop character, it was otherwise in Israel. To serve Yahwè aright involved spiritual effort and personal sacrifice, and consequently led to growth in righteousness.

Essential superiority of Yahwism consisted in the righteous character of Yahwè.

The people had hardly attained a certain religious level when the messengers of Yahwè urged them on to loftier heights in life and thought than their present achievement. Thus one by one the false views attaching to Yahwè in Israel were in the course of its divine education expelled. Hence we conclude that the essential superiority of Yahwism to the neighbouring Semitic religions lay not in its moral code, in which indeed it was unquestionably

CHAP. I.

superior, but in the righteous character of Yahwè which was progressively revealed to His servants.

We have now touched on some of the leading characteristics of Yahwism in its first stage, when it was monolatrous, that is, claimed to be the true religion of Israel: "Thou shalt have none other gods but Me." We have now to touch briefly on the next stage, when it is monotheistic, and its teaching then is: "There are no other Gods but Me."

II. Monotheistic Yahwism, from 800 B.C. onwards.

II. *Monotheistic Period of Yahwism.* — This development appears as already achieved in the eighth- and seventh-century prophets. These prophets were not founders of religion, but reformers in a true sense. For true reform, whilst returning to earlier beliefs, is yet also progressive. Thus the prophets went back to the old essentially Mosaic thought, that the bond existing between Yahwè and Israel had been the result of a free act of the former, attested by their deliverance from Egypt. Through Canaanitish influence, however, this bond had come to be regarded popularly by Israel as a *natural* one in accordance with which the god and his people mutually possessed each other, and could not exist in isolation. But the prophets teach that Israel's relation to Yahwè is *ethically* conditioned. Israel had been chosen in order to carry out the moral purposes of Yahwè. If Israel is faithless therein, its nearness to Yahwè must entail a proportionately severer punishment. Should their disobedience prove irremediable, then Yahwè must destroy the nation, for righteousness is the measure of all

Israel's relation to Yahwè ethically conditioned.

things, and even the world-empires subserve its decrees. As Yahwè's agent, Assyria will destroy Israel.

Although the preachers of the destruction of the nation of Israel, the prophets became the saviours of its religion. Through their living communion with God, they made it known, in terms that could never be forgotten, that Yahwè pursued His own righteous purposes independently of Israel. Thus it was that Yahwism did not perish with the nation, and that true religion survived the destruction of the state. In the religion thus enfranchised from national limitations, the individual becomes the religious unit, and is brought into immediate communion with God. Thus the way is prepared for the coming of Christianity.

Individualisation of religion by the prophets.

From the period of the Exile onwards there are two parallel developments of monotheism. In the truer and nobler development, as it appears in Jeremiah and his spiritual successors, monotheism is a living doctrine which shapes the teachings of its adherents on the religious duties and destinies not only of Israel but also of the nations. In the parallel development initiated by Ezekiel, monotheism is a living and fruitful doctrine for Israel, but not for the nations. From the legitimate scope of its blessings they are absolutely excluded. So far as they are concerned, it has become a lifeless dogma. Such a false conception of Yahwè's relation to the nations in due time reacted on Judaistic monotheism, and explains in large measure its subsequent barrenness.

Parallel but inconsistent developments of monotheism from the Exile onwards.

In studying a great religion the inquirer seeks

CHAP. I.

In universal religions an organic connection should exist between their theology and their eschatology.

naturally to trace an organic connection between its central conceptions and the most remote portions of its system. He expects to find a certain degree of logical coherence existing between all its parts. And in his expectations he is not disappointed when dealing with such religions as Christianity, Mohammedanism, or Buddhism, for in these the eschatology, or the teaching on the final condition of man and of the world, follows in the main from the fundamental doctrines of these religions. But the student must not approach the early religion of Israel with such an expectation; for though an organic connection exists between its theology and the eschatalogy of *the nation as a whole*, this connection does not extend to the eschatology of *the individual Israelite*. The eschatology of the individual in early Israel is not only wholly independent of Yahwism, but it actually stands in implicit antagonism to it, an antagonism which becomes explicit and irreconcilable in the subsequent developments of Yahwism, and which results in the final triumph of the latter. At the close of this conflict Yahwism will be found to have developed an eschatology of the individual more or less consistent with its own essential conceptions. Thus it is only in respect of the nation that Yahwism can be said to have possessed a definite eschatology till long after the return from Exile.

This connection holds with regard to the eschatology of the nation, but not of the individual in Israel.

Yahwism had no eschatology till after the Exile.

The explanation of this defect.

The explanation of this defect in the early religion of Israel is not far to seek. The sphere of that religion was, like the sway of Yahwè, confined, as we have found above, to this world, and indeed to a small portion of it. The dominion of Yahwè being so circumscribed had no concern whatever with any future existence of man, and hence it possessed no eschatology of the individual. Accordingly we must look elsewhere for that eschatology.

Old Testament eschatology of the individual and of the nation, and their ultimate synthesis.

We shall deal with Old Testament eschatology under three heads—(i.) The eschatology of the individual; (ii.) The eschatology of the nation,[1] *i.e.* Israel; (iii.) The synthesis of these two eschatologies in the fourth century B.C.

Primitive eschatology of the individual in Israel is derived from heathen sources, *i.e.* from Ancestor Worship.

Eschatology of the Individual.—The ideas that prevailed in pre-Mosaic times regarding the future life, and that were indeed current in some degree down to the second century B.C., were in many respects common to Israel and other Semitic nations. These were naturally not the outcome of revelation, but were mere survivals of Semitic heathenism. According to Stade, Schwally, and other scholars, they belong to what is known as Ancestor Worship. Prior to the legislation of Moses this phase of religion dominated to a great degree the life of the Israelite. But Yahwism from the first was implicitly engaged with it in irreconcilable strife. For several centuries, however, many of the tenets and usages of this worship were left unaffected by Yahwism; for, as we have already seen, early Yahwism had no eschatology of the individual, and concerned

[1] As Israel in the course of history necessarily enters into relations with Gentile powers, the final destinies of the latter are naturally dealt with by the prophetic writers.

CHAP. I.

itself only with the existence of the nation. Thus the individual was left to his hereditary heathen beliefs, and these can be best interpreted as part and parcel of Ancestor Worship.[1]

Ancestor Worship.

According to this belief the dead were not regarded as dead, but as in a certain sense living and sharing in all the vicissitudes of their posterity, and as possessing superhuman powers to benefit or injure. With a view to propitiate these powers the living offered sacrifices. By these sacrifices the vitality of the dead was preserved, and their honour in the next world upheld. A man made sacrifices naturally to his own ancestors:[2] the departed ancestors and their living descendants formed one family. We shall now give some of the evidence for the existence of such beliefs in Israel, under the three following heads—I. The ancestors or their images, the household gods, namely the teraphim, were honoured with sacrifices, and the right of offering these sacrifices was restricted to a son of the departed. II. The primitive mourning usages in Israel are part and parcel of Ancestor Worship.

Evidence for existence of Ancestor Worship in Israel.

[1] Cf. Schwally, *Das Leben nach dem Tode*, chap. i. "Der alte Glaube," pp. 5-74, and Stade, *Gesch.* i. 387-427, to whom the present writer is immeasurably indebted on this subject; also Marti, *Gesch. der israel. Religion*, 22-26, 40-43, 47-49, 193; Budde on Judg. xi. 37, xvii. 5; Holzinger on Gen. xxxi., xxxv. 8-14, xxxvii. 29-34, xxxviii. 30, and appendix on p. 269; Wildeboer on Eccl. xii. 7; Nowack on Hos. iii. 4. This view has been recently attacked by Frey, *Tod, Seelenglaube und Seelenkult im alten Israel*, 1898, but on the whole unsuccessfully. His contention is that, whereas a *Seelenglaube* existed in Israel, it is not true that this *Seelenglaube* was ever developed into a *Seelencult*. Davidson, Hastings' *B.D.* ii. 200, 201, is disinclined to accept the view in the text.

[2] Sacrifices could be offered to departed heroes of the nation, with a view to gain their counsel and advice, as in the case of Saul and Samuel. This was customary also in the Babylonian and Greek religions.

III. The beliefs regarding the departed are essential constituents of the same cult.

I. Our first thesis, that the ancestors or their images, the teraphim, were honoured with sacrifices performed by a son of the departed, can best be treated under the following heads—(i.) The teraphim or images of the ancestors were the object of family worship; (ii.) To these certain sacrifices were offered; (iii.) The right of offering such sacrifices was limited to a son of the departed, that is, a son of his own body begotten or adopted; (iv.) But since a man might die without male offspring of his own or adopted, the necessities of Ancestor Worship gave birth to the levirate law, in accordance with which it became the duty of a surviving brother to marry the childless widow of the deceased in order to raise up a male offspring to his brother for the performance of the sacrificial usages due to his deceased brother; (v.) The family formed a sacramentally united corporation.

Teraphim, or household gods, probably images of the ancestors,

(i.) First, then, as to the teraphim. The teraphim mentioned in Gen. xxxv. 4 were clearly gods.[1] Their sacred character is recognised by their burial under a sacred tree, the terebinth. They could be buried but not profaned, else such profanation might provoke the powers they represented. In the above passage they are called "strange gods," and their

[1] Stade (*Gesch.* i. 467) and Schwally's (*Leben nach dem Tode*, 35 *sqq.*) contention that these teraphim are images of departed ancestors is practically accepted by Budde on Judg. xvii. 5; Holzinger on Gen. xxxi. 17; Nowack on Hos. iii. 4, and in his *Hebräische Archäologie*, ii. 23; but disputed by Frey, 102-112.

CHAP. I.

worship is regarded as incompatible with that of Yahwè. An earlier mention of these is found in Gen. xxxi. 19, 30-35, where Rachel steals her father's teraphim. Further, they were household gods. Thus from 1 Sam. xix. 13, 16 it follows that they had a human form, and also that they formed part of the usual equipment of a well-to-do family—observe "*the* teraphim." In the next place they are most probably, with Stade and Schwally, to be identified with images of ancestors; for they were consulted as oracles: thus they are enumerated with the 'oboth and yiddeʿonîm in 2 Kings xxiii. 24. In Exod. xxi. 2-6 we have a passage attesting the worship of these gods. According to this section there was a god close to the door in private houses to which the slave who desired enrolment in his master's family had to be brought: "Then his master shall bring him unto the god, and shall bring him to the door and to the doorpost, and his master shall bore his ear through with an awl; and he shall serve him for ever." This was originally admission to the family cult, with all its obligations and privileges. It is quite wrong to take this door to be that of the temple with the older interpreters; for this sacrificial action which made the slave a member of his master's family would have been meaningless unless the door, on which his ear was pierced by the awl, was that of his master's house.[1] As regards the use of the word

[1] So Schwally (37 *sqq.*), who rightly rejects the older view which takes האלהים to mean the judges (so Revised Version in margin). Frey, 104-110, disagrees with both these interpretations, but his own, that הגיש אל־אלהים means no more than to take an oath, seems clearly to be impossible. His words are

"elohim," or god, here, we should remember that the dead when invoked were termed elohim (see 1 Sam. xxviii. 13). In Deut. xv. 12-18 this heathen ceremony is robbed of all its primitive religious significance by the omission of the term "god," and given a wholly secular character. Later these teraphim were regarded as images of Yahwè (cf. Judg. xvii. 5 and xviii. 17 *sqq.*; see also 1 Sam. xix. 13-16); for we can hardly regard it as possible that David, the champion of the religion of Yahwè, would have worshipped the teraphim in their original character as household gods. In Hos. iii. 4 and Zech. x. 2 they may retain their original character as images of ancestors, or, as images of Yahwè, they may have been used like the Ephod in consulting the Deity. They are represented in Ezek. xxi. 26 (ver. 21 in E.V.) as being consulted by Nebuchadnezzar. Thus this cult of household gods (Dillmann, *Alttest. Theologie*, 90, 98) was firmly established in the family of Jacob before it went down into Egypt, and must have been observed by Israel during its entire stay in Egypt, seeing that it flourished among the people after their settlement in Canaan, and prevailed down to the latest period of the Monarchy.

but later regarded as images of Yahwè.

(ii.) *Sacrifices were offered to the dead.*—The object of these sacrifices is clear from Deut. xxvi.

Sacrifices offered to the dead.

(p. 109): "Liegt nichts im Wege, die Bedeutung der Handlung nur in dem Heften des Ohres an den Thürpfosten zu sehen, während das Bringen אל־האלהים, wodurch der Handlung nur ein eidlicher Character aufgeprägt wird, bei Wiederholung dieser Verordnung, weil nicht konstitutives Merkmal, unbeschadet wegfallen konnte." The omission referred to in the concluding words is found in Deut. xv. 12-18.

CHAP. I.

14: "I have not eaten thereof in my mourning, neither have I put away thereof, being unclean, nor given thereof *for the dead*"; Jer. xvi. 7 (?). They are probably implied in Is. viii. 19, xix. 3; for when a man wished to consult the dead, he would naturally present an offering. They are referred to in Ezek. xxiv. 17: "Make no mourning for the dead, bind thy headtire upon thee, and put thy shoes upon thy feet, and cover not thy lips, and eat not the bread of mourning."[1] See also xxiv. 22; 2 Chron. xvi. 14 (see Schwally, 16, 24, 48), xxi. 19. The object of these sacrifices was to give sustenance to the dead and to win their favour.[2] In later times this object was lost sight of, and these sacrifices came to be regarded as mere funeral feasts. But this does not seem to

[1] I have here followed Bertholet and Toy in emending אנשים into אונים. Thus, instead of the senseless "bread of men" we obtain "the bread of mourning" (cf. Hos. ix. 4). This verse refers to four of the mourning usages: uncovering the head in order to strew it with ashes, putting off the shoes, covering the beard, and eating the bread of the offering to the dead (see pp. 28-30).

[2] See Schwally, 21-25; Stade, *Gesch.* i. 389, 390; Nowack, *Arch.* i. 192-198; Wellhausen, *Isr. v. jüd. Gesch.*[3] 100, 101, 1899; Benzinger, *Hebräische Archäologie*, 164-167. Just as in the old Semitic, so in the Greek religion, libations were made to gain the favour of the departed (cf. Euripides, *Or.* 119, 789; *El.* 676-683; *Herc. Fur.* 491-494; Sophocles, *El.* 454. See Rohde, *Psyche*,[2] i. 242, 243; ii. 250). But the value of these is questioned in Eur. *Troad.* 1248-1250, where Hector declares that rich offerings on the grave are of no service to the dead, but only minister to the vanity of the living.

δοκῶ δὲ τοῖς θανοῦσι διαφέρειν βραχύ,
εἰ πλουσίων τις τεύξεται κτερισμάτων·
κενὸν δὲ γαύρωμ' ἐστὶ τῶν ζώντων τόδε.

These lines represent the real view of Euripides. But still more important than these Greek analogies are the similar usages which prevailed in Babylonia. The close affinities existing between the early Hebrew and the Babylonian views of the departed are beyond the reach of questioning (see pp. 23, 24, 34, 39-41). The burial couch was filled with various kinds of spices, which were of the nature of offerings (cf. 2 Chron. xvi. 14). Offerings of food

have come about even in the second century B.C. Sacrifices to the dead appear to be commended in Sir. vii. 33, "From a dead man keep not back grace";[1] Job iv. 17, "Pour out thy bread on the tomb of the just"; but derided in Sir. xxx. 18, 19; Ep. Jer. 31, 32; Wisdom xiv. 15, xix. 3; Or. Sibyl. viii. 382-384. They are referred to in Jubilees xxii. 17 as prevailing among the Gentiles.

Right of offering such sacrifices limited to a son.

(iii.) *The right of offering such sacrifices was limited to a son of the departed.*—Ancestor Worship enables us to explain the importance of male offspring.[2] The honour and wellbeing of the dead depended on the worship and sacrifices offered by their malc descendants. According to this belief, even in the after-life men could be punished by Yahwè through the destruction of their posterity

and water were presented to the departed, not only at the time of burial, but afterwards at certain seasons by their surviving relatives. The comfort of the departed depended on their reception of the proper burial rites and offerings. If they were deprived of the rites of burial, their shades were forced to wander restlessly. Any mutilation of the dead body affected the departed shade. Furthermore, if after burial the body were disinterred, no food could be offered or sacrifice tendered to the shade. In such a case not only the disentombed shade suffered, but also the survivors; for the shade assumed the form of a demon and afflicted the living. The shades, moreover, possessed great power. They could direct the affairs of the living. To gain their favour offerings and prayers were made to them. They were consulted regarding the future. Hence their abode is at times called Shuâlu, or "the place of oracles" (so Jastrow, p. 561, who denies Jeremias' explanation as "the place of decision," p. 559). At times also they are said to dwell in Ekur, where likewise the gods were supposed to dwell. Thus the departed were brought into close association with the gods. Indeed, certain of the dead received the honour of deification. In Israel, it is true, the departed had no association with any gods. They were, however, themselves addressed as gods by those who consulted them (see pp. 23, 40). See Jeremias, *Bab-Assyr. Vorstellungen vom Leben nach dem Tode*, pp. 53-58; Jastrow, *Religion of Babylonia and Assyria*, 511, 512, 568, 582, 598, 599.

[1] ἐπὶ νεκρῷ μὴ ἀποκωλύσῃς χάριν.

[2] Besides Schwally and Stade, see Benzinger, *Arch.* 354 *sqq.*; Nowack, *Arch.* i. 348 *sqq.*

CHAP. I.

(Exod. xx. 5; xxxiv. 7; Num. xiv. 18; Deut. v. 9), for with the destruction of the latter, sacrifices ceased to be made to the former. On the same principle a man destroyed his enemy and all his sons originally with the object of depriving him of respect and worship in the lower world. We have already remarked that sacrifices could be offered only by the son. But as not unfrequently a man might fail to have male offspring, the difficulty was surmounted by adoption. By such adoption a man passed from his own family or clan to that of the father who adopted him, and thereby took upon himself all the obligations attaching to the latter. Even a slave could be so adopted. Thus in Gen. xv. 2, 3 Eliezer is regarded as Abraham's heir in default of male issue. It is to be presumed, with Stade (*Gesch. Isr.* i. 391) and Holzinger (on Gen. xv. 2), that he had already been adopted into the family cult. Thus the right of inheritance is derived in principle from Ancestor Worship.[1] Only the son

[1] The duty of the avenging of blood is to be traced originally to the worship of ancestors. This obligation was in Greek religion limited to a body of relations of three generations (an ἀγχιστεία), who in the male line had the same man for father, grandfather, and great-grandfather. Now this was the very body to whom the right of succession belonged. With succession to an inheritance the obligation of the avenging of blood was at the same time undertaken. In the earliest times the soul of the departed could be appeased only by the blood of the murderer; but subsequently, even before the Homeric era, when the worship of ancestors had retired largely into the background, the custom arose of taking compensation or blood-money. In this case the matter is a transaction wholly between the living, and no account is taken of the dead. In the centuries immediately subsequent to Hesiod, when there was a great revival of the worship of the dead, the nearest relative was obliged to avenge the dead. Being a member of an organised community, he was not allowed to do so with his own hand, but could proceed against the slayer before a court of justice, as the State refused to allow a money ransom. If the relative in question failed in this duty through

or heir could fulfil its rites. Illegitimate sons could not inherit (Stade, *Gesch. Isr.* i. 391), because their mother had not been admitted by marriage into the cult (cf. Judg. xi. 2). In Num. xxxvi. we see that the law regulating inheritance has already undergone a change. Thus a daughter is there allowed to inherit on condition she married a man belonging to the same family or tribe as her father. In Athens, on the other hand, the property descended to the next heir male, but he was obliged to marry the daughter of the deceased. Thus from the above facts it appears that the living and the dead formed one family, and the departed participated in the vicissitudes of their living descendants. Rachel in her grave shared in the troubles of her children in northern Israel (Jer. xxxi. 15, "A voice is heard in Ramah, lamentation and bitter weeping, Rachel weeping for her children: she refuseth to be comforted for her children; because they are not").

Hence is to be explained the levirate law.

(iv.) But the necessity of a son for the performance of Ancestor Worship gave birth, where there was no such offspring, to the *levirate law.*[1]

negligence, the soul of the slain visited with its wrath its faithless avenger: for such a soul had no rest until its wrongs were avenged. This was the general belief at Athens down to the tenth century (see Rohde, *Psyche*, 260 *sqq.*) This stage of ransom was already reached by Israel long before the Monarchy. The legislation of the Priests' Code is directed against this custom of compensation (see Num. xxxv. 31, 32). In Israel the homicide was clearly distinguished from the murderer; but no such distinction existed in Greece in Homeric times; but at a later period, when the community took into its own hands the right of the avenger, this distinction was carefully observed.

[1] This custom (according to Stade, *Gesch. Isr.* i. 394) still prevails among the Indians, Persians, Afghans, Circassians, and Gallas, amongst whom Ancestor Worship exists. See also Schwally, 28 *sqq.*; Marti,[3] 48, 49; Nowack, *Arch.* i. 343 *sqq.*; Benzinger, *Arch.* 134, 136, 345, 346.

CHAP. I.

According to this law, it was the duty of surviving brothers to marry the childless widow of their deceased brother, or where there was no brother, the duty fell on the nearest male relation of the deceased. The firstborn son of such a marriage was registered as the son of the deceased. Thus the deceased was secured the respect and sacrifices due to him. These could be rendered only by a son legitimately begotten or adopted. This law appears to have been in force in Gen. xxxviii. 16, but its significance is forgotten in Deut. xxv. 5-10. Tamar fulfilled according to old Israelitish views a duty of piety towards her dead husband (Stade, i. 394) and similarly Ruth. The daughters of Lot may have had the same end in view.

Family was a sacramentally united corporation.

(v.) The family formed a sacramentally united corporation, within which the above rites were celebrated. The father of the family was its priest. This title was afterwards actually transferred to the priest (Judg. xvii. 10, xviii. 19). Even in historical times the family preserved its special festivals (1 Sam. xx. 29). These undoubtedly point back to the family cult.

II. Mourning usages originally derived from Ancestor Worship.

II. The Primitive Mourning Usages in Israel were Part and Parcel of Ancestor Worship.[1] Such usages had originally a religious significance, and not merely a psychological, as they came subsequently to possess. They indicate reverence for the

[1] Schwally, *Das Leben nach dem Tode*, pp. 9-16; Stade, *Gesch. d. Volks Israel*, i. 387 *sqq.*; Benzinger, *Arch.* 102, 165-167; Nowack, *Arch.* i. 192-198.

dead, and the confession of dependence upon them. Thus (1) the mourner girt himself with sackcloth (2 Sam. iii. 31; 1 Kings xx. 31; Is. iii. 24, xv. 3, xxii. 12; Jer. vi. 26), or laid it on his loins (Gen. xxxvii. 34; Jer. xlviii. 37). This practice expresses submission to a superior. Thus the servants of Benhadad go forth in sackcloth from Aphek to Ahab (1 Kings xx. 31, 32). (2) The mourner put off his shoes (2 Sam. xv. 30; Ezek. xxiv. 17). The removal of the shoes was required in approaching holy places (Exod. iii. 5, 6; Jos. v. 15). This explains its connection with the dead. (3) Mourners cut off their hair (Is. xxii. 12; Jer. vii. 29; Am. viii. 10; Mic. i. 16; Ezek. vii. 18, xxvii. 31) and beards (Jer. xli. 5), or both (Is. xv. 2; Jer. xlviii. 37); and made baldnesses between the eyes (Deut. xiv. 1, 2). The hair so cut off was designed as an offering for the dead (Robertson Smith, *Rel. Sem.*[2] 323-336). These rites are condemned as idolatrous in the latter half of the seventh century in Deut. xiv. 1, 2; for they are forbidden on the ground "for thou art a holy people to the Lord thy God" (cf. Deut. xviii. 11, 12; Lev. xix. 27, 28). Yet these rites are mentioned by the prophets of the eighth century without any consciousness of their impropriety (cf. Am. viii. 10, "I will bring up sackcloth upon all loins, and baldness upon every head"; Mic. i. 16, "Make thee bald, and poll thee for the children of thy delight"; see also Is. xv. 2, xxii. 12). They appear still to have been the universal custom (Jer. xli. 5). At this period their original significance may have largely

CHAP. I.

been forgotten. (4) Mourners made cuttings in their flesh for the dead. Such incisions were regarded as "making an enduring covenant with the dead" (Rob. Smith, *Rel. Sem.* 322, 323). Like incisions were made by the priests of Baal (1 Kings xviii. 28). These rites were forbidden by the Hebrew law in Deut. xiv. 1; Lev. xix. 28, on the same grounds as (3). (5) The covering of the head by the mourner (2 Sam. xv. 30; Esth. vi. 12; Jer. xiv. 3) is probably, with Schwally, to be regarded as a substitute for cutting off the hair, and similarly the covering of the beard for its removal (Ezek. xxiv. 17). This practice on the part of the mourner expresses his reverence for the dead. The same custom was observed by the worshipper in approaching God. Thus Elijah covered his head in the presence of God on Horeb, and such is the universal usage in the synagogue and mosque at the present day.

We have now considered the household gods of Ancient Israel, the sacrifices that were offered to them, that is, to the departed whom they represented, and the restriction of the right of offering such sacrifices to the eldest son, or to the son through a levirate marriage, or the nearest male heir. We have also touched on the mourning usages. All these are essential parts of Ancestor Worship, and for the most part regulate *the conduct of the living* in their approach to the dead. We have now to consider the beliefs that prevailed regarding *the dead themselves*, *i.e.* their place of abode, and the nature

CHAP. I.

Heathen beliefs regarding the dead survive till 70 A.D.

of their existence there. These beliefs regarding the dead are essential constituents of Ancestor Worship no less surely than those we have already considered. They had, moreover, a much more extended lease of life; for, long after the other constituents of this worship had become unintelligible, or sunk into complete desuetude, these still flourished in the high places of Judaism, and claimed the adherence of no small portion of the priesthood down to the destruction of the temple by Titus.

III. Beliefs regarding the dead.

III. Beliefs regarding the Dead.—We shall consider these under the heads of—(i.) *Burial;* (ii.) *The family grave;* (iii.) *Sheol;* (iv.) *The dead, or the inhabitants of Sheol.*

(i.) Burial.

(i.) *Burial* was regarded as indispensable to the comfort of the departed, just as in the religions of Greece and Rome. It was hardly ever withheld in Israel. Criminals who were hanged (Deut. xxi. 22, 23) or stoned (Jos. vii. 24-26), and suicides (Joseph. *Bell. Jud.* III. viii. 5), were accorded burial, and even the most hostile of the national foes of Israel (Ezek. xxxix. 12). One of the most grievous calamities that could befall a man was loss of burial. This is the sentence pronounced on Jezebel (2 Kings ix. 10). It was the fate that awaited the enemies of Yahwè (Jer. xxv. 33[1]). This horror at the thought

[1] Even the materialistic writer of Eccl. vi. 3 regards such a misfortune as outweighing a whole lifetime of material blessings on earth. But the context is against this reference to the loss of burial, and so we must either strike out the entire phrase "and moreover he have no burial," with Hitzig, or else the negative, with Wildeboer.

of being unburied cannot be explained as in the Greek and Roman religions, where it involved the penalty of non-admission to Hades; for according to Hebrew views all without exception descended into Sheol. It may be explained on two grounds: (1) In earlier times no sacrifices could be offered to the dead unless they had received burial. Sacrifices were offered at the grave; for the grave was in some measure the temple in Ancestor Worship. (2) The soul was conceived as connected with the body even after death. Hence every outrage to the dead body was also an outrage to the departed soul. This view appears as late as Job's time (see xiv. 22).

(ii.) The family grave.

(ii.) *The family grave.*—Not burial only but burial in the family grave was the desire of every Israelite. Hence the frequent mention that a man was gathered to his fathers (Gen. xv. 15; Judg. ii. 10), or his people (Gen. xlix. 29-33; Num. xxvii. 13). The object of burial not merely in a grave but in the family grave was clearly to introduce the departed into the society of his ancestors. In the earliest times this society was conceived to exist either in the family grave or in its immediate neighbourhood. Every one wished to be buried with his father and mother (2 Sam. xvii. 23, xix. 38). The deprivation of such a burial was an act of condemnation (1 Kings xiii. 22). Jacob and Joseph direct that their bodies should be carried back to Canaan to be buried in the family grave (Gen. xlvii. 30, l. 25; Exod. xiii. 19). The family grave was originally in the house.[1] Thus Samuel was buried in his own house (1 Sam. xxv. 1), and Joab (1 Kings, ii. 34).[2] But as no family stood in isolation, but was closely united with others, and as those together made up the clan or tribe, and these tribes in due time were consolidated into the nation, a new conception arose. According to this all the graves of the tribe or nation were regarded as united in one; and to this new conception the designation Sheol was given. How early this new conception arose we have no means at present of determining.

(iii.) Sheol.

(iii.) *Sheol.*—We have just seen that in all probability Sheol was originally conceived as a combination of the graves of the clan or nation, and as thus its final abode. In due course this conception was naturally extended till it embraced the departed of all nations, and thus became the final abode of all mankind, good and bad alike. It has already reached this stage in Ezek. xxxii.; Is. xiv.; Job xxx. 23 ("the house appointed for all living"); Eccl. xii. 5 ("his eternal house"). Strictly regarded, the conceptions of the abode of the dead in the grave and in Sheol are mutually exclusive. But being popular notions they do not admit of scientific definition, and their characteristics are

1 The same usage is said to have prevailed in Ancient Greece (see Rohde, *Psyche*,[2] i. 228), and in Babylonia (see Jastrow's *Rel. of Babylon*, 599).

2 Certain kings of Judah (2 Kings xxi. 18, 26) were buried close to the temple. Seeing that graves had originally a sacred character, such sites as human dwellings and the immediate neighbourhood of the temple were natural. But in later times just because of their old association with Ancestor Worship they were declared to be unclean (Ezek. xliii. 7; Num. xix. 16), and were marked with white (cf. Matt. xxiii. 27, τάφοις κεκονιαμένοις) in order to guard wayfarers from impurity through contact with them.

CHAP. I.

treated at times as interchangeable (cf. Is. xiv. 11, "Thy pomp is brought down to Sheol . . . the worm is spread over thee, and the worms cover thee").[1] The family grave, with its associations of Ancestor Worship, is of course the older conception. But the conception of Sheol goes back to the period when the Hebrew clans lived in the Valley of the Euphrates, and shared this and other beliefs with the Babylonians of that time.[2] Just as a man required burial in the family grave in order to join the circle of his ancestors, so honourable burial was a precondition to an honourable place in Sheol, *i.e.* to union with his people there. Otherwise they are

[1] The same confusion is to be found frequently in the Greek religion. See Rohde, *Psyche*, i. 257 *note;* ii. 240 *note*, 366 *note*, 381 *note*, 384 *note*. Rohde is of opinion that the cult of the dead can have no legitimate relation to the soul that has once entered Hades (i. 257 *note*), though such a relation is often assumed in Greek religion. The same confusion appears also in the Babylonian religion.

[2] That the Hebrew and Babylonian conceptions of Sheol are ultimately from the same source is clear if we compare them together. Thus Aralû, the Babylonian Sheol, is a mighty palace situated under the earth, in the depths of the mountain Aralû (cf. Jonah ii. 6). It is approached by the great ocean into which the sun dips at evening. Hence it appears to be in the west, and in this respect differs from the Hebrew Sheol. It is without light, surrounded by seven walls, and provided with gates and bars. It is covered with dust and filth. The food of its inhabitants is dust, unless offerings of food are received from the living. There is no distinction made between good and bad. They are withdrawn from the control of the gods of the upper world just as the inhabitants of Sheol were supposed to be removed from the jurisdiction of Yahwè. But Aralû, unlike Sheol, had its own gods, Nergal and Allatu. The departed cannot enter Aralû unless they have received burial. In this respect also the Hebrew view differs. It is probable also that in the Babylonian Shuâlu we have the same word as the Hebrew Sheol (so Delitzsch, Jeremias, Jastrow. Jensen, however, doubts the existence of this word in Babylonian; Zimmern regards the question as still open). The inhabitants of Aralû are naked (cf. Job i. 21). But the more usual Hebrew view was that the departed wore in shadowy guise the customary attire of earth (cf. Ezek. xxxii.; Is. xiv.) See especially Jeremias (*Bab.-assyr. Vorstellungen vom Leben nach dem Tode*, pp. 106-126) on the relations existing between Babylonian and Old Testament views of the after-life.

thrust into the lowest and most outlying parts of the pit (Ezek. xxxii. 23). Sheol is said to have different divisions or chambers, חדרי מות (Prov. vii. 27). It is provided with gates (Ps. ix. 14, cvii. 18; Job xxxviii. 17; Is. xxxviii. 10). These are secured with bars (Job xvii. 16). It is the land of disorder (Job x. 22), and of dust (Dan. xii. 2; Job vii. 21, xvii. 16). As regards its position, Sheol was supposed to be situated in the lowest parts of the earth (Ps. lxiii. 9, lxxxvi. 13; Ezek. xxvi. 20, xxxi. 14, xxxii. 18, 24), below the sea (Job xxvi. 5), yet above the subterranean waters (Ps. lxxi. 20). It is likewise known as "the pit," בּוֹר (Ezek. xxvi. 20, xxxi. 14, 16, xxxii. 18, 24, 25, 29, 30; Lam. iii. 53, 55; Is. xiv. 15, 19; Prov. i. 12, xxviii. 17; Ps. xxviii. 1, xxx. 3, lxxxviii. 4, cxliii. 7), or שַׁחַת (Is. xxxviii. 17, li. 14; Ezek. xxviii. 8; Job xvii. 14, xxxiii. 18, 22, 24, 28, 30). So situated, Sheol is naturally without light. It is "the land of darkness," of thick darkness as darkness itself, "where the light is as darkness" (Job x. 21, 22).

CHAP. I.

Two characteristics of Sheol.

In the next section we shall deal at some length with the condition of the dead in Sheol. It will be sufficient here to point out two of its main characteristics—(*a*) Sheol was in early times quite independent of Yahwè, and outside the sphere of His rule. For, as we have seen, Yahwè was originally but the God of the tribe or nation, and His sway for many centuries after Moses was conceived to extend not to the whole upper world, much less to the lower, *i.e.* Sheol, but only to His

CHAP. I.

own people and His own land. Sheol preserved its independence undiminished in many respects down to the fourth century. The persistence of this heathen conception of Sheol[1] side by side with the monotheistic conception of Yahwè as Creator and Ruler of the world for several centuries is hard for the Western mind to understand; for the conceptions are mutually exclusive. Thus Israel believed that when a man died he was removed from the moral jurisdiction of Yahwè (Ps. lxxxviii. 5:—

> Like the slain that lie in the grave
> Whom thou rememberest no more
> And they are cut off from thy hand.

Ps. xxxi. 22), and his relations with Yahwè ceased (Is. xxxviii. 18):—

> For Sheol cannot praise thee;
> Death cannot celebrate thee.
> They that go down into the pit cannot hope for thy truth.

(*b*) As Sheol is independent of Yahwè, the moral distinctions that prevailed on earth had no currency in Sheol.

(iv.) The inhabitants of Sheol.

(iv.) *The Dead, or the Inhabitants of Sheol.*—Death, according to the Old Testament, means an end of the earthly life, but not the cessation of all existence. After death the person still subsists. In

[1] Though God's power is conceived from the eighth century onward (cf. Am. ix. 2; 1 Sam. ii. 6 (very late); Job xxvi. 6, xxxviii. 17; Prov. xv. 11; Ps. cxxxix. 7, 8:—

> Whither shall I go from thy spirit?
> Or whither shall I flee from thy presence?
> If I ascend into heaven, thou art there,
> If I make my bed in Sheol, behold thou art there)

to extend to Sheol, yet Sheol maintains its primitive character. In the earlier centuries the powers that bore sway in Sheol were the ancestors of the living.

CHAP. I.

order to understand so far as possible the nature of existence in Sheol, we must first consider the composite personality of man in the Old Testament. Man consists of two elements, spirit or soul and body, according to the older view, and of three elements, spirit and soul and body, according to the later view. Now a knowledge of the Old Testament doctrine of the soul is of paramount importance if we wish to understand the eschatological development of the Old Testament. For convenience sake we shall treat it under the following heads:—

Old Testament anthropology—the earlier and the later.

(1) *The soul, or nephesh* (נפשׁ), *is identical with the blood.*—As the shedding of blood caused death, the soul was conceived to be in the blood (Lev. xvii. 11[a]), or was actually identified with it (Deut. xii. 23; Gen. ix. 4, 5). Hence the eating of blood was shunned, and the blood offered to God. Hence likewise blood unjustly spilt on the earth (Gen. iv. 10) cried to heaven for vengeance, *i.e.* the soul. Again, since the soul was the blood, and the heart was the central seat of the blood, the heart was regarded as the organ of thought. A "heartless" man was a man without intelligence (Hos. vii. 11); when a man thought, he was said to "speak in his heart." Thought is not ascribed to the soul, though intelligence in a limited degree is.

(1) The soul identical with the blood.

(2) *The soul is the seat of feeling and desire, and, in a secondary degree, of the intelligence, and is identified with the personality.*—Not only are purely animal functions attributed to the soul, such as hunger (Prov. x. 3), thirst (Prov. xxv. 25), sexual desire (Jer. ii. 24),

(2) The seat of feeling and the personality.

CHAP. I.

but also psychical affections, such as love (Is. xlii. 1), joy (Ps. lxxxvi. 4), fear (Is. xv. 4), trust (Ps. lvii. 1), hate (Is. i. 14), contempt (Ezek. xxxvi. 5).[1] Indeed these are so essentially affections of the soul that they are hardly ever attributed to the spirit; yet see p. 46. To the soul also are ascribed wish and desire (Gen. xxiii. 8; 2 Kings ix. 15; 1 Chron. xxviii. 9), and likewise, but very rarely, memory (Lam. iii. 20; Deut. iv. 9) and knowledge (Ps. cxxxix. 14). As the seat of feeling and desire and intelligence (in a limited degree) it becomes an expression for the individual conscious life. Thus "my soul" (נפשׁי) = I, "thy soul" = thou, etc. (Hos. ix. 4; Ps. iii. 3, vii. 2, xi. 1). So many souls = so many persons (Gen. xlvi. 18; Exod. i. 5). This designation of the personality by soul (nephesh) points to the limited conception of the personality that prevailed in Israel. "My spirit" (רוחי) was never so used.

Soul leaves the body in death.

(3) *The soul leaves the body in death* (Gen. xxxv. 18; 1 Kings xvii. 21; 2 Sam. i. 9; Jonah iv. 3).—But this did not always necessarily take place immediately, but it did so apparently on the corruption of the body. In certain cases after outward death the soul was regarded as being still in some sense either in or near the body; for a dead person is called a "soul," *i.e.* nephesh (Lev.

[1] This Semitic view of the soul is quite distinct from that of the Greeks as it appears in Homer. There the soul is not the seat of any of the mental activities; for these belong to the θυμός, which is merely a function of the body, and disappears on the death of the body. It is only the soul that survives death according to Homer (see Chap. III. pp. 137-139).

xix. 28, xxi. 1, xxii. 4; Num. ix. 6, 7, 10; Hag. ii. 13), or a "dead soul," *i.e.* נפשׁ מת (Num. vi. 6; Lev. xxi. 11). This usage, however, can be far more satisfactorily explained from Gen. ii. 7, where the living man is called "a living soul" (see pp. 42, 43).

Two conflicting, and to some extent concurrent, views of life in Sheol.

(4) *In death the soul dies, but not in an absolute sense, according to primitive Hebrew anthropology.*— We have here to deal with a very important question, and one which brings to light in the Old Testament conflicting, and to a certain extent concurrent, views on the nature of the after-life in Sheol. At this stage we are obliged to part company with our predecessors in this field.[1] The older view (*a*) which originated in the period of Semitic heathenism, attributes to the departed a certain degree of knowledge and power in reference to the living and their affairs; the later (*b*), which is derived logically from the monotheistic doctrine of man's nature taught in Gen. ii., iii., but was unknown in preprophetic times, declares that there is neither knowledge, nor wisdom, nor life in the grave. We shall deal with the latter in due course. To return, according to the older view (*a*), the departed possessed a certain degree of self-consciousness and the power of speech and movement (Is. xiv.); a large measure of knowledge, hence their name ידעונים, "the knowing ones"[2] (Lev. xix. 31, xx. 6;

The older view. The departed are acquainted with the affairs of their descendants, and possess the power of helping them.

1 Only Stade appears to have apprehended this fact, and that but partially, so far as we may judge from his published works.

2 The departed spirit when consulted was also termed אוב. A necromancer was said to possess an אוב, or familiar spirit (Lev. xx. 27; 1 Sam. xxviii. 7); he was called "a questioner of the אוב" (Deut. xviii. 11).

CHAP. I.

Is. xix. 3); acquaintance with the affairs of their living descendants, and a keen interest in their fortunes—thus Rachel mourns from her grave for her captive children (Jer. xxxi. 15[1]); ability to forecast the future, hence they were consulted by the living regarding it (1 Sam. xxviii. 13-20, where observe that the dead person invoked is called elohim; Is. viii. 19, xxix. 4). Hence the practice of incubation (Is. lxv. 4). We have already shown that the departed were believed to have the power of helping or injuring their descendants (see p. 24). It will be sufficient to observe here that it follows from Is. lxiii. 16 that Abraham and Israel were conceived as protectors of their descendants (see Cheyne and Duhm *in loc.*)

Customs of this life reproduced in Sheol.

The relations and customs of earth were reproduced in Sheol. Thus the prophet was distinguished by his mantle (1 Sam. xxviii. 14), kings by their crowns and thrones (Is. xiv.), the uncircumcised by his foreskin (Ezek. xxxii.) Each nation also preserved its individuality, and no doubt its national garb and customs (Ezek. xxxii.) Those

[1] According to the Greek religion also, the inhabitants of Hades were acquainted with the affairs of the living. Cf. Pindar, *Pyth.* v. 98-103; *Olymp.* viii. 81-84, xiv. 20-24. See Rohde, *Psyche*, i. 201. This view is expressed doubtfully by Demosthenes, *Leptin.* 87, but it is presupposed in Aeschylus, *Choeph.* 324, 325, *φρόνημα τοῦ θανόντος οὐ δαμάζει πυρὸς μάλερα γνάθος*, and also by the words of invocation addressed to the soul of Agamemnon (139, 147, 148, 156, 157, 477-509); cf. *Eum.* 598. This knowledge of what occurs on earth is ascribed to the dead also in Sophocles, *El.* 1066 *sqq.*; the dead can avenge themselves on the living (*Trach.* 1201, 1202), or help them (*El.* 454, 1419, 1420). Similarly in Euripides the soul of the slain father is invoked to help his children (*El.* 676 *sqq.*), who are convinced that their father hears their appeal (683). The soul of the dead sweeps round the living, and knows all their concerns (*Or.* 667 *sqq.*)

slain with the sword bear for ever the tokens of a violent death in Sheol (Ezek. xxxii. 25), and likewise those who died from grief (Gen. xlii. 38). Indeed the departed were regarded as reproducing exactly the same features as marked them at the moment of death. Hence we can appreciate the terrible significance of David's departing counsel to Solomon touching Joab: "Let not his hoar head go down to Sheol in peace" (1 Kings ii. 6).

In many respects the above view is identical with that of Ancestor Worship, and, though this worship had already withdrawn entirely into the background before the prophetic period, yet many of its usages still persisted in the popular belief till long after the Exile. The leading characteristic of these survivals may be said to be the *comparatively large measure of life, movement, knowledge, and likewise power* attributed to the departed in Sheol. The importance of this characteristic will become obvious when we deal with the later and antagonistic views of the condition of the departed in Sheol.

Composite nature of man according to Gen. ii., iii.

(*b*) This later view, which practically denies knowledge and life to the inhabitants of Sheol, follows logically from the account in Gen. ii. 4–iii., according to which the material form when animated by the spirit became a living soul. "Yahwè Elohim formed man of dust from the ground, and blew into his nostrils breath of life (נשמת חיים), and man became a living soul" (Gen. ii. 7, J). The breath of life (נשמת חיים) here mentioned is identical with the spirit of life (רוח חיים) in vi. 17, vii. 15 (P).

CHAP. I.

Thus the spirit of life is found also in the brute creation according to both these passages (see also Ps. civ. 29, 30). A conflation of both these phrases is given in vii. 22 (J), "the breath of the spirit of life" (נשמת-רוח חיים), which the lower creation is said to possess. Since, therefore, "the breath of life," or "the spirit of life," is common to man and the rest of the animal creation,[1] the spirit of life conceived as thus existing in all living things is life in an impersonal sense. The spirit, therefore, in man can never in this sense be the bearer of the personality. On the other hand, though the spirit is not personally conceived, yet, since it remains in the man so long as he lives and forms in him a thing apart by itself, it must be regarded as forming part of man's composite personality. Accordingly, we have here a real trichotomy of spirit (רוח), soul (נפשׁ), and body (בסר). But if we examine these elements more closely we see that the soul is the result of the indwelling of the spirit in the material body, and has no independent existence of its own. It is really a function of the material body when quickened by the spirit. So long as the spirit is present, so long is the soul "a living soul" (נפש חיה), but when the spirit is withdrawn, the vitality of the soul is destroyed, and it becomes a dead soul (נפשׁ מת), or corpse (Num. vi. 6; Lev. xxi. 11). The dead body is sometimes simply termed "a

Spirit impersonally conceived.

Man a trichotomy.

Soul a function of the quickened body.

[1] According to the story worked up by a late priestly writer in Gen. i. 24 (P), the brute creation is only indirectly the product of the divine creation, whereas man is such directly (i. 26).

soul" (Lev. xix. 28, xxi. 1, xxii. 4; Num. ix. 6, 7, 10; Hag. ii. 13). According to this view the annihilation of the soul ensues inevitably at death, that is, when the spirit is withdrawn. This dissolution of the personality at death is frankly recognised in Eccl. xii. 7, and the impersonal breath of life returns to the Supreme Fount of Life: "the spirit shall return to God, who gave it." Thus this anthropological view is logically and historically the parent of later Sadduceism, which taught that there is neither angel nor spirit (Acts xxiii. 8). Thus the consequences of this view were fully drawn in the second and first centuries before the Christian era, but in the three preceding centuries the logic of its representatives was less consistent. They still believed that the soul *subsisted* after death, though it *did not exist*. This subsistence is indeed purely shadowy and negative—so negative that in it all the faculties of the soul were suspended, and Sheol, the abode of the souls, became a synonym of Abaddon or destruction (Job xxvi. 6; Prov. xv. 11, xxvii. 20).

Hence personality is extinguished at death.

If the teaching of Gen. ii., iii. is taken as a complete account of man's composite nature, the soul must be regarded not only as the vital principle of the body, but as the seat of all the mental activities.[1] With these the spirit, which is really the impersonal basis of life in man, stands in no direct relation.

The soul is on this view the seat of the mind.

[1] It is noteworthy that the soul, according to this view, corresponds to the Homeric conception of the mind (θυμός). See p. 137.

CHAP. I.

Such a theory makes the doctrine of a future life inconceivable.

From these facts it is clear that no advance in the direction of an immortality of the soul can be made with such an anthropology; for in death the soul is extinguished and only the spirit survives. But since the spirit is only the impersonal force of life common to men and brutes, it returns to the Fount of all Life, and thus all personal existence ceases at death. So the Sadducees concluded, and if we start from the same premises we must inevitably arrive at the same conclusion (cf. the Pauline psychology, p. 409).

Soul and spirit thus differ in essence and origin.

In the above threefold division of man's personality the spirit and soul are distinct alike in *essence and origin*. The former is the impersonal basis of life coming from God, and returning on death to God. The latter, which is the personal factor in man, is simply the supreme function of the quickened body, and perishes on the withdrawal of the spirit.

This doctrine of Gen. ii., iii. never succeeded in dispossessing the older and rival doctrine.[1] Their conflicting views of soul and spirit were current together, and not unfrequently the same writers in the Old Testament have used these terms, sometimes

[1] Its prevalence is attested by the Second Isaiah xlii. 5. It is presupposed probably by Deuteronomy, certainly by Ezek. xxxvii., and its diction and influence are conspicuous in Job and certain psalms. Thus in Job xxvii. 3 we find: "The spirit of God is in my nostrils"; and in xxxiii. 4, "The spirit of God hath made me and the breath of the Almighty giveth me life"; and in xxxiv. 11-15, "If he cause his spirit to return unto him, and gathereth unto him his breath, all flesh shall perish together" (so Duhm emends). Similarly in Ps. civ. 30-29, "Thou sendest forth thy spirit, they are created, and thou renewest the face of the earth. Thou takest away their spirit; they die, and return to their dust"; and in Ps. cxlvi. 3, 4, "Put not your trust in princes, in a son of man who cannot save. His spirit goeth forth, he returneth to his earth; in that very day his thoughts perish."

with one meaning, sometimes with another. Greece furnishes us with good analogies (see pp. 137, 138, 141-145). CHAP. I.

Having now dealt with the later doctrine of man's personality which is taught in Gen. ii., iii., we shall now return to the earlier view with which we have already dealt at some length above. According to this primitive Hebrew view, man was composed not of three essentially distinct elements —a trichotomy—spirit, soul, and body, but only of two—a dichotomy—spirit *or* soul and body. The spirit and soul were really one and the same. They were synonymous in their primitive signification as "breath" or "wind." The conception of both was arrived at in the way of observation. When the breath (nephesh or ruach, נפש or רוח) left the body, death ensued. Thus the principle of life was identified with the soul or spirit. The partial differentiation of these two naturally arose in the course of time. The term "spirit" was appropriated to mark the stronger side of the soul and, as Stade (*Gesch. d. Volks Israel*,[2] i. 418) has remarked, designated the stronger and stormier emotions.

Earlier Hebrew view. Man not a trichotomy but a dichotomy.

The spirit.

When once it became customary to personify the psychical affections as nephesh, the practice began of naming the stronger expressions of this personification as spirit or ruach. Thus anger is an affection of the ruach (Judg. viii. 3; see later).

So long as a man was wholly master of his powers, he still possessed his ruach, but when he became lost in amazement, as the queen of Sheba (1 Kings x. 5), or despair (Jos. ii. 11), or fainted (1 Sam. xxx. 12), his ruach left him, though on his reviving it returned (Gen. xlv. 27; Judg. xv. 19). In keeping with this view of the spirit, it is said to be the subject of trouble (Gen. xli. 8), anguish (Job vii. 11), grief (Gen. xxvi. 35; Is. liv. 6), contrition (Ps. li. 17; Is. lxvi. 2), heaviness (Is. lxi. 3). It is the seat of energetic volition and action. Thus the "haughty spirit" (Prov. xvi. 18), the "lowly spirit" (xxix. 23), the impatient spirit (Prov. xiv. 29), etc.

As the departure of the ruach entailed a paralysis of the will (see above), it expresses therefore the impulse of the will (Exod. xxxv. 21); the purposes of man are the outcome of the spirit, מעלות רוח (Ezek. xi. 5): the false prophets follow their own spirit rather than that of Yahwè (Ezek. xiii. 3); God tries men's spirits (Prov. xvi. 2). Further, it seems to express character as the result of will in Num. xiv. 24, "Caleb . . . had another spirit in him."

These various applications were evolved in connection with the earlier conception of ruach.

Soul and spirit identical in essence and origin, but differentiated in function.

In the course of a natural development, the ruach had become the seat of the highest spiritual functions in man. To sum up, then, soul and spirit are at this early stage identical in essence and origin, though differentiated in function.

The primitive doctrine of the soul has already been discussed (see pp. 37-40). If we compare the doctrine of the soul there given with that of the spirit, which we have just investigated, it will be

CHAP. I.

obvious that soul and spirit at this early stage were *identical in essence and origin, though differentiated in function*, whereas according to the later doctrine of Gen. ii., iii. they *differed alike in essence, in origin, and function.*

Difference between earlier and later views.

According to the primitive view of the spirit as the stronger side of the soul, it is clear that it could not descend into Sheol. The soul, on the other hand, did descend, and enjoyed a considerable degree of life and knowledge there.

Spirit could not descend into Sheol.

We are now in a position to contrast the earlier and later views on the state of the departed in Sheol.[1]

State of the departed in Sheol according to the earlier and later views.

Thus in opposition to the older view that in Sheol there is a certain degree of life, movement, and remembrance, the later view teaches that it is the land of forgetfulness (Ps. lxxxviii. 12), of silence (Ps. xciv. 17, cxv. 17), of destruction (Job xxvi. 6, xxviii. 22); in opposition to the belief that the dead return to counsel the living, the later teaches that the dead cannot return to earth (Job vii. 9, xiv. 12); in opposition to the belief that they are acquainted with the affairs of their living descendants, the later teaches that they no longer know what befalls them on earth (Job xiv. 21, "His sons come to honour, and he knoweth it not; and they are brought low, but he perceiveth it not of them"); in opposition to the belief in their superhuman knowledge of the future—as the "knowing ones"—the later teaches

[1] Logically, as we have seen above, there could be no future life for the soul in Sheol according to the later teaching of Gen. ii., iii.

CHAP. I.

that all knowledge has forsaken them (Eccl. ix. 5), that they have neither device nor knowledge nor wisdom (Eccl. ix. 10). And whereas according to the older view they were called elohim in invocation, they are termed in the later "dead ones," מתים (Is. xxvi. 14; Ps. lxxxviii. 10).[1]

Finally, the relations of the upper world appear to be more faintly reproduced, if at all; for all the inhabitants of Sheol, kings and slaves, oppressor and oppressed, good and bad, are all buried in profound sleep (Job iii. 14-20). Indeed all existence seems to be absolutely at an end. Thus Ps. xxxix. 13, "O spare me, that I may recover strength before I go hence and be no more"; Job xiv. 7, 10, "There is hope of a tree, if it be cut down, that it will sprout out again—but—man giveth up the ghost, and where is he?"

Departed in Sheol not designated as souls till a late period.

We have now to call attention to one point more before leaving this subject, and this is that *though the soul leaves the body in death, the departed in Sheol are hardly if ever designated as souls in the Old Testament.* This fact is probably to be explained by the metaphysical inability of early Israel to conceive the body without psychical functions, or the soul without a certain corporeity. Thus the departed were conceived as possessing a soul and a shadowy body. In the older days they were called

[1] The term "shades," רפאים (used also in the Phœnician religion; see Driver, *Books of Samuel*, p. xxix), was applied to the departed by both views, but possibly with a difference: contrast Is. xiv. 9, 10; xxvi. 14, 19, with Ps. lxxxviii. 10 (Prov. ii. 18, ix. 81, etc.), where it is synonymous with the dead.

shades (rĕphāîm), or, when addressed, elohim. During the later times when such a doctrine of man's being became current as that in Gen. ii., iii., the departed were called "dead ones," or "shades," as in the older days. We should probably recognise in Job xiv. 22 an instance of the later usage of designating the inhabitants of Sheol as souls: "Only for himself his flesh hath pain, and for himself his soul mourneth."[1] Here the soul is in Sheol, with all its feeling and interests limited to itself, and the body is in the grave. In this passage Job reflects the popular eschatology of his day. Furthermore, in xix. 26, 27, where he abandons this eschatology, and rises to the expression of his highest hopes, he declares that without the body he will see God, that is, *his soul* or *spirit* will enjoy the divine vision at some period after death. Since only the highest powers of man's soul were capable of the divine vision, it is clear that the writer had a lofty conception of the capabilities of the soul apart from the body. We cannot emphasise too strongly the importance of this point, since it is almost universally taught that the Jew had no such conception of the soul till he came under the influence of the Greek (see pp. 71, 72).

According to the higher theology, the soul after death is capable of the divine vision.

We have now done with the treatment of Ancestor Worship. We have considered it only in

Short résumé of chapter.

[1] We seem here to have an idea which is also found in ancient Greek religion. So long as the body in any form still existed, the soul, though separated from it, was conscious of what befell it. This is the presupposition underlying Achilles' ill-treatment of Hector's dead body (see Rohde, *Psyche*, i. 27).

its eschatological aspects, only so far as it supplied to the individual a doctrine of the future life.

We have found that the individual Israelite derived from this source his views as to the nature of the soul and spirit, Sheol, and the condition of the departed there. On these questions no revelation was furnished by Yahwism for many centuries; Yahwism had no eschatology relating to the individual to begin with. But with the first proclamation of Yahwism by Moses the doom of Ancestor Worship and its teachings was already pronounced, though centuries might elapse before this doom was fully accomplished. We have already seen partial fulfilments of this doom in the destruction by Yahwism of all life in Sheol. This step was necessary with a view to the truly ethical doctrine of the future life. In the next chapter we shall deal with the positive preparation made by Yahwism for such a higher doctrine. This preparation proceeded essentially from the new value which came to be set on the individual through Yahwism.

CHAPTER II

ESCHATOLOGY OF THE INDIVIDUAL—RISE OF THE DOCTRINE OF AN INDIVIDUAL IMMORTALITY

Résumé of Chapter I.

In the preceding chapter we pointed out that it would be impossible to understand the eschatology of the individual Israelite in preprophetic times apart from some knowledge of his conception of God.

For even a superficial study of the former is sufficient to show that down to the Exile and later the beliefs of Israel in reference to a future life were heathen to the core, and irreconcilable with any intelligible belief in a sole and supreme God. The question therefore naturally arose: Since Israel's preprophetic conception of God was not monotheistic, of what nature was it? In our short inquiry into this question, we found that Yahwè had revealed Himself to Israel as a God of justice, righteousness, and purity, and was thereby sundered essentially and absolutely from the other Semitic deities of the time, and yet that He was not regarded by Early Israel as the sole God of the earth, but

CHAP. II.

only as the sole God of Israel, whose influence and authority were in the main limited to His own people and country. As a national God, further, He was popularly conceived as being concerned only with the wellbeing of the nation, and as possessing neither interest nor jurisdiction in the life of the individual beyond the grave. Hence since early Yahwism possessed no eschatology of its own, the individual Israelite was left to his hereditary heathen beliefs. These beliefs we found were elements of Ancestor Worship. Thus the individual Israelite possessed teraphim, or household gods, which he worshipped with sacrifices with a view to secure their favour or avert their wrath. This worship was performed by a son of the departed, and thus in connection with this worship arose the importance of securing a male offspring. The primitive mourning usages in Israel belonged to this worship, and likewise the beliefs entertained regarding the family grave, Sheol, and its inhabitants. Finally we discovered that we have herein a key to difficulties that have hitherto proved insoluble in relation to the conceptions of the soul and spirit in the Old Testament. For the Old Testament attests, not a single and uniform doctrine of the soul and spirit, but two essentially distinct views of these conceptions, the earlier derived ultimately from Ancestor Worship, the later from the monotheistic account in Genesis.

The primitive beliefs of the individual Israelite regarding the future life, being thus derived from

Ancestor Worship, were implicitly antagonistic to Yahwism from its first proclamation by Moses. In its subsequent developments this antagonism becomes explicit, and results in the final triumph of Yahwism. During the progress of this conflict Yahwism annihilates all existence in Sheol, since the nature of this existence was heathen and non-moral, and could in no sense form a basis on which to found an ethical and spiritual doctrine of the future life. Thus the first stage in this conflict was eminently destructive in character, but this only with a view to a higher reconstruction. For whilst Yahwism was destroying the false life in Sheol it was steadily developing in the individual the consciousness of a new life and a new worth through immediate communion with God. Now it is from the consciousness of this new life, and not from the moribund existence in Sheol, that the doctrine of a blessed future—whether of the soul only immediately after death, or of the soul and body through a resurrection at some later date—was developed in Israel. Thus this doctrine was a new creation, the offspring of faith in God on the part of Israel's saints.

A large body of the nation, however, took the provisional stage above referred to to be one of true and eternal significance. This defective view, named in later times the Sadducean, arose in the fifth century B.C., and maintained itself down to the destruction of Jerusalem in 70 A.D.

When Yahwism had destroyed the false view of

CHAP. II.

Doctrine of individual retribution derives its origin from Yahwism.

the future life, it began to develop an eschatology of the individual in harmony with its own essential conceptions. We have now to deal with the foundation laid by Yahwism for this higher doctrine of the future life. This foundation is based on the new value set on the individual through Yahwism. The rise of individualism in Israel must therefore presently engage our attention.

Preludings of the doctrine of a blessed future.

But before we enter on this study we must not fail to observe certain beliefs in pre-Exilic religion, which, though they could not be regarded as forming actual stages in the development of the doctrine of a blessed future life, are nevertheless heralds and preludings of this doctrine. Regarded from the standpoint of our present investigation, these beliefs are of various worth. Of such beliefs there are four. Two of these, which ought to have had a determining influence on subsequent Jewish development, but which apparently had not, we shall discuss first. These are (i.) the creation of man in God's image and likeness in Gen. i. 26, 27. (ii.) The presence of the tree of life in the Garden of Eden (Gen. ii., iii.) We need not linger long over either of these. As regards the former, however we interpret Gen. i. 26, 27, we cannot adopt it as the foundation of a Biblical anthropology, since this doctrine of man's creation in the divine likeness[1]

Man's creation in God's likeness not made the basis of Biblical anthropology.

[1] Does the likeness refer to moral qualities? This is possible. Yet it is to be observed that Adam transmits this likeness to Seth v. 3, and that all men possess it after the fall (ix. 6). On the other hand, it is contended that the divine likeness consists in the fact that man rules all other living creatures on the earth just as God rules the universe. It is to be observed that, had the likeness been one of essence, and *this view been accepted in Israel*, the

CHAP. II.

References to tree of life in Gen. ii., iii. intrusions in the text.

does not appear, with the exception of Gen. i. 26, 27; v. 1, 3; ix. 6, throughout the rest of the Old Testament. (ii.) Next, as to the tree of life. The presence of this tree in the Garden of Eden would seem to indicate that primitive man was intended from the outset to become immortal. But Budde (*Biblische Urgeschichte*, pp. 48-59) has shown that only one tree was spoken of in the original narrative, and that this tree was the tree of the knowledge of good and evil. Thus, according to iii. 3, there is only one tree in the midst of the Garden, and the same presupposition underlies iii. 5, 6, 11, 12. We find the first mention of the tree of life in ii. 9. But the latter half of this verse, which is in itself syntactically questionable, is irreconcilable with iii. 3. Further, though according to ii. 9 the tree of life occupied the chief place in the Garden, man was not forbidden to eat of it. Yet the eating of it would, according to iii. 22, have made man immortal. But this last idea is at variance with iii. 19. Man's mortality follows not from his being forbidden to eat of the magical tree of life: it rests simply on the will of Yahwè.[1] Hence ii. 9^b, iii. 22, 24 are intrusions in the original narrative.

These passages regarding the tree of life, whether we take them as interpolations or not, were without effect on the Old Testament doctrine of a future life.

Having disposed of these two apparent herald-

doctrine of a future life would have been developed some centuries earlier than it actually was.

[1] See Holzinger on Genesis, pp. 40, 41 in the *Kurzer Hand-Commentar*.

CHAP. II.

Two beliefs which provide essential characteristics and presuppositions of the doctrine of a future life.

ings of a higher theology in Israel, we are now at liberty to deal with two beliefs which, though not furnishing in themselves the basis for this theology, yet provide some of its essential characteristics and presuppositions. These beliefs have to do with (i.) the translation of Enoch and Elijah; (ii.) the power of Yahwè to bring back the soul from Sheol. The former involves certain essential characteristics of the higher doctrine of the future life, and the latter one of its necessary presuppositions.

The translations of Enoch and Elijah supply an essential characteristic of this doctrine—the future life follows from present life in God.

(i.) *The translations of Enoch and Elijah.*—These translations of Enoch (Gen. v. 22-24) and Elijah (2 Kings ii. 11) are essentially miraculous in character, and on such exceptional incidents, therefore, the doctrine of a future life for man *as man* cannot be built. They are significant, however, in that they teach that death does not end the full and conscious life of all, and that Sheol does not engulf every living energy. They belong to an early period in Hebrew thought when immortality was inconceivable for man if soul and body were sundered. Hence soul and body must be translated together. The belief in such translations does not controvert the ancient view of Sheol as a place whence none can return. It probably springs from a time when the authority of Yahwè was still limited to this side the grave, and the dead were regarded as beyond the exercise of His grace. The dead were beyond recall, but the living could be raised to immortality—that is, to an immortality with the body, not without it, before death, not after it. But since these translations, though miraculous, follow distinctively from the moral uprightness of Enoch and Elijah, we see herein an essential characteristic of the subsequent development. As it was a *life of communion with God* that led, though uniquely, to the translation of Enoch and Elijah,[1] so it was from the same spiritual root that the immortality of all who enjoyed such communion was derived in later centuries.

A blessed future life presupposes Yahwè's power to restore the soul from Sheol.

(ii.) *The power of Yahwè to bring back the soul from Sheol.*—This view could not have arisen till monotheism had in some form been accepted. Yahwè's power now extends to Sheol, though it does not influence its non-moral character. This belief is attested in 1 Kings xvii. 22 and 2 Kings iv. 35, xiii. 21, where Yahwè restores the dead to life through the instrumentality of His prophets. Here again the incidents in question are exceptional, but they are important as showing that *Yahwè's power can reach the dead.*

With this preface we shall now turn to the rise and development of individualism in Israel.

[1] What an infinite gulf yawns between the old Greek conception of the translation of Heroes to the Isles of the Blessed and that of the translation of Enoch and Elijah in Israel! For the translation of the Greek Heroes was due, not to their *moral* character or merits of any kind, but to their *physical* relationship to some of the gods. It is on this ground that the "cowardly" Menelaus (μαλθακὸς αἰχμητής, *Il.* xvii. 588) is translated (*Od.* iv. 561-565). See pp. 39, 40; and Rohde, *Psyche*, i. 79-81. In the Babylonian religion there is one instance of translation—that of Parnapishtim and of his wife to the confluence of the waters, where they enjoy the immortal life of the gods. For this translation no distinctively ethical grounds were advanced. This place at the "confluence of the waters" may be an island, according to Jeremias. See Jastrow, *Rel. of Bab. and Assyr.* pp. 488, 493, 494, 577; Jeremias, *Bab.-assyr. Vorstellungen vom Leben nach dem Tode*, pp. 94-99.

CHAP. II.

No individual retribution looked for in preprophetic times.

No individual retribution looked for in preprophetic times.—The early Israelite was not alarmed by the prosperity of the wicked man or the calamities of the righteous; for Yahwè was concerned with the well-being of the people as a whole, and not with that of its individual members. The individual was not the religious unit, but the family or tribe. The individual was, as in Ancestor Worship, identified with his family; a solidarity existed between him and the line of his ancestors and descendants. This identification led to strange consequences. Hence it was regarded as natural and reasonable for God to visit the virtues and vices of the fathers on the children (Exod. xx. 5; Lev. xx. 5; Jos. vii. 24; 1 Sam. iii. 13), of an individual on his community or tribe (Gen. xii. 17, xx. 18; Exod. xii. 29), while His mercy was shown in postponing the punishment of the sinner till after his death[1] and allowing it to fall on his son (1 Kings xi. 12, xxi. 29). This principle of retribution gave no difficulty to the prophets of the eighth century. Their message is still directed to the nation, and the judgments they proclaim are collective punishment for collective guilt. It is not till late in the seventh century that the problem of individual retribution really emerged and received its first solution in the teaching of Jeremiah.

Popular seventh-century view of the responsibility of the individual.

Towards the close of the kingdom of Judah the popular sentiment expressed itself in the proverb:

[1] Rewards and punishments were necessarily conceived as limited to the earthly life; for Sheol was regarded as outside the jurisdiction of Yahwè.

"The fathers have eaten sour grapes, and the children's teeth are set on edge" (Jer. xxxi. 29). In this the people *explicitly* denied their own responsibility in the overthrow of the nation. It was their fathers that had sinned, and they were involved as by an iron fate in their guilt. Such a view naturally paralysed all personal effort after righteousness, and made men the victims of despair. But *implicitly* in the same proverb there is expressed, not an humble submission to the divine judgments, but rather an arraignment of the divine method of government. The righteousness of the individual could not deliver him from the doom befalling the nation.

Criticism of this view by Jeremiah, and his statement of the new doctrine of the individual springing from his personal relation to Yahwè.

Now in opposition to this popular statement of the law of responsibility Jeremiah answers as follows: the days come "when they shall say no more, The fathers have eaten sour grapes, and the children's teeth are set on edge; but every one shall die for his own iniquity" (Jer. xxxi. 29, 30). And yet the same prophet had already himself declared that the children suffered for the sins of the fathers: "I will cause them to be tossed to and fro among all the kingdoms of the earth because of Manasseh, the son of Hezekiah" (Jer. xv. 4). How, then, are we to account for this new departure in his teaching? It is to be explained from the new relation which God would establish in the coming days between *Himself and the individual Israelite*,[1] which would

[1] See Duhm, *Theologie der Propheten*, 242-247; Giesebrecht, *Das Buch Jeremia*, Einleit. xiii. xiv. pp. 171, 172; Marti, *Gesch. d. isr. Rel.* 153-156.

CHAP. II.

supersede the old relation which had existed between *Himself and the nation as a whole* (Jer. xxxi. 31-34). Heretofore the individual was related to Yahwè only as a member of the nation, and as such shared, whatever his nature and character, in the national judgments, and thus had no individual worth. The nation was the religious unit. Henceforth the individual would step into the place of the nation in its relation to Yahwè, and the individual would henceforth constitute the religious unit.

Nature of new covenant determined by man's need

Two great facts determined the nature of this new relation or covenant, *i.e.* man's need, and God's essential character.

First as to man, Jeremiah affirms man's total incapacity for self-reformation, his inability to convert himself. Just as easily might the Ethiopian change his skin or the leopard his spots (xiii. 22, 23). The law imposed under Josiah (*i.e.* Deuteronomy) had failed to touch the evil: it had led to a righteousness merely legal (vii. 4 *sqq.*; viii. 9, 10), as external as the physical rite of circumcision (iv. 4), to an outward reformation which cannot stand before Him who tries the reins and the heart (xi. 20, xvii. 10, xx. 12). Hence, since the old covenant had failed to preserve, much less to redeem Israel, Jeremiah promises the institution of this new covenant. Under this new covenant man's spiritual incapacities for obedience to God's law would be removed; for God would write His law in their hearts, and so beget a willing obedience. Jeremiah has arrived at this conclusion from his own experience, his own relation to the law. To him the law is not an external commandment provoking opposition, but the word of God written in his heart, renewed from day to day, and evoking within him a passionate loyalty and obedience. His life is fed through constant communion with God. If then God so entered into communion with him, He will likewise in the coming time redeem the nation by writing His law in their hearts (Jer. xxxi. 31-34), that is, by establishing an immediate relation with each individual, such as God has already established with the prophet. Thus in the face of the coming exile, when the nation would cease to exist and only the individuals remain, Jeremiah was the first to conceive religion as the communion of the individual soul with God. Thus each individual enters into the privileges of the prophet. Moreover, the character of God led to a like conclusion. Since God could accept none but a true and spiritual worship (xi. 20, xvii. 10), and, since, if this is to be offered, it must spring from the heart of the individual, then God must enter into relation with the individual, and make known His will to him, and hereby a personal relation of the individual with God is established. Thus through Jeremiah the foundation of a true individualism was laid, and the law of individual retribution proclaimed. The further development of these ideas led inevitably to the conception of a blessed life beyond the grave.

and God's essential character.

This teaching of Jeremiah was taken up and developed by Ezekiel. In pre-Exilic times the

CHAP. II.

Jeremiah's doctrine of the individual developed by Ezekiel.

individual soul had been conceived as the property of the family and the nation, but Ezekiel[1] now teaches that every soul is God's, and therefore exists in a direct and immediate relation to God (Ezek. xviii. 4). Ezekiel's individualism here receives its most noble and profound expression. Never hitherto had the absolute worth of the individual soul been asserted in such brief and pregnant words as those of the prophet speaking in God's behalf: "Behold all souls are mine." From this principle Ezekiel concluded that if the individual is faithful in his relation to Yahwè, he is unaffected whether by his own past (xviii. 21-28), or by the sins or the righteousness of his fathers (xviii. 20, xiv. 12-20). Righteousness raises him above the sweep of the dooms that befall the sinful individual or the sinful nation. And since this righteousness is open to his own achievement, he possesses moral freedom,[2] and his destiny is the shaping of his own will (xviii. 30-32). Hence there is a strictly individual retribution: judgment is daily executed by God, and finds concrete expression in man's outward lot. Thus the outward lot of the individual harmonises perfectly with his inner character. According to ix. 3-6 Ezekiel expected that no righteous man would perish in the fall of Jerusalem. This expectation naturally followed

[1] Ezekiel's individualism is stated in iii. 16-21, xiv. 12-23, xviii., xxx. 1-20.

[2] On the other hand, we must recognise that Ezekiel emphasises beyond all other Old Testament prophets the absolute sovereignty of God. With this he makes no attempt to reconcile man's free will.

from his doctrine of individual retribution. Only once does he fall into forgetfulness of it, when in xxi. 3, 4 he foretells the indiscriminate destruction of the righteous and the wicked.

False elements in Ezekiel's doctrine of the individual.

In these statements Ezekiel has enunciated a great spiritual truth, but has hampered its acceptance and development by associating it with positions which are demonstrably false. It is true, on the one hand, that the individual can in communion with God break with the iron nexus of his own past and that of his people, and make a new beginning which is different in essence from that past and inexplicable from it as a starting-point; but, on the other hand, it is no less true that this new beginning is always conditioned in some degree by the past of the individual and that of his fathers.

Ezekiel's doctrine rooted itself firmly in the national consciousness. The evil results of such a doctrine are not far to seek. Thus, since in Ezekiel's view all retribution is necessarily limited to this life, and since, further, it has mainly to do with material blessings and is strictly proportioned to a man's deserts, it inevitably follows that a man's outward fortunes are the infallible witness to his internal character and to the actual condition in which he stands before God.

Thus by Ezekiel's individualism the community is dissolved into a mass of individual units, each of which pursues independently his own way wholly unaffected by the rest, responsible only for his own acts, and working out his own salvation or his own

CHAP. II.

doom. But his individualism proceeds farther still. The very individual is no longer conceived in his unity, but is dismembered into so many outward manifestations of life. Righteousness is not for Ezekiel a uniform divine temper shaping the whole life in conformity to God's will, but a mass or congeries of separate righteous acts. Hence *the individual act* is taken to be *a true expression of the whole man at the moment of its occurrence.* If this act is wicked on the moment of the advent of the kingdom, then the man will rightfully be destroyed, but if righteous he will be preserved.

Religious atomism of Ezekiel.

This doctrine of a strictly individual retribution is taught and applied in detail in the great popular handbooks, the Psalter and the Book of Proverbs. Though the righteous may have many afflictions, the Lord delivereth him out of them all: all his bones are kept, not one of them is broken, but evil slays the wicked (Ps. xxxiv. 19-21; see also xxxvii. 28, etc.) Similarly, the righteous and the wicked are to be recompensed on earth (Prov. xi. 31). Life is the outcome of righteousness, and this is to be understood as physical life, just as physical death is the outcome of wickedness (Prov. ii. 21, 22; x. 2; xi. 19; xv. 24, 25; xix. 16, etc.) Doubts, however, as to the truth of this doctrine are found from time to time in the Psalms.

Currency of Ezekiel's doctrine in Psalms and Proverbs.

Naturally such a doctrine was a continual stumbling-block to the righteous when in trouble. So long as all went well with him, he was assured of the favour of God, but misfortune or pain

This doctrine a stumbling-block to the suffering righteous,

destroyed this certainty; for as such they were incontrovertible evidence of sin. Hence the righteous man looked to God to be justified by an outward judgment. If this was granted, then his righteousness was attested to his own conscience, and before men; but if it was withheld, no other conclusion could be drawn save that his case was one, not of afflicted righteousness, but hidden wickedness, now unmasked and visited with its fitting retribution.

and an absolute hindrance to any progress to a true solution of the problem.

Nor was it to the sufferer alone that this doctrine of retribution proved an insuperable difficulty. So long as the nation was convinced that there was a perfectly adequate retribution in this life, no true solution of the problem[1] was possible, nor was there any occasion to question the justice of the prevailing views of the condition of the departed in Sheol, and thus every possibility of progress in this direction was at a standstill. Hence, as a preparation to the attainment of truer views of the after-life, it was necessary that this theory of retribution should be questioned and rejected. This was done subsequently in Job and Ecclesiastes.

Now, before dealing with the later developments of the doctrine of Ezekiel, it would be of advantage to define in the briefest compass those elements in it which received the sanction of subsequent religious thought, or called forth its opposition. Now whilst Ezekiel's undying merit in this respect was his assertion of the independent worth of the indi-

[1] According to Ezekiel's theory, there was no problem to solve. Every man received his exact due in this life.

CHAP. II.

Erroneous elements in Ezekiel's doctrine.

vidual, his defects lay in two misstatements—(*a*) the individual does not suffer for the sins of his fathers, but only for his own; (*b*) the individual is at present judged in perfect keeping with his deserts. In other words, sin and suffering, righteousness and wellbeing, are always connected: the outward lot of the individual is God's judgment in concrete form.[1]

Now as regards (*a*), the experience of the nation must always have run counter to this statement. Indeed, subsequent Jewish literature attests the persistence of the older view, and rightly so, for the elements in every man's nature and lot *which lie outside the sphere of his volition* are undoubtedly shaped for better or worse in accordance with the merits or demerits of his father and people. Thus in Ps. cix. 13 the writer prays that the posterity of the wicked may be cut off. The son of Sirach declares that such is the fate of the children of sinners (xli. 6), that the offspring of the ungodly put forth few branches (xl. 15), that the children of an adulterous wife will be destroyed (xxiv. 25). That men are punished for the iniquities of their fathers and brethren is freely acknowledged in Ps. cvi. 6; Dan. ix. 7, 8, 16; Jud. vii. 28; Tob. iii. 3; Ass. Mos. iii. 5; Matt. xxiii. 35; Baruch i. 18-21, ii. 26, iii. 8; Apoc. Bar. lxxvii. 3, 4, 10.

Ezekiel's views controverted by the writers of Job and Ecclesiastes.

Ezekiel's second error (*b*), that the individual's experience agrees with his deserts, is the corollary

1 Both (*a*) and (*b*) seemed to Ezekiel to follow logically from God's righteousness.

of (*a*). We find that this thesis gave birth to a lengthened controversy, of which two notable memorials have come down to us, *i.e.* Job and Ecclesiastes. Although Ecclesiastes is much the later in time we will, for convenience sake, deal with it first.

Protest of Ecclesiastes.

Against the statement in (*b*), that the individual is at present judged in perfect keeping with his deserts, the writer of Ecclesiastes enters at once a decided negative. He declares, in fact, that there is no retribution at all.[1] Thus he maintains that evil may prolong a man's days and righteousness curtail them (vii. 15), that the destiny of the wise man and of the fool is identical (ii. 14), and likewise that of the righteous and the wicked (ix. 2): "All things come alike to all: there is one event to the righteous and to the wicked; to the good and to the evil; to the clean and to the unclean; to him that sacrificeth and to him that sacrificeth not. The good man fares like the sinner, and he that sweareth as he that feareth an oath"; finally, that the wicked attain to the honour of burial, whilst this is often denied to the righteous (viii. 10). However extravagant the attack of this writer, his book is nevertheless valuable as a counterblast to the no less extravagant and superficial doctrine of Ezekiel,

[1] The passages where judgment is threatened (iii. 17, xi. 9^b, xii. 14) are, according to an increasing number of critics, intrusions in the text, being at variance with the entire thought of the writer. viii. 12, 13 is likewise an interpolation, or else no longer exists in its original form. Yet in certain cases the man who fears God has, he thinks, an advantage over others (ii. 26, vii. 18, 26). For a very interesting discussion of this book, see Cheyne's *Jew. Rel. Life*, pp. 183-203.

CHAP. II.

that the previsions and claims of faith are realised in the world of sight.

Job's criticism of the Ezekelian doctrine.

In the Book of Job the principal elements of Ezekiel's teaching reappear, and are dealt with in dramatic form. It is here shown that the doctrines of man's individual worth and a strictly individual retribution are really irreconcilable. The former receives in the person of Job its noblest exposition in all ancient literature, whilst in his actual fortunes the extravagance and untruth of the latter are demonstrated to the full. Conscious in the highest degree of his own worth and rectitude, Job claims that God should deal with him in accordance with his deserts. Like his contemporaries, he believes (for Job and the author of the dialogues may be identified for the present) that every event that befalls a man reflects God's disposition towards him ; misfortune betokens God's anger, prosperity His favour: in short, that there is a strictly retributive judgment enforced in this life. But this belief, Job discovers, is not confirmed by the fortunes of other men (xxi. 1-15), for the wicked prosper, grow old and go down to the grave in peace, and their seed is established on the earth. Most of all, his own experience emphasises this conflict between faith and experience, and teaches him to conclude that in the world, governed as it is, faith may be without recognition, and the righteous be visited with the penalty of the wrongdoer. Faith, indeed, in order to be sure of its own reality, claims its attestation by the outward judgments of God ; yet, despite the absence of all such attestation, Job resolves to hold on in the way of righteousness independently of both God and man (xvii. 7-9). The world as it is is out of joint; hence Job appeals from the God of outer providence, from the God of circumstance, to the God of faith.[1] The fact that the writer does not seek to solve the antinomies of the problem, by making his argument lead up to the doctrine of a future life, shows that this doctrine had not yet won acceptance even amongst the religious thinkers of Israel.

The writer's conclusions point to the moral conception of the future life.

And yet the main views and conclusions of Job point in this direction. The emphasis laid on man's individual worth, with his consequent claims upon a righteous God, and the denial that these claims meet with any satisfaction at the hands of the God of the wrongful present, lead naturally to the conclusion that at some future time all these wrongs will be righted by the God of faith. And this thought is not wholly absent from Job. A momentary anticipation of it appears in xiv. 1-15. May not man revive as the tree that has been cut down? May not Sheol be only a temporary place of sojourn,[2] where man is sheltered from the wrongs of the present life till God, who had once communion with him, summons him back to its renewal? But the time for realising this axiom of the faith had not yet

[1] In keeping with the high conception of the worth of the individual in Job is that of the conscience also, which is unique as regards the Old Testament. Job accepts its verdict over against that of his contemporaries and of the outward events of Providence.

[2] This idea of Sheol as an intermediate abode which is here suggested became shortly after 200 B.C. the prevailing doctrine. In xix. 25-27 also Sheol is conceived in some sense as an intermediate place.

CHAP. II.

come. It is but a passing gleam that dispersed the gloom of Job's perplexities, and the darkness speedily prevailed as before.

But what appears only as an impassioned desire in chap. xiv. rises into *a real, though possibly only momentary, conviction* in xix. 25-27:—

> But I know that my Avenger liveth,
> And that at the last he will appear above (my) grave:
> †And after my skin hath been thus destroyed,† [1]
> Without my body shall I see God:
> Whom I shall see for myself,
> And mine eyes shall behold, and not another.

Although line 3 is hopelessly corrupt, the rest of the passage is clear. Job declares that God will appear for his vindication, and that after his death (*i.e.* without the body) he shall witness this vindication, and enjoy the vision of God. But we cannot infer that this divine experience will endure *beyond the moment of Job's justification by God.* It is not the blessed immortality of the departed soul that is referred to here, but its actual entrance into and enjoyment of the higher life, however momentary its duration. The possibility of the continuance, much less the unendingness, of this higher life does not seem to have dawned on Job, though it lay in the line of his reasonings. If it had, its overwhelming significance could not have been ignored through the

[1] See Duhm *in loc.*, who declares that, with the exception of line 3 and a slight transposition in line 2, not a single letter in the rest of the text need be changed. Dr. Cheyne, on the other hand (*J.Q.R.* Oct. 1897, pp. 15, 16), regards the present form of xix. 26, 27 as corrupt. His restoration removes all reference to a future life. I cannot herein follow him. Both text and thought seem to me to be against him.

rest of the book. Nevertheless, the importance of the spiritual advance here made cannot be exaggerated. In order to appreciate this advance we have only to compare the new outlook into the future which it provides with the absolutely hopeless view that was then accepted on all hands. The Book of Job reflects all the darkness of the popular doctrine (see chaps. iii., vii., xiv.), and likewise exhibits the actual steps, whereby the human spirit rose gradually to the apprehension that *man's soul is capable of a divine life beyond the grave.*[1] Two points require here to be emphasised. The first is that this new view of the next life springs from a spiritual root, and owes nothing to any animistic doctrines of the soul then existing. The second is no less weighty. We have here a new doctrine of the soul. The soul is no longer cut off from all communion with God on death and shorn of all its powers, even of existence, as Job and his contemporaries had been taught to conceive it, but is regarded as *still capable of the highest spiritual activities, though without the body*[2] (see

Book of Job exhibits the steps whereby the human spirit rose to the apprehension of a blessed life beyond the grave.

A new doctrine of the soul involved therein.

[1] I cannot but regard as misleading in the highest degree the statement of Gunkel (*Schöpfung und Chaos*, p. 291 *note*) that the rise of the resurrection doctrine cannot be traced in the Old Testament. He holds that this belief originated neither in prophetical eschatology nor in the piety of the psalmists. It is owing to the piecemeal and unhistorical method in which the doctrine of a future life in the Old Testament and in Apocryphal and Pseudepigraphal literature has been studied in Germany and England that such assertions are possible. The spiritual basis for the resurrection doctrine is laid in Job and the Psalms, which in part suggest and in part teach the doctrine of a future blessed life *of the individual.* When we take one step farther, and combine the hope of the individual and that of the nation together, we arrive forthwith at the doctrine of the resurrection. But, according to Gunkel, this doctrine arose in Israel neither from the previsions of faith nor from religious reflection, but was borrowed in its fully developed form from the East!

[2] Thus the new and lofty idea of the after-life has arisen, not from the old animistic conceptions, but amid their ruins.

CHAP. II.

pp. 48, 49). We thus see that it was not necessary for Israel to borrow from Greece the idea that the soul could preserve its powers independently of the body.

Though the Book of Job did not teach categorically the "higher theology," it opliged its readers to take up a definite attitude to it.

Though the Book of Job does not teach categorically, it undoubtedly suggests, the idea of a future life. *That this idea was in the air* is clear from xiv. 13-15 and xix. 28, 29, but even if they were entirely absent, it would still be true; for throughout the rest of this book the antinomies of the present are presented in so strong a light that the thinkers of Israel who assimilated its contents were forced to take up a definite attitude to the "higher theology." Some made the venture of faith and postulated the doctrine of a future life; others, like the writer of Ecclesiastes, declining this challenge of the Spirit, made the "great refusal," and fell back on unbelief and materialism. We have here arrived at the parting of the ways.

It only remains to consider the evidence of the Psalms touching a blessed future life of the soul.

The doctrine of a blessed future of the soul in the Psalms.

Those who maintain the existence of this hope in the Psalter base their view on Pss. xvi., xvii., xlix., lxxiii. As regards the two former, the evidence fails to bear out their view. There is nothing that necessarily relates to a future life in Ps. xvi., which expresses the fears and hopes not of the individual but of the community. In Ps. xvii. likewise the psalmist does not speak as an individual (cf. the plurals, vers. 7 and 11), but as the mouthpiece of the Jewish people, who are to Yahwè as the apple of the eye (ver. 8). In fear of a foreign invader (vers. 9, 13) the psalmist prays for help. Hence instead of "I shall be satisfied, when I awake with thy likeness" we expect some reference to God's help (so Cheyne and Smend [1]). The former reads "I shall feast mine eyes when thy zeal awakes." In any case the context does not admit of a reference to a future life.

Psalm xlix.

But with regard to Pss. xlix. and lxxiii. the case is different. The doctrine of a blessed future life appears to be implied. With the present text of xlix. we seem compelled to adopt one or other of two interpretations. In vers. 14, 15 the speaker announces speedy destruction for the wicked, but complete redemption from death for himself. But who is the speaker? Does the "I" here denote the psalmist as a representative pious Israelite or the righteous community? In favour of the latter it is argued that the psalmist is here speaking in the name of the righteous who are poor and oppressed over against the wicked who are rich and oppressive: and in the next place that ver. 10 states that "all die, alike the wise man (*i.e.* the righteous) and the fool." Thus the immortality here expected is that of the righteous community.[2] This

[1] Smend, *ZATW*, 1888, p. 95; Cheyne, *Jew. Rel. Life*, 240 f. Duhm, on the other hand, in his new *Commentary on the Psalms*, maintains that no change of text is necessary. "To behold God's face" = to visit the temple, as in Ps. xxvii. 4; and "the awaking" here mentioned means nothing more than the awaking next morning, when the psalmist will join afresh in the temple worship (cf. v. 3).

[2] See Cheyne's *Bampton Lectures on the Psalter*, 381-425, where it is contended that the belief of a future life is implied in Pss. xvi., xvii., xlix., lxxiii. In Pss. xlix. and lxxiii. he finds a protest against the old Hebrew view of Sheol. Dr. Cheyne has since abandoned this view of the psalms in question.

CHAP. II.

is the view of Smend, Schwally, and Cheyne. But in favour of a future life of the individual it is to be argued that Sheol is represented in ver. 14 as clearly *penal* in character—a place where the wicked rich men are punished. This is still clearer from Dr. Cheyne's attractively emended text (*Jew. Rel. Life*, 238):—

Sheol having penal character in Pss. xlix. and lxxiii. never becomes the abode of the righteous.

> Like sheep they sink into Sheol
> Death rules them, terrors affright them;
> They go down straight into the grave
> Sheol is their mansion for ever.

Thus in Pss. xlix. and lxxiii. Sheol is conceived as the future abode of the wicked only; heaven as that of the righteous. This conception of the penal character of Sheol is all the more credible from the fact that in the Old Testament two other places of punishment for special offenders are already developed. Thus in Is. xxiv. 21, 22 the angelic rulers of the nations and the kings will be imprisoned in "the pit" for "many days," after which they shall receive their (final) punishment. This "pit" must not be confounded with Sheol (cf. Eth. En. 54). Again, Gehenna is alluded to in Is. lxvi. 24 as the final abode of Jewish apostates.

Other penal abodes in the Old Testament.

But apart from all emendation, Sheol appears here as the place of punishment for the wicked, and the same view returns in some degree in ver. 20. From Sheol so described the righteous is to be delivered (ver. 15). But the force of the argument will be seen best by bringing forward the salient points of the thought. Thus in vers. 7-9 bodily death is declared to be the inevitable lot of all: the righteous and wicked alike must physically die (ver. 10). But after death a difference in their respective lots sets in. As regards the wicked rich men, they must perish as the beasts (ver. 12); their bodies will be housed for ever in the grave[1] (ver. 11), and their souls descend as helpless sheep into Sheol, there to be shepherded by death; Sheol will consume their phantom forms (ver. 14). But as for the righteous, though they too must die[2] (ver. 10), God will ransom them, from the hand of Sheol will He take their soul[3] (ver. 15).

As a place of penal punishment, therefore, Sheol could never become the abode of the righteous. Hence in ver. 15 the righteous expect to escape it after death, and be taken immediately to heaven: "Surely my soul God will set free; for from the hand of Sheol will he take me."

Psalm lxxiii.

In Ps. lxxiii., as in xlix., the writer is troubled by the prosperity of the wicked (vers. 11, 12). He is even tempted to declare that all things fall out

[1] Here I follow the LXX, Syr., Vulg. and Targum, which, by transposing two letters (קִבְרָם for קִרְבָּם), read—

Their graves are their houses for ever,

instead of

Their inward thought is their houses for ever.

[2] All must submit to bodily death is the teaching of ver. 10. Duhm, however, thinks that "the wise" spoken of here are not the wise in a religious sense, but are "the wise of this world," and this, he believes, is proved by their being contrasted with "the fools" and "brutish persons" in the parallel member of the verse. But the usage of almost the entire Wisdom literature is against this view, and particularly the usage of the Psalms, which always take the terms "wise man" and "fool" in a religious and ethical sense. This misinterpretation of ver. 10 has led Duhm into his impossible exposition of ver. 15 (see note 2 on p. 76).

[3] נפשי is here taken collectively of all the faithful, as in Ps. xi. 1.

CHAP. II.

well with the sinner, but ill with the righteous, but from such an utterance he refrains out of loyalty to the Jewish community (vers. 13-15). Nevertheless, his trouble of heart has driven him to study this inversion of right and wrong in life, but the problem remained an unsolved burden upon him (ver. 16) till he entered into the knowledge of God's secret mysteries (מקדשי־אל), and learnt the fate of the ungodly, how that they do not escape punishment, but are already the prey of self-delusion (משׂואות—so Duhm), and will become the victims of a speedy and utter destruction (vers. 17-19). From such false views of life the righteous are preserved through God's daily chastisements (ver. 14), and enjoy His guidance continually. Their highest blessedness consists in unbroken communion with Him—unbroken even by death; for after this life God takes them to Himself (vers. 23, 24). What earth or heaven, therefore, has in store for them matters not. In comparison with God all the universe is as nothing (ver. 25): this life ended, God is the true portion of the *souls*[1] of the righteous for evermore (ver. 26).

In interpreting this psalm as referring to individual immortality the present writer has the support of Delitzsch, Davidson, Baethgen, Duhm,[2] and

[1] Duhm appears to be right in striking out צור לבבי as a false variant of שׁארי ולבבי; we should then render: "When my flesh and my heart have perished, God is my portion for ever."

[2] Duhm interprets Ps. xlix. 15 of an actual *bodily* translation, on the ground that לקח has here the same technical meaning as in 2 Kings ii. 9, 10; Gen. v. 24; Ps. lxxiii. 24. Such an interpretation is simply impossible. Indeed on Ps. lxxiii. 24 he is obliged to abandon this view, and take the verb as simply meaning translation from this life to a higher state of being. Of what nature this state of being is we gather from lxxiii. 26, which takes for

originally Cheyne,[1] though there is great divergence in the exposition of details.

Conclusions as to how far the doctrine of an individual immortality of the righteous existed in the Old Testament.

We have now done with the question of individual immortality so far as it is dealt with in the Old Testament. Its attestation is meagre. In Job it emerges as a strong aspiration, but falls short of being an abiding spiritual conviction. To the latter stage it has already risen in Pss. xlix. and lxxiii. But even if the evidence of the Psalms were doubtful, the evidence of Job is in itself sufficient to prove that, amongst a few at any rate in Israel, the hopes of the individual had at last come in sight of their destined goal, even the future blessed life of the righteous. But, further, even if all such evidence were wanting, we should be obliged to postulate the existence of this doctrine from the logical necessities of thought; for the doctrine of the resurrection which was developed towards the close of the fourth century, or at latest early in the third, is a complex idea, and presupposes in Israel[2] the prior existence of its two chief components, namely, the doctrine of an individual immortality of the righteous and that of the Messianic kingdom. When once the

The historical attestation of this doctrine confirmed by the logical necessities of thought.

granted the *disembodied* existence of the righteous after death. In Ps. xlix. also the writer is dealing with the destinies of the righteous and of the wicked *after death*. Death leads off the latter to Sheol (ver. 14), whereas God takes the souls of the former to Himself (ver. 15). We should observe that *μετατίθημι*, which is the LXX rendering of לקח in Gen. v. 24, is used in Wisdom iv. 10 of the translation of the *soul*.

[1] Dr. Cheyne now regards ver. 24 as corrupt, and reads "And will make known to me the path of glory," *i.e.* the divine glory which will be revealed in the Messianic age.

[2] That is, unless we assume that Israel borrowed the resurrection doctrine in its completeness. But the Book of Job, supported by Pss. xlix., lxxiii., makes this assumption at once gratuitous and groundless.

CHAP. II.

Early superseded by the doctrine of the resurrection.

doctrine of an individual immortality was subsumed in the larger doctrine of the resurrection, and had thus played its part in the evolution of truth, it could no longer exist side by side with this larger conception, but fell perforce into the background, and for a prolonged period appears to be unknown and undesired in the thoughts and aspirations of the faithful. But with the lapse of nigh 200 years or more it again comes of necessity to the front, when the growing dualism of the times leads to the disintegration of the resurrection hope (as then conceived) into its original constituents, in order that these may pursue afresh and independently their paths of development with a view to their final synthesis in Christianity.

The ground for this supersession.

If we should ask why the doctrine of an individual immortality so soon gave place to that of the resurrection, the answer is at hand. The common good was still more dear to the faithful in Israel than that of the individual : in other words, the Messianic kingdom was a more fundamental article of their faith than that of a blessed future life of the individual. Hence when these doctrines were fused together, the doctrine of the resurrection, which was the direct outcome of this fusion, soon displaced that of the individual immortality of the righteous ; for the latter doctrine could never gain the full sympathies of the Jew, who loved his nation, and had his heart fixed on its blessed future. Thus the resurrection, stripped of its accidents and conceived in its essence, marks the entrance of the

Essential significance of the resurrection.

individual after death into the divine life of the community, the synthesis of the individual and the common good. Thus the faithful in Palestine looked forward to a blessed future only as members of the holy people, as citizens of the righteous kingdom that should embrace their brethren. And herein, as throughout this evolution of religion, we can trace the finger of God; for it was no accident that His servants were unable to anticipate any future blessedness save such as they shared in common with their brethren and nation. The self-centredness, if not selfishness, that marked the Greek doctrine of immortality[1] is conspicuous

[1] Thus in the religious philosophy of Plato, where the immortality of the soul is set forth in its loftiest and purest form, the individual who would secure this immortality is taught to live an ascetic life: not to concern himself with the community, but with himself (ἰδιωτεύειν ἀλλὰ μὴ δημοσιεύειν, *Apol.* 32 A); to lead a quiet life and mind his own business, like a man who has fallen among beasts (ὥσπερ εἰς θηρία ἄνθρωπος ἐμπεσών, *Rep.* vi. 496 D). "Human affairs are not worth any real trouble" (τὰ τῶν ἀνθρώπων πράγματα μεγάλης οὐκ ἄξια σπουδῆς, *Leg.* vii. 803 B). From these and many other passages of like import (see Rohde, *Psyche*, ii. 288-294) it follows that in pursuit of his own individual good a man should ignore the interests of the community; for that all the present life is corrupt, and the aim of the individual is to adopt a hostile attitude towards its manifold expressions, and fashion his conduct wholly with a view to his own immortality. Even in his own ideal Republic, the civic and social virtues had no independent value for the philosopher. "Der vollendete Weise hat nicht mehr die oberste Bestimmung, den Andern, draussen Stehenden, Pflichten zu erweisen; sein eigenes inneres Leben reif machen zur Selbsterlösung, das ist seine wahre und nächste Pflicht" (p. 293).

Thus the Greek development was one-sided. It was individualistic. And yet it could not well be otherwise with its peculiar doctrine of immortality, namely, its view that the soul was not only immortal but eternal, alike without beginning and end, and that it was capable of repeated incarnations in human and animal bodies. From this doctrine it follows that the present environment of the soul is only one of the many in which it exists from age to age, and accordingly this community or that can have no abiding significance. Such a soul can only consider God and itself. In Israel, however, as we have above seen, the soul was not in itself immortal, but only won such immortality through life in God.

by its absence in the religious forecasts of the faithful in Judaism. In true religion unlimited individualism is an impossibility. The individual can only attain to his highest in the life of the community alike here and hereafter.

CHAPTER III

THE ESCHATOLOGY OF THE NATION AND THE SYNTHESIS OF THE TWO ESCHATOLOGIES IN THE DOCTRINE OF THE RESURRECTION. DOCTRINE OF THE SOUL AND OF THE FUTURE LIFE AMONG THE GREEKS.

In the preceding chapters we have studied the eschatology of the individual, and in the course of this study we have come down to within a couple of centuries of the Christian era. We have now to study the eschatology of the nation, and for this purpose we must retrace our steps and go many a hundred years back into Israel's past.

Though Israel became a nation at the Exodus, it would be difficult to express what were the hopes and aspirations they cherished at that early date or for many subsequent centuries. Long before they came into existence as a nation, promises are expressed in connection with Abraham, Isaac, and Jacob (Gen. xii. 2, 3; xvii. 2, 4-6; xviii. 18; xxii. 17, 18; xxvi. 3, 4; xxvii. 29; xxviii. 14; xxxii. 12) as to the ultimate greatness of Israel and its destination as a source of blessing to all mankind. But since the

CHAP. III.

passages in question were, according to recent criticism, written eight hundred years or more subsequently to the Exodus, we shall confine ourselves in the present work to such eschatological facts and hopes as appear in the prophets. As these cluster *at the outset* round the familiar conception, "the day of Yahwè," we may with advantage study the eschatology of the nation in connection with this conception from preprophetic times down to the close of the Old Testament. But the day of Yahwè does not in itself constitute the blessed future, but only the divine act of judgment which inaugurates it. Hence the eschatology of the nation centres in *the future national blessedness introduced by the day of Yahwè.* This future is variously conceived. According to the popular conception which was current down to the eighth century, it was merely a period of material and unbroken prosperity which the nation was soon to enjoy through Yahwè's victorious overthrow of Israel's national foes. With this non-ethical expectation we shall not occupy ourselves further than to notice the conception of the day of Yahwè, associated with it.

Eschatology of nation may be treated as starting from the conception, "the day of Yahwè."

Eschatology of the nation centres in the future national blessedness to be introduced by the day of Yahwè.

Popular non-ethical conception of this period.

But this conception of the future gave place in the eighth century, at all events amongst the spiritual leaders of the people, to the prophetic doctrine of the coming kingdom. According to the prophets, this kingdom was to consist of a regenerated nation, a community in which the divine will should be fulfilled, an organised society interpenetrated, welded together, and shaped to ever

Prophetic conception = a regenerated community existing under national forms in which the divine will should be fulfilled.

CHAP. III.

higher issues by the actual presence of God. This ideal we shall henceforth, for convenience sake, designate shortly as the *Messianic* or *theocratic kingdom.*

The Messiah no organic part of this Old Testament conception.

Whether this kingdom was constituted under monarchical, hierarchical, or purely theocratic forms was in itself a matter of indifference. Since the Messiah formed no organic part of the conception, He was sometimes conceived as present at its head, sometimes as absent. Two factors, and only two, were indispensable to its realisation. First, it must be a *community* of Israelites, or of these together with non-Israelites. Secondly, it must be a community *in which God's will is fulfilled.* If we lose sight of either factor, our view of the kingdom is untrue.

Two factors indispensable.

No eighth-century prophet foretold the advent of this kingdom save Isaiah, according to a growing body of scholars.

That the prophetic conception of the kingdom prevailed from the seventh century onwards is admitted on all hands, but of late years there is a growing body of scholars who maintain that, with the exception of a single passage in Isaiah, no prophet of the eighth century preached the advent of this kingdom, and that the unceasing burden of their message to Israel was solely one of fast approaching and inevitable doom. That most of the passages in Amos, Hosea, Isaiah, and Micah which promise the advent of the Messianic kingdom and of the Messiah are intrusions in the text from a later time, may be regarded, on the whole, as a sound conclusion of criticism. But that they are all with one exception interpolations of a later date, and particularly that all the passages which tell of the Messiah are without exception of this character,

CHAP. III.

cannot be regarded as an established result of criticism.

But this conclusion is still to be taken provisionally.

If the following pages betray at times signs of indecision, they do but reflect the present attitude of the writer ; for though he has elected to follow the conclusions of the more advanced critics, it is with great hesitation that he has done so.

All the following statements on the above controversy regarding the eighth-century prophets are to be regarded as provisional.

Our study begins with the day of Yahwè, and develops into a description of the kingdom it introduces.

As regards the day of Yahwè, no such critical difficulty exists. Our study of the eschatology of the nation, therefore, will begin with this unquestioned element in Israel's expectations of the future, and trace its subsequent enlargement and various developments from a judgment of individual nations to a judgment of all mankind. In pre-Exilic times this conception constitutes all but exclusively the subject of the prophetic teaching as to the future ; but from the Exile onwards this is not so. Henceforth it serves only to introduce the eternal kingdom of God on earth. From the Exile onwards eschatological development begins to grow in complexity, for from that period the nation, no less than the individual, begins to maintain his claims to righteous treatment.

The Day of Yahwè

This conception relates to the nation, and not to the individual.

This conception is related to the people as a whole, and not to the individual. It means essentially the day on which Yahwè manifests Himself in victory over His foes, that is, the national foes of Israel.

Day amongst the Hebrews, as among the Arabs, occasionally had the definite signification of "day of battle." Thus in Is. ix. 4 "the day of Midian" is the day of victory over Midian. The belief in this day was older than any written prophecy. It was a popular expectation in the time of Amos. This popular conception, which was as unethical and nationalistic as the kingdom it was expected to establish, was adopted by the prophets and transformed into one of thoroughly ethical and universal significance. We shall now deal with the various forms it assumed in the Old Testament.

Popular and unethical conception of day of Yahwè.

I. *The popular conception of the day of Yahwè as a judgment on Israel's national enemies*, eighth century B.C. and earlier.—This conception originated, no doubt, from the old limited view of Yahwè as merely the national God of Israel. The relation of Yahwè to Israel, in the minds of Amos' contemporaries, was not an ethical, but, to a large extent, a *natural* one. They conceived themselves to be solely Yahwè's people, and Yahwè to be solely Israel's God (Am. iii. 2). Israel's duty was to worship Yahwè, and Yahwè's to protect Israel. This worship consisted in ritual and sacrifice, and to its due discharge the morality of the worshipper was a thing indifferent. Hence, as they were faithful in the duties of worship and sacrifice and tithing (iv. 5; v. 5, 21, 22), they could with confidence not only look forward to, but also pray for, "the

CHAP. III.

day of Yahwè" as the instrument of their vindication against their enemies. The "day of Yahwè" is thus the *day of Israel's vindication against their enemies through Yahwè.*[1] But "the day of Yahwè," Amos warns Israel, is no such day as they expected. The day of Yahwè, the God of righteousness, cannot for an unrighteous people be a day of salvation, but of woe; not a day in which Israel would be vindicated against its enemies, but in which Yahwè's righteousness would be vindicated against wrongdoing, whether in Israel or its enemies.

AMOS (*circa* 760 B.C.)

Prophetic conception of the day of Yahwè. I. Pre-Exilic period. (*a*) directed against Israel in Amos

This assault of Amos on the popular conceptions of the day of Yahwè provides us, at the same time, with the prophetic conception of this day. According to the prophets of the eighth century, this day was to be one (*a*) *of judgment directed, first and chiefly, against Israel.* In opposition to the popular view that Yahwè is Israel's national God, Amos avoids the very phrase "God of Israel," and designates Him as "the Lord Yahwè," "the God of Hosts," or "Yahwé of Hosts."[2] Yahwè is the Moral Ruler of all the earth. His "day,"[3] therefore, is, as we have seen, the day

[1] This belief that Yahwè must save His people survived, despite the prophets, till the captivity of Judah in 586 B.C.

[2] Yahwè of Hosts means in the prophets the Omnipotent, the Lord of the armies of heaven as well as of earth. See p. 9 for an earlier meaning.

[3] The day of Yahwè, in its double character as a day of punishment and blessing, is also spoken of as "that day" (Is. xvii. 7, xxx. 23, xxviii. 5, xxix. 18; Hos. ii. 18; Mic. ii. 4, iv. 6, v. 10; Zech. ix. 16, xiv. 4, 6, 9), "that time" (Jer. xxxi. 1, xxxiii. 15, l. 4; Zeph. iii. 19, 20; Joel iii. 1), "the day" (Ezek. vii 10; Mic. iii. 6), "the time" (Ezek. vii. 12).

in which He manifests Himself for the *vindication of Himself and of His righteous purposes, and not of Israel.* In Amos, to whom we owe this new meaning of the phrase, the day of Yahwè appears *only in its darker side,*[1] as directed against Israel. It will bring about the overthrow of the kingdom (v. 1-3), Samaria will be destroyed (iii. 11, 12), and Israel carried into captivity (v. 5, 27; vi. 7; vii. 11; ix. 4). This day is "darkness and not light" for Israel (v. 18). Other nations will feel it in proportion to their unrighteousness, but since unrighteous Israel is specially related to Yahwè, they will, for that reason, experience His severest judgments (iii. 2): "You only have I known of all the families of the earth: therefore will I visit upon you all your iniquities."

[1] ix. 8-15, which promises a happy future for Israel and the house of David, is rejected as an Exilic addition by Wellhausen, Smend, Cheyne, G. A. Smith, Marti, Nowack, Volz. Driver, on the other hand, defends this passage, but with some hesitation (*Joel and Amos*, 119-123).

In this rejected passage we have the promise of the restoration of the dynasty of David in all its former splendour over reunited Ephraim and Judah (ix. 11):—

> In that day will I raise up the fallen tabernacle of David,
> And close up the breaches thereof;
> And I will raise up his ruins,
> And I will build it as in the days of old.

The land is to be blessed with prosperity (ix. 13), and the exiles to be restored (ix. 14):—

> And I will bring again the captivity of my people Israel,
> And they shall build the waste cities and inhabit them, etc.

And Israel thus restored will never again be removed from its own land (ix. 15).

The Messianic kingdom is limited strictly to Israel. The neighbouring nations, particularly Israel's ancient foe Edom, should come under the suzerainty of Israel, as in David's time (ix. 12).

CHAP. III.

Hosea (746-734 B.C.)

and in Hosea.

Hosea is of one mind with Amos.[1] It is against Israel that the day of Yahwè is directed. Though the phrase itself is not found in Hosea, the judgment it designates is foretold.

The whole nation is utterly corrupt: "There is no truth, nor mercy, nor knowledge of God in the land" (iv. 1). They have gone after Baal, and become worshippers of graven images (v. 3, viii. 4, xi. 2). Wherefore Israel "shall fall by the sword: their infants shall be dashed in pieces, and their women with child shall be ripped up" (xiii. 16). So dire will be their tribulation that "they shall say to the mountains, Cover us; and to the hills, Fall on us" (x. 8). It was a fate from which there was no escape.[2] "The iniquity of Ephraim is bound up:

[1] The clauses referring to Judah in i. 7; iv. 15; v. 5, 10, 12, 13, 14; vi. 4, 11; viii. 14; x. 11; xi. 12; xii. 2 are rejected by Marti as interpolations. Nowack, *Die kleine Propheten*, 1897, excises all these references except v. 5.

[2] Most of the passages which predict the establishment of the kingdom under the Messianic King are rejected by a variety of scholars. Thus i. 10–ii. 1, iii. 5, iv. 15^a are condemned as interpolations by Stade (*Gesch.*[2] 577 *note*). In addition to these, ii. 16, vi. 11, and most of xiv. 1-9, have been rejected by Wellhausen. The latter, however, and Nowack, defend some of the passages which promise the future blessedness of Israel. "The complete destruction of Israel is for him (Hosea) an inconceivable thought" (Wellhausen, *Gesch.*[3] 116). Similarly Nowack (*Die kl. Propheten*, p. 81). Nowack, notwithstanding, denies the originality of i. 7; i. 10–ii. 1, 14-16, 20-23; iii. 5; iv. 15^a; vi. 11; xiv. 7, 9. The passages of a similar character which he accepts are v. 15–vi. 3; xi. 8; xiv. 6, 8. G. A. Smith adopts a like attitude to Wellhausen and Nowack. Cheyne (in W. R. Smith, *Proph.*[2] pp. xvii, *sqq.*) rejects i. 7; i. 10–ii. 1; iii. 5; iv. 15^a; v. 15–vi. 4, 11; vii. 1; viii. 14; and xiv. 1-9 in its entirety. Marti (*Gesch. d. isr. Rel.* pp. 181, 182) appears to regard Hosea as the prophet of inexorable doom like Amos. Similarly Volz (*Vorexilisch. Yahweprophetie*, 32 *sqq.*) See Driver, *Introd. to Old Testament*,[7] 306, 307.

Taking the text as it stands, the eschatology is as follows: "At the end

his sin is laid up in store. . . . From the hand of Sheol shall I ransom them: from death shall I redeem them: . . . compassion is hid from mine eyes" (xiii. 12-14).

CHAP. III.

ISAIAH (740-701 B.C.)

(*b*) directed mainly against Judah.

(*b*) *Day of Yahwè mainly against Judah.*—In Isaiah and Micah the day of Yahwè receives a new application: it is directed against Judah. Like the two preceding prophets, Isaiah[1] aimed his warnings of judgment against Israel (ii. 6-21, viii. 1-4, ix. 8-20, xvii. 1-11, xxviii. 1-4). By Yahwè's wrath should the land be burnt up; its people should be as the fuel for fire (ix. 19); in one day should head and tail, palm-branch and rush be cut off (ix. 14); its warriors shall not be spared, nor its widows nor orphans receive compassion (ix. 17). The doom shall come like a tempest of hail, a destroying storm, as a tempest of mighty waters (xxviii. 2). And the lofty looks of man shall be brought low, and the haughtiness of men shall be bowed down, and the

First against Israel, as in preceding prophets.

of days" (iii. 5) Israel will be converted and return to God (v. 15), for He will revive them from their spiritual death (vi. 2), and betroth them to Him for ever "in righteousness, and in judgment, and in loving kindness, and in mercies" (ii. 19). And Israel will be called "sons of the living God," and become innumerable as the sand of the sea, and Judah and Ephraim will be reunited under one king (i. 10, 11), even under a scion of the house of David (iii. 5). And the exiles will return to their own land (xi. 10, 11). In this period the earth will be blessed with fruitfulness (ii. 22), the wild beasts will become tame, and all the weapons of war will be destroyed (ii. 18).

[1] In my references to Isaiah I have adopted Dr. Cheyne's critical results in his *Introduction to Isaiah*, 1895. It is due pre-eminently to this scholar that it is possible to give some coherent account of the various eschatological systems that are to be found in the composite book of Isaiah.

CHAP. III.

Lord shall be exalted in that day (ii. 11-17). And men shall cast away their idols of silver and of gold to the moles and the bats, and go into the caves of the rocks to hide themselves from before the terror of the Lord, when He ariseth to shake mightily the earth (ii. 19-21). Thus judgment fell on Israel, and since Judah was no less corrupt, it too must be destroyed (i. 10-17, 21-26; iii. 1-15; v. 8-24; xxviii. 14-22; xxix. 1-4; xxx. 8-17; xxxi. 4), and all the more surely as it sought help from the neighbouring world-powers (xxviii. 14-22, xxxi. 3). The judgment on Jerusalem shall come suddenly: it shall receive doom from the Lord of Hosts with thunder and with earthquake and great noise, with whirlwind and tempest, and the flame of a devouring fire (xxix. 6[1]).

Judgment on Judah.

Thus Isaiah was, like Amos, a prophet of doom. In one passage, however, he prophesies the advent of the kingdom, but in a very modest form.

Isaiah once prophesied the advent of the kingdom.

i. 24-26. "Therefore this is the oracle of the Lord, Yahwè Sebáoth, the Hero of Israel: Ha! I will appease me of mine adversaries, and avenge me on mine enemies; 25. and I will bring back mine hand upon thee, and will smelt out in the furnace thy dross and will take away all thy alloy; 26. and I will bring back thy judges as at the first, and thy counsellors at the beginning: afterwards thou shalt

[1] If we accept the last as it stands, the views of Isaiah as to the inviolability of Jerusalem wavered. Thus in xxix. 7, 8; xxxi. 5 he definitely prophesies that Zion can never be taken by its foes. This latter view is rejected by Cheyne, who pronounces xxix. 5, 7, 8 an intrusion, and xxxi. 5 to be hopelessly corrupt.

be called Citadel of Righteousness, Faithful City" (Cheyne's translation). CHAP. III.

The nation is thus to be restored as aforetime, but on a righteous foundation. All that was evil was to be purged out of it. It is to be observed, however, that there is no mention of the Messiah in connection with it.

No world-judgment in Isaiah.

There is no world-judgment in Isaiah. Judgment, it is true, will be executed on Egypt, Ethiopia, Tyre, Philistia, Moab, and Syria, and all nations will be concerned in Yahwè's purpose of "breaking Assyria." These nations, however, are dealt with by the prophet *only in relation to his own people*. The conception of a world-judgment wherein every nation was to be judged independently of Israel was of a later date.[1]

In iii. 13, where there appears to be a reference to it, the text is corrupt.[2] The idea of its universality seems to be given in ii. 11-21, but the language is poetical.

Isaiah nowhere extends the blessings of the kingdom to the heathen world. Israel alone should enjoy them. Most of the Messianic passages in Isaiah i.-xxxix. are due to later interpolations.[3]

1 Cheyne, *Introd.* pp. 53, 246.

2 *Ibid.* 391 *note.*

3 All the Messianic passages save one (Is. i. 24-26) are rejected as the work of a later age by Cheyne: also wholly or in part by Duhm, Hackmann, Marti, Volz, Brückner, G. A. Smith, etc. The chief passages are Is. ii. 2-4, iv. 2-6, ix. 1-7, xi., xvi. 5, xix. 18-25, xxv. 6-8, xxviii. 16, xxix. 16-24, xxx. 18-26, xxxii. 1-8[c], xxxv. 1-10. With ii. 2-4, xix. 18-25 we shall deal under post-Exilic prophecy. The post-Exilic date of iv. 2-6 is practically admitted by G. A. Smith (Hastings' *Bible Dictionary*, ii. 488); likewise of xi. 10-16, xvi. 5, xxv. 6-8, and xxxv. 1-10, pp. 492, 493. On the other

MICAH (*circa* 723-700 B.C.)

Destruction of Jerusalem. No Messianic kingdom.

In Micah the doom of Jerusalem is pronounced, and no hope of ultimate redemption is

hand, this scholar strongly contends against Marti, Volz, and Brückner, who deny that the Messiah appeared at all in pre-Exilic prophecy.

Apart from arguments based on language and historical allusions, these writers argue that the functions of the Messiah are purely political and not religious. He is a national leader, and exercises the offices of neither prophet, priest, nor leader, and belongs therefore to the Exilic and post-Exilic periods. G. A. Smith vigorously assails this view. He contends (Hastings' *Bible Dictionary*, ii. 488, 489) that this national conception of the Messiah suits the pre-Exilic and not the later periods: that it belongs naturally to the pre-Exilic forms of the Messianic kingdom: that the Isaianic passages ascribe to the Messiah the duties prescribed by the time, the deliverance of Israel from the Assyrian invasion, and the establishment of a righteous kingdom over the people of Yahwè.

If we accept the chief Messianic passages as Isaianic, we obtain a very striking picture of the Messiah. Thus, according to ix. 6, 7 (Cheyne's translation):—

A child is born unto us, a son is given unto us,
And the government is upon his shoulders, and his name is called
Wonder-counsellor, God-hero, Father of booty, Prince of Peace.
Increased is the government and of peace there is no end,
Upon the throne of David and over his kingdom,
In establishing and supporting it by justice and righteousness from henceforth even for ever.
The zeal of Yahwè Sebáoth will accomplish this.

In these verses we have a description of the Messiah as a great warrior and ruler. In the following verses as a righteous judge, inspired by the Spirit of Yahwè, equally great in knowledge and in practice. xi. 1-5:—

And a shoot shall come forth from the stock of Jesse,
And a scion from his roots shall bear fruit,
And the spirit of Yahwè shall rest upon him,
A spirit of wisdom and discernment, a spirit of counsel and might, a spirit of knowledge and of the fear of Yahwè.
And he shall not judge according to that which his eyes have seen,
Nor arbitrate according to that which his ears have heard,
But with righteousness shall he judge the helpless,
And arbitrate with equity for the humble in the land;
And he shall smite tyrants with the rod of his mouth,
And with the breath of his lips shall he slay the ungodly.
And righteousness shall be the girdle of his loins,
And faithfulness the girdle of his reins.

held out:[1] iii. 12. "Zion, for your sake, shall be ploughed as a field, and Jerusalem shall become heaps, and the mountain of the house as the high places of the forest."

In the above prophets the judgment of the Gentiles is *never conceived independently, but only in relation to the judgment on Israel or Judah.*

NAHUM (664-607 B.C.) and HABAKKUK (605-600 B.C.)

When we pass from these four great prophets of the eighth century to those of the latter half of the seventh, namely Nahum, Habakkuk, and Zephaniah, we find that religious thought on our subject has in

The nature of the lower creation will be transformed, xi. 6-8:—

And the wolf shall lodge with the lamb, and the leopard lie down with the kid,
And the calf and the young lion, and the fatling together, whilst a little child leadeth them.
And the cow and the bear shall feed, together shall their young ones lie down,
And the lion shall eat straw like the ox;
And the suckling shall play at the hole of the asp,
And the weaned child shall stretch out his hand to the eyeball of the basilisk.

xxx. 26:—

Moreover the light of the moon shall be as the light of the sun,
And the light of the sun shall be sevenfold, as the light of seven days.

[1] Only chaps. i.-iii. (with the exception of ii. 12, 13, which promise the return from the Exile) are assigned to Micah. Chaps. iv.-vii. (with the exception of iv. 9, 10, and v. 1, 10-14) are, according to Nowack (*Kleine Propheten*, 187, 188, 204 *sqq.*), derived from different authors and different periods. Stade, Smend, Wellhausen, Marti, and Cheyne reject iv., v. in their entirety, and most critics since Ewald's time reject vi., vii. See Stade, *ZATW*, 1881, pp. 161-172; 1883, 1-16; 1884, 291-297; Smend, *ATliche Theol.* 225; Driver, *Introd.* vii. 329-334.

According to the rejected chapters, Yahwè will again restore the kingdom to Israel (vii. 7-9). The exiles will be restored (ii. 12; iv. 6, 7). The Messiah from Beth Ephratah will rule in Yahwè's name (v. 2), and with His reign will begin the eternal Messianic kingdom (v. 3-7), and He will crush Assyria (v. 5-7), and henceforth idolatry and wickedness and warfare will be at an end (v. 10-14).

CHAP. III.

Modification of conception of day of Yahwè in seventh century.

part advanced and in part retrograded. The retrogression is manifest in the books of Nahum and Habakkuk. In these prophets we have a modified renewal of the old popular conception of the day of Yahwè; for they conceive it as an intervention on behalf of *righteous* Israel against the *wicked* Assyria.

Yahwè must intervene for Israel because Israel is righteous.

According to the primitive view, Yahwè was bound to intervene on behalf of His people on the ground of the supposed *natural* affinities existing between them, whereas according to the view of Nahum and Habakkuk[1] His intervention must follow on the ground of *ethical* affinities; for Israel and the Gentiles are related to each other as the righteous, צדיק, and the wicked, רשע (Hab. i. 4, 13).

The grounds for this renewal in a modified form of the old view of the day of Yahwè are to be found partly in the sufferings experienced by Israel at the hands of their oppressors, and partly in the confidence which Josiah's reforms had begotten in the people that they were truly Yahwè's people.

Israel's sufferings at the hands of their oppressors had given birth to unutterable bitterness and resentment. The pressure of foreign influences in worship and morals also naturally made the religious leaders in Judah set all the higher value on their national worship and ancestral customs. The religious party therefore tended to become more and more

[1] Hab. i. 5-11 is an interpolation according to Giesebrecht, Wellhausen, Nowack, etc. Likewise chap. iii. The former passage is probably earlier and the latter much later in date than Habakkuk. With the later date of iii. Davidson and Driver agree, but both defend i. 5-11. ii. 11-14 is rejected by Nowack.

national in sympathy and aims. Nahum appears as the spokesman of this party. He does not stand, as the preceding prophets, in opposition to the ruling party in the state, but rather gives expression to their sentiments. The cause of Yahwè and of Israel is one and the same.

CHAP. III.

In the next place, owing to the reforms under Josiah, the people felt themselves to be Yahwè's people, and accordingly were confident of His help. They felt themselves to be righteous—neither in Nahum nor Habakkuk is there any mention of Israel's sin—hence over against the glaring wickedness of the Gentiles the *actual* Judah was regarded as righteous (see Hab. i. 4, 13). The righteousness of Judah was thus, it is true, only a *relative* righteousness. Judah could claim to be righteous only in contrast with the wickedness of the heathen. We have herein the beginnings of the thought that Israel is right over against the world—the beginnings; for in Nahum and Habakkuk this view is applied only to the single nation of the Assyrians and not, as in later times, to all the Gentiles. Hence the impending judgment will strike, not righteous Israel, but the godless Gentiles. Under the influence of Habakkuk's example the usage was developed later of designating the Gentiles absolutely as the godless, רשע, and Judah as the righteous, צדיק (cf. Is. xxvi. 10; Pss. ix. 5, 17, x. 2, 3, 4, lviii. 10, lxviii. 2, cxxv. 3. Henceforth in most subsequent representations of the future the destruction of the Gentiles stands as a central thought.

This the beginnings of the belief that Israel is right over against the world.

CHAP. III.

In Nahum i.–ii. 2 we have a description of the day of Yahwè and the setting up of the Messianic kingdom. It begins with a reference to the attributes of Yahwè and their manifestation in nature (i. 2-6). The writer then deals with the utter end that is to be made of the enemies of His people, particularly of Assyria (i. 7-14). The Messianic kingdom is apparently to follow on the destruction of Nineveh. For the humiliation of Judah is at an end (i. 12): "Though I have afflicted thee, I will afflict thee no more."[1] The hour of redemption is at hand (i. 15): "Behold upon the mountains the feet of him that bringeth good tidings, that publisheth peace." God will restore Israel and Judah (ii. 2): "Yahwè bringeth again the excellency of Jacob, as the excellency of Israel."

The Messianic kingdom to follow on the destruction of Assyria in Nahum.

If, however, Bickell, Gunkel, and Nowack are right in their views that i. 2–ii. 2 is not a prophecy but an alphabetical psalm describing under traditional forms the coming of Yahwè to judge the enemies of His people and the establishment of the Messianic kingdom,[2] they will be no less right in maintaining that it is not from Nahum's hand but from a much later date. In that case the original prophecy of Nahum would deal with the judgment of Nineveh (ii. 3–iii.) and *not possess a single reference to the Messianic*

But i. 2–ii. 2 may be post-Exilic. In that case Nahum would possess no reference to the Messianic future.

[1] These words might be rendered: "When I afflict, I will afflict thee no more," that is, the affliction would be thorough and final. In this case the verse would apply to Assyria.

[2] See Gunkel, *ZATW*, 1893, pp. 223 *sqq.*; Bickell, *Sitzungsberichte der kaiserl. Akad. der Wiss. in Wien*, Abhandl. v. 1894; Gunkel, *Schöpfung und Chaos*, 102, 103, 1895; Nowack, *Kleine Propheten*, pp. 227, 231-237, 1897; Davidson on *Nahum*, pp. 18-20, criticises this view unfavourably.

CHAP. III.

future. The real beginning of this prophecy was according to this view thrust out when i. 2–ii. 2 was amalgamated with ii. 3–iii.

In Habakkuk

In Habakkuk the only words that could be construed as referring to the kingdom are ii. 4, "The just shall remain in life through his integrity," at the judgment, and ii. 14, "the earth shall be filled with the knowledge of the glory of Yahwè, as the waters cover the sea."[1]

ZEPHANIAH (before 621 B.C.)

But whilst Nahum and Habakkuk are retrogressive, an important advance in the development of the idea of divine judgment is attested in Zephaniah, by whom the *day of Yahwè is conceived as the judgment of the whole world resulting in the survival of a righteous remnant of Israel.*

Day of Yahwè = world-judgment resulting in survival of a righteous remnant in Israel.

In Zephaniah the judgment appears for the first time to be universal. Its universal scope is the necessary corollary to the monotheistic faith of the prophet; for Yahwè as the God of the whole earth, and pre-eminently as the God of righteousness, must summon all the nations to judgment.

The judgment deals with Jerusalem (i. 8-13), with Philistia, Ethiopia, and Assyria (ii. 1-6), with all nations (iii. 8), with all the inhabitants of the earth (i. 18). It extends even to the brute creation (i. 2, 3). There is, however, a certain inconsistency in the picture. The instruments of judgment are a

[1] This verse, however, is regarded by many scholars as a later addition.

CHAP. III.

mysterious people, called "the guests" of Yahwè (i. 7)—probably the Scythians—who do not themselves come within the scope of judgment. Thus the conception is wanting in definiteness and comprehension. Zephaniah moves in the footsteps of Isaiah in the account of the impending judgment, but, whereas, in the latter, judgment on Israel and the nations stands in inner connection with his conception of the divine character and purposes, in Zephaniah it is without definite aim,[1] if with certain critics we reject ii. 8-11, iii. 8-10: its various constituents appear to represent already current eschatological expectations, while its wide sweep shows the operation of the prevailing monotheism. The day of Yahwè is a day of battle and assault on the defenced cities (i. 16), a day of trouble and distress, of wasteness and desolation, of supernatural terrors, of darkness, clouds and thick darkness (i. 14-18). The nations are to be assembled in order to be destroyed by the fierce anger of Yahwè (iii. 8).

Zephaniah first treats of the judgment of all nations.

This last feature, that is, the destruction of *the nations generally*, appears first in Zephaniah. This idea is a further development of the earlier doctrine that only the nations *hostile to* Judah should be destroyed, which is found in ii. 1-7 (*i.e.* the Philistines, Moab, and Ammon, etc.), Jer. xxv. 15-24 (*i.e.* the genuine portions), and Is. xvii. 12, 13 (*i.e.* the Assyrians). In the eighth-century prophets

[1] ii. 8-11 are rejected by Wellhausen and Nowack (*l.c.* 275-277); also by Budde and Cornill. iii. 9, 10 generally held to be later. Davidson defends the integrity of the entire book. See Driver, *Introd.* 342, 343.

in this connection it is the destruction of *definite and present foes* that is announced, but in the later it is that of *the nations generally*. Of these later prophets it forms a prominent and constantly recurring characteristic, as we see in Jer. xxv. 32, 33 (the addition of a reviser); Ezek. xxxviii.-xxxix., the fifth-century passages in Is. xxxiv., lxiii. 1-6; Zech. xii. 1-3, and the much later anonymous fragments in Is. lxvi. 16, 18, 19; Zech. xiv. 1-3, 12-15. The scene of this judgment on the nations, which Zephaniah leaves indeterminate, is declared by later prophets to be Jerusalem (Zech. xiv. 2, 12, 13; Joel iii. 2; Is. lxvi. 15).

The Messianic kingdom.

At the close of the judgment there will be left a small and righteous remnant in Israel (iii. 12, 13): "I will leave in the midst of thee an afflicted and poor people, and they shall trust in the name of Yahwè. The remnant of Israel shall not do iniquity, neither shall a deceitful tongue be found in their mouth: for they shall feed and lie down, and none shall make them afraid." These are those who are urged in ii. 3 to seek righteousness, if haply they may be hid in the day of Yahwè.

All the nations are to serve Yahwè.

There is a wide universalism in Zephaniah if ii. 11 and iii. 9, 10 are original. ii. 11. "Men shall worship him, every one from his place, even all the coast lands of the nations." iii. 9. "Then will I turn to the peoples a pure lip, that they may all call upon the name of Yahwè, to serve him with one consent."

No Messiah.

In Zephaniah, as in Nahum and Habakkuk, there is no mention of a Messianic king.

CHAP. III.

JEREMIAH[1] (626–586 B.C.) and EZEKIEL (593-571 B.C.)

Contrast between the pre-Exilic and Exilic conceptions of judgment.

We have now done with the pre-Exilic conceptions of the day of Yahwè. In pre-Exilic times divine judgment was *mainly* conceived collectively as one of doom on the nation *as a nation:* in Exilic and subsequent times the divine judgment is conceived as dealing with the individual Israelite, and thus as presenting a favourable or unfavourable side according to the character of the individual. As a result of this judgment a righteous community was to emerge, forming the nucleus of the Messianic kingdom. This difference in the conceptions of the two periods was brought about, at all events externally, by the destruction of the State. For the political annihilation of Israel may be regarded from two standpoints: from the one it was the inevitable doom of the impenitent nation; from the other, and that the one of most moment to our present study, it formed an indispensable factor in the development of religion; for it contributed to the individualisation of religion, alike in its essential nature and its expectations of the future. Thus the eschatology of the individual becomes henceforth a factor in the eschatology of the nation.

The Exile contributes to the individualisation of religion.

[1] Jeremiah (626-586 B.C.) belongs, it is true, to the pre-Exilic period. Since, however, his teaching on the relation of man to God is so diverse from that of his contemporaries and predecessors, and in many respects so nearly akin to that of Ezekiel (who was herein his disciple), I have thought it best to discuss their doctrines together, and treat Jeremiah as though he were a prophet of the Exile.

CHAP. III.

Contrast between pre-Exilic and subsequent prophecy as to the Messianic kingdom.

We have seen above that the message of the pre-Exilic prophet to Israel was mainly one of condemnation, and that only in a few cases was the prospect held out of a regenerated national life. But with the Exile the burthen of prophecy is no longer doom and destruction, but promise and blessing, and such is its unfailing characteristic till the close of the Canon. Judgment is still of necessity preached. But its character is very differently conceived in the succeeding centuries accordingly as we study the spiritual founders of Judaism or the large-hearted prophets who prepared the way for Christianity. According to Jeremiah and his spiritual successors, the rôle of judgment is only vindictive with the finally impenitent: in the case of all others its character is corrective and disciplinary. Its object is to prepare the way for the external Messianic kingdom in which all the nations shall participate.

The kingdom for Israel and all the nations, according to Jeremiah.

But, according to Ezekiel and subsequent writers of the same school, judgment was conceived as a purging of Israel from its evil elements with a view to the establishment of the eternal Messianic kingdom; but for the nations it meant only destruction, partial or complete, or, under the most favourable construction, absolute political subjection to Israel.

For Israel only, according to Ezekiel.

According, therefore, to the eschatology of the Exile, the Messianic kingdom was placed in the forefront of both prophetic and popular expectation. This kingdom was to be introduced by the day of

Conflicting Exilic conceptions of the day of Yahwè and of the Messianic kingdom.

CHAP. III.

Yahwè—conceived no longer merely as inflicting collective punishment for collective guilt, but as meting out individual retribution. As the result of this judgment a new and regenerate Israel emerges —the Messianic kingdom. Into this kingdom the nations enter by conversion, according to Jeremiah, but according to Ezekiel, even those which had survived the day of Yahwè are for ever excluded from it.

We have above dealt with Jeremiah and Ezekiel's doctrine of Individualism (see pp. 59-67). The individualising of religion in these prophets was the *precondition* of the restoration of Israel after the fall of Jerusalem. In God's visitations only the wicked in Israel, according to Ezekiel, should be destroyed. When a new Israel was thus created, Yahwè would further intervene to vindicate His honour and sole sovereignty over the world, and Israel would be restored to its own land, and the Gentiles destroyed. In Ezekiel a synthesis of the eschatologies of the nation and of the individual is attempted wholly within the sphere of this life.

Ezekiel's synthesis of the eschatologies of the nation and of the individual.

We have now arrived at a new period in the development of eschatological thought in Israel. Israel is on the eve of exile. But this exile is to be only of temporary duration. Yahwè's thoughts to Israel are thoughts of peace and not of evil (Jer. xxix. 11). After an exile of 70 years[1] in Babylon (xxv. 11, xxix. 10), Israel will be converted and brought back to its own land, and an ever-

Prophecy of the Messianic kingdom by Jeremiah.

[1] What a fruitful source of apocalyptic systems this number became we shall see later (see pp. 171-173).

lasting Messianic kingdom be established. This kingdom will be ruled over either by Yahwè or His servant the Messiah. Some scholars, it is true, maintain that the references to the Messiah in this prophet do not belong to the original text.[1]

Although the judgment of Israel is not strictly individualistic in Jeremiah, as it is in Ezekiel, we shall give his eschatological views with those of Ezekiel; for the latter are built on the former.

In Jeremiah the day of Yahwè is directed first and principally against Judah: the enemy will come in from the north (i. 11-16); the city and the temple will be destroyed (xxxvii. 6-10). But account is taken also of other nations, which are to drink of the cup of the wine of the fury of Yahwè—Egypt, Palestine, Edom, Moab, Ammon (xxv. 15-24; cf. i. 18). The further details of the judgment (xxv. 27-33, which expand it into a day of universal judgment) are interpolations from a later date. But there is a hopeful outlook. Israel will be restored (xxiii. 7, 8; xxiv. 5, 6). This restoration will be preceded by repentance (iii. 13, 19-25), and accompanied by a change of heart wrought by Yahwè. Through this change of heart each member of the nation will know Yahwè and obey Him (xxiv. 7): "And I will give them a heart to know me, that I am Yahwè; and they shall be my people, and I will be their God: for they shall return unto me with their whole heart"; cf. xxxii. 39. The same

Restoration of Israel to be accompanied by a change of heart.

[1] So Volz, who rejects all the passages which speak of the Messiah in Jeremiah. See *Vorexilische Yahweprophetie*, pp. 78-80.

promise is made, but more clearly and fully, in xxxi. 33, 34: "But this is the covenant that I will make with the house of Israel after those days, saith Yahwè: I will put my law in their inward parts, and in their heart will I write it; and I will be their God, and they shall be my people; and they shall teach no more every man his neighbour, and every man his brother, saying, Know Yahwè, for they shall all know me, from the least of them unto the greatest of them, saith Yahwè: for I will forgive their iniquity, and their sin will I remember no more." When restored to their own land, Yahwè will give them a righteous Branch of the house of David to rule over them (xxiii. 5, 6): "Behold the days come, saith Yahwè, that I will raise unto David a righteous Branch, and he shall reign as king and deal wisely, and shall execute judgment and justice in the land. In his days Judah shall be saved, and Israel shall dwell safely: and this is his name whereby he shall be called, Yahwè is our righteousness." Elsewhere Jeremiah speaks of the rulers of restored Israel as Shepherds (iii. 15, xxiii. 4). The Messiah, therefore, is conceived of as a dynasty, and not as an individual. Other Messianic passages, as xxx. 8, 9, 21; xxxiii. 14-26, are rejected by Giesebrecht.

Messianic kingdom and the Messiah, the latter representing a dynasty.

But the blessings of the kingdom will not be limited to Israel. The nations also will be converted, even those who have been hostile to Israel (xii. 14, 15): "Thus saith Yahwè: Against all mine evil neighbours, that touch the inheritance which I

The nations will be converted and incorporated in the kingdom.

have caused my people Israel to inherit: Behold I will pluck them up from off their land, and will pluck up the house of Judah from among them. And it shall come to pass, after that I have plucked them up, I will return and have compassion on them; and I will bring them again, every man to his heritage, and every man to his land." And elsewhere it is declared (iv. 2): "The nations shall bless themselves in Yahwè, and in him shall they glory"; (xvi. 19): "O Yahwè, my strength and my stronghold, and my refuge in the day of affliction, unto thee shall the nations come from the ends of the earth, and shall say, Our fathers have inherited nought but lies, even vanity and things wherein there is no profit." iii. 17, which gives evidence in the same direction, is rejected by Giesebrecht. All the nations shall be converted, and only the impenitent will be destroyed (xii. 16, 17): "And it shall come to pass, if they will diligently learn the ways of my people, to swear by my name, As Yahwè liveth; even as they taught my people to swear by Baal; then shall they be built up in the midst of my people. But if they will not hear, then will I pluck up that nation, plucking up and destroying it, saith Yahwè."

Only the finally impenitent will be destroyed.

The individualism appearing in Jeremiah is, as we have seen above, developed in Ezekiel to an extreme degree. Judgment will proceed individually on Israel, but collectively on the Gentiles. Yahwè will give a new heart to Israel (xi. 17-21, xxxvi. 25-32), and restore Israel and Judah to their

Teaching of Ezekiel.

CHAP. III.

Messianic kingdom.

own land, where, as the Messianic kingdom (xvii. 22-24), they shall be ruled by the Messiah (xxi. 27), by one king, even David (xxxiv. 23-31, xxxvii. 21-28). But the Messiah is not conceived here as an individual, but as a series of successive kings (cf. xlv. 8, xlvi. 16).

The Messiah not an individual, but a series of successive kings.

But after the establishment of the kingdom under the Messiah in Palestine, the heathen powers will join in a vast confederation against it. Under Gog, from the land Magog, will they march, but will all be destroyed through the might of Yahwè (xxxviii., xxxix.) This is the foe whose invasion of Israel from the north had been prophesied by Jeremiah (iii.-vi.) and Zephaniah (i. 7), but whose coming had hitherto been looked for in vain. Since this prophecy had remained unfulfilled, Ezekiel edits it anew, and adjourns its accomplishment. It is of Gog that Ezekiel thus speaks: "Thou art he of whom I spake by my servants the prophets of Israel, which prophesied in those days for many years, that I would bring thee against them" (xxxviii. 17[1]). This reduplication of judgment first appears in Ezekiel.

Invasion of Palestine by Gog.

This prophecy arises from an unfulfilled prophecy of Jeremiah and Zephaniah.

To this re-editing of unfulfilled prophecy is to be traced one of the main sources of Apocalyptic.

Unfulfilled prophecy a source of Apocalyptic.

On the Gentiles which survive the final overthrow in the land of Israel, no gleam of divine compassion will for ever light.[2]

Hopeless destiny of the surviving Gentiles.

I have given side by side the views of Jeremiah

[1] See Bertholet on Ezekiel xxxviii. 17.

[2] Some scholars find in xvii. 23 a promise that the Gentiles will seek refuge under the rule of the Messiah; but xvii. 24 shows that this interpretation is unsound. The Gentiles are symbolised not by the "birds of every

and Ezekiel, the great prophets of the Exile and the years immediately preceding it, as the best means of displaying their undoubted affinities, and their no less indubitable diversities. This parallel presentation of their views will be helpful, since these two prophets were the sources of two concurrent but very diverse streams of development.

Jeremiah and Ezekiel founders of two very diverse schools of development.

Both prophets are teachers of monotheism. With Jeremiah this doctrine was a living and fruitful principle, and teaches him to see, not in Israel only but in all the nations, the objects of the saving purposes of Yahwè. Jeremiah's universalism marks him out as the true spiritual successor of the great prophets of the eighth century. Ezekiel's particularism, on the other hand, shows his affinities to Nahum and Habakkuk of the seventh. For in Ezekiel monotheism is but a barren and lifeless dogma. Though theoretically he conceives Yahwè to be the sole Creator and God of all the earth, his belief has no influence on his views as to the destinies of the Gentiles. Israel alone will experience the salvation of Yahwè: but as for the Gentiles, their end is partly destruction and partly an unblessed existence under the malign rule of an ever hostile and ever unappeasable deity.

We shall deal first with those prophets who followed in the wake of Jeremiah, and developed his teaching to its legitimate consequences. In this

wing" in xvii. 23, but by "the trees of the field," xvii. 24. As "the cedar," xvii. 23, represents the kingdom of Israel, so "the trees of the field" represent the Gentile kingdoms. The only object with which the latter seem to be spared is that they may recognise the omnipotence of Yahwè.

CHAP. III.

Universalistic conception of the Messianic kingdom.

post-Exilic development (550-275 B.C.) *the thought of judgment, of the day of Yahwè, all but wholly disappears before that of an all-embracing Messianic kingdom—a kingdom initiated not through judgment but through the missionary efforts of Israel and the willing conversion of the nations.*

THE SECOND ISAIAH, xl.-lv. (545-539 B.C.)

Restoration of the exiles: rebuilding of Jerusalem and the temple.

According to the Second Isaiah, there is in store for Jerusalem not punishment but mercy, for already she has received double for all her sins (xl. 2). Moreover the Chaldean power will be overthrown through Cyrus (xli. 25; xliii. 14; xlv.-xlvii.; xlviii. 14, 15). Yahwè's people will then come forth from Babylon (xlviii. 20, lii. 11, 12). All difficulties in the way of the returning exiles will be removed (xl. 3-5; xli. 18, 19; xliii. 2-7; xlviii. 20-22; xlix. 8). Jerusalem and the temple will be rebuilt by the help of Cyrus (xliv. 28, xlv. 13). The desolation of Zion will be at an end, her wilderness will become like Eden and her desert like the garden of the Lord (li. 3), and Jerusalem will be built of precious stones (liv. 11, 12), and its inhabitants will be disciples of Yahwè (liv. 13). And the land will be too strait for its inhabitants (xlix. 18-23, liv. 1). And never more shall Jerusalem be assailed nor any arm raised up against her (xlix. 24-26, liv. 8-10, 14-17). The cities of Judah shall again be inhabited (xl. 9, xliv. 26), and Israel will possess the nations (liv. 3). Egypt and Ethiopia will of their own free will submit themselves unto

Voluntary conversion of nations, and their submission to Israel.

Israel, confessing: "Only in thee is God, and there is none beside—no Godhead at all" (xlv. 14). Yea, all the nations will become subject to Israel (xlix. 22, 23).[1]

The kingdom embracing Israel and the nations to be established through "the Servant of Yahwè," according to "Songs of the Servant."

But the conception of Israel's purpose and future is more nobly conceived in the "Songs of the Servant" (xlii. 1-4, xlix. 1-6, l. 4-9, lii. 13–liii. 12), which can hardly be of the same authorship as the rest of Isaiah (xl.-lv.) "They form a connected cycle of poetical meditations."[2] In this poem the Servant is the pious remnant of the people. They have been elected by God to a special service, and this service is the conversion of mankind to the worship of Yahwè. Hence the function of this true Israel is a missionary one. Their first task is the conversion of the rest of the nation—to "bring back Jacob unto him, and that unto him Israel might be gathered" (xlix. 5). Then their work is to extend to all the ends of the earth. The Servant should become the light of the nations; judgment shall be established on the earth, and the coast lands shall wait for His law (xlix. 6, xlii. 4). In these "Songs" the nations are considered only as subjects of the divine mercy, and never of judgment, as in Is. xlii. 13-17. There is no thought of Israel's political supremacy.

The nations to put themselves under the tutelage of Yahwè (Is. ii. 2-4).

A representation of the future somewhat similar to that in the Second Isaiah appears in the post-

[1] In xlii. 13-17 we have a description of the day of Yahwè in the Second Isaiah. In this passage it is the heathen and idolatrous world that is judged. Israel does not come within its scope (cf. li. 23).

[2] Cheyne, *Introd.* p. 305.

CHAP. III.

Exilic passages Is. ii. 2-4 = Mic. iv. 1-3, according to which the nations should of their own free will submit themselves to Yahwè.

Isaiah ii. 2-4: "And it shall come to pass in the latter days that the mountain of Yahwè's house shall be established in the top of the mountains, and shall be exalted above the hills; and all nations shall flow unto it. And many peoples shall go and say, Come ye, and let us go up to the mountain of Yahwè, to the house of the God of Jacob; and he will teach us of his ways, and we will walk in his paths: for out of Zion shall go forth the law, and the word of Yahwè from Jerusalem. And he shall judge between the nations, and reprove many peoples, and they shall beat their swords into plowshares, and their spears into pruning hooks; nation shall not lift up sword against nation, neither shall they learn war any more."

A like conception is probably at the base of the post-Exilic Is. xi. 9 = Hab. ii. 14 (both editorial additions?), which declare that the earth shall be full of the knowledge of Yahwè as the waters cover the sea.

PSALMS xxii., lxv., lxxxvi., lxxxvii.

In the Psalms.

The same thought[1] is set forth in the Psalms: "All the ends of the earth shall remember and turn to Yahwè, and all the kindreds of the nations shall worship before him" (xxii. 27-31): yea, "all nations . . . should come and worship," for God is their

[1] Cf. also the addition in Zeph. iii. 9, 10.

Creator (lxxxvi. 9).[1] God is said to be "the confidence of all the ends of the earth" (lxv. 5); all flesh is to come to Him as "the hearer of prayer" (lxv. 2).[2] But in Ps. lxxxvii. we have a noble conception which sums up in itself all the highest thought of the past in this direction. Jerusalem is to be the mother city of all the nations, "the metropolis of an ideally Catholic Church" (Cheyne); whole nations should enter the Jewish Church (lxxxvii. 4), but as individuals (lxxxvii. 5); and this should be their universal song: "All my fresh springs are in thee" (lxxxvii. 7).

Only two more works, Malachi and Is. xix. 16-25, call for attention, but these are beyond measure remarkable.

MALACHI (before 458 B.C.)

Recognition of monotheistic element in heathen religions by Malachi.

A wide universalism is apparently found in Mal. i. 11, where, in regard to the surrounding nations, the prophet declares: "From the rising of the sun even unto the going down of the same, my name is great among the Gentiles; and in every place incense is offered unto my name and a pure offering." Here the writer recognises the monotheism underlying the heathen religions. At this date the divine

[1] Cf. also xxv. 6 in the small apocalypse in Is. xxiv.; xxv. 6-8; xxvi. 10-20; xxvii. 1, 12, 13. This Cheyne assigns to the fourth century, Duhm to the second. This later date, which is, however, impossible on other grounds, would help to explain the very advanced eschatology which appears in xxiv. 21-23, which speaks of a preliminary judgment, and then after a very long interval of the final judgment. On the latter follows the theocratic kingdom (xxiv. 23).

[2] On the expectation that proselytes shall be admitted into the congregation of Yahwè's worshippers, see also Is. xiv. 1, xxv. 6, lxv. 3, 6.

designation "the Most High God" existed contemporaneously among the Phœnicians, Samaritans, and Jews. The words, however, are not to be taken in an absolute, but in a relative sense. The offerings of the heathen are made, though unconsciously, to Yahwè, and are more pleasing to Him than the faulty and deceitful sacrifices of Israel. That the words are to be construed in some such limited sense is clear from the next chapter (ii. 10), where Yahwè is represented as the Father and Creator of all the members of Judaism, and of these alone;[1] for on this statement is based an argument against the taking of heathen wives. And yet, however much we limit the words, it is indisputable that in Malachi heathenism is not conceived as a power hostile to God, as it is in Haggai and Zechariah.

Despite the severe visitations which the nation had experienced in the past, Israel proved again unfaithful when restored to its own land. Some seventy years earlier Haggai and Zechariah had promised the advent of the kingdom on the rebuilding of the temple. Within a few years the temple had been rebuilt, but the promise remained unfulfilled.

With Malachi the temple still holds this central position. Yahwè will suddenly come to it after that His messenger has prepared the way. But this coming will be for judgment; for Israel has, alike in

[1] These conflicting views show that although the monotheistic conception of God was a central article of the Jewish creed of the time, it was not a living and growing principle, and so its transforming influence on the rest of this creed was in the main nullified.

private morals (iii. 5, 14) and public worship (i. 6, 14), gone back to evil pre-Exilic ways.

Day of Yahwè on Israel only.

Judgment was therefore impending, but before that "great and terrible day" Elijah should be sent to "turn the heart of the fathers to the children and the heart of the children to the fathers" (iv. 5, 6). This judgment, which in Hag. ii. 5 *sqq.*, 21-23, and Zech. i. 15, ii. 1 *sqq.*, vi. 1-8, was conceived as an annihilation of the heathen powers, is in Malachi limited to Israel (ii. 17, iii. 3, 5, 13 *sqq.*) This day will "burn as a furnace," and destroy "all the proud and all that work wickedness." Only the righteous will be delivered. For them there is a book of remembrance written before Yahwè. "And they shall be a peculiar treasure unto me, saith Yahwè of Hosts, in the day that I prepare; and I will spare them as a man spareth his own son that serveth him" (iii. 17); "and all nations shall call you happy; for ye shall be a delightsome land, saith Yahwè of Hosts" (iii. 12).

Only the righteous will inherit the kingdom.

ISAIAH xix. 16-25 (*circa* 275 B.C., Cheyne)

In Is. xix. 16-25 the hopes of Ps. lxxxvii. reappear, but are far outbid in universality. Jerusalem, though the source of spiritual blessedness to Egypt and Assyria (Syria), is neither nationally nor spiritually paramount over them; rather do they form a spiritual and national confederacy in which Israel holds not the first but the third place (Is. xix. 21, 23-25): "And

Israel, Egypt, and Assyria to form a spiritual confederacy.

CHAP. III.

Yahwè shall be known to Egypt, and the Egyptians shall know Yahwè in that day; yea, they shall worship with sacrifice and oblation. . . . In that day shall there be a high way out of Egypt to Assyria, and the Assyrians shall come into Egypt and the Egyptians into Assyria; and the Egyptians shall worship with the Assyrians. And in that day shall Israel be the third with Egypt and with Assyria, a blessing in the midst of the earth; for that Yahwè of Hosts hath blessed them, saying: Blessed be Egypt my people, and Assyria the work of my hands, and Israel mine inheritance."

We have now dealt with the prophetic writers who, following in the wake of Jeremiah and the Second Isaiah, foretold the incorporation of the Gentiles into the Messianic kingdom. But concurrently with this large-hearted universalism there existed a variety of narrow and one-sided views, which held more or less closely to the particularism which originated with Nahum and Habakkuk, but especially with Ezekiel. According to Ezekiel and his successors, the future world, the Messianic age, belonged to Israel—to Judah and Israel reunited (Hos. iii. 5; Mic. v. 3[b]; post-Exilic) under the Messianic descendant of David (Is. ix. 1-6, xi. 1-8; Mic. v. 2-4; all Exilic or later): in it the Gentiles had no share at all, or only in a subordinate degree as dependants or servants of Israel. Their destiny was subjection or destruction, generally the latter, and always so in the case of those that had been hostile to Israel. According to these teachers—

The future, according to Ezekiel and his successors.

CHAP. III.

Particularistic conception of the day of Yahwè and the Messianic kingdom.

The day of Yahwè was to be a day of deliverance, initiating the Messianic kingdom on earth for Israel, but (a) *a period of ministry or bondage, or* (b) *else of partial or complete destruction for the Gentiles.*[1]

Some post-Exilic Fragments of Isaiah

Various post-Exilic fragments of Isaiah.

(*a*) In the Messianic future the Gentiles are to escort the returning Israelites to Jerusalem, and become their servants and handmaids (Is. xiv. 1-3,[2] lxvi. 12-16, 18^{a}-20[3]): they should build up its walls (lx. 10), and bow themselves and become subject to Israel (lx. 14), or else perish (lx. 12); they should become Israel's herdsmen, and ploughmen, and vinedressers (lxi. 5).[4] Very noble descriptions of the Messianic kingdom are given in iv. 2-6, xxvii. 6, xxix. 16-24, xxxv. 1-10, but these speak only of Israel in relation to the Messianic age.

(*b*) But at times the partial or complete destruction of the Gentiles predicted. In Is. xxxiv., xxxv. (450-430 B.C., Cheyne) there is a universal judgment described in which all the nations are to be destroyed (xxxiv. 1-3).[5] In the fifth-century

[1] Though in Haggai and Zechariah, and other post-Exilic writings, the day of Yahwè is essentially a day of destruction for the Gentiles, in Malachi, as we have already seen, its range is limited to Israel (see ii. 17–iii. 6, iii. 17–iv. 3).

[2] Cheyne regards these verses as alien to Is. xiii. 2–xiv. 21. This idea of the nations escorting the exiles back to Zion is found also in the Second Is. xlix. 22, 23.

[3] According to Cheyne, lx. and lxvi. 6-16, 18^{b}-22 belong to the age of Nehemiah and Ezra.

[4] These passages are post-Exilic, lx., lxi. being about 432 B.C. (Cheyne).

[5] We have a world-judgment described in xiii. 6-22, though the judgment is there directed primarily against Babylon (cf. xiii. 11, 19), just as in xxxiv. it is specially against Edom.

CHAP. III.

fragment lix. 15^b-20 the nations hostile to Yahwè and Israel [1] are singled out for destruction, while those that are spared fear the name of Yahwè (lix. 18, 19); [2] whereas in another fragment of the same date, lxiii. 1-6, which closely resembles the preceding passage in subject and phraseology, only the destruction of the Gentiles is announced.

Haggai (520 B.C.)

Messianic kingdom will be established on the completion of the building of the temple.

The exiles have already returned sixteen years, and the Messianic kingdom has not yet come.[3] That it is at hand the prophet Haggai is assured. A few years more and it will be manifested. So he infers from the political upheavals of the time. But Israel has not done its part. The temple is still lying in ruins. When it is rebuilt, the time will have arrived. Yahwè will in a little while shake the heavens and the earth, and the kingdoms of the nations will be overthrown, and their wealth will be brought to the temple, and though all the world round about be tumbling into ruin, peace will reign in Jerusalem (i. 8, ii. 6-9). That the dawn of this kingdom has

[1] In the post-Exilic (?) passage ix. 1-7 it is the Messiah that destroys the oppressors of Israel (ix. 1). This active rôle of the Messiah is rare in the Old Testament.

[2] Cf. the world-judgment in the small apocalypse Is. xxiv., xxv. (fourth century according to Cheyne, second century according to Duhm, but latter date not possible), where after the judgment (xxiv. 18-23) the surviving Gentiles shall be admitted to the worship of Yahwè (xxv. 6). It is very remarkable that in xxiv. 21, 22 *an intermediate place of punishment* is spoken of. The judgment, therefore, is conceived as consisting of two distinct acts. It is possible that we have here some traces of Mazdean influences. See Stave, *Ueber den Einfluss des Parsismus auf das Judenthum*, 176, 177.

[3] The prophecies of Jeremiah and Ezekiel imply that the return from the Exile and the advent of the kingdom will synchronise.

CHAP. III.

The heathen powers to be destroyed, and Zerubbabel chosen to be Messiah.

already appeared is made clear by a prophecy delivered two months later. For Yahwè will presently overthrow all the heathen powers, and set on the throne of the Messianic kingdom a prince of the house of David, even Zerubbabel, who was already in their midst (ii. 20-23).

Thus the establishment of the Messianic kingdom was expected to follow on the completion of the building of the temple;[1] and the day of Yahwè was conceived to be a destruction of the heathen powers.

What a falling-off there is in Haggai as compared with the great pre-Exilic prophets! No religious reformation of the individual and of the community is demanded by this prophet to prepare for the kingdom. They have only to build the temple.

ZECHARIAH i.-viii. (520-518 B.C.)

Advent of Messianic kingdom on building of the temple.

The thoughts of Haggai are more fully developed by his contemporary Zechariah. He expects the immediate advent of the kingdom when once the temple is rebuilt. As in Haggai (ii. 20-22), so in Zechariah there will be a day of Yahwè in which all the hostile heathen powers will be destroyed (i. 18-21). In this passage the complete heathen world is symbolised by the "four horns," *i.e.* the four quarters of the world. Since this world was

[1] For Yahwè the temple is indispensable as His dwelling-place. This thought is apocalyptic. It is not through moral reformation, but through divine intervention, that the kingdom is to be introduced. The importance of the temple also testifies to the growing importance of the priesthood. Hence the Messiah is less important in Haggai and Zechariah than in Jeremiah.

CHAP. III.

hostile to Israel, which was to Yahwè as the apple of His eye (ii. 8), it must be annihilated. This destruction of the heathen powers is a precondition of the Messianic time. We have in Haggai and Zechariah further developments of that opposition between the kingdom of God and of the world-kingdoms which has already appeared in Nahum, Habakkuk, and Ezekiel, and which is presented in its sharpest features in Daniel.

Zerubbabel to be the Messiah and to build the temple.

Zechariah agrees also with Haggai in naming Zerubbabel as the Messianic king. After the example of Jeremiah (xxiii. 5, xxxiii. 15), he names him the Branch (iii. 8, 9; vi. 12). But whereas Jeremiah designated a dynasty by this term, in Zechariah it is applied to an individual already in their midst. Zerubbabel will rebuild the temple (vi. 12), and thus Yahwè will dwell among them (ii. 12, 13; viii. 23). The exiles will return (ii. vi.)

Entrance into the kingdom ethically conditioned for Jews and surviving Gentiles.

Zechariah differs from Haggai in requiring moral purity and uprightness in the members of the kingdom (vii. 9, 10; viii. 16, 17). The nations also that survive the day of Yahwè will become worshippers of Yahwè (ii. 11, viii. 20, 21, 23).

Joel (about 400 B.C.)

Judgment and annihilation of all the Gentiles.

In Joel the enemies of Judah are not actual and present foes, but *the nations generally*. These are to be gathered together in order to be annihilated (iii. 1, 2). The place of judgment is mentioned—the valley of Jehoshaphat—which is obviously chosen on the ground of the etymological meaning of the term. Yahwè will there sit in judgment upon them (iii. 12), and all the Gentiles will be destroyed. Here we have a nearer approximation to the idea of a final world-judgment than elsewhere in the Old Testament save in Dan. vii. 9, 10. But the judgment is one-sided. Yahwè appears as an advocate for Israel against the nations (iii. 2). The day of Yahwè does not morally sift Israel, as in the pre-Exilic and some Exilic prophets, and the exceptional post-Exilic Mal. iii. 2-5, iv. 1-3, 5, but serves only to justify Israel (ii. 25-27, iii. 16, 17) against the world.[1] On the other hand, it is to be observed that Israel here is not the *actual* but the purified and restored Israel, a spiritually transformed people (ii. 28, 29) worthy of Yahwè's presence (iii. 21). This spiritual transformation, however, is not extended to any of the nations. They are to perish irrevocably.

Before the day of Yahwè all the members of the nation will be filled with the spirit of God (ii. 28, 29): "And it shall come to pass afterward, that I will pour out my spirit upon all flesh; and your sons and your daughters shall prophesy, your old men shall dream dreams, your young men shall see visions: and also upon the servants and upon the handmaids in those days will I pour out my spirit."

Signs of the day of Yahwè.

Then signs of the approaching judgment will appear in nature (ii. 30, 31): "And I will show wonders in the heaven and in the earth, blood and

[1] Cf. the interpolation in Second Isaiah, *i.e.* xlv. 25.

CHAP. III.

fire, and pillars of smoke. The sun shall be turned into darkness, and the moon into blood, before the great and terrible day of Yahwè come."

Jerusalem the centre of the eternal Messianic kingdom.

Those who call upon Yahwè in Jerusalem (ii. 32) will be saved. Henceforth Jerusalem is to be holy, and there will be no heathen to defile it; (iii. 17): "So shall ye know that I am Yahwè your God, dwelling in Zion, my holy mountain: then shall Jerusalem be holy, and there shall no strangers pass through her any more"; (iii. 18, 20): "And it shall come to pass in that day, that the mountains shall drop down sweet wine, and the hills shall flow with milk, and all the brooks of Judah shall flow with waters; and a fountain shall come forth of the house of the Lord, and shall water the valley of Shittim. . . . But Judah shall abide for ever, and Jerusalem from generation to generation." There is no mention of the Messiah.

Joel apocalyptic in character.

With Joel and his successors prophecy has largely changed into apocalypse. The forecasts of these prophets do not as a rule stand in a living relation with the present and its needs, but are frequently the results of literary reflection on former prophecies. This is specially clear in Joel's "day of Yahwè," which has no organic relation with the present, as it has in the earlier prophets.

ZECHARIAH xii.-xiv. (before 300 B.C.)

According to the late post-Exilic fragment Zech. xii. 1–xiii. 6, all the Gentiles will attack Jerusalem and be destroyed before it (xii. 3, 4, 9), whereas in the still later fragment xiv. it is only the hostile nations that are to be annihilated (Zech. xiv. 12, 13), and the remnant to be converted to Judaism, and to attend the yearly Feast of Tabernacles (Zech. xiv. 9, 16-21). This fragment is further peculiar in that divine help does not intervene till Jerusalem is in the hands of the Gentiles (xiv. 2, 3).

The non-hostile nations to be converted to Judaism.

Daniel (168-167 B.C.)

We shall now touch on the salient points in the Apocalypse of Daniel, but only in the briefest manner, as we shall have to deal with it later at greater length under various heads. When evil reaches its culmination, and the need of the saints is greatest (vii. 21, 22; xii. 1) (in the time of Antiochus Epiphanes), the Ancient of Days will intervene, and His throne of judgment will be set up (vii. 9), and the world-powers overthrown (vii. 11, 12), and everlasting dominion given to His saints (vii. 14, 22, 27), and these will "break in pieces and consume" all the kingdoms of the world (ii. 44), and all the surviving nations will serve them (vii. 14). And the righteous dead of Israel shall rise to share in this Messianic kingdom, but the apostate Jews shall be cast into Gehenna (xii. 1-3). With the question of the resurrection we shall deal presently.

When evil reaches its climax, God will intervene and judge the world.

The Messianic kingdom and the resurrection.

The view that the world's history will terminate in the culmination of evil, and that Israel will be delivered by supernatural help in the moment of its

That the world's history will terminate on the culmination of

CHAP. III.

evil henceforth an apocalyptic dogma.

greatest need, derives originally from Ezekiel, and after reproduction in various forms in his spiritual successors attains to classical expression in Daniel, and henceforth becomes a permanent factor in Jewish Apocalyptic.

ISAIAH lxv., lxvi. (before 400 B.C.)

The doctrine of a new heavens and a new earth an interpolation in Is. lxv. 17 and lxvi. 22 (from Mazdean sources?)

In defiance of historical sequence I have reserved the consideration of the composite chapters Is. lxv., lxvi. to the last. These call for special treatment, because *apparently* they present a new development as regards the scene of the Messianic kingdom: it was to be a new heavens and a new earth. In lxv. Jerusalem is to be especially blessed: it is to undergo a spiritual, but not a physical transformation [1]—there appears to be no question here of the New Jerusalem: it is the same material Jerusalem as before, but supernaturally blessed. They still build houses and plant vineyards in it (lxv. 21, 22), sinners are still found in it (lxv. 20), and death still prevails. Hence lxv. 17, where a novel doctrine is proclaimed—the creation of a new heavens and a new earth [2]—seems impossible in its present context. In

[1] The word ברא does not appear to imply a physical or actual creation in lxv. 18, therein differing from its sense in lxv. 17.

[2] The older doctrine was the eternity of the present order of things. This doctrine is attested in Ps. civ. 5, "Who laid the foundations of the earth, that it should not be removed for ever"; Eccl. i. 4, "The earth abideth for ever." See also Pss. xciii. 1, xcvi. 10, cxlviii. 6. This was the received view in Palestine down to the close of the second century B.C., with the exception of a few passages in the Old Testament, which we shall deal with presently. About or after 100 B.C. the destruction of the present heaven and earth was taught in Eth. En. xci.-civ., and some decades later this doctrine, together with the creation of a new heavens and a new earth, in Eth. En. xxxvii.-

the Messianic age here foreshadowed men live to a patriarchal age, and the animal world, as in an earlier prophecy (xi. 6-9), loses its ferocity, and shares in the prevailing peace and blessedness (lxv. 25).

In lxvi. 6-16, 18[b]-22 we have a fragmentary apocalypse (see Cheyne, *Introd. to Isaiah*, 374-385) which describes the judgment of the hostile nations (lxvi. 16, 18[b], 19). Those of the Gentiles who escape are to go to the more distant nations and declare to them the divine glory (lxv. 19). There-

lxx. In this last book the doctrine of a new heaven and a new earth is set forth for the first time in Jewish literature with logical consistency. In the Old Testament passages where such a view appears, it is, as we have seen above, at variance with other eschatological features therein described. Is. li. 16, which apparently speaks also of a new heavens and a new earth is, as Cheyne (*Introduction*, p. 303) and Duhm (*Isaiah*, p. 359) have shown, a piece of mosaic interpolated at a later date. Hence the doctrine of a new heaven and a new earth appears to be adopted eclectically in the Old Testament, and is thus of the nature of a foreign element. It may therefore be a loan from Mazdeism, as Kohut has pointed out (*ZDMG*, xxx. 716, 717). On the other hand, it must be recognised that the way for such a doctrine was prepared for in the Old Testament by the post-Exilic view that the present heavens and earth should be destroyed. Thus in Is. li. 6 this view is expressed, not indeed as an eschatological doctrine, but purely poetically. Not only the inhabitants of the world but the world itself will perish; only God's salvation and God's righteousness abide for ever. "The heavens shall vanish away like smoke, and the earth shall wax old like a garment, and they that dwell therein shall die in like manner, but my salvation shall be for ever, and my righteousness shall not be abolished." The further dissolution of the heavens and earth is pronounced in a distinctly eschatological passage of a late date, *i.e.* Is. xxxiv. Thus in ver. 4, "The heavens shall be rolled together as a scroll, and all their host shall fade away." Finally, in Ps. cii. 25, 26, which, according to Baethgen, was probably, and, according to Duhm, was certainly, written in Maccabean times, the destruction of the present heaven and earth, and their creation anew, are poetically described: "Of old thou hast laid the foundation of the earth, and the heavens are the work of thy hands. They shall perish, but thou shalt endure: yea, they shall all wax old like a garment: as a vesture thou shalt change them, and they shall be changed." The important thought here, it is true, is not the transitoriness of the world, but the eternity of God: though heaven and earth pass away, God abides. But if this psalm be Maccabean, we have probably here the reflection of the new doctrine of the future heaven and earth, though there is no other reference to it in the literature of the second century.

CHAP. III.

upon the latter are to go up to Jerusalem, escorting the returning exiles. This apocalypse concludes with the promise: "For as the new heavens and the new earth, which I will make, shall remain before me . . . so shall your seed . . . remain" (lxv. 22). This verse is all but unintelligible. Does the new creation take place at the beginning of the Messianic kingdom, or at its close? By neither supposition can we overcome the inherent difficulties of the text. If the new creation is to be taken literally, it can only be supposed to be carried out at the close of the Messianic kingdom; but this kingdom has apparently no close. Either, then, the expression is used loosely and vaguely; or, and I incline to this view, lxvi. 22 is a later intrusion.[1]

We have now completed the study of the eschatologies of the individual and of the nation, in their concurrent and separate developments, from pre-prophetic times to the fourth century before the Christian era and somewhat later. Down to the period of the Exile these developments pursue an independent course, but from the Exile onwards they begin to exert a mutual influence on each other. This mutual interaction, however, does not lead to any true synthesis till the close of the fourth century or the early decades of the third, when they are both

[1] Is. li. 16 and lx. 19 can hardly be quoted in support of lxv. 17, lxvi. 22; for in the two last passages the language is obviously meant to be literal, whereas in the former it is metaphorical.

It is possible that the idea is derived from the Persian religion. The renewal of the earth, according to this faith, was to follow after the final judgment and the destruction of the evil powers. Yet see note on pp. 123, 124.

seen to be the two complementary sides of a religious system, that subsumes and does justice to the essential claims of both. Thus, when the doctrine of the blessed immortality of the faithful is connected with that of the coming Messianic kingdom, *the separate eschatologies of the individual and of the nation issue finally in their synthesis:*[1] *the righteous individual, no less than the righteous nation, will participate in the Messianic kingdom, for the righteous dead of Israel will rise to share therein.*

Synthesis of the two eschatologies in the resurrection of the righteous in Israel to the Messianic kingdom.

We have considered the question of the day of Yahwè and the Messianic kingdom in relation to Israel and the Gentiles as they were conceived by pre-Exilic, Exilic, and post-Exilic writers. We have seen that whereas the advent of Yahwè to exercise judgment meant all but universally a crisis of doom for Israel in the pre-Exilic period, in subsequent times it came all but universally to be regarded as marking the advent of Messianic blessedness for Israel.

Concurrently with the establishment of the Messianic hope in the national consciousness the claims of the individual had, as has already been shown, pressed themselves irresistibly on the notice of religious thinkers—so irresistibly, in fact, that no representation of the future could ultimately hope for acceptance which failed to render them adequate

[1] A synthesis of these two eschatologies was attempted by Ezekiel wholly within the sphere of this life. But this reconciliation was achieved only through a misconception and misrepresentation of the actual facts of the problem. And yet this theory of retribution gave such general satisfaction that the need of a theory that did justice to the facts of the problem was not experienced, save by isolated thinkers, till the era of the Job literature.

CHAP. III.

satisfaction. Thus naturally these two questions came to be considered as essentially related, as in fact they were. The righteous individual and the righteous nation should be blessed together—or rather the righteous individual should ultimately be recompensed—not with a solitary immortality in heaven or elsewhere, but with a blessed resurrection life together with his brethren in the coming Messianic kingdom. We saw above how the doctrine of an individual immortality failed to establish itself permanently in the Old Testament, and the grounds for such a failure were not far to seek. But the objections against the belief in a blessed immortality of the righteous man apart from the righteous community are actual arguments in favour of the resurrection of the righteous to share in the Messianic kingdom. The obvious lesson in such a development is that the individual should not seek to be blessed *apart from his brethren*—nay, rather that his blessedness, his highest well-being, is impossible of realisation except through the common life.

The doctrine of the resurrection is clearly enunciated in two passages of great interest: as a spiritual conception in Is. xxvi. 1-19, and as a mechanical conception in Dan. xii. 2, 3.

Doctrine of the resurrection spiritually conceived in Is. xxvi.

Is. xxvi. 1-19 forms an independent writing, according to Cheyne, composed about 334 B.C.[1] He calls it "a Liturgical Meditation."

[1] Smend (*ZATW*, 1884, pp. 161 *sqq.*) and Kuenen assign chaps. xxiv.-xxvii. to the fourth century; Driver to an early post-Exilic date; Duhm (*Das Buch Jesaia*, p. xii.) to the close of the second century B.C.

CHAP. III.

The writer looks forward to the setting up of the kingdom, to the city of strength, whose walls and bulwarks are salvation, and whose gates will open that the righteous nation may "enter in" (xxvi. 1, 2). And since the nation was but few in numbers, the righteous dead shall rise and share the blessedness of the *regenerate* nation (xxvi. 19). This notable verse should, with Duhm and Cheyne, be read as follows: "Thy dead men (Israel!) shall arise, and the inhabitants of the dust shall awake[1] and shout for joy;[2] for a dew of lights is thy dew, and the earth shall produce the shades."

Criticism of this doctrine.

In this passage of Isaiah, as we have above remarked, there is a true synthesis of the eschatologies of the nation and of the individual. A true synthesis, and yet defective. A true synthesis; for justice is done to the claims of the righteous nation and the righteous individual, and the blessedness of the individual and that of the nation receive their perfect consummation together. A defective synthesis; for the righteous who die before the advent of the Messianic kingdom are, till that kingdom appears, committed to the unblessed existence of Sheol,[3] where they are shut out from the life of God.

[1] The designation of death as a sleep did not arise from the resurrection hope; for it is found in books that were unacquainted with this hope. Thus death is described as "sleep" in Gen. xlvii. 30; Deut. xxxi. 16; Job vii. 21, xiv. 12; as "the eternal sleep" in Jer. li. 39, 57. Hence in later times, when the belief in the resurrection was firmly established, and the state of the departed is described as a "sleep," the word must in no case be taken in its literal meaning.

[2] יחיו and נבלתי are omitted by these scholars as interpolations, and instead of הָקִיצוּ וְרַנְּנוּ they read וְהֵקִיצוּ וְרִנְּנוּ.

[3] In this synthesis Sheol on the one hand maintains its primitive heathen

CHAP. III.

Yet if we are to disregard this defect, which was inevitable under the circumstances, this passage of Isaiah presents us with a truly spiritual doctrine of the future life; for that life stands in organic and living relation to the present life in God, which the faithful enjoy on earth. And since the faithful alone stood in this relation, only the resurrection of the righteous was conceivably possible. This limitation of the resurrection to the righteous is the primitive form of this conception. It is the genuine product of Jewish inspiration, and not derived from any foreign source. For even if the Mazdean doctrine of the resurrection of the righteous and the wicked be of an earlier date, it could not be the parent of the higher spiritual form with which we have just dealt.

The doctrine that only the righteous are raised a genuine product of Jewish inspiration.

This spiritual form of the resurrection doctrine is the genuine product of Jewish inspiration; for all its factors are indigenous to Jewish thought. The way was prepared for it, as we have seen, in the independent and concurrent eschatologies of the individual and the nation, the synthesis of which could not admit of any other resurrection save that of the righteous. But long before any such synthesis was effected the idea of a spiritual resurrection had

character in that it is still an unspiritual, godless region; but on the other it undergoes a certain transformation in that, though heretofore the eternal abode of all the departed, it henceforth becomes only the intermediate abode of righteous Israelites, though it continues to be the eternal abode of all else. Thus for the time being the progress achieved by the writers of Pss. xlix. and lxxiii. is lost sight of. These, we remember (pp. 72-77), held that death could not break off the communion of the righteous with God, and accordingly that the soul of the faithful could not descend into Sheol, as popularly conceived, but must be taken home to God.

established itself in Israel. Thus in Hos. vi. 2 (possibly of Exilic or post-Exilic origin) a religious transformation of character is described as a spiritual resurrection: "After two days will he revive us: on the third day he will raise us up so that we shall live before him." This is done on a large scale in Ezek. xxxvii. The resurrection there described of the dry bones imports, no doubt, a political restoration of Israel, but it is a restoration ethically conditioned. The people so restored are to be God's people (xxxvii. 13); they will be cleansed from all their sins and transgressions (xxxvii. 23); they will walk in the statutes and judgments of God, and be ruled by the Messiah of David's line (xxxvii. 24, 25); God will make an everlasting covenant of peace with them, and dwell with them for ever (xxxvii. 26, 27). Hence the resurrection in Ezekiel, though national, postulates a moral regeneration of the people. This harmonises with the view enforced elsewhere in Ezekiel that the conversion of the individual Israelites is the pre-condition for the restoration of the kingdom.

CHAP. III.

The idea of a spiritual resurrection—one of its chief sources—already familiar to Judaism through Hosea and Ezekiel.

We have on an earlier page (see pp. 78-80) referred to the thought underlying this spiritually conceived doctrine of the resurrection. We must here deal with it more closely. According to Is. xxvi. the righteous individual is at some period after death to be restored to *communion with God and with the righteous community. This double restoration to communion with God and to communion with the community of the faithful after death* constitutes the resurrection in its essential aspects. That there

Determination of the essential thought underlying this doctrine.

The resurrection implies a double restoration: (*a*) restoration to communion

CHAP. III.

with God, and (*b*) with the righteous community.

should be any delay to this restoration to *communion with God* after death in Is. xxvi. is, as we have above seen, due to the imperfect thought conditions of the time. Till the Messianic kingdom was established, even the righteous must abide in Sheol apart from God. In later times, however, when this heathen idea of Sheol was displaced by the doctrine of Paradise, or heaven, as the abode of the faithful immediately after death, death made no breach in the communion of the faithful with God. Hence the first constituent of the resurrection doctrine is not really subject to any time-conditions. The second constituent, however, restoration to communion with the community of the righteous, seems at first sight to be so conditioned; for this second requirement cannot be *fully* realised till the kingdom of God is *consummated* either in this world or in the next. In other words, *the blessedness of the individual is conditioned by that of the community as a whole.* But further. If in the definition "restoration to communion with God and to communion with the community of the faithful after death" we omit the words "after death," we have in what remains a description of the spiritual change which the faithful must already experience in the present life, and which really forms in itself the essence of the resurrection. Such a spiritual change constitutes, in Pauline language, a spiritual resurrection. Thus it appears that man can appropriate the spiritual side of this doctrine already here: can, through abjuring the life of self and sin, enter into the new life of God

(*a*) Restoration to communion with God not temporally conditioned because unbroken by death.

(*b*) Restoration to communion with the righteous community is temporally conditioned as regards its consummation,

but not as regards its spiritual essence, for the spiritual resurrection can be experienced in the present.

and of the community of the faithful. Thus the *spiritual* resurrection can already be experienced by the faithful on this side of the grave.

Moreover, since the life of the faithful beyond the grave is in communion with God and the faithful departed, this life is the resurrection life, though but in its beginnings.

But we may press on farther, and ask: If this Old Testament doctrine of the *time* of the resurrection of the faithful is manifestly based on the faulty conceptions of that age, when do the faithful rise to the resurrection life beyond the grave? The answer is clear in the light of later developments. Since the life of the faithful beyond the grave consists in communion with God and communion with the faithful who form the kingdom of God, though but in its beginnings, then the faithful in a certain degree enter into the resurrection life immediately after death, into the true resurrection life, though not indeed into its consummated form; for that cannot be realised till the consummation of the righteous community, or the kingdom of God. Thus it is only from the standpoint of its *consummation* that the second essential factor of the resurrection can be said to be temporally conditioned.

Prevalence of resurrection doctrine indirectly attested.

The currency of the doctrine of the resurrection is attested in Ps. lxxxviii. 10, where, indeed, the resurrection of the righteous is only mentioned in order to be rejected: "Wilt thou show wonders to the dead? Shall the shades arise and praise thee?" That this psalmist should reject the resurrection hope is not to be wondered at; for in the Psalter this psalm stands solitary and alone as the expression of a pessimistic despair. A similar

CHAP. III.

rejection of the resurrection doctrine may possibly be found in Ecclesiastes vii. 14.

Doctrine of the resurrection mechanically conceived.

We must assume that a considerable period of time elapses between the promulgation of this doctrine in Isaiah and the next and final form in which it appears in the Old Testament, *i.e.* in Dan. xii. 2: "And many of them that sleep in the land of dust shall awake, some to everlasting life, and some to shame and everlasting contempt."

The resurrection doctrine has already degenerated into lifeless dogma.

Here there is an absolute transformation of the resurrection doctrine. Heretofore it was the sole prerogative of the righteous Israelite; now it is extended to the pre-eminently good and bad in Israel. Accordingly, between the rise of the doctrine enunciated in Isaiah and that in Daniel there must have been a considerable interval—an interval sufficiently long to account for the loss of the original significance of the resurrection as a restoration to the life of communion with God which had been broken off by death. During this interval, at all events within a small circle of pious Israelites, the spiritual doctrine has passed into a current and somewhat lifeless dogma, in which the real essence of the conception has been forgotten; for without any consciousness of impropriety, the writer of Daniel can speak of the resurrection of the wicked. The resurrection is thus severed from the spiritual root from which it sprang, and transformed into an eschatological property or device, by means of which all the members of the nation are presented in the body before God for judgment.

CHAP. III.

Thus the doctrine of the resurrection must have been familiar to the Jews for many generations previous to Daniel; unless we are to assume that the later conception in Daniel is due to Mazdean influences.

Grounds for this extension of the resurrection to the wicked.

But though the possibility of extending the resurrection to the wicked is to be explained by the lifelessness of this article of the faith, we have not as yet learnt why the writer was obliged to resort to this idea. The ground for such a necessity is clearly to be discovered in his belief that Sheol is still exempt from the divine sway, and that, though God can raise souls from thence, He cannot influence them for good or evil *so long as they are there.* Hence, if any inhabitants of Sheol are to be rewarded or punished, they must first through resurrection return to earth and come within the bounds of the divine rule. Thus *this new application of the resurrection conception*[1] *in Daniel follows logically from two beliefs of the writer—the doctrine of God's retributive righteousness, and the heathen conception of Sheol.*[2]

It is most noteworthy that this doctrine of the resurrection of the wicked[3] is attested only three or,

[1] This doctrine of a partial resurrection of the wicked is taught also in Eth. En. i.-xxxvi. (see Chap. XXII.) This section may be earlier than Daniel. A general resurrection of all Israel is found probably in 2 Macc. xii. 42, 43, and Eth. En. li. 1.

[2] Sheol is still the "land of dust," Dan. xii. 2.

[3] This resurrection to punishment, or a belief perfectly akin, is found in contemporary work, xxiv.; xxv. 6-8; xxvi. 20, 21; xxvii. 1, 12, 13, a fragmentary apocalypse of 334 B.C. (Cheyne), a date which seems too early, as that of Duhm (*Das Buch Jesaia*, p. xii.), *i.e.* 128 B.C., is much too late. Thus in xxiv. 21, 22, the "host of heaven," *i.e.* angelic rulers of the nations, and the kings of the earth, are to be imprisoned in the "pit," and "after many days to be visited"

CHAP. III.

at most, four times in Jewish literature prior to the Christian era.

In these two conflicting doctrines of the resurrection we have the parents of all subsequent speculation on this subject in Judaism and Christianity.

Resurrection doctrine of Is. xxvi. 19 the product of Jewish inspiration, and in no sense borrowed from Mazdeism.

We have now traced the rise and development of the doctrine of a blessed future so far as it appears in the Old Testament. We have seen how thoroughly native to the Jewish genius has been the nature of this development. It is therefore a matter of surprise that some scholars have sought to affiliate this doctrine on that of the Mazdean religion, and to treat it accordingly as borrowed from the teaching of Zoroaster. But in the case of any religion such a method of explanation is mechanical, and only to be admitted when it is clearly proved that the elements for an internal and organic development were wanting. In the case of Israel, however, these elements were present, and that in a very high degree, and were slowly but surely shaped under the influence of the supreme and formative idea of God. Further, even were the resurrection doctrine in Israel the exact equivalent of that in Mazdeism, the evidence would not justify us in concluding that the former was borrowed from Mazdeism, but only that the latter exercised a formative influence in shaping the Jewish doctrine. But as a matter of fact the

with punishment. This punishment of the angelic rulers of the nations and the kings is found also in Eth. En. liv., xc. 25.

According to later views, God did not punish a nation until He had first humiliated its angelic patron (Shir. rabba xxvii.[b]) Moreover, the future judgment of the Gentile nations will be preceded by the judgment of these angelic chiefs (Tanchuma, Beshallach 13); see Weber, *L. d. Talmud*,[2] 170.

Jewish doctrine, as it appears in its earliest form in Is. xxvi., is essentially different from the Mazdean. Thus (i.) Whereas the former is spiritually conceived as the prerogative of only the righteous in Israel, the latter is a mechanical and ethically indifferent dogma, in accordance with which good and bad alike are raised. Thus whereas the former is specifically the result of right conduct, the latter has no relation to conduct at all. (ii.) According to the former, only a limited number—the faithful in Israel—are raised; according to the latter, all men of all nationalities and of all times. (iii.) According to the former, the resurrection was at the beginning of the Messianic kingdom; according to the latter, at its consummation in connection with the final judgment. Thus we see that the resurrection doctrine in Is. xxvi. cannot in any sense be derived from that of the Mazdean religion. We may observe here, in the way of anticipation, that this spiritual form of the resurrection is the prevailing one in Judaism down to the Christian era.

Resurrection doctrine in Daniel has certain affinities with that of Mazdeism,

But as regards this doctrine as it appears in Daniel, the case is very dissimilar. There are several points in common between Daniel's doctrine of the resurrection and that in Mazdeism. Thus—(i.) both alike teach a resurrection of the righteous and the wicked; and (ii.) both alike combine it with the final judgment. Since there are some other points of contact between the eschatologies of the two, it is not impossible that we have here traces of the influence of the Mazdean religion. On the other

CHAP. III.

but in other respects is strongly at variance with it.

hand, we must recognise that certain differences exist. Thus the resurrection in Daniel is not extended to all Israelites, but is limited to the martyrs and the apostates, whereas in Mazdeism it is absolutely universal. Again in Daniel, Sheol—the intermediate abode of the saints and apostates—preserves its ancient godless character, whereas in Mazdeism the intermediate abode of the souls of the righteous and of the wicked are respectively heaven and hell. Finally, in Daniel the final judgment is at the beginning of the Messianic kingdom, in Mazdeism at its close. Thus even in Daniel's eschatology the influence of Mazdeism was, on the most favourable assumption, but slight.

We conclude, therefore, that though Mazdeism may have exerted some influence in shaping the mechanical doctrine of the resurrection in Daniel, the evidence is wholly against the assumption of any such influence on the spiritual doctrine of the resurrection as taught by Is. xxvi.

Grounds for a short study of the Greek doctrines of the soul and the future life.

Judaism, as we are aware, came under Greek influences as early as the third century B.C. It is a matter, therefore, of great moment to ascertain to what extent these influences operated in the formation of the Jewish doctrines of the soul and of the future life. It has long been the fashion to exaggerate these influences, and to derive from Greek sources certain undoubtedly indigenous developments. Such exaggerations have been due in many instances to indefinite ideas both of Judaism and of Greek religion. Their best refutation will be to append to our history of Jewish eschatology a short sketch of Greek religion in so far as this relates to the soul and the future life. CHAP. III.

Doctrine of the Soul and the Future Life among the Greeks[1]

Homeric doctrine of the soul.

Only one part of man's composite nature survived death according to Homer. This was the soul (ψυχή). But the Homeric conception of the soul is peculiar. It enjoys an independent and secret existence in the body, and on the death of the body independently withdraws itself. It exercises no function of the human spirit, whether of thought, will, or emotion. These belong to the "mind" (θυμός), which resided in the diaphragm (φρένες, *Il.* xxii. 475). The θυμός is the most comprehensive expression in Homer for the various mental activities. Now this θυμός, and such faculties of the mind as are represented more or less definitely by νόος, μένος, or physical expressions such as ἦτορ, καρδίη, κῆρ, στῆθος, etc., are all *functions of the body and not of the soul*, and disappear with its resolution into its original elements.[2] Homer never

[1] The present writer is indebted beyond measure in this sketch of Greek religion to Rohde's *Psyche*,[2] 1898. He has also used Zeller's *History of Greek Philosophy*, likewise that of Ueberweg, Campbell's *Religion in Greek Literature*, 1898, and Fairbairn's *Studies in the Philosophy of Religion*, 168-230, which, though written over twenty years ago, is valuable and suggestive. Dieterich's *Nekuia* has occasionally been found helpful.

[2] Only once is the θυμός said to descend into Hades (vii. 131); but this can only be an oversight or carelessness of expression. In *Od.* xi. 221, 222 the θυμός and ψυχή are distinguished. The latter alone goes down to Hades.

CHAP. III.

ascribes any activity to the soul in the *living* man. The soul is not mentioned till its separation from the body is impending, or has actually taken place. Accordingly after death, or rather after entrance into Hades,[1] the soul loses consciousness and thought (*Il.* xxiii. 103, 104); it knows naught of the upper world; it cannot return thither[2] (*Il.* xxiii. 75, 76); it cannot exert any influence on the living; it is as incapable of anguish as of affection. Wherein the personality consists in Homer is difficult of comprehension. At times the body, as opposed to the soul (*Il.* i. 3-5), is described as the person, at times the soul (*Il.* xv. 251, where it is the soul that speaks). The person fully conceived appears to be the living man, that is, the combination of the visible body and the invisible soul.

Conflicting views due to survivals of Animism in the Homeric poems.

Such is the normal, and all but universal, view of the soul in Homer.[3] On the other hand, passages are occasionally to be met with in the *Odyssey* which

[1] The soul possessed a certain degree of consciousness and thought before it entered Hades (*Il.* xxii. 65-67).

[2] Hence the Homeric world had no ghosts. The living were at rest from the dead.

[3] The Homeric conceptions of the soul and of Hades find an excellent parallel in the fourth- and third-century views of these in Israel. In the case of the latter this result was brought about, as we have seen, by the action of Yahwism directly and indirectly. The soul in Sheol possessed in early Israel a certain degree of energy and power to benefit or injure the living—an idea which was derived from a primitive Ancestor Worship, but in the course of 1000 years this idea was overcome by Yahwism, the soul reduced to all but annihilation in Sheol, and Sheol itself transformed into a synonym for destruction and death. In Greece, on the other hand, the Homeric conceptions were the result of very different influences. What these were it is perhaps impossible to enumerate exhaustively. Amongst them, however, undoubtedly was first the separation of the Ionic Greeks from the land of their forefathers, where were the ancestral graves—the temples of the dead. A further cause was the adoption of the custom of burning the dead. By this means the soul was confined at once and for ever to Hades.

assign a larger degree of consciousness, thought, and vitality to the shades. These passages attest belated survivals of Ancestor Worship. They are to be found especially in books x. and xi. of the *Odyssey*. In these books the poet attributes the restoration of the consciousness of the shades to their enjoyment of the blood of the slaughtered animals; but this is a pure misapprehension of the poet, who lived in an age that had forgotten the original significance of these rites. The shades, even according to these books, possess the faculties of thought, will, and action before drinking the blood. The blood is simply an offering to the souls of the departed to comfort and feed them, but not to restore to them faculties which they had never lost. Moreover, the poet's account provides us with an exact and detailed description of a sacrifice to the dead (see Rohde, i. 55-59).

Hence, according to the specific view of the Homeric times, the soul had no consciousness in Hades; but occasional survivals of the older view belonging to Animism are reproduced in the *Odyssey* without any consciousness of their true significance.

Immortality possible only through translation to Elysium or heaven, according to Homeric views.

We have now to ask: How are the Homeric views related to the question of immortality? The soul, as we have seen, when it had once descended into Hades could never return. Hence if immortality was to be vouchsafed to any individual man, it had of necessity to be given to him when living through translation into Elysium (as in the case of

CHAP. III.

Menelaus) or heaven (as in that of Ganymede). Thus this immortality was mainly a material immortality, and such was the immortality of the Homeric gods. Moreover, as immortality was of necessity a privilege limited in the main to mortals who were *physically* related to the gods, it is of no service in preparing the way for a doctrine of human immortality as such.

Further survivals of Animism in Hesiod.

From Homer we pass on to Hesiod, but in this connection we shall only pause to draw attention to the vigorous survivals of Animism which are apparent in his poems. Souls cannot exist outside Erebus and possess consciousness in Homer; yet such is Hesiod's belief. Thus, according to his *Works and Days*, 109-201, the men of the golden age became after death δαίμονες ἐπιχθόνιοι, watchers over mankind in a good sense, and endowed with large powers. Similarly, men of the silver age became δαίμονες ὑποχθόνιοι (not in Hades). Men of the bronze age (namely of Hesiod's own time) became phantoms (εἴδωλα) in Hades. Now these views regarding the two earlier ages are not inventions of Hesiod, but survivals in the outlying Boeotia of a worship of souls which had existed long anterior to Homer; and that such views prevailed with regard to earlier generations and not to the later is due to the fact that in Hesiod's age the Homeric doctrine had become supreme.

Such views as to the conscious and independent activity of souls after life were undoubted helps to the formation of a doctrine of immortality. Certain classes of souls in the past belonging to the gold and silver ages could, it is true, become immortal, but this was not possible for members of the bronze age.

Doctrine of the soul in the Dionysiac cult.

The first real contribution towards this doctrine comes from the Dionysiac cult in Thrace. Underlying this cult is the presupposition of the original kinship of God and man. This being presumed, man could through certain ritual ceremonies and ecstasies become one with the gods. In such experiences the soul burst, as it were, the fetters of the body. But even so, the old Homeric view of the indispensableness of the body to the soul is not yet fully transcended. The soul has an eternal existence, but *not apart from the body.* A full and divine life apart from the body for men in general was still inconceivable. Hence the doctrine of the transmigration of souls was of necessity a factor in this belief. The soul could maintain its immortality only through successive incarnations.[1]

A vigorous life of the soul apart from the body still inconceivable.

Hence doctrine of transmigration adopted.

Transformation of the Dionysiac doctrines of soul and of transmigration in the Orphic teaching.

With the Orphic teaching we enter on a new stage of development. So far from the body being the necessary complement of the soul, the union of body and soul has become an actual bar to the consummation of the latter. And this is easy to understand; for when the conviction that the soul and body can exist independently rises into a belief in the godlikeness and immortality of the soul, as opposed to the transitoriness of the body, the distinction

[1] For a full treatment of the Dionysiac cult in Thrace and Greece, Rohde, *Psyche*, ii. 1-69.

CHAP. III.

between soul and body naturally leads to an antagonism of both. Thus the body comes to be conceived as the prison-house (δεσμωτήριον) or tomb of the soul (σῶμα—σῆμα, Plato, *Crat.* 400 C), and the connection of the soul and body to be regarded as a punishment of the former. Under this view the tenet of transmigration changes of necessity its character. It is no longer the means whereby the soul preserves its vitality, as the Dionysiac religion conceived it, but has become a spiritual punishment and discipline of the soul, and the soul does not attain to its highest till it is freed from this cycle of necessity or rebirths (κύκλος ἀνάγκης or τροχὸς τῆς γενέσεως), and lives eternally in God.[1] As opposed, therefore, to the Homeric doctrine of the soul, we have here a new and well-defined doctrine as to the origin, essence, and destiny of the soul.

This transformation is to be traced to the Orphic doctrine of the indissoluble connection of guilt and expiation.

Hades becomes an intermediate abode and a place of moral distinctions.

In this phase of religion Hades becomes an intermediate abode where the soul meets with retributive judgment. There the initiated and purified live in communion with the gods of the lower world till the time for their return to the upper life has come. At last when the soul has passed through its cycle of rebirths and is fully cleansed, it ascends, as we have above remarked, to enjoy a never-ending existence with God.

The soul, whether of the impure or of the purified,

[1] See Rohde, *Psyche*, ii. 129, 130, 133-136; Dieterich, *Nekuia*, 88, 89.

is in itself immortal. But it is not only immortal, it is eternal, without beginning or end.

The soul eternal—without beginning or end.

In the speculative systems of the philosophers to which we must now turn, the term "soul" assumes a new meaning, and becomes a comprehensive designation for all the human powers of thought and will. From the fifth century onwards it is used in this sense in prose writers and non-philosophical poets. When the soul was thus absolutely identified with the mind, its individual existence after death was inconceivable in the speculative systems of such philosophers as Thales of Miletus, Anaximander, Anaximenes, Heraclitus. Indeed, such a question would have been meaningless; for the soul was in their philosophies conceived merely as a function of the various elements of the body or as a transient individualisation of the one primitive substance or force, and this individualisation terminated at death.

New meaning attached to the term "soul" by the philosophers. No room in their systems for the existence of the soul after death in its older meaning, nor yet in its new.

In the pantheistic theories of the Eleatic philosophers Xenophanes of Colophon, Parmenides, and Zeno, there is no room for the future individual existence of the soul. And yet Parmenides quite inconsistently taught the pre-existence of the soul and its survival on the death of the body,[1] but this he did as a disciple of the Orphic and Pythagorean schools.

According to Pythagoras, the soul of man is immortal, and is confined in the body only in

Pythagoras' doctrine of the soul.

[1] See Ritter and Preller's *Historia Philosophiae*, § 151, *καὶ τὰς ψυχὰς πέμπειν ποτὲ μὲν ἐκ τοῦ ἐμφανοῦς εἰς τὸ ἀιδές, ποτὲ δὲ ἀνάπαλίν φησιν.* This view, however, is disputed by Zeller, *Pre-Socratic Philosophy*, i. 604 (English transl.)

CHAP. III.

the way of punishment. It has no inner connection with the body in which it dwells; any soul may live in any body. It possesses a divine knowledge through memory (Dieterich, *Nekuia*, p. 122; Rohde, *Psyche*, ii. 186 *note*). When death separates the soul from the body, the soul must after an interval of purification in Hades return to the upper world, and be reborn. Its conduct in the earlier life determines the nature of its new incarnation. Finally, after a series of transmigrations, it is raised from the earthly life and restored to a divine existence.

Empedocles.

Empedocles' doctrine of the soul is peculiar. The office of the soul, which is a stranger in the world of sense, is neither perception nor thought, which are merely functions of the body, but the philosophic vision into the complete truth of being and becoming which it brings with it out of its divine existence in the past (Rohde, *Psyche*, 185, 186). The faculty of thought (*νόος*) and the daimonic being which we may call soul (though Empedocles never uses this term) thus exist side by side in man, the former of which perishes with the body, while the latter is not immortal, indeed, but longlived. This dualism in the inner life which appears in Homer thus reappears in Empedocles, and later in Plato and Aristotle. The doctrine of transmigration naturally formed a part of his system; but between the various incorporations of the soul it did not, as in the Orphic or Pythagorean belief, descend into an underground Hades. Finally, when all the elements and powers return into their original unity, all souls and even the gods will be reunited in the divine universal spirit, in order again to come forth in individual existence in a newly restored world.

The immortality of the soul was inconceivable from Anaxagoras' principle of an all-pervading mind. For though this mind individualised itself in certain material combinations, it retired into itself on the dissolution of these.

Anaxagoras.

The views of Pindar on the soul and the after-life form an interesting study. Side by side we find two distinct and irreconcilable views on these questions. Thus at times—(i.) his poems reproduce the old Homeric doctrine of the soul and of Hades, the everlasting abode of the shades, combined with certain elements of soul worship; (ii.) at others they present us with a theology of an essentially Orphic type.

Pindar's divergent views on the soul and its destiny.

In the former he uses the language of the popular theology of the day, which was a medley of Homeric and animistic elements. This was indeed practically at all times the orthodox belief. Thus the soul departs after death to Hades (*Pyth.* xi. 19-22; *Ol.* ix. 33-35), where it is still acquainted with the affairs of the living (*Pyth.* v. 96-104). No rewards await it save the praise its virtues have won on earth. If individuals were to enjoy a blessed life, they were translated in the body, as in the Homeric view a perfect life was otherwise inconceivable. Yet instances of deification after death were also acknowledged, as of Semele.

(i.) The popular view.

CHAP. III.

(ii.) The Orphic view—Pindar's own.

The second view is closely connected with the first. The soul is, as in the former, the invisible double of the man. It is to a large degree dormant—though not wholly, as in Homer—during a man's living activities on earth. Soul is never used by Pindar in its philosophic meaning (see above). Thus far, therefore, Pindar's conception corresponds mainly with the Homeric, but to this conception he adds, with the Orphics, that it is of divine origin, "an image of eternity" (*αἰῶνος εἴδωλον*), and springs from the gods only (*μόνον ἐκ θεῶν*, *Frag.* 131). Its descent into the body is due to ancient guilt. After death retributive judgment follows in Hades, and the condemned are plunged into Tartarus (*Ol.* ii. 57-60). The soul must be embodied at least three times before it can hope for an end of its earthly course. The past life determined the conditions of the present, and the present those of the future. After a final course of nine years in Hades the purified soul could "ascend the path of Zeus" and enter "the Isles of the Blessed" (*Ol.* ii. 69-75) and become heroes.[1]

Aeschylus reflects the popular views of the soul and of Hades.

Aeschylus reproduces the old Homeric conceptions of Hades and the soul, but he goes beyond these in speaking in a few cases of a judgment beyond death in Hades. This judgment, however, is only a completion of the retribution which is generally executed on earth (*Suppl.* 230, 231, 416; *Eum.* 273-275; *Choëph.* 61-65). On the other hand, the belief in the community of interests existing

1 According to certain tomb-inscriptions of the fourth century found near Sybaris the blessed become gods (see Rohde, *Psyche*, ii. 217-221).

between the living and the dead is reflected strongly—in other words, an essential factor belonging to Ancestor Worship (see p. 40 *note*). This same belief is attested also in Sophocles and Euripides, though the latter does not himself accept it (see p. 24 *note*).

Plato at first held the popular views.

The immortality of the soul was not originally a part of Plato's system.[1] We have in the *Republic* the various stages through which his views passed before he arrived at his maturest convictions on the subject.

His own doctrine of the soul.

It is not necessary to our present purpose to do more than give a few of the salient points in the later Platonic doctrine of the soul. The soul is a purely spiritual being. It is uncreated (ἀγένητος, *Phaedr.* xxiv.), apparently eternal[2] (ἀΐδιος, *Rep.* x. 611 B). In compliance with a universal cosmic law, according to the *Timaeus* (41 D *sqq.*), or else in consequence of an intellectual declension of the soul from its original destiny, according to the *Phaedrus*

[1] This has been established by Krohn, *Der Platon. Staat*, p. 265; Pfleiderer, *Platon. Frage*, pp. 23, 24, 35 *sqq.*; Rohde, *Psyche*, ii. 265-267. Thus no trace of this doctrine is to be found in the oldest part of the *Republic*, iii. 368–v. 460 C. The next portions that were composed were v. 460 D–471 C, viii., ix. (all but 580 D–588 A), x. (608 C to end). In this part the doctrine of immortality is introduced and discussed, and further established in the third part, v. 471 C–vii., ix. 580 D–588 A, x. 595–608 B. Books i.–ii. 367 were finally written as an introduction to the whole. In this introduction a harmonising of the above parts is attempted. This statement is drawn from Rohde.

[2] Plato's doctrine of the soul's immortality and pre-existence are bound up together. The mythical representation of the *Timaeus*, where the creation of souls is attributed to the Demiurge, cannot be allowed any weight in the face of his frequent assertions that this pre-existence had no beginning (cf. *Phaedr.* 245 C, ψυχὴ πᾶσα ἀθάνατος. The soul is ἀρχὴ κινήσεως, ἀρχὴ δὲ ἀγένητον . . . . ἐξ ἀνάγκης ἀγένητόν τε καὶ ἀθάνατον ψυχὴ ἂν εἴη. See Zeller, *Plato*, 398, 399, 405 (English transl.)

CHAP. III.

(246 *sqq.*) and the *Phaedon* (246 C), it enters into the body. In the body the soul lives as in a prison. However closely united, there can never be any true harmony between them. Yet this connection with the body can become the cause of unlimited impurity and degradation.

Soul, according to his earlier views, a trichotomy of reason, courage, and desire.

In his earlier speculations, *i.e.* the *Phaedrus*,[1] Plato had ascribed a trichotomy of reason (τὸ λογιστικόν), courage (τὸ θυμοειδές), and desire (τὸ ἐπιθυμητικόν), to the soul in its pre-existent state, and explained its fall by the presence of the two latter. Subsequently, however, the thought that such lower powers were indissolubly connected with the soul became inconceivable, since this conjunction would have logically involved the soul in a never-ending cycle of rebirths, and, henceforth, the soul was regarded by him as simple and indivisible, a power of pure thought (λογιστικόν [2]). According, therefore, to his later speculations in the *Timaeus*, it was not until a soul was enclosed in the body that courage and desire were associated with it, these being proper to the body only. Though the passions are on this view left behind by the soul at death, yet the association of the soul with these in the body produces an inward deterioration of the soul—an idea by means of which Plato explains its desire for rebirth in the body.

Afterwards held to be purely rational.

Courage and desire added to the soul on its birth in the body.

[1] See Zeller, *Plato and the Older Academy*, 391, 392 (English transl.); Lewis Campbell, *Religion in Greek Literature*, p. 353.

[2] When the entire content of the soul came to be regarded as λογιστικόν, a soul could no longer consistently be ascribed to animals, who only possessed θυμός and ἐπιθυμία. Further, if a soul could not justly be ascribed to animals, it follows further that a human soul could not rightly be said to descend into the body of an animal. Plato, however, maintained this view to the end, probably for ethical reasons.

Judgment after death, and subsequent transmigrations.

Immediately after death the soul is judged, and placed in heaven or under earth by way of reward or punishment, where it remains for 1000 years. When this interval has elapsed the soul is forced to be incorporated anew. The nature of the new body is determined by the character of the soul in the former life. The soul must pass through a series of such transmigrations.[1] In the course of these it can descend to the beast,[2] or ascend into nobler forms of existence. Incurable sinners are cast into Tartarus. The aim of the soul is finally to be delivered from the body and to depart into the realm of pure being, that is, of the divine, the invisible, and the pure.

Aim of the soul.

Pre-existence and immortality lead to doctrine of recollection.

In Plato pre-existence and immortality stand or fall together,[3] and if these are admitted, the doctrine of recollection follows of necessity. This doctrine, which appears first among the Orphics, receives at Plato's hands a philosophical exposition. It is necessary, he holds, in order to explain the facts of learning and knowledge. "We could not seek for what is yet unknown to us, nor recognise in what we find the thing that we sought for, if we had not unconsciously possessed it before we recognised and were conscious of it (see *Meno*, 80 D *sqq.*) We could form no conception of Ideas, of the eternal essence of things which is hidden from our percep-

[1] At least three (as in Pindar, *Ol.* ii. 68 *sqq.*), according to the *Phaedrus*, 249 A. Between each of the births there is a period of 1000 years (cf. *Rep.* x. 615 A).

[2] See *note* 2, p. 148.

[3] Zeller, *Plato*, 405 *sqq.*

CHAP. III.

tion, if we had not attained to the intuition of these in a former existence."[1]

Earlier teaching on retribution.

Two phases of teaching on the question of retribution appear in Plato. In the earlier the unconditional worth of morality in itself is set forth without reference to a hereafter. Thus, according to the *Republic*, iii. 1 *sqq.*, the guardians are to pay no heed to what follows after death, but to make it their chief task to show that virtue carries with it its own reward. But this doctrine is handled very differently when Plato became convinced of the soul's immortality. Retribution hereafter appeared to follow necessarily from this doctrine, else divine justice would be at fault, and discord disturb the moral order of the universe.[2]

Later teaching.

We have now touched on the chief features of Plato's doctrine of immortality.

An immeasurable gulf divides Greek from Jewish and Christian eschatology.

It is obvious that an immeasurable gulf divides it from Jewish no less than Christian doctrine. We do not refer to such obvious differences as appear in his doctrine of the soul's transmigrations, its eternal pre-existence, and its antagonism to the body, but to the two following points: (i.) it is not a human soul that Plato's final teaching deals with, but a pure intelligence; (ii.) his doctrine, as set over against the Jewish and Christian, is the glorification of an unbridled individualism. The individual soul owes no duty practically but to itself. Its appearance in any single human community or family

[1] Zeller, *Plato*, 406, 407.

[2] *Rep.* x. 612 A *sqq.*; cf. *Phaedo*, 63 C, 95 B, 114 D.

is of the nature of an accident. It existed before any such came into being, and will outlive them. However nobly the virtues relating to one's neighbour or the State are expounded in the Platonic system, they are related to the individual mainly as elements in its discipline and self-culture.

Popular eschatology still Homeric down to the Christian era.

Despite all the teaching of individual poets, philosophers, and schools, the popular beliefs of the Greeks remained from century to century in the main unaffected. The immortality of the soul never became a part of the national creed, but remained the peculiar property of individual theologians and philosophers.[1] This is conclusively established by the evidence of Greek epitaphs.

[1] Prof. Percy Gardner, *New Chapters in Greek History*, 333, 334; Rohde, *Psyche*, ii. 378.

CHAPTER IV

SUMMARY OF OLD TESTAMENT TEACHING ON INDIVIDUAL CONCEPTIONS

Short summary of development of doctrine of a future life.

In the preceding chapters we have tried to trace the history of Old Testament eschatology; but before entering on the subsequent developments of this eschatology in Jewish literature, it will be helpful to sum up shortly the results we have already gathered from the writers of the Old Testament on this question. In these results we are provided with an eschatology that *to a large extent* takes its character from the conception of Yahwè. So long indeed as Yahwè's jurisdiction was conceived as limited to this life, a Yahwistic eschatology of the individual could not exist; but when at last Israel reached the great truth of monotheism, the way was prepared for the moralisation of the future no less than of the present. The Exile also contributed to this development by making possible a new and truer conception of the individual. Henceforth the individual and not the nation became the religious unit. Step by step through the slow processes of the religious life, through the ofttimes halting logic of spiritual experience, the religious thinkers of Israel were led to a moral conception of the future life, and to the certainty of their share therein. These truths were reached, not through questionable assumptions and metaphysical processes, as in Greece, but through spiritual crises deep as the human personality and wide as human life. Only thus could they be won if they were to last for ever. The eternal life, the life in God, cannot admit of death as its goal, and to the apprehension of this truth Israel's saints rose through first realising that life to be the one supreme fact of the present, before the necessities of their spiritual experience forced them to postulate its continuance in the future. Thus in fact they reasoned: he that hath God hath eternal life.

We shall now enumerate the views of the Old Testament on such conceptions as soul, spirit, Sheol, Gehenna, etc., which are partly developed from Yahwism, and, partly as heathen survivals, are still independent of it.

Soul and spirit. Earlier and later doctrines of these.

Soul and Spirit.—There were two conflicting views on the nature of these, as we have seen above. According to the older dichotomic view, the soul and spirit were all but practically identical. The spirit represented the stronger side of the soul. But according to the later trichotomic view (Gen. ii. 4^b–iii.), which is current from the time of the Deuteronomist onwards side by side with the former, the spirit is the breath of God, which on death returns to God. This different conception should be borne in mind in order to appreciate the psychology of subsequent periods. For a full account of the two views, see above, pp. 39-48.

CHAP. IV.

We should observe that the departed in Sheol are spoken of as "gods," "shades," or "dead ones," but never as "spirits" nor as "souls" except in Job. See above, pp. 48, 49. The way for this last usage is prepared by such passages as Pss. xvi. 10, "Thou wilt not give over my soul to Sheol"; xxx. 3, etc. On the other hand, that the soul of *the righteous* was conceived as capable of exercising its highest capacities after death follows incontestably from Job xix. 26, 27, and also, we may safely conclude, from Pss. xlix. 15, lxxiii. 24.

Judgment, preliminary and final.

Judgment, preliminary and final, on all Israel, on the surviving Gentiles, and on the faithless angelic rulers.—In the Old Testament the conception of a final judgment is developed, but in a limited sense. It always precedes the Messianic kingdom. It deals only with the living Jew and Gentile, and not with the dead, in Ezekiel and Joel; in its latest Old Testament development in Daniel it takes account, of course, of all the living, whether Jew or Gentile, but it is also extended to certain classes of departed Israelites—the martyrs and apostates. The Gentiles were apparently visited with temporal penalties only, *i.e.* loss of this life. But it is possible that even in the third century, or much earlier, pains and penalties were conceived to attend on them in Sheol; for Sheol was in all cases the final abode of the Gentiles, whether bad or good, and had already in some instances come to be regarded as penal in character.

The final never embraced all men in the Old Testament.

But though the final judgment in the Old Testament was never conceived as embracing all men, living and dead, a very remarkable extension of the idea of judgment is found in Is. xxiv. 21, 22, where the faithless angelic patrons and departed kings are brought within its venue.[1] Here there is definitely a preliminary as well as a final judgment.

This division of the judgment into two distinct catastrophes is to be found in Ezekiel, where the first consists of the triumphal restoration of Israel to its own land, and the second in the judgment of the Gentile world. But still more clearly in Daniel, where the first act of judgment is executed by the saints (ii. 44), and the final by God Himself on all the nations.

Places of abode of the departed.

Of abodes for the departed there are Heaven, Sheol, Gehenna, and the Pit.

Heaven.

Heaven.—Heaven appears to be the final abode to which the writers in Pss. xlix. 15, lxxiii. 24 look forward. It was to heaven also that Enoch and Elijah were translated.

Sheol—its various meanings.

Sheol[2] appears in the Old Testament either as (i.) the eternal abode of all the dead; (ii.) the eternal abode of the wicked only; (iii.) the intermediate abode of certain classes in Israel. (i.) Of the former conception there were two varieties, as we have already seen: (*a*) the older represents Sheol as the scene of considerable life, movement, and knowledge;

[1] See pp. 133 *note*, 159.

[2] As synonyms for Sheol in meaning (i.) we find "pit" (בּוֹר), Pss. xxviii. 1, xxx. 3, lxxxviii. 4, cxliii. 7; Is. xiv. 19, xxxviii. 18; Ezek. xxvi. 20, xxxi. 14, 16, xxxii. 18, 24, 29, 30; Prov. i. 12. We must carefully distinguish this sense of "pit" (בּוֹר) from that in Is. xxiv. 22, where it is the intermediate abode of angels and kings. "Pit" is also a rendering of שַׁחַת, and in this case also it is a synonym for Sheol in the following passages: Pss. xvi. 10, xxx. 9, lv. 23, ciii. 4; Is. xxxviii. 17; Ezek. xxviii. 8; Job xvii. 14, xxxiii. 18, 22.

CHAP. IV.

(*b*) the later represents it as the practical negation of all existence, and all but a synonym for annihilation. Greek religion furnishes us with a remarkable parallel to these two conflicting views of Sheol (see above, pp. 40-43). Hades was similarly conceived in Greece at two different periods (see p. 138 *note*). (ii.) Sheol is depicted as the eternal abode of the wicked only in Pss. xlix. 14, 15; lxxiii. 19, 20. (iii.) The transformation of Sheol into an intermediate abode of the departed was due to the rise of the higher theology. The transformation, however, is very slight. Though Sheol is regarded as the intermediate abode of righteous Israelites in Is. xxvi. 19, it remains the eternal abode of all the rest of mankind. In Dan. xii. 2 it is again presupposed as the intermediate abode of Jewish martyrs and apostates, but the eternal abode of all else.

Gehenna—its various meanings.

Gehenna.—The word Gehenna, Γέεννα in Tischendorf and WH (or Γεέννα according to other scholars, on the ground of its derivation from the Aram. גְּהִנָּם), is derived ultimately from the Hebrew expression גֵּי הִנֹּם = "Valley of Hinnom" (Jos. xv. 8, xviii. 16; Neh. xi. 30), which is an abbreviated form of גֵּי־בֶן הִנֹּם = "Valley of the Son of Hinnom" (Jos. xv. 8, xviii. 16; 2 Chron. xxviii. 3, xxxiii. 6; Jer. vii. 31, 32, xix. 2, 6), or in the *Kethib* of 2 Kings xxiii. 10 (גֵּי בְנֵי־הִנֹּם). But this place became so notorious through its evil associations that it was simply called "the Valley," κατ' ἐξοχήν (Jer. ii. 23, xxxi. 40), and the gate of Jerusalem leading to it "the Valley-gate" (2 Chron. xxvi. 9; Neh. ii. 13, 15, iii. 13). In Eth.

En. xxvii. 2 it is termed "the accursed gê or valley," "the deep gê or valley" (liv. 1), and "the gê or valley" (Ass. Mos. x. 10). This valley lay to the S. and S.W. of Jerusalem (Robinson, *BRP*. ii. 273, 274). The derivation of הִנֹּם is quite uncertain. This term is used in a variety of meanings in the course of Israelitish and Jewish history.

I. Its use in the Old Testament falls under three heads. (*a*) It is used in a merely *topographical sense.* Thus it formed the boundary between Judah and Benjamin (Jos. xv. 8, xviii. 16), and the northern limit of the district occupied by the tribe of Judah after the Captivity (Neh. xi. 30), and lay in front of the gate Harsith of Jerusalem (Jer. xix. 2).

(*b*) It is used in a *religious significance as implying a place of idolatrous and inhuman sacrifices.* These were first offered by Ahaz and Manasseh, who made their children to "pass through the fire" to Moloch in this valley (2 Kings xvi. 3; 2 Chron. xxviii. 3; and 2 Kings xxi. 6; 2 Chron. xxxiii. 6). These sacrifices were probably made on the "high places of Tophet, which is in the Valley of the Son of Hinnom" (Jer. vii. 31; cf. Jer. xxxii. 35). In order to put an end to these abominations, Josiah polluted it with human bones and other corruptions (2 Kings xxiii. 10, 13, 14). But this worship of Moloch was revived under Jehoiakim (Jer. xi. 10-13; Ezek. xx. 30). In consequence of these idolatrous practices in the Valley of Hinnom, Jeremiah prophesied that one day it would be called the "Valley of Slaughter," and that they should "bury in Topheth till there be no place to bury" (Jer. vii. 32, xix. 11). Many scholars have accepted the statement of Kimchi (*circa* 1200 A.D.) on Ps. xxvii: "Gehinnam fuit locus spretus, in quem abjecerunt sordes et cadavera, et fuit ibi perpetuo ignis ad comburendum sordes illos et ossa; propterea parabolice vocatur judicium impiorum Gehennam." But this is denied by Robinson (i. 274), who writes that "there is no evidence of any other fires than those of Moloch having been kept up in this valley" (Rosenmüller, *Biblisch. Geogr.* II. i. 156, 164).

(*c*) It signifies the *place of punishment for rebellious or apostate Jews in the presence of the righteous.* Gehinnom or Gehenna is not actually mentioned with this signification in the Old Testament, but it is it and no other place that is implied in Is. l. 11, "in a place of pain shall ye lie down," and lxvi. 24, with this new connotation. Both these passages are very late, and probably from the same hand—not earlier than the third century B.C. (see Cheyne, *Introd. to the Bk. of Isaiah*, p. 380; Smend, *Alttestamentliche Religionsgeschichte*, p. 506). Further, the punishment of the apostate Jews in Is. lxvi. 24 is conceived as eternal: "They shall look upon the carcases of the men that have transgressed against me; for their worm shall not die, neither shall their fire be quenched, and they shall be an abhorring to all flesh." The punishment of Gehenna is implied also in Dan. xii. 2, "some to shame and everlasting abhorrence." We should observe that the same word דֵּרָאוֹן, "abhorrence," occurs in these two pass-

CHAP. IV.

ages, and in these only, and the reference in both is to Gehenna.[1]

The Pit as the intermediate abode of angels and kings.

The Pit (בּוֹר) is the intermediate abode or place of punishment of the guilty angels and kings (Is. xxiv. 22). The fact that there is a special intermediate place for these makes it easier to understand Sheol as an intermediate place for the righteous. Yet the ideas in Is. xxiv. 22 appear as a foreign element in the Old Testament, and may be derived from the Mazdean religion.[2]

Resurrection.

Though the doctrine of an individual immortality emerged in Job and the Psalms, it failed to establish itself permanently in the religious expectations of Israel. Not to a future of individual bliss, even though in the divine presence, but to a resurrection to a new life (Is. xxvi. 19) as members of the holy people and citizens of the Messianic kingdom, did the righteous aspire. The individual thus looked forward to his highest consummation in the life of the righteous community. This resurrection as the necessary spiritual sequel and the true organic development of the righteous life on earth was of necessity limited to the righteous; but, as we have seen, the author of Dan. xii., writing at a time when this spiritual significance of the resurrection was forgotten, extended it to the unfaithful in Israel, and thus wholly secularised it, and gave it a meaning absolutely at variance with its original one.

[1] Most of these paragraphs on Gehenna have already appeared in my article on Gehenna in Hastings' *Bible Dictionary*, ii. 119.

[2] See Stave, *Einfluss des Parsismus auf das Judenthum*, pp. 176, 177.

CHAP. IV.

Messianic kingdom always of eternal duration in the Old Testament.

The Messianic kingdom was always conceived as eternal on earth save in Is. lxv. 17, lxvi. 22, where a new heavens and a new earth are spoken of; but these verses are at issue with their contexts, and should no doubt be rejected (see pp. 122-124).

Gentiles.—Apart from the few wider teachers who looked for the redemption of the Gentiles, the prevailing view, and the view that was strong and effective in later Judaism, was that all the Gentiles were to be destroyed (Is. xxxiv., xxxv.; Joel) or all that were hostile to Israel (Ezekiel, Haggai, Zechariah), while the rest were for ever to rest under the shadow of Yahwè's omnipotent but pitiless supremacy (Ezekiel), or to be converted to His worship (Haggai, Zechariah, etc.[1])

[1] Eschatological ideas, which are proper to Apocalyptic, are by no means rare in later Jewish prophecy. Thus we have the *Book of Life*. A roll of citizens seems to have been kept in Israel from the end of the ninth century onwards (Ezra ii. 62; Neh. xii. 22, 23, vii. 5, 64) as a security against aliens (Bertholet, *Stellung d. Isr. zu d. Fremden*, p. 80). This burgher list is referred to in Ezek. xiii. 9 (Jer. xxii. 30). From this seems to have been derived the expression "God's Book" in Exod. xxxii. 32, 33; Ps. cxxxix. 16; "Book of the living," Ps. lxix. 28: cf. also Ezek. ix. 4; Ps. lxxxvii. 6. In all these passages to have one's name in the book of life meant participation in the *temporal* blessings of the theocracy; but in Dan. xii. 1 the idea is transformed, and to have one's name in the Book of Life means participation in the spiritual blessings of a future life. For further details see Charles' *Book of Enoch*, 131-135.

New heavens and a new earth.—This idea, though found in Is. lxv., lxvi., is really inoperative there (see above, pp. 122, 123).

Angelic patrons of the nations.—This idea, which is referred to in Is. xxiv. 21, 22, where the angelic rulers and kings are committed to prison, was used by the Jews to explain the oppression of Israel consistently with the belief in the supremacy of Yahwè (see Cheyne, *Introd. Is.* p. 151; Smend, *A.T. Rel. Gesch.* 395, 396). God did not rule the world directly, but through the agency of angels. The mention of this judgment is here so brief that obviously it is a current belief. The writer counts on the ready intelligence of his readers, and so touches on it shortly. This idea is referred to in Deut. xxxii. 8; Pss. lviii. 2, 3-lxxxii.; Dan. x.-xii., and is reproduced,

BIBLIOGRAPHY.—For the older literature on this subject see *Alger, a Critical History of the Doctrine of a Future Life, with a Complete Bibliography*, by Ezra Abbot, pp. 783-970, New York, 1871. Schulze, *Voraussetzung der Christ. Lehre v. d. Unsterblichkeit*, 1861. Stade, *Die ATliche Vorstellungen vom Zustand nach dem Tode*, 1877; *Geschichte des Volks Israel*,[2] i. 415-427, 503-506, 1889. Briggs, *Messianic Prophecy*, 1886. Jeremias, *Die Babyl.-Assyr. Vorstellungen vom Zustand nach dem Tode*, 1887. Schwally, *Das Leben nach dem Tode*, 1892—original and most helpful. Toy, *Judaism and Christianity*, 1892. Cheyne, *Origin of the Psalter*, see pp. 381-452 on "Rise of Doctrine of Judgment after Death," 1891; *Introduction to the Book of Isaiah*, 1895—invaluable both on critical and exegetical grounds; *Jewish Religious Life after the Exile*, 1898. Robertson Smith, *Religion of the Semites*, 1894. Salmond, *Christian Doctrine of Immortality*, 3rd ed., 1897. Davidson, Art. "Eschatology" in Hastings' *B.D.* i. 734-741. See also the relative sections in the Biblical Theologies of Oehler, Schultz, Dillmann, and particularly Smend's *ATliche Religionsgeschichte*, 1893, and Marti's *Geschichte der Israelitischen Religion*, 1897.

but in a different form, in Eth. En. lxxxix. 59, xc. 17. According to Jubilees xv. 31, 32, angels are set over the nations, but only God is over Israel.

Mountain of God in the North.—This mountain in the north is referred to in Is. xiv. 13 (Ezek. i. 4) and in Job xxxvii. 22 (according to Siegfried's emendation) and in Ps. xlviii. 2 (?). In Ezek. xxviii. 13, 14, 16 this idea is combined with that of the Garden of Eden in Gen. iii. In this form the myth is further developed in Eth. En. xviii. 6-9, xxiv. 1-3, xxv. 3. The Mountain of God in the North is found amongst the Assyrians, Babylonians, Indians, etc. It is a late idea in Israel; for their sacred mountain was anciently in the south (Judg. v. 4, 5; Deut. xxxiii. 2; Hab. iii. 3; Ps. lxviii. 8, 9; Zech. ix. 14).

CHAPTER V

THE ESCHATOLOGY OF APOCRYPHAL AND APOCALYPTIC LITERATURE DURING THE SECOND CENTURY B.C.

Higher theology of Old Testament further developed in subsequent non-Canonical literature, but not in Ecclesiasticus and Tobit.

IN the preceding chapters we have dealt with the eschatological thought of the Old Testament Canonical books, and the rise of the higher theology in Job, the Psalms, Isaiah, and Daniel. The main ideas of this theology are reproduced and further developed in the subsequent Apocryphal and Apocalyptic literature. Of the Apocryphal books, however, Ecclesiasticus and Tobit have no part in this development, but reflect the earlier and more conservative views of the Old Testament. Since these are the last chief witnesses to some of the still surviving heathen elements in Judaism, and lie off the main path of religious development, we shall consider them at the outset together, and then pass on to the writings, which are important in an eschatological regard.

Doctrine of retribution in Ecclesiasticus.

In Ecclesiasticus the problem of retribution takes a peculiar form. On the one hand it is uncompromisingly tory, and refuses to admit the possibility of the new views as to the future life.

Retribution confined to this life.

All retribution without exception is confined to this life: "Fear not death," exclaims the Son of Sirach, "whether it be ten or a hundred or a thousand years, there are no chastisements[1] for life in Sheol" (xli. 3, 4). On the other hand, this writer supplements Ezekiel's theory of exact individual retribution with the older view which Ezekiel attacked, and seeks to cover its obvious defects with the doctrine of the solidarity of the family. A man's wickedness must receive its recompense either in his own person in this life, or, failing this, in the persons of his surviving children, since Sheol knows no retribution. Thus on the one hand he teaches the doctrine of individual retribution:

> Look at the generations of old and see:
> Who did ever put his trust in the Lord and was ashamed?[2]
> (ii. 10, 11).
>
> There shall no good come to him that continueth to do evil,
> Nor to him that giveth no alms (xii. 3).
>
> The ungodly . . . shall not go unpunished unto Hades
> (ix. 12).
>
> For it is an easy thing in the sight of the Lord
> To reward a man in the day of death according to his ways, . . .
> And in the last end of a man is the revelation of his deeds
> (xi. 26, 27^b).

But this theory of individual retribution was inadequate, for obviously all men did not meet with their deserts. Hence a man's sins are visited through

[1] So the marginal reading of the new Hebrew text. This reading is supported by the LXX.

[2] Some suffering is disciplinary and educational, and as such is a proof of God's love. Thus "gold is tried in the fire, and acceptable men in the furnace of humiliation" (ii. 5; cf. Prov. iii. 12; Ps. cxix. 71).

CHAP. V.

the evil remembrance of his name and in the misfortunes of his children after him. Thus our author declares that a man's character shall be manifest in the fortunes of his children :—

A man shall be known in his children (xi. 28).
The children of the ungodly shall not put forth many branches ;
For the root of the impious is on the point of a crag (so Heb.) (xl. 15).

The inheritance of sinners' children shall perish,
And with their posterity abideth poverty (Heb. and Syr.) (xli. 6 ; cf. xxiii. 24-26).

On the other hand, the children of the righteous are blessed. Thus :—

With their seed shall remain continually a good inheritance ;
Their children are within the covenants.
Their seed standeth fast
And their children for their sakes.
Their seed shall remain for ever,
And their glory shall not be blotted out (xliv. 11-13).

Since there is thus no retribution beyond the grave, there is no organic relation between this life and the life in Sheol.[1] Sheol is out of the sphere of moral government ; for there no account is taken of man's past life on earth (xli. 4) ; there is there no recognition of God : "Thanksgiving perisheth from the dead as from one that is not" (xvii. 28). In that region there is no delight of life (xiv. 16) ; its inhabitants are bereft of light (xxii. 11) ; they are plunged in an eternal sleep (xlvi. 19).

The reference to Gehenna in vii. 17, ἐκδίκησις

[1] In xxi. 10 thoughts of the penal character of Sheol do seem to be present, though not in harmony with the doctrinal system of the author.

ἀσεβοῦς πῦρ καὶ σκώληξ, is undoubtedly corrupt; for belief in an abode of penal character is contrary to the whole outlook of the writer as to the future: moreover, it is without the support of the Hebrew, of the Syriac Version and the best MSS. of the Ethiopic Version.

CHAP. V.

As regards the future of the nation, the writer looks forward to the Messianic kingdom (xxxvi. 1-17), of which Elijah is to be the forerunner (xlviii. 10), when Israel will be delivered from evil (l. 23, 24), the scattered tribes restored (xxxvi. 11; Greek, xxxiii. 13), the heathen nations duly punished (xxxvi. 18, 19; Greek, xxxii. 22-24). This kingdom of Israel will last for ever (xxxvii. 25, xliv. 13).[1]

Tobit.

Tobit.—The eschatology of this book is very slight. It entertains, like the Old Testament, high hopes for the nation. Thus Jerusalem and the temple will be rebuilt with gold and precious stones, the scattered tribes restored, and the heathen, forsaking their idols, will worship the God of Israel (xiii. 10-18, xiv. 4-6). This author takes Sheol in its Old Testament sense. Thus it is called the eternal place (ὁ αἰώνιος τόπος) in iii. 6. Here Hades (cf. iii. 10, xiii. 2) is a region where existence is practically at an end, as in Job and Ecclesiasticus, for Sarah, the daughter of Raguel, prays in iii. 6: "Command my spirit to be taken from me, that I . . . may

[1] This last statement is questionable, as it has the support of the Greek Version only; for xxxvii. 25 is not found in the Syriac, and in xliv. 13, while the Greek gives "their seed (=וזרעם) shall remain for ever," the Heb. and Syr. "their remembrance (=וזכרם) shall remain for ever."

CHAP. V.

become earth . . . and go to the everlasting place." This deathlike character of Sheol is due to the current theory of the soul and spirit derived from Gen. ii., iii.

A developed form of the Old Testament higher theology the creed of the Chasids.

When we pass from the Old Testament to apocalyptic literature at the beginning of the second century B.C., we find that what had been tentative and exceptional on the part of two or more Old Testament writers has now become normal and settled in the creed of a small body of zealous Jews known as Chasids or Asidaeans. Since these came forward as the representatives and champions of the higher theology in Israel, we must turn aside for a few minutes to notice their history. For many years it was one of patient martyrdom. The first reference to these as forming a religious organisation is found in Eth. En. xc. 6, and the date of its initiation appears to be about 200 B.C. In this passage they are described in the following allegorical terms: "But behold lambs were borne by those white sheep, and they began to open their eyes, and to see and to cry to the sheep." "The white sheep" here are the faithful adherents of the Theocracy, the lambs are the Chasids. The lambs are distinguished from the white sheep, because the movement initiated by the Chasids marked a new and severer rule of life and worship than had hitherto been observed. The next reference to them is to be found in 1 Macc. ii. 29-38, where we are told of a large body of men who, with their wives and children, forsook all that they had, and

Their history.

took refuge in the caves in the wilderness, in order to worship without let or hindrance. When the officers of Antiochus were informed of this exodus, they went in pursuit, and put 1000 Chasids to the sword (Joseph. *Ant.* xii. 6, 2) on their refusal to return and comply with the edicts of Antiochus. The victims offered no resistance, for it was the Sabbath. But many escaped and gave their support to Mattathias in the great Maccabean struggle on behalf of the Law of God, but only after much indecision (1 Macc. vii. 13 *sqq.*); because the Maccabean movement put them in strife with the high priest of the time, the legitimate and religious head of the nation. So long, however, as the Maccabean family fought simply for the restoration of the Theocracy, they carried with them the support of the Chasids; but the moment that Jonathan laid hands on the high priesthood, from that moment began the alienation of the Chasids, and their withdrawal from the arena of public life. For almost half a century they are unknown to history; when they once more reappear in history, they are known as the Pharisees, and from henceforth they mould for good or ill the destinies of the nation. However corrupt this movement became in later times, it was incomparably noble in its early days. It incorporated within it all the enthusiasm and religious faith of the nation, and, though spiritual children of the Scribes, they drew within their membership the most zealous of the priestly as well as the non-priestly families. Though first appearing

CHAP. V.

as the champions of the Law against the Hellenising Sadducees, they were still more the representatives of advanced forms of doctrine on the Messianic kingdom and the resurrection. To this comparatively small body of men was entrusted for some decades the defence, confirmation, and development of the religious truths that were to save the world. How nobly and with what prodigal self-sacrifice they proved themselves worthy guardians of this sacred trust is told for all time in the Enoch and Maccabean literature, and set forth in pregnant strength and simplicity in the New Testament book of the Hebrews (xi. 35-39), which describes them as those "of whom the world was not worthy." Through their agency the spiritual aspirations of the Old Testament few became in the course of a century the unshakeable convictions of Palestinean Judaism.

Their tasks and achievements.

Apocalyptic springs from prophecy, but is differentiated from it in certain respects.

Before we enter into the study of apocalyptic literature, it will be well to touch briefly upon its origin[1] from prophecy, and likewise on its essential differentiation from the latter. On the appearance of apocalyptic features in the Old Testament, we have from time to time remarked in the last chapters.[2] We shall now give a short but comprehensive account of Apocalyptic.

Apocalyptic springs from the reinterpretation of unfulfilled prophecy.

The origin of Apocalyptic is to be sought in prophecy, or rather, indeed, in unfulfilled prophecy. For that certain prophecies had not been fulfilled was clearly a matter of religious difficulty as early

[1] On this question see Wellhausen, *Skizzen und Vorarbeiten*, viii. 225-231.
[2] See pp. 102, 106, 116, 117, 120-122, 160, 161, *notes*.

CHAP. V.

First re-interpretation due to Ezekiel.

as the Exile. Thus Ezekiel takes up one such prophecy and reinterprets it in such a way as to show that its fulfilment is yet in the future. The prophets Jeremiah (iii.-vi.) and Zephaniah had foretold the invasion of Judah by a mighty people from the North. But this northern foe had failed to appear. And yet appear he must; for was not inspired prophecy pledged thereto?[1] Hence Ezekiel re-edits this prophecy in a new form, and adjourns its fulfilment. Thus, according to Ezek. xxxviii. 8, 16, a mighty host (*i.e.* Gog) in the future will attack Jerusalem from the North (see above, p. 106). This host, Ezekiel declares, is the foe foretold by the prophets: "Thou art he of whom I spake by my servants the prophets of Israel, which prophesied in those days for many years that I would bring thee against them" (xxxviii. 17[2]).

It was probably the re-editing of these unfulfilled prophecies that led Ezekiel to divide the final judgment into two great catastrophic events—the glorification of the united Israel in Jerusalem

[1] The source of a prophecy, whether from Yahwè or not, was, according to Deut. xviii. 21, 22, to be shown by what followed. If the prophecy was fulfilled, then it was from Yahwè, but otherwise not. That this cannot, however, be regarded as a true canon follows from the fact that many prophecies of the greatest prophets remained unfulfilled. This canon, moreover, is to some extent questioned in Deut. xiii. 1-4, where it is said that false prophets, who would lead Israel to worship other gods, will foretell signs and wonders, and that though these come to pass the false prophets are not to be hearkened to. Thus the fulfilment of prophecy did not in itself prove that the prophet was from Yahwè. Yet another canon is given by Jer. xxviii. 8, 9: "The prophets which have been before me and before thee of old prophesied against many countries, and against great kingdoms, (only) of war and of evil and of pestilence. (But) the prophet which prophesieth of peace, when the word of the prophet shall come to pass, then shall the prophet be known that Yahwè hath truly sent him."

[2] So LXX and Vulgate, which omit the interrogative in this verse.

CHAP. V.

(xxxvii. 23-28) and the subsequent destruction of the heathen powers (xxxviii., xxxix.)

Other apocalyptic features in Ezekiel.

Other traces of the apocalyptic type of thought discover themselves in Ezekiel. Thus the word of God has become identical with a written book (ii. 8–iii. 4), by the eating of which he learns the will of God—an idea that is to be compared with the tree in Paradise, the eating of which imparted spiritual knowledge. Moreover, when the divine word is thus conceived as a written message, the sole office of the prophet is that of merely communicating what is written. Thus the human element is reduced almost to zero, and the conception of prophecy becomes mechanical. Man stands over against God as the involuntary instrument of the Absolute. And as the personal element disappears in the conception of the prophetic calling, so it tends to disappear in the prophetic view of history, and the future comes to be conceived, not as the organic result of the present under the divine guidance, but as mechanically determined from the beginning in the counsels of God, and as arranged under certain artificial categories of time.

It is therefore not without reason that Duhm[1] has called Ezekiel the spiritual founder of Apocalyptic.

Non-fulfilment of prophecies of the date of the Messianic kingdom the main source of Apocalyptic.

The non-fulfilment of prophecies relating to this or that individual event or people served, no doubt, to popularise the methods of Apocalyptic, but only in a very slight degree in comparison with the non-

[1] *Theologie der Propheten*, p. 210.

CHAP. V.

fulfilment of the greatest of all prophecies—the advent of the Messianic kingdom. Thus, though Jeremiah had promised that after seventy years (xxv. 11, xxix. 10) Israel should be restored to their own land (xxiv. 5, 6), and there enjoy the blessings of the Messianic kingdom under the Messianic King (xxiii. 5, 6), this period had passed by, and things remained as of old. A similar expectation was cherished by Ezekiel, but this no more than that of Jeremiah was destined to be fulfilled.[1] Next, Haggai and Zechariah promised that, when the temple was rebuilt, the Davidic kingdom should be established and the glories of the Messianic time. The temple was presently rebuilt, but the kingdom failed to appear. Through century after century the hope for the advent of the kingdom still persisted, and was possibly sustained with fresh reinterpretations of ancient prophecy.

Advent of kingdom after seventy years, according to Jeremiah; after forty years, according to Ezekiel.

After rebuilding of temple, according to Haggai and Zechariah.

At any rate, in the first half of the second century B.C. we have two notable reinterpretations of the old prophecy of Jeremiah. In both of these works the problem is solved by adjourning the hour of fulfilment. In the first—the Book of Daniel, *circa* 168 B.C.—the writer (ix. 25-27) interprets the 70 years of Jeremiah as 70 weeks of years = 490 years. Since $69\frac{1}{2}$ of these had already expired, there were only $3\frac{1}{2}$ years to run before the destruction of the Greek power and the consummation of the

According to two writers (*circa* 168-161), advent of kingdom within a few years, or at most a generation.

[1] According to Ezek. iv. 6, the captivity was to last forty years. Thus the present generation was to atone for its own guilt. But since the children were not to suffer for the parents, the next generation was to witness their restoration to Palestine. Ezekiel hoped to survive it (xxix. 21).

CHAP. V.

Theocracy. In the second, and almost contemporaneous work—Eth. En. lxxxiii.-xc., *circa* 166-161 B.C.—a somewhat analogous solution of the problem is given. The writer takes the 70 years of Jeremiah to denote the 70 successive reigns of the 70 angelic patrons to whom God had committed the care and administration of the world. Since the sway of these angelic rulers was to terminate within the present generation, the Messianic kingdom was, therefore, at hand.

Both the above periods came and passed by, and again the expectations of the Jews were doomed to disappointment. The Greek empire in the East was indeed overthrown, and an independent kingdom of Judah set up under the Maccabean dynasty. But this latter speedily showed itself to be in many respects the antithesis of the promised kingdom of God. Thenceforward the Messianic hopes undergo an absolute transformation. They are still cherished, indeed, but their object is no longer an *eternal* but only a *temporary* theocracy established on the present earth. The solutions of Daniel and Enoch (lxxxix., xc.) have been perforce abandoned for the time, but the number seventy still possesses a strong fascination for the Jewish writer of Apocalyptic. Thus in Eth. En. xci.-civ. (*circa* 105-95 B.C.) the whole history of the world is divided into ten weeks, each apparently of seven generations. The Messianic kingdom is to be established at the beginning of the eighth week, and to terminate with the seventh

After 100 B.C. only a temporary Messianic kingdom expected, but that immediately.

day of the tenth. The writer is living at the close of the seventh week (Eth. En. xciii. 10). Hence the kingdom is close at hand. But this hope no more than its predecessors met with fulfilment.

Book of Daniel recovers its prestige, and its prophecy of the fourth kingdom now interpreted of Rome in the Apocalypse of Baruch and 4 Ezra.

We shall now pass over a period of a century and a half. During this interval the Book of Daniel has more than recovered the loss its prestige had sustained in the second century through its unfulfilled prophecies of the kingdom. During the same interval, however, a new and more ruthless power had taken the place of the Greek empire in the East. This new phenomenon called, therefore, for a fresh reinterpretation of Daniel. The fourth and last empire, which, according to Dan. vii. 19-25, was to be Greek, was now declared to be Roman by the writer of the Apocalypse of Baruch xxxvi.-xl. (*circa* 50-70 A.D.), and likewise by the author of 4 Ezra x. 60–xii. 35 (*circa* 90 A.D.) In the latter work the writer implies that the vision in Dan. vii. 7, 8 was misinterpreted by the angel in vii. 23-25.[1]

We have now shown sufficiently that unfulfilled prophecy has been a perennial source of Apocalyptic. We shall now point out in what respects Apocalyptic is distinguished from Prophecy.

Apocalyptic distinguished from Prophecy by the transference of interest from the present to the future, from the mundane to the supermundane,

(1) *Prophecy still believes that this world is God's world, and that in this world His goodness and truth*

[1] Thus in reference to the fourth kingdom, symbolised by the eagle in this book (see xi. 1 *sqq.*), God says to Ezra: "Aquilam quam vidisti ascendentem de mari, hoc est regnum quartum quod visum est in visu Danieli fratri tuo. Sed non est illi interpretatum quomodo ego nunc tibi interpretor" (xii. 11, 12).

CHAP. V.

will yet be justified. Hence the prophet addresses himself chiefly to the present and its concerns, and, when he addresses himself to the future, his prophecy springs naturally from the present, and the future which he depicts is regarded as in organic connection with it. *The apocalyptic writer, on the other hand, almost wholly despairs of the present; his main interests are supermundane.* He cherishes no hope of arousing his contemporaries to faith and duty by direct and personal appeals; for though God spoke in the past, "there is no more any prophet." This pessimism and want of faith in the present, alike in the leaders and the led, limited and defined the form in which the religious ardour of the former should manifest itself. They prescribed, in fact, as a necessity of the age, and as a condition of successful effort, *the adoption of pseudonymous authorship.* And thus it is that the apocalyptic writer approaches his countrymen with a work which claims to be the production of some great figure in the past, such as Enoch, Moses, Isaiah, Daniel, or Baruch.

and by the adoption of pseudonymous authorship.

Also by its determinism and its mechanical conception of history.

(2) Another feature of Apocalyptic, as distinguished from Prophecy, was imposed upon it by the necessities of the time, *i.e. its indefinitely wider view of the world's history.* Thus, whereas ancient Prophecy had to deal with *temporary* reverses at the hands of some heathen power, Apocalyptic arose at a time when Israel had been subject for centuries to the sway of one or other of the great world-powers. Hence in order to harmonise such diffi-

culties with God's righteousness, it had to take account of the rôle of such empires in the counsels of God; to recount the sway and downfall of each in turn till, finally, the lordship of the world passed into the hands of Israel, or the final judgment arrived. The chief part of these events belonged, it is true, to the past; but the apocalyptic writer represented them as still in the future, arranged under certain artificial categories of time, and as definitely determined from the beginning in the counsels of God, and revealed by Him to His servants the prophets. *Determinism thus became a leading characteristic of Jewish Apocalyptic; and accordingly its conception of history, as distinguished from that of Prophecy, was mechanical rather than organic.*[1]

Having now dealt with the origin of Apocalyptic and its differentiation from Prophecy, we shall now address ourselves to a detailed consideration of the literature of the former throughout the three centuries from 200 B.C. to 100 A.D. The literature of each century can be considered best by itself. It will thus fall into three divisions. Each division will be treated under four heads. I. The authorities. II. General eschatological development of the century. III. Eschatological systems of the various writers of the century. IV. Development of special conceptions.

[1] These two paragraphs are repeated from my article on Apocalyptic in Hastings' *Bible Dictionary*, i. 109, 110.

CHAP. V.

I. *Authorities for* 200-100 B.C.

Ethiopic Enoch i.-xxxvi.
Daniel.
Ethiopic Enoch lxxxiii.-xc.
Sibylline Oracles—Procemium and iii. 97-818.
Test. xii. Patriarchs—Some of its apocalyptic sections.

We have given the above authorities in their chronological order, and in the following discussion this order will be observed save in the case of the third book of the Sibylline Oracles (*i.e.* iii. 97-818). Since this shallow *rechauffé* of Old Testament ideas makes no single contribution to the eschatological expectations of the time, and confines its forecasts to the final destinies of Israel as a nation and of the Gentiles, we will at once reproduce its main teaching in these respects. Belonging, moreover, to Hellenistic Judaism, and observing an esoteric (?) reticence as to the higher doctrines of a future life, its evidence is only of very secondary importance in this study of Palestinean eschatology, and really lies outside the stream of religious development that drew within it all the noblest elements in Palestinean Judaism.

Eschatology of Sibylline Oracles iii. 97-818 confined to the nation.

Its eschatological forecasts are, as we have already observed, confined to this world.

Ultimate destinies of Israel and the Gentiles.

Though so limited, it gives, nevertheless, a vivid account of the Messianic kingdom. Very soon the people of the Mighty God will grow strong (iii. 194, 195), and God will send the Messiah from the East, who will put an end to evil war, slaying some, and fulfilling the promises in behalf of others, and He will be guided in all things by God. And the temple will be resplendent with glory, and the earth teem with fruitfulness (iii. 652-660). Then the nations will muster their forces and attack Palestine (iii. 660-668), but God will destroy them, and their judgment will be accompanied by fearful portents (iii. 669-697). But Israel will dwell safely under the divine protection (iii. 702-709), and the rest of the cities and the islands will be converted, and unite with Israel in praising God (iii. 710-731). The blessings of the Messianic age are recounted (iii. 744-754; cf. also iii. 367-380, 619-623). And the kings of the earth will be at peace with one another (iii. 755-759). In the later section of this book the forecast is somewhat different. Though in the earlier part, as we have seen above, it was the Messiah that conducted the war against the hostile nations, in this it is the prophets of God. Thus God will establish a universal kingdom over all mankind, with Jerusalem as centre (iii. 767-771), and the prophets of God will lay down the sword and become judges and kings of the earth (iii. 781, 782), and men will bring offerings to the temple from all parts of the earth (iii. 772, 773).

II. *General Eschatological Development in the Second Century* B.C.

Eschatological doctrine and development of the second century B.C.

In the apocalyptic literature of the second century we enter into a region of definite ideas

CHAP. V.

as to the destinies of the individual and the nation.

Despairing of the present, the writers of this century have fixed their entire hopes on the future. This future is sketched in firm, unwavering lines. In order to encourage the faithful under the unsparing persecutions of Antiochus, religious thinkers of the period consolidated and developed into more or less consistent theodicies the various eschatological systems of the Old Testament. In these theodicies there is no vagueness or doubt as to the ultimate destinies of the righteous and the wicked. The doctrine of retribution in the next life is held all the more firmly in proportion to the uncertainty of its sway in the present. These writers are convinced that the essential distinctions already existing between these classes must one day be outwardly realised. Hence, all with one accord proclaim, in the most emphatic tones, the certainty of judgment on the advent of the Messianic kingdom, while some further teach that on death men enter immediately on a state of bliss or woe in Sheol, which is but the prelude to their final destiny.

The righteous dead rise to share in the eternal Messianic kingdom on earth.

The righteous, both quick and dead,[1] will be recompensed to the full in the eternal Messianic kingdom, and the blessed future of the righteous individual and of the righteous nation will be realised and consummated together.

Old Testament synthesis of the two hopes prevails throughout this century.

Thus the synthesis between the eschatologies of the nation and the individual, that was established on Old Testament soil, is still maintained

[1] This is true only of the martyred righteous in Daniel.

throughout this century. There are not wanting, however, signs of its approaching resolution into its original factors, in order that these may again pursue their separate lines of development, and, on attaining their full-grown stature, may once more coalesce in the final and complete synthesis which they receive in the New Testament.

Sign of the approaching resolution of this synthesis

The sign of this impending detachment of the hopes of the individual from those of the nation is to be seen in the fact that the writer of Enoch lxxxiii.-xc. has become conscious that the earth, however purged and purified, is no fitting theatre for an eternal Messianic kingdom. If the Messianic kingdom is to be of eternal duration, and God is to be present with men, His habitation and that of the blessed must be built, not of things earthly and corruptible, but of things heavenly and incorruptible. Hence the writer represents the erection of the heavenly Jerusalem in the place of the earthly as the centre of the kingdom.

owing to the growing dualism of the times.

This device is clearly of the nature of a compromise, and springs from the dualism that was making itself increasingly felt in Judaism. In the following century we shall find that it had established itself so firmly in Jewish thought that an eternal Messianic kingdom on the present earth became inconceivable.

We must not fail to notice here a development of this century to which we have already called attention. This is the extension of the prerogative of resurrection from the righteous to the wicked. That this marks a declension in religious thought we have

CHAP. V.

already pointed out. The currency, however, of this lower view was far from general. The older and higher conception is retained in Eth. En. lxxxiii.-xc., which presents the fullest picture of the last things in the literature of the second century.

III. *Eschatological Systems of the various Writers of the Second Century* B.C.

THE BOOK OF DANIEL (168 B.C.)

We have already discussed the Book of Daniel in certain aspects amongst the Old Testament books. But since it belongs in character specially to this literature; since, further, it forms an indispensable link in eschatological development, it finds here its natural place.

Book of Daniel mainly concerned with the world-empire of Israel—the Messianic kingdom—and only partially with the future lot of the individual.

Although this book is the forerunner and herald of most subsequent apocalyptic developments, its own outlook is in the main confined to this world. Its hopes are directed, not to the after-world, with its retributions for the individual, but to the setting up of a world-empire of Israel which is to displace the heathen, to an eternal Messianic kingdom on earth. Accordingly, it extends neither promise nor threatening to *the individual as such*, but only to those individuals who have *in an extraordinary degree* helped or hindered the advent of this kingdom. To the former, the martyrs, the great saints and teachers (xii. 2, 3), it holds forth the blessedness of a resurrection to life; to the latter, the Jewish apostates, it proclaims a resurrection to shame and everlasting contempt.[1] As for the great majority of the nation, who are of average character, and are neither overmuch righteous nor overmuch wicked, their lot is of no concern to the kingdom, and Sheol remains their eternal abode. Thus the claims of the individual are only very partially recognised in the eschatological system of Daniel.

This world-empire of Israel is to be of eternal duration, and all the nations are to be subject to it (vii. 14). We are probably right in assuming that all the surviving nations will be converted. There is no Messiah.

Sheol here used in its non-moral sense.

Sheol, which is called "the land of dust"[2] (xii. 2), retains its Old Testament sense as a non-moral region. This is not incomprehensible in a writer whose paramount interest is in the nation and not in the individual, in this world and not in the next. If he had ever experienced a profound concern in the problem of individual retribution, he could no longer have tolerated such a heathen conception. Sheol thus possesses a peculiar character in our author. It is the *intermediate* abode of the very good and the very bad in Israel, and the *eternal* abode of the rest of Israel and of all the Gentiles. It is not improbable, likewise, that after the special class of righteous Israel have enjoyed "an aeonian life"[3] in the kingdom,

Very peculiarly conceived in this book.

[1] This is probably to be taken as describing Gehenna.

[2] אַדְמַת עָפָר. For Sheol so described compare Job vii. 21, xvii. 16, and the Babylonian view.

[3] חַיֵּי עוֹלָם. That this is not an eternal life follows from the general presuppositions of the writer. The above Hebrew phrase = ܚ̈ܝܐ ܕܠܥܠܡܐ

CHAP. V.

they will descend finally and for ever to Sheol. Thus ultimately Sheol becomes sooner or later the eternal abode of all mankind, save the small class of Jewish apostates who are condemned to Gehenna.

Angelic patrons of the nations.

In this book the writer uses the belief in the angelic patrons of the nations to explain the national reverses, and likewise the delay in the establishment of the Messianic kingdom. Thus Persia has its angelic guardian (x. 13, 20), likewise Greece (x. 20), and Israel (x. 21, xii. 1), *i.e.* Michael.[1] We shall find another application of this idea in the almost contemporaneous work Eth. En. lxxxiii.-xc., which we shall now deal with.

Ethiopic Enoch i.-xxxvi. (probably before 170 B.C.)

Ethiopic Enoch i.-xxxvi. an early theodicy.

This fragmentary work represents the earliest and in some respects the most primitive theodicy of the second century. The problem of its author is

ζωὴ αἰώνιος. The indefinite meaning of this phrase is seen in the contemporary work Eth. En. i.-xxxvi. Thus in x. 10 it is said that the ζωὴ αἰώνιος = 500 years, and εἰς τοὺς αἰῶνας in x. 5 = a period of 70 generations. In the next century the phrase εἰς αἰῶνας ἅπαντας (*Sibyl. Or.* iii. 50) denotes merely a very long time. This same use is attested also in Apoc. Bar. xl. 3, lxxiii. 1, where the Syriac = εἰς τὸν αἰῶνα = "for the age." See below, p. 226. The phrase in Daniel might possibly be taken to mean everlasting life if we could accept the view advocated by Berthold, *Daniel neu übersetzt und erklärt* (1806), and later by Lagarde, and by Barton, *Composition of the Book of Daniel*, 1898, which regards Dan. x.-xii. as an independent writing.

[1] In the Targ. Jer. i. on Gen. xi. 7, 8 the seventy angels of God are apparently appointed to preside over the seventy nations which originated through the confusion of tongues. So also Deut. xxxii. 8 (LXX). These guardian angels are referred to in Ecclus. xvii. 17, but are limited to the Gentiles—Israel has God as its portion. But according to the prevailing tradition Michael represents Israel.

to justify the ways of God to man. Unlike the author of Daniel, this writer is more concerned with the problem of individual retribution than with the future of the nation. The righteous will not always suffer, and the wicked will not always prosper (i. 1). The limits to such evil experience are set by death (xxii.) and by great world-judgments. But in order to apprehend the remedy of the world's ills, we must apprehend their cause, and their cause, according to our author, is to be discovered, not in the primal fall of Adam, but in the lust of the fallen angels for the daughters of men referred to in Gen. vi. 1-4. Original sin, therefore, stands not in the following of Adam, whose transgression seems limited in its effects to himself, but in the evil engendered through the fallen watchers or angels (ix. 6, 9, 10; x. 8). But sin of necessity entails its due retribution, and this retribution has already in part befallen the sinful angels, their children, and antediluvian man in the first world-judgment (x. 4-10, xii. 1-3.) By this first act of judgment the fallen angels are confined in caverns under the mountains as an intermediate abode of punishment (x. 4, 5, 12), and the souls of men are committed to Sheol (xxii.) To an account of this place we will return presently. It is well to observe the definiteness with which the intermediate abodes of angelic and human beings are here conceived. But though only a few righteous survived the Deluge, sin afresh asserted itself in the world through the agency of the demons. These demons, according to our author, were the spirits that had

CHAP. V.

gone forth from the slaughtered children of the fallen angels and the daughters of men. For some reason unexplained, these invisible agents of evil were allowed to pursue their wicked activities through all the interval elapsing between the Deluge and the Final World-judgment (xvi. 1), a belief that was still current in New Testament times.[1] But with regard to the generations of men subsequent to the Flood, the due recompense of their conduct is not postponed till the last judgment. Immediately after death they enter on a foretaste of their final doom in Sheol (xxii.) We must now treat somewhat fully this important conception.

Certain Old Testament views of Sheol prepare the way for the teaching of chap. xxii.

We have shown in the preceding chapters that the conception of Sheol as an intermediate abode underlies at least certain passages of the Old Testament (see pp. 155, 156, 181), though in other respects it preserves in these passages its traditional non-moral character. In two of the Psalms it assumes the character of a place of retribution; but since some doubt possibly attaches to this view, there is all the more reason here for dwelling on the ancient and very full description of Sheol given by our author in chap. xxii., written probably before 170 B.C. This chapter[2] I will give in the words of the author, who represents himself, like Dante, as visiting this region under the guidance of an angel.

Description of Sheol. Fourfold division.

xxii. 1. "And thence I went to another place,

[1] See Matt. viii. 29.

[2] The translation given in the text is a revised form of that which is given in my *Book of Enoch*, pp. 93-97. It incorporates the emendations made on pp. 359-362 on the basis of the Gizeh Greek Fragment of Enoch.

CHAP. V.

and (Uriel) showed me in the west[1] a great and high mountain and hard rocks. 2. And there were in this (mountain) four hollow places, deep, wide, and very smooth. Three of them were gloomy and one bright, and there was a spring of water in its midst. And I said: How smooth are these hollow places, and deep and black to look at. 3. And this time Rufael answered me, one of the holy angels who was with me, and spake to me: These hollow places, whereon the spirits of the souls of the dead are assembled, have been created to this very end, that all the souls of the children of men should assemble here. 4. These places are appointed as their habitation till the day of their judgment and till their appointed period, and the appointed time in which the great judgment comes upon them. 5. And I saw the spirits of the children of men who were dead, and their voice penetrated to the heaven and complained. 6. This time I asked the angel Rufael who was with me, and spake to him: Whose spirit is that one yonder whose voice thus penetrates (to heaven) and complains? 7. And he answered me, and spake thus to me, saying: This is the spirit which went forth from Abel, whom his brother Cain slew, and he keeps complaining of him till his seed is destroyed from the face of the earth, and his seed disappears from amongst the seed of men. 8. And therefore at that time I asked regarding it, and regarding all the hollow places, Why is one separated from the

First division for the righteous who had met with an undeserved death.

[1] The geographical position assigned to Sheol here agrees with Babylonian (?), Greek, and Egyptian ideas, but not with the ancient Hebrew. It is most probably Greek views that have influenced the text.

CHAP. V.

other? 9. And he answered me, and spake to me: These three divisions are made to separate the spirits of the dead. And thus a division is made for the spirits of the righteous, in which there is a bright spring of water. 10. Such a (division) likewise has been made for sinners when they die and are buried in the earth without incurring judgment in their lifetime. 11. Here their spirits are placed apart in this great pain, till the great day of judgment and punishment and torment of the accursed for ever, and vengeance for their spirits, there will they be bound for ever. 12. And such a division has been made for the spirits of those who complain and make known their destruction when they were slain in the days of the sinners. 13. Thus it has been made for the spirits of men who were not righteous but sinners, complete in their crimes: they will be with criminals like themselves, but their spirits will not be slain on the day of judgment, nor will they be raised from thence."[1]

Second division for the other righteous.

Third for sinners who have died without suffering due retribution.

Fourth for sinners who have met with retribution in life. These will remain here for ever.

This elaborate description of Sheol with its four divisions, two for the spirits of the righteous and two for those of the wicked, cannot have leapt into life full grown, as it appears here, but must have passed through several stages of development. This fact in itself serves to confirm the view urged in previous chapters, that different conceptions of Sheol springing from the higher theology had already shown themselves in the Old Testament.

[1] Since the wicked in this division are confined here for ever, Sheol has in this instance become synonymous with Hell.

CHAP. V.

Great moral advance in this picture of Sheol.

From this view of Sheol the chief heathen features have disappeared. We have thus here a vast advance on the conception of Daniel. Instead of being a region where existence was at its lowest possible ebb, and the presence of moral distinctions was inconceivable, it has now become a place where there is a vigorous conscious existence, where ethical considerations are paramount, and the soul's lot is determined on moral grounds, and on moral grounds alone.

It is difficult to exaggerate the importance of this revolution in Jewish thought on the nature of the after-life.

Its shortcomings.

But whilst we recognise the ethical importance of this forward movement, we must not conceal its shortcomings. For its conception of Sheol is only imperfectly ethical. The destiny of each soul is regarded as accomplished at death, and its place in Sheol is absolutely and irrevocably defined according to its character on earth. Thus, however prolonged its abode may be in Sheol, it is held to be incapable of progress either upward or downward, and its character is regarded as mechanically fixed. Hence, at its best, Sheol thus conceived is only a place of petrified moralities and suspended graces. It aims at being moral but ends in being mechanical, and thus constitutes an amalgam formed of heterogeneous elements.

To return, however, to the description of our author, we should observe that of the four classes of souls or spirits in Sheol, three are raised to

CHAP. V.

Sheol = hell for the wicked who have met with judgment on earth, but only an intermediate abode for other Israelites.

The wicked who had escaped judgment in life raised as disembodied spirits to be punished for ever in Gehenna.

receive their final award, but the fourth, which consists of the wicked who have already been punished for their crimes in the upper world, is not raised from Sheol, but remains there for ever. Of the three other classes, one is composed of the wicked who had escaped punishment in this life, and after a preliminary course of "great pain" in Sheol, are raised at the great day of judgment in order to receive the punishment and torment of the accursed in Gehenna (xxvii. 2). Thus though the wicked are here said to rise, they do not share in the resurrection truly so called, they are simply transferred from Sheol to everlasting punishment in Gehenna, where "their spirits are slain."[1] This phrase appears to teach that the writer conceived the wicked to rise as disembodied spirits at the resurrection.[2] As for the two remaining classes, composed of the righteous, these rise with their bodies: they eat of the tree of life (xxv. 4-6), and thereby enjoy patriarchal lives (v. 9, xxv. 6), in the Messianic kingdom on a purified earth (x. 7, 16, 20-22), with Jerusalem as its centre (xxv. 5). All the Gentiles become righteous and worship God (x. 21). In this Messianic kingdom, in which there is, however, no Messiah, but the immediate presence of God with men (xxv. 2), the felicity of the blessed is of a very sensuous character. The powers of nature are increased indefinitely.

The righteous raised in the body to enjoy a very long life and a material prosperity,

[1] The fourth class escapes this severest form of condemnation (Eth. En. xxii. 13).

[2] xxii. 10, 11 (cf. xxii. 13). It is true that in xxvii. 3 the wicked in Gehenna are visible to the risen righteous, but this does not necessarily imply the possession of a body by the wicked.

Thus the righteous will beget 1000 children (x. 17); of all the seed that is sown each measure will bear 10,000 grains (x. 19); and each vine will have 10,000 branches, and each branch 10,000 twigs, and each twig 10,000 clusters, and each cluster 10,000 grapes, and each grape 25 measures of wine.[1] The allowance is liberal. We must not, however, neglect the ethical side of this felicity. Thus "light and joy and peace and wisdom" will be bestowed upon them, and "they will all live and never again sin either through heedlessness or through pride," and "their lives will grow old in peace, and the years of their joy will be many in happiness, and the peace of the age all the days of their life" (v. 7-9): "And the store-chambers of blessing which are in heaven will be opened" and "poured down upon the work and labour of the children of men," and "peace and justice will be wedded throughout all the generations of the world" (xi. 1, 2).

yet of a strongly ethical character.

ETHIOPIC ENOCH lxxxiii.-xc. (166-161 B.C.)

Enoch lxxxiii.-xc. a Chasid defence of the Maccabees.

We have now to study that most interesting fragment of the Book of Enoch which was written when Judas the Maccabee was still warring against Antiochus (166-161 B.C.) It consists of only eight chapters, *i.e.* lxxxiii.-xc. Their author was a Chasid, writing in support of the Maccabean movement. Its value is all the greater as it is the chief literary memorial emanating from the short period when

[1] See my *Apocalypse of Baruch*, p. 54, where I show that such was probably the full and original form of this expectation.

CHAP. V.

a coalition existed between the Chasids and the Maccabees.

His eschatological views are in advance alike of Daniel and Eth En. i.-xxxvi.

The writer has advanced considerably beyond the naïve and sensuous views of the kingdom presented in the earlier fragment i.-xxxvi. His conceptions are more spiritual. He writes a few years later than the Daniel Apocalypse. To this apocalypse his own forecasts of the future are on the whole closely allied, but in certain respects his outlook is more logically ethical: he reflects the earlier and more spiritual view of the resurrection, and does fuller justice to the problem of individual retribution. To these points we will return presently.

Like Eth. En. i.-xxxvi. this also a theodicy.

Like the previous writers of his century, our author is concerned with the undeserved calamities of the elect people, and with the task of reconciling the belief in God's righteousness with the suffering condition of His servants on earth.

His solution of this problem took the form in short compass of a Semitic philosophy of religion. In this treatise, though he describes the first world-judgment, and traces it to the sin of the angels, his interest centres mainly in the disastrous history of Israel since the Exile. That Israel indeed has sinned grievously, and is deserving of punishment, our author amply acknowledges, but not a punishment so immeasurably transcending its guilt. But these undue severities have not come upon Israel from God's hands. They are the doing of the seventy shepherds or angels into whose care God committed

Israel's undue sufferings due to the seventy angels to whom God had committed Israel for chastisement.

Israel (lxxxix. 59) for the due chastisement of Israel. But these angels had proved faithless to their trust, and treacherously destroyed those whom God willed not to destroy—but not with impunity. For an account has been taken of all their excesses, and of all those whom they had wickedly destroyed (lxxxix. 61, 62). And judgment is fast approaching. When the oppression is at its worst a righteous league will be established in Israel (xc. 6). This league is composed of the Chasids, with whom we have already dealt. These embrace within their ranks a family from which will come forth the deliverer of Israel (xc. 9-16). The deliverer here referred to is Judas the Maccabee, who was fighting against Syria when our author was writing. At this point the writer has completed his description of the past. He now completes his representation with a forecast of the future. The Syrians and other enemies of Israel, and finally all nations of the earth, will put forth every effort to destroy the God-sent hero, but in vain. While the struggle is still raging, God will intervene in person, and the earth will open her mouth and swallow them up (xc. 19, 16, 18). Then a throne will be "erected in the pleasant land" (xc. 20), and first the lustful angels, who had wrought such woe through their sin with women, will be judged and condemned to the abyss of fire, which is full of fire and flame and pillars of fire, and likewise the seventy angels who had dealt treacherously with Israel (xc. 20-25). The apostate Jews are next judged, and cast into Gehenna

The Chasids or Asidaeans the forerunners of the Pharisees.

Judas the Maccabee.

The final judgment.

CHAP. V.

(xc. 26, 27). With this last act the great Assize will close. Then God Himself will set up the New Jerusalem (xc. 28, 29), and the surviving non-Jewish nations will be converted and serve Israel (xc. 30), and the dispersion will be brought back, and the righteous dead of Israel will be raised to take part in the kingdom (xc. 33). Then the Messiah will appear amongst them, and all the righteous will be transformed into His likeness (xc. 38); and God will rejoice over them.

The resurrection.

Signs of dualism in this apocalypse.

In the above apocalypse there are one or two features that call for further attention. We remark first of all the consciousness of a dualism in the mind of the writer. The earthly Jerusalem, however purified, is no longer regarded as a fitting abode for God amongst men. Hence the heavenly Jerusalem must take the place of the earthly, as the spiritual and temporal metropolis of the Messianic kingdom, which is co-extensive with the world.

Only the righteous are raised to an eternal life.

In the next place only the righteous dead are raised. Thus our writer holds fast to the original and spiritual view of the resurrection, that the risen life is the organic development of the righteous life on earth. Finally, after the resurrection follows a transformation of all the members of the kingdom into a higher form of life. From this transformation of the righteous into the likeness of the Messiah we naturally conclude their eternal risen life. Thus we have this idea for the first time in Jewish literature.

TESTAMENTS OF THE XII. PATRIARCHS

Only one more work calls for consideration in this century—the Testaments of the XII. Patriarchs. It seems indubitable that some apocalyptic fragments of this book belong to this century, though the body of the book originated over a century later. Some of the oldest sections appear to have constituted originally a defence of the warlike Maccabean high priests in the latter half of the second century B.C., while others[1] seem to attack the later chiefs of that family in the first century B.C. It is hardly possible to interpret otherwise such a statement regarding Levi as in Reub. vi. *ad fin.*: "He shall die for us in wars visible and invisible" (cf. Sim. v.) One or more of these sections may possibly be from an earlier date, whereas many of them may belong to the first century B.C. Since, however, their eschatological thought in some respects belongs to the second century, we will give a brief outline of it, though we will not build any conclusions upon it.

This is all that can be done till a critical edition of this book appears. In the following references I have availed myself of the better readings of the Armenian Version.

Levi has been chosen by God to rule all the Gentiles with supreme sovereignty (Reub. vi.) The Messiah of the tribe of Levi,[2] who will appear at the

[1] Cf. Levi xiv., xix. *in init.* These passages resemble the Psalms of Solomon where these assail the Sadducean priesthood.

[2] Sometimes a Messiah of the tribe of Judah is spoken of. There is nothing against the Jewish origin of such passages, but others which combine the two ideas are Christian.

CHAP. V. close of the 7th Jubilee, will possess an eternal priesthood (Levi xviii.; Apocalyptic sections of Levi = ii.-v., viii., x., xiv.-xviii.) This will endure till God comes and restores Jerusalem and dwells in Israel (Levi v.) This Messiah will judge as a king: He will bind Beliar, open the gates of Paradise, and give His saints to eat of the tree of life (Levi xviii.; cf. Eth. En. xxv. 4-6). To the Messianic kingdom on earth all the righteous patriarchs will rise (Sim. vi.; Zeb. x.; Jud. xxv.) Then the spirits of deceit will be trodden under foot (Sim. vi.; Zeb. ix.) and Beliar destroyed (Levi xviii.; Jud. xxv.) And there will be only one people and one tongue (Jud. xxv.) The surviving Gentiles are in all cases to be converted save in Sim. vi., where they are doomed to annihilation. According to Benj. x. there is to be a resurrection, first of the Old Testament heroes and patriarchs, and next of the righteous and of the wicked. Thereupon the judgment is to follow, first of Israel and then of the Gentiles. Many of the above views are very late.

The designation of Michael in Dan. vi. (cf. Levi v.; Jud. xxv.) as a "mediator between God and man" is noteworthy.

Development of Special Conceptions

Soul and Spirit.—The later view of the spirit as the divine breath of life probably underlies Ecclus. xxxviii. 23; Bar. ii. 17 ("the dead also who are in Hades whose spirit is taken from their

CHAP. V.

bodies"); Tob. iii. 6 ("Command my spirit to be taken from me, that I may depart and become earth . . . command therefore that I may now depart unto the everlasting place"); and Jud. x. 13, where man is called a breath of life (πνεῦμα ζωῆς). In the Baruch and Tobit passages the spirit and the soul are regarded as essentially different. The spirit goes back to God and the soul continues to subsist in Sheol.

The older anthropology prevails in a developed form.

Elsewhere in the second century only the older Semitic view of the soul and spirit is attested, but *the older view in a further stage of development.* At this stage the difference that had hitherto distinguished these conceptions has now wholly disappeared. The soul and spirit, which according to the older view had been identical in essence but not in function, are now identical in both. The terms have become absolutely synonymous. What can be predicated of one can be predicated of the other.

Departed in Sheol called souls or spirits indifferently.

Of this new development we find several examples in the oldest chapters of the Ethiopic Enoch. Thus the inhabitants of Sheol are called "souls" in xxii. 3 (cf. also ix. 3), but generally "spirits" (xxii. 5, 6, 7, 9, 11, 12, 13[1]). The obvious result of this development is the high degree of life and consciousness now attributed to the inhabitants of Sheol. On death the entire personality so far as this is immaterial descends into Sheol. Thus, though according to the old Semitic view *the spirit*

[1] A very peculiar phraseology appears in ix. 10 and xxii. 3, where we find "the spirits of the souls of the dead." In the Syncellus Version of ix. 3 we have "the spirits and the souls of men."

CHAP. V.

never descended into Sheol, now it always does so, and the departed in Sheol are more frequently called "spirits" than "souls."[1] From this time forward, when the departed are spoken of as "asleep," the term is to be regarded as a mere metaphor. The departed are henceforth conceived as possessing life and consciousness as much as the living.

Before leaving this subject it is worth observing that the fallen angels and demons are always spoken of as "spirits," the former in xiii. 6, xv. 4, 6, 7, the latter in xv. 9, 11; xvi. 1. The term "soul" is never used of angels, fallen or otherwise, in the Old Testament, or elsewhere in Jewish or Christian literature.

Final judgment on the living and on certain classes of the dead.

Judgment.—Besides the preliminary judgment there was, on the advent of the Messianic kingdom, to be the final judgment on all men living, and on certain classes of the dead of Israel, or on all Israel, on the faithless angelic rulers and the impure angels.

Judgment, according to Eth. En. i.-xxxvi., already in Sheol.

Judgment, according to Daniel, on the living and certain dead Israelites.

The second century thus marks a great development upon the past. This development is not seen in Daniel so much as in the Ethiopic Enoch. In Daniel there is a preliminary judgment of the sword executed by the saints (ii. 44), and the final world-judgment in vii. 9, 11, 12 by God Himself to initiate the Messianic kingdom. There is no mention of

[1] In Daniel the word "soul" is not found. The writer always uses "spirit" when he could with perfect propriety have used "soul." That he had likewise the idea of the spirit existing apart from the body after death may probably be concluded from vii. 15, "my spirit was grieved in its sheath" (reading נִדְנַהּ instead of נִדְנֶה with Nöldeke). But the text is doubtful.

the judgment of angels; but this must be supposed in the case of the angelic patrons of Persia and Greece, who were hostile to Israel. In Eth. En. i.-xxxvi. the question of retribution has advanced with mighty strides. Judgment is conceived as setting in immediately on death in an intermediate abode of souls (xxii.) There is also a preliminary judgment on the angels who married the daughters of men, and likewise on all mankind at the Deluge (x. 1-12). The final judgment will take place before the advent of the Messianic kingdom on the impure angels (x. 12, 13), on the demons who have hitherto gone unpunished (xvi. 1), and on all Israel with the exception of a certain class of sinners. In Eth. En. lxxxiii.-xc. there is the first world-judgment of the Deluge (lxxxix. 1-8), the judgment of the sword executed under Judas the Maccabee (xc. 19, 16), and the final judgment on the impure angels and the faithless angelic patrons (xc. 20-25) and the apostate Jews (xc. 26, 27). This judgment serves to introduce the Messianic kingdom on *the present earth.*

Judgment in Eth. En. lxxxviii.-xc.

Places of Abode for the Departed.—Of these there are four.

(i.) We have already dealt with the transformation which Sheol has undergone in Daniel (see p. 181) and Eth. En. i.-xxxvi. (see pp. 184-188).

(ii.) *Paradise.*—In the second century only two men, Enoch and Elijah, were conceived as admitted to Paradise immediately on leaving this world (Eth. En. lxxxvii. 3, 4; lxxxix. 52). This view was

Paradise only for those who had been translated in the flesh.

CHAP. V.

evidently due to Old Testament accounts of their translation (see above, p. 58).

Gehenna becomes the final abode of apostates.

(iii.) *Gehenna.*—The conception of Gehenna preserves for the most part during this century its Old Testament signification. But whereas in Is. l. 11, lxvi. 24 it signifies the immediate place of punishment of apostate Jews, it is definitely conceived in Dan. xii. 2; Eth. En. xxvii. 1, 2, xc. 26, 27 as the *final* and *not the immediate* abode of apostates in the next world.[1]

Final abodes of the faithless and the impure angels.

(iv.) *The Abyss of Fire.*—This abyss is the final place of punishment for the faithless angelic rulers and for the impure angels (Eth. En. xviii. 11–xix., xxi., xc. 21-25). In Eth. En. xviii. 11-16, xxi. 1-6 the fiery abyss for the impure angels is distinguished from another fiery abyss in xxi. 7-10. This latter may be for the faithless angelic rulers.

Resurrection—various conceptions.

Resurrection.—There is only a resurrection of some of the righteous and some of the wicked in Dan. xii. 2, 3, of all the righteous and some of the wicked in Eth. En. i.-xxxvi. (see pp. 184-188), of all the righteous but of none of the wicked in Eth. En. lxxxvii.-xc. In all cases only Israelites attain to the resurrection. The ethical character of this second-century development we have already discussed (see pp. 178-180). In all cases where the righteous rise they rise to participate in the Messianic kingdom.

Messianic kingdom in all cases on the earth and for ever.

Messianic Kingdom.—The scene of this kingdom

[1] In Eth. En. xc. 26, 27 apparently only the living apostates are judged and cast into Gehenna.

was to be on the earth in Daniel, and in Eth. En. i.-xxxvi. But the growing consciousness of the evils and imperfections of the present world shows itself in Eth. En. lxxxiii.-xc., where the centre of this kingdom is to be, not the earthly Jerusalem, but the New Jerusalem brought down from heaven. This is the first trace in this century of a sense of the unfitness of the present world for this kingdom. In all cases the kingdom itself was to last for ever, and its members were to enjoy a patriarchal life, Dan. xii. and in Eth. En. v. 9, xxv. 6, or a never-ending one in xc.

Messiah only referred to twice in second century.

Messiah.—There is no mention of the Messiah in this century save in Eth. En. lxxxiii.-xc. (see xc. 37) and the Sibylline Oracles III. 652-654. But there He has no part to play in the kingdom, and His introduction seems due merely to literary reminiscence.

Since there is such great doubt attaching to the date of the Testaments of the XII. Patriarchs, I have refrained in the sequel from building on its evidence.

Non-hostile Gentiles to be converted.

Gentiles.—According to Eth. En. x. 21, all the Gentiles are to become righteous and worship God. Only the hostile Gentiles are to be destroyed (Dan. ii. 44, vii. 11, 12; Eth. En. xc. 9-16, 18). The rest will be converted (?) and serve Israel (Dan. vii. 14; Eth. En. xc. 30).

CHAPTER VI

ESCHATOLOGY OF APOCRYPHAL AND APOCALYPTIC LITERATURE DURING THE FIRST CENTURY B.C.

I. *Authorities for* 104-1 B.C.

Ethiopic Enoch xci.-civ.
Ethiopic Enoch xxxvii.-lxx.
1 Maccabees.
Judith.
Psalms of Solomon.
Sibylline Oracles III. 1-62.
2 Maccabees.

This last book was composed indeed in this century, but its eschatology belongs to the second century B.C., as we shall see in the sequel.

II. *General Eschatological Development in First Century B.C.*

Absolute breach with the expectations of the past.

A great gulf divides as a whole the eschatology of this century from that of the past. Thus the hope of an *eternal* Messianic kingdom *on the present earth*, which had been taught by the Old Testament prophets and cherished by every individual Israelite, is now at last absolutely abandoned.[1] The earth, as it is, has now come to be regarded as wholly unfit for the manifestation of this kingdom. Thus the dualism which had begun to affect the forecasts of religious thinkers in the preceding century has in this century succeeded in leavening their entire expectations. As a consequence of this breach between the things of earth and the things of heaven, the writers of this century are forced to advance to new conceptions touching the kingdom. Hence some boldly declare (Eth. En. xci.-civ.) or else imply (Pss. Sol. i.-xvi.) that the Messianic kingdom is only of temporary duration, and that the goal of the risen righteous is not this transitory kingdom but heaven itself. From this abandonment of the hope of an eternal Messianic kingdom it follows further that not only the resurrection but also the final judgment must be adjourned to its close.

Henceforth only a temporary Messianic kingdom expected on the present earth, and the resurrection and the final judgment adjourned to its close.

In the thoughts of these writers *the belief in a personal immortality has thus dissociated itself from the doctrine of the Messianic kingdom. Thus the synthesis of the two eschatologies achieved two centuries earlier* (see pp. 125-131) *is anew resolved into its elements, never again, save once* (Eth. En. xxxvii.-lxx.), *to be spiritually fused together within the sphere of Judaism.* Their true and final synthesis became the task and achievement of Christianity.

Synthesis of the two eschatologies resolved into their original factors,

But quite another line of thought was possible,

[1] See also p. 203.

CHAP. VI.

except in the Similitudes, Eth. En. xxxvii.-lxx., which teach the doctrine of a new heavens and earth as the scene of the kingdom and the goal of the risen righteous.

and this was pursued by the author of the Similitudes (Eth. En. xxxvii.-lxx.) The present earth could not, it is true, be regarded as the scene of an eternal Messianic kingdom, but a renewed and transformed earth could. Hence the scene of the eternal Messianic kingdom would be such a new earth, and not only so, but also a new heaven, and to a share in this eternal kingdom the righteous should rise. Here the idea of a new heaven and a new earth, which appeared illogically in Is. lxv., lxvi., is applied for the first time with reasonable consistency.

Elsewhere in this century only a resurrection of the spirits of the righteous expected.

It is further to be observed that these writers who hope only for a temporary Messianic kingdom anticipate a resurrection of the righteous only, and of the spirit, not of the body (Eth. En. xci.-civ.; Pss. Sol.), at the close of this temporary Messianic kingdom, whereas the writer of the Similitudes looks forward to a resurrection of all Israel (Eth. En. xxxvii.-lxx.) at the beginning of the eternal Messianic kingdom. In 2 Maccabees, which diverges in some respects from both classes, a bodily resurrection of the righteous is expected, and possibly of all Israel; but this doctrine belongs, as we shall discover presently, to the second century B.C.

Unique doctrine of the Messiah.

Again, in contradistinction to the preceding century, a vigorous, and indeed a unique, doctrine of the Messiah is developed in this century—that of the supernatural Son of Man in the Similitudes, and of the militant Messiah in the Psalms of Solomon.

Object of suffering in regard to Israel.

Finally, the present sufferings of Israel at the hands of the Gentiles are explained as of a disciplinary character.[1] Israel is at once chastened for its sins lest they should come to a head; but the Gentiles are allowed to fill up the cup of their iniquity.[2]

CHAP. VI.

III. *Eschatological Systems of the various Writers of the First Century* B.C.

Ethiopic Enoch xci.-civ. (134-95, or more nearly 104-95, B.C.)

We begin the study of the eschatological literature of this century with a most fascinating and original work. It dates at latest from the first years of the century, and attests in unmistakable terms the revolution that has passed over Jewish thought.

Century opens with a revolutionary doctrine of the future.

In the preceding century it was still conceivable, as in the Old Testament prophets, that God could take up His abode with men. But this conception has now become impossible. God is of such unapproachable purity on the one hand, and humanity so sinful and defiled on the other, that His abiding on earth with men has now become inconceivable. Thus the doctrine of the divine immanence has given place to that of the divine transcendence, and the time-honoured hope of an eternal Messianic kingdom which should abide for ever on earth, ruled and sustained by the immediate present Deity, has at last been sorrowfully abandoned by the Jews of

No longer an eternal but only a temporary Messianic kingdom expected.

1 See 2 Macc. vi. 12-17; cf. Jud. viii. 27; Wisdom xii. 22.

2 See Dan. viii. 23, ix. 24; cf. Gen. xv. 16.

CHAP. VI.

Hence the resurrection and final judgment can no longer initiate the kingdom, but must be relegated to its close.

this later age. According to the universal expectations of the past, the resurrection and the final judgment were to form the prelude to an everlasting Messianic kingdom on earth, but from this time forth these great events are relegated to its close, and the Messianic kingdom is for the first time in literature conceived as of temporary duration. On this revolutionary view of the Messianic kingdom follows another no less revolutionary. Such a temporary earthly kingdom cannot be the goal of the hopes of the risen righteous. Their faith can find satisfaction only in a blessed immortality in the eternal heaven itself.

Debate on the nature of retribution.

Another question of surpassing interest dealt with by the author is that of the nature of retribution in this and in the after life. His views on this subject he brings forward in the course of a debate which he represents as taking place between himself and some Sadducees. The latter uphold the still orthodox and tory view found in the Old Testament, our author that of the higher theology. We will not, however, recount this discussion till we have first sketched the eschatology of this work. Our author acknowledges that the wicked are seemingly sinning with impunity; but this is not so: their evil deeds are recorded every day (civ. 7), and immediately on death "their spirits will be cast into the furnace of fire" (xcviii. 3): yea, they "will be slain in Sheol" (xcix. 11); and from this hell of darkness and flame and grievous condemnation, into which their souls enter on death, they will never escape (ciii. 7, 8). Thus Sheol is here conceived as hell.

The author's scheme of the world's history (Eth. En. xci. 12-17).

But turning from our author's views of the immediate lot of the wicked at death to his scheme of the world's history, we find that he divides the history of mankind into ten world-weeks of varying duration. The first seven weeks embrace all events from the Creation till the advent of the Messianic kingdom. This kingdom lasts three world-weeks, and thus terminates with the close of the tenth week. In the words of the writer, "And after that there will be another week, the eighth, that of righteousness, and a sword will be given to it, that judgment and righteousness may be executed on those who commit oppression, and sinners will be delivered into the hands of the righteous. 13. And at its close they will acquire houses through their righteousness, and the house of the Great King will be built in righteousness for evermore. 14. And after that in the ninth week the righteous judgment will be revealed to the whole world, and all the works of the godless will vanish from the whole earth, and the world will be written down for destruction, and all mankind will look to the path of uprightness. 15. And after this, in the tenth week in the seventh part, there will be the great eternal judgment, in which he will execute vengeance amongst the angels. 16. And the first heaven will depart and pass away, and a new heaven will appear, and all the powers of the heavens will shine sevenfold for ever. 17. And

CHAP. VI.

after that there will be many weeks without number for ever in goodness and righteousness, and sin will no more be mentioned for ever" (Eth. En. xci. 12-17[1]). Here we see that the final judgment will be held at the close of the Messianic kingdom, that the former heaven and earth will be destroyed and a new heaven created. To share in this new heaven the righteous dead will rise; but in the meantime their spirits will be at rest, guarded by angels (c. 5). From this intermediate abode (probably in Sheol, cf. 4 Ezra iv. 41) they will be raised (xci. 10, xcii. 3), but not in the body, but as spirits only (ciii. 3, 4), and the portals of heaven will be opened to them (civ. 2), and they shall joy as the angels (civ. 4), and become companions of the heavenly hosts (civ. 6), and shine as the stars for ever (civ. 2).

Spirits of the departed righteous kept in safety till the final judgment. Heaven henceforth their abode.

We now return to our author's treatment of the question of retribution. He enters the arena against the doctrine as taught by Ezekiel. According to Ezekiel's teaching and that of his spiritual successors, the wealthy could appeal to their riches as a proof of their righteousness; for according to them prosperity was a divine token of God's approval.

Our author denies Ezekiel's doctrine of retribution.

Our author, on the other hand, so far from regarding prosperity as the mark of divine favour, charges it with being the source of delusion to

Prosperity is no mark of divine favour, but only a source of delusion to those who experience it.

[1] From the present writer's edition of the *Book of Enoch*. The rest of the quotations from the Ethiopic Enoch are from the same edition, with occasional slight changes in the renderings.

those who possess it: "Woe unto you, ye sinners, for your riches make you appear like the righteous, but your hearts convict you of being sinners" (xcvi. 4). To their own conscience, therefore, this writer appeals against the orthodox view of retribution. Yea, further, he declares that their very personality through giving itself up to such external possessions will at last lose itself: "in grandeur, and in power, and in silver, and in gold, and in purple, and in splendour, and in food, they will be poured out as water. Therefore they will be wanting in knowledge and wisdom, and they will perish thereby, together with their possessions and with all their glory and their splendour, and in shame and in slaughter and in great destitution will their spirits be cast into the furnace of fire" (xcviii. 2, 3). And as regards the experience of the righteous, our author considers Ezekiel's doctrine of retribution as equally false. He teaches that there is often no difference in the outward lot of the righteous and the wicked, either in life or in death. Nay, more, he can contemplate the righteous as enduring undeserved tribulation all their days, and yet address them with words of hope and encouragement: "Fear ye not, ye souls of the righteous, and be hopeful, ye that die in righteousness. 5. And grieve not if your soul descends in grief into Sheol, and that in your life your body has not fared as your goodness deserved, but truly as on a day on which ye became like the sinners, and on a day of cursing and chastisement" (cii. 4, 5). These words

There is often no difference in the outward lot of the righteous and the wicked.

CHAP. VI.

This concession seized by the Sadducean opponents.

conceding the unhappy experience of the righteous in this life are immediately fastened upon by the Sadducean opponents in this debate. cii. 6. "As we die, so die the righteous, and what benefit do they reap from their deeds? 7. Behold, even as we, so they die in grief and darkness, and what advantage have they over us? From henceforth we are equal. 8. And what will they receive and what will they see for ever? For, behold, they too have died, and from henceforth they will never see light." To this the author replies that the life of the wicked is fashioned by material and temporal aims only, and so all their desires find satisfaction in this world, but the life of the righteous is moulded by spiritual and eternal aims. 9. "I tell you, ye sinners, ye find your satisfaction in eating and drinking . . . in robbery and sin, in the acquisition of wealth and in seeing good days. 10. Have ye seen the righteous how their end falls out? for no manner of violence is found in them till the day of their death" (cii. 9, 10). Thereto the wicked rejoin that this difference in character is of no advantage: "Notwithstanding they perished, and became as though they had not been, and their souls descended into Sheol in tribulation" (cii. 11).

Our author's rejoinder. The righteous and the wicked differ in character and ideals.

"These make no difference in destiny," say the wicked.

Our author here abandons the form of a debate, and henceforth addresses the righteous and their Sadducean opponents alternately.

At this point the context ceases to bear the form of a debate, and thenceforward the author develops the contention at issue in alternate addresses to the righteous and their Sadducean opponents. At first, in opposition to the statement of the latter that the same lot awaits the good and bad alike, our author

CHAP. VI.

declares: ciii. 1. "I swear to you, ye righteous, by the glory of him that is great and honoured, and mighty in dominion; yea, by his greatness I swear to you. 2. I know this mystery and have read it in the heavenly tables, and have seen the book of the holy ones, and have found written therein and inscribed regarding them: 3. That all goodness and joy and glory are prepared for them, and are written down for the spirits of those who have died in righteousness, and that manifold good will be given to you in recompense for your labours, and that your lot is abundantly beyond the lot of the living. 4. And your spirits—(the spirits) of you who die in righteousness, will live and rejoice and be glad, and their spirits will not perish, and their memorial will be before the face of the Great One unto all the generations of the world: wherefore, then, fear not their contumely."

He assures the righteous of their future blessedness,

Having thus assured the righteous, he turns to the wicked with words of denunciation and woe: ciii. 5. "Woe unto you, ye sinners, when ye die in your sins, and those who resemble you say regarding you: Blessed are the sinners: they have seen good all their days. 6. And now they have died in prosperity and in riches, and have not seen tribulation or slaughter in their life; and they have died in honour, and judgment has not been executed on them during their life. 7. Know ye that their souls will be made to descend into Sheol, and they will become wretched, and great will be their tribulation. 8. And into darkness and chains and a burning fire,

and declares the future torment of the wicked.

CHAP. VI.

where there is grievous condemnation for the generations of the world. Woe unto you, for ye will have no peace."

It is noteworthy here that, though our author declares that the anticipations of the godless as to their future destiny are wholly false, he tacitly admits their claim to having seen good all their days. Moreover, in keeping with this admission, he accepts as true the derisive description which the ungodly give of the righteous in the immediately subsequent verses ciii. 9-15: "In the days of their life they are worn out with their troublous toil, and have experienced every trouble, and met with much evil and suffered from disease, and have been minished and become small in spirit. 10. And they have been destroyed, and there has been none to help them (even) in word, and have attained to nothing: they are tortured and destroyed, and have not hoped to see life from day to day. 11. And they hoped to be the head, and they have become the tail: they toiled laboriously, and attained not to the fruit of their toil; and they became the food of sinners, and the unrighteous laid their yoke heavily upon them. 12. And they that hated them and smote them have had dominion over them; and they have bowed their necks to those that hated them, and they have had no compassion on them. 13. And they have desired to get away from them that they might escape and be at rest, but have found no place whereunto they should flee and be safe from them. 14. And they have complained to their

The evil lot of the righteous in the present life.

rulers in their tribulation, and cried out against those who devoured them, but they did not attend to their cries, and would not hearken to their voice. 15. And they helped those who robbed and devoured them, and those who made them few; and they concealed their oppression, and they did not remove from them the yoke of those who devoured, and dispersed, and murdered them, and they concealed their murder, and have thought not of the fact that they had lifted up their hands against them."

Yet the day of their recompense is at hand.

This terrible picture, which the godless gave of the condition of the Chasids, is, as we have remarked, accepted by our author as true. He, therefore, makes no attempt to charge it with exaggeration or weaken a single detail, but turns to the righteous, and urges them to continued faithfulness and hope, for that the day of recompense and of the great judgment will soon appear: civ. 1. "I swear unto you, that in heaven the angels are mindful of you for good before the glory of the Great One: your names are written before the glory of the Great One. 2. Be hopeful; for aforetime ye were put to shame through ills and affliction; but soon ye will shine as the stars of heaven, ye will shine and ye will be seen, and the portals of heaven will be opened to you. 3. And persist in your cry for judgment, and it will appear to you; for all your tribulations will be visited on the rulers, and on all their helpers, and on all those who plundered you. 4. Be hopeful, and cast not

CHAP. VI.

away your hope, for ye will have great joy as the angels of heaven. 5. What will ye be obliged to do then? Ye will not have to hide on the day of the great judgment, and ye will not be found as sinners, and the eternal judgment will be far from you for all the generations of the world. 6. And now fear not, ye righteous, when ye see the sinners growing strong and prospering in their ways, and be not like unto them and have no companionship with them, but keep afar from their violence; for ye will become companions of the hosts of heaven. 7. Ye sinners, though ye say, Ye cannot ascertain it, and all our sins are not written down, still they will write down all your sins continually every day."

We cannot part from this book without confessing how nobly it maintains the cause of goodness in the face of triumphant evil, how unhesitatingly it concedes that this world gives its best to the unrighteous and the sinner, and that godliness can find no stay or encouragement therein. Yet though the lot of the latter is thus one of contumely and rebuke and shame, they are not for one moment to regret their high calling, but to be steadfast and hopeful; for the day of their glorification is at hand. It is a noble work, yet falls far short of what was noblest in the past. It never reminds the faithful, as do some of the psalmists, that present life and communion with God more than outweigh the loss of every temporal blessing.

Ethiopic Enoch xxxvii.-lxx. (94-64 B.C.)

From this interesting work we now pass to the consideration of one of still greater interest, namely, the well-known "Similitudes," which consist of chaps. xxxvii.-lxx. of the Ethiopic Book of Enoch. This book presents us with many difficulties. In several respects it stands alone among Jewish apocalyptic writings. Thus, though all other writers of this and the next century abandoned the Old Testament idea of an everlasting Messianic kingdom, the author of the Similitudes clings fast to this hope. The scene of this kingdom, indeed, was not to be the present earth, but a new heavens and a new earth (xlv. 4, 5[1]); for, owing to the prevalent dualism, such a conception had already become impossible. Thus the writer for the last time in Judaism combines in one blessed future the separate hopes of the individual and the nation, and thus unites in a high spiritual synthesis the severed eschatologies.

The unique conception of the Messiah.

Of no less startling character is the conception entertained by the writer of the coming Messiah. He is here regarded not as of human descent, but as a supernatural being. Four titles applied to Him

[1] This thought lay ready to hand in Is. lxv., lxvi. But there, as we have already seen, the thought is an interpolation, being incompatible with other facts in the context. Thus the wicked still live on the new earth (lxv. 20). The writer of the Similitudes seems to guard against such a misconception, for in the words following on the declaration of a new heaven and a new earth, he declares "the sinners and the evildoers will not set foot thereon."

CHAP. VI.

Variously described as "the Christ," "the Righteous One," "the Elect One," "the Son of Man."

here for the first time in literature are afterwards reproduced in the New Testament. These are "the Christ" (xlviii. 10, lii. 4); "the Righteous One" (xxxviii. 2, liii. 6; Acts iii. 14, vii. 52, xxii. 14); "the Elect One" (xl. 5, xlv. 3, 4, etc.; Luke ix. 35, xxiii. 35); and, most important of all, "the Son of Man."[1] This last title is found in its definite form for the first time in the Similitudes, and is historically the source of the New Testament designation, if the date assigned to the former is correct. The conception, indeed, is so lofty and wide-reaching that in treating of it we are treating likewise of the writer's eschatology. Thus he is conceived as the Judge of the world, and the Champion and eternal Ruler of the righteous.

[1] Eerdmans (*Theol. Tijdschrift*, 1894, pp. 153-176) and Lietzmann (*Der Menschensohn*, 1896) have sought to show that "Son of Man" in the Similitudes is never a title of the Messiah, and that it simply means "man." To prove this contention, they point out that "Son of Man" is almost always accompanied by the demonstrative "this" or "that," and allege that in only one passage (lxii. 7) is it without the demonstrative. Since this passage is contrary to his thesis, Lietzmann rejects it, while Eerdmanns seeks to weaken its evidential value by reference to the context. Wellhausen (*Skizzen und Vorarbeiten*, vi. 199) builds an hypothesis also on the presence of the demonstrative. He holds, with the two scholars already mentioned, that the expression "Son of Man" simply = man, and that if it has to convey a definite signification, it must be preceded by a demonstrative pronoun, as is always the case in the Ethiopic Enoch, according to Lietzmann. Wellhausen presses home the fact that the use of the demonstrative before the expression "Son of Man" proves conclusively that "Son of Man" cannot be a Messianic title; for that such a phrase as "this Messiah" or "that Messiah" is an impossibility. Since, therefore, so much turns on the presence or absence of the demonstratives, it is of the highest moment to determine whether these demonstratives, when they are present, are renderings of Greek demonstratives, or of the Greek article. That they are renderings of the Greek article will, I think, be clear from the following evidence. Now, if we examine the way in which the Ethiopic translator frequently renders the Greek article in those passages where the Greek Version is preserved, we shall be able to deal with the meaning of the Ethiopic demonstratives which are prefixed to the phrase "Son of Man." Now as regards "this" (= ze and zentû), we find that in chaps. xxv. 1, xxvii. 2, xxviii. 2, xxxii. 5 it is a rendering of the

CHAP. VI.

The Messiah the Judge of the world.

The Messiah is conceived in the Similitudes as (i.) the Judge of the world and the Revealer of all things; (ii.) the Messianic Champion and Ruler of the righteous. (i.) As Judge, He possesses righteousness, wisdom, and power (cf. Pss. xlv. 4-8, lxxii.; Is. xi. 3-5; Jer. xxiii. 5, 6). He is the Righteous One in an extraordinary sense (xxxviii. 2, liii. 6): He possesses righteousness, and it dwells with Him (xlvi. 3), and on the ground of His essential righteousness (xlvi. 3) has He been chosen no less than according to God's good pleasure (xlix. 4). Wisdom, which could find no dwelling-place on earth (xlii.), dwells in Him, and the spirit of Him who giveth knowledge (xlix. 3): and the secrets of wisdom stream forth from His mouth (li. 3), and wisdom is poured forth

Greek article. But the result is startling if we compare the small Greek fragment of chap. lxxxix. 42-49 with the Ethiopic Version, for we find that zekû or zektû (=that), though occurring ten times in these verses, is nine times a rendering of the Greek article. That it is very frequently used in this sense in Ethiopic translations generally is stated by Dillmann's *Ethiopic Lexicon*, col. 1057. W'etû (=that) is also twice used to render the Greek article in lxxxix. 42-49. Thus it appears that the demonstratives very frequently represent the Greek article, and it is these very demonstratives that are prefixed to the expression "Son of Man." Hence we may, with some reason, conclude that before the latter expression the demonstratives zekû and zentû stand for the article, and nothing more, in xlvi. 2, 4; xlviii. 2; lxii. 9, 14; lxiii. 11. This conclusion is supported by lxii. 7, where the demonstrative is wanting. But the evidence is still stronger. In xlvi. 3; lxix. 26, 29[a b]; lxx. 1; lxxi. 14, 17 the demonstrative w'etû (=that) is prefixed. Now that in all these cases, except xlvi. 3, lxxi. 14, where it stands for the copula, w'etû represents the article I feel convinced, for in the first place this is one of its commonest uses in translations from the Greek (see Dillmann's *Lexicon*, col. 919), and in the next place the Ethiopic translator actually uses it in this sense, as I have shown above. Finally, in two other passages (lxiii. 10, lxii. 2), where w'etû precedes the phrase "Lord of Spirits," it is beyond the reach of question the equivalent of the Greek article. In xlvi. 3, lxxi. 14 w'etû serves as a copula. Indeed, it cannot be taken here in any other sense. Thus we conclude that in the Ethiopic expression "Son of Man" we have a Messianic title, and that this expression represents the Greek ὁ υἱὸς τοῦ ἀνθρώπου.

CHAP. VI.

like water before Him (xlix.) In Him abides the spirit of power (xlix. 3), and He possesses universal dominion (lxii. 6). He is the revealer of all things. His appearance will be the signal for the revelation of good and the unmasking of evil: will bring to light everything that is hidden, alike the invisible world of righteousness and the hidden world of sin (xlvi. 3; xlix. 2, 4): and will recall to life those that have perished on land and sea, and those that are in Sheol and hell (li. 1, lxi. 5). Evil when once unmasked will vanish from His presence (xlix. 2). Hence all judgment has been committed unto Him (lxix. 27), and universal dominion (lxii. 6), and He will sit on the throne of His glory (xlv. 3, lxii. 3, 5), which is likewise the throne of God (xlvii. 3, li. 3), and all men, righteous and wicked, and all angels, fallen and unfallen, will be judged before Him (li. 2, lv. 4, lxi. 8, lxii. 2, 3), and no lying utterance will be possible before Him (xlix. 4, lxii. 3), and by the mere word of His mouth will He slay the ungodly (lxii. 2).

The Champion and Ruler of the righteous.

(ii.) He is the Messianic Champion and Ruler of the righteous. He is the stay of the righteous (xlviii. 4), and has already been revealed to them (lxii. 7): He is the avenger of their life (xlviii. 7), the preserver of their inheritance (xlviii. 7): He will vindicate the earth as their possession for ever (li. 5), and establish the community of the righteous in unhindered prosperity (liii. 6, lxii. 8): their faces will shine with joy (li. 5), and they will be vestured with life (lxii. 15), and be resplendent with light (xxxix. 7), and "become angels in heaven" (li. 4), and He will abide in closest communion with them for ever (lxii. 14), in the immediate presence of the Lord of Spirits (xxxix. 7), and His glory is for ever and ever, and His might unto all generations, (xlix. 2). I have given with some fulness this description of the expected Messiah; for it forms the centre of this writer's expectations of the future. To the revival of the Messiah hope in this century we shall advert later.

This writer's solution of the moral problem of the world.

Before leaving this author we shall briefly recount his solution of the difficulties affecting the moral government of the world. This he discovers in a comprehensive view of the world's history. Only by tracing evil to its source can the present wrongness of things be understood, and only by pursuing the world's history to its final issues can its present inequalities be justified. The author has no interest save for the moral and spiritual worlds, and this is manifest even in the divine name "Lord of Spirits," and in the peculiar form he gives to the trisagion (xxxix. 12): "Holy, holy, holy, is the Lord of Spirits: he filleth the earth with spirits." Whole hierarchies of angelic beings appear in lxi. 10-12, and the doctrine of the Satanic world is further developed. The origin of sin is traced back not to the Watchers or angels, as in an earlier work, but to the Satans, the original adversaries of man (xl. 7).

Sin traced to the Satans.

The Watchers fell through becoming subject to these, and leading mankind astray (liv. 6). Punishment was at once meted out to the Watchers, and they were confined in a deep abyss (liv. 5) to

CHAP. VI.

await the final judgment (liv. 6, lv. 3, lxiv.) In the meantime sin flourishes in the world: sinners deny the name of the Lord of Spirits (xxxviii. 2, xli. 2), and of His Anointed (xlviii. 10); the kings and the mighty of the earth trust in their sceptre and glory (lxiii. 7), and oppress the elect of the children of God (lxii. 11). But the prayer of the righteous ascends, and their blood goes up before the Lord of Spirits crying for vengeance (xlvii. 1); and the angels unite in the prayer of the righteous (xlvii. 2). But the oppression of the kings and the mighty will not continue for ever: suddenly the Head of Days will appear, and with Him the Son of Man (xlvi. 2, 3, 4; xlviii. 2), to execute judgment upon all alike—on the righteous and wicked, on angel and on man. All are judged according to their deeds, for their deeds are weighed in the balance (xli. 1). The fallen angels are cast into a fiery furnace (liv. 6); the kings and the mighty confess their sins, and pray for forgiveness, but in vain (lxiii.); and are given into the hands of the righteous (xxxviii. 5); and their destruction furnishes a spectacle to the righteous as they burn and vanish for ever out of sight (xlviii. 9, 10; lxii. 12), to be tortured in Gehenna by the angels of punishment (liii. 3-5, liv. 1, 2). The remaining sinners and godless are driven from off the face of the earth (xxxviii. 3, xli. 2, xlv. 6). The Son of Man slays them with the word of His mouth (lxii. 2). Sin and wrongdoing are banished from the earth (xlix. 2); and heaven and earth are transformed (xlv. 4, 5); and the

The Head of Days and the Messiah appear to judge the world.

A new heavens and a new earth.

righteous and elect have their mansions therein (xxxix. 5, xli. 2). And the light of the Lord of Spirits shines upon them (xxxviii. 4); they live in the light of eternal life (lviii. 3). And they seek after light and find righteousness and peace with the Lord of Spirits (lviii. 3, 4); and grow in knowledge and righteousness (lviii. 5).

Of the peculiar character of the resurrection in this book we shall treat presently.

1 MACCABEES (100-64 B.C.)

1 Maccabees the work of a Sadducee.

From the Similitudes, the work of an original and highly gifted member of the Pharisaic school, we turn for a few minutes to First Maccabees, the work of a contemporary who belonged to the Sadducean party. As we might expect, this book is entirely wanting in eschatological teaching. Of the hope of a future life beyond the grave there is not a trace. All the rewards of faithfulness enumerated by the dying Mattathias (ii. 52-61) are limited to this life. Thus this writer ignores the entire Chasid movement, which embodied within it all that was best and most spiritual from the Maccabean revolt for many generations onwards. God has no longer direct dealings with men. With the Maccabean psalmist who wrote—

> We see not our signs:
> There is no more any prophet,
> Neither is there among us any that knoweth how long
> (Ps. lxxiv. 9)—

this writer too deplores the extinction of prophecy

CHAP. VI.

(ix. 27). And yet he seems to look forward to some prophet in the future; for Simon the Maccabee was appointed to be high priest "until there should arise a faithful prophet" (xiv. 41), and the stones of the profaned altar of burnt offerings were laid up "in the mountain of the temple . . . until there should come a prophet to show what should be done with them" (iv. 46).

Psalms of Solomon (70-40 B.C.)

Psalms of Solomon of Pharisaic authorship,

are from different authors, and present two distinct eschatological systems.

The next work that calls for consideration is the so-called Psalms of Solomon, which were written some decades later than the Similitudes. These Psalms are eighteen in all. They appear to be derived from various authors. With this diversity of authorship we are only here concerned in a limited degree. Our present subject requires us to distinguish the first sixteen psalms carefully from the last two. The eschatological systems presented by these differ in essential respects.

Pss. xvii., xviii.

We shall deal with Pss. xvii., xviii. first. These psalms cannot be regarded as possessing great originality. There is hardly a statement in them relative to the hopes of Israel which could not be accounted for on the grounds of literary reminiscence. And yet the representation on the whole is vigorous and fascinating. Where, however, they do display decided originality, their influence is distinctly hurtful; for, by connecting the Messiah with the popular aspirations of the nation, they secularised it, and with it the teaching of Pharisaism, and thus prepared the way for the ultimate destruction of the nation. The Messiah, certainly, is finely conceived. As in the Similitudes, He is called the Christ (xvii. 36, xviii. 6, 8). He is to be of the house and lineage of David: thus the psalmist prays (xvii. 23-25):—

CHAP. VI.

The Messiah of Pss. xvii., xviii.

Behold, O Lord, and raise up unto them their king,
The Son of David, in the time which thou, O God, knowest,
That he may reign over Israel thy servant.
And gird him with strength to break in pieces unrighteous rulers,
To purge Jerusalem from the heathen that tread her down and destroy.[1]

Moreover, the Messiah will be "a righteous king and taught of God" (xvii. 35); He will "be pure from sin, so that he may rule a mighty people" (xvii. 41). He will bring back the dispersion also (xvii. 28):—

And he shall gather together a holy people, whom he shall lead in righteousness.
And he shall judge the tribes of the people that have been sanctified by the Lord his God.

And having purged Jerusalem and made it holy as in the days of old (xvii. 33), He will make Israel a holy people (xvii. 29, 30^a, 36):—

And he shall not suffer iniquity to lodge in their midst
And none shall dwell with them that knoweth wickedness;
For he shall take knowledge of them that they are all the sons of their God.

[1] These and the following quotations from this book are drawn from Ryle and James's edition. They are, however, occasionally modified in accordance with Gebhardt's new text. For "to purge" (*καθαρίσαι*), conjectured by Geiger and accepted by Gebhardt, Ryle and James give the MSS. reading *καθάρισον*, "purge."

CHAP. VI.

And there shall be no iniquity in his days in their midst
For all shall be holy and their king is the Lord Messiah.

And no stranger shall dwell within the gates: "the sojourner and the stranger shall dwell with them no more" (xvii. 31[a]).

But as for the ungodly nations, He will destroy them with the word of His mouth (xvii. 27; cf. xvii. 39). His weapons will not be carnal (xvii. 37):—

For he shall not put his trust in horse, and rider, and bow,
Nor shall he multiply unto himself gold and silver for war,
Nor by means of many peoples[1] shall he gather confidence for the day of battle.

But he shall (xvii. 41)—

Rebuke princes and overthrow sinners by the might of his word.

When at last the hostile nations are destroyed, the rest will become subject to Him (xvii. 31[b], 32[a], 38[b], 34):—

He shall judge the nations and the peoples with the wisdom of his righteousness
And he shall possess the nations of the heathen to serve him beneath his yoke.
And he shall have mercy on all the nations that come before him in fear.
(Yea) the nations shall come from the ends of the world to see his glory,
Bringing as gifts her sons that had fainted.

The Messiah is mortal.

And the Messiah will not faint all His days (xvii. 42).

[1] So Gebhardt, adding λαοῖς after πολλοῖς. Ryle and James emend πολλοῖς into πλοίοις ("by means of ships"), Hilgenfeld into παλτοῖς or ὅπλοις.

I have given at some length this very vigorous presentation of the Messiah hope. The nearly contemporaneous appearance of this picture of the Messiah and that in the Similitudes attests the strength and vitality to which this hope, though practically dead in the preceding century, had already attained, before many decades had elapsed in its successor. By means of these two writings we are enabled to understand in some degree the intensity with which the expectation of a personal Messiah was cherished in the first century of the Christian era, and likewise the guise in which the people expected Him to appear.

The Messianic kingdom of temporary duration.

The Messianic kingdom in these psalms is apparently of temporary duration, for there is no hint of the righteous dead rising to share in it. Only the surviving righteous become members of it. Cf. xvii. 50:—

> Blessed are they that shall be born in those days.
> To behold the blessing of Israel, which God shall bring to pass in the gathering together of the tribes.

Further, we might infer the transitory nature of the Messianic kingdom from the fact that the Messiah here is a single person, and not a series of kings. The duration of His kingdom, therefore, is to be regarded as conterminous with that of its ruler.

Pss. i.-xvi. contain no references to the Messiah.

We now proceed to discuss the remaining sixteen psalms of this book. In these psalms there are hardly any references to the future, and there are none to the Messiah.

A Messianic kingdom, however, was expected;

CHAP. VI.

but dwell on the Messianic kingdom.

for they paint in glowing colours the restoration of the tribes (xi. 1-8[1]):—

1. Blow ye the trumpet in Zion, yea the holy trumpet of Jubilee.

2. Proclaim ye in Jerusalem with the voice of him that bringeth good tidings,
That God hath had mercy upon Israel: he hath visited them.
3. Stand up on high, O Jerusalem: and behold thy children
Gathered from the East and the West together by the Lord.
4. From the North they come in the gladness of their God:
From the islands afar off hath God gathered them.
5. Lofty mountains did he make low: yea even unto the plain before them.
6. The hills fled before their entering in,
The woods gave them shelter as they passed by.
7. Every tree of sweet savour did God make to spring up before them
That Israel might pass by in the day when the glory of their God shall visit them.
8. Put on, O Jerusalem, the garments of thy glory:
Make ready thine holy apparel,
For God hath spoken comfortably unto Israel, world without end.

But the righteous do not rise to share in this kingdom, but to an eternal life in the spirit.

This future is regarded as a promised and appointed period when God would succour His people (vii. 9). But the psalmists do not dwell on the gracious side of this promised time, but on the vengeance that will befall the hostile nations and the sinners amongst men. With their main burden, therefore, we are not here concerned. Whatever degree of importance they may attach to the expected kingdom, they do not regard it as the recompense of the righteous. The righteous rise not to a kingdom of temporal prosperity but to eternal life. Thus iii. 16:—

[1] Cf. also viii. 34.

CHAP. VI.

They that fear the Lord shall rise unto life eternal,
And their life shall be in the light of the Lord, and it shall fail no more.

And they will "inherit this life in gladness" (xiv. 7), and "live in the righteousness of their God" (xv. 15). There seems to be no resurrection of the body.

The wicked descend to Hades, their eternal abode of torment.

As for the wicked, on the other hand, they descend on death into hell (xvi. 2). Further, the psalmist declares (xv. 11):—

And the inheritance of the sinners is destruction and darkness,
And their iniquities shall pursue them as far as Hades beneath.

And again (xiv. 5[a], 6):—

They remembered not God:
Therefore is their inheritance Hades and darkness and destruction
And they shall not be found in the day of mercy for the righteous.

We thus observe a remarkable agreement between the teaching of the first sixteen psalms of this book and that of Eth. En. xci.-civ.

JUDITH (*circa* 50 B.C.[1])

In the next book of which we have to take account, *i.e.* Judith, there is only one eschatological reference. This is found in xvi. 17, which runs:—

Judith attests a new development of Gehenna.

Woe to the nations that rise up against my kindred:
The Lord Almighty will take vengeance of them in the day of judgment.
By putting fire and worms in their flesh,[2]
And they shall weep and feel their pain for ever.

[1] The date of this book is uncertain. Most probably it belongs to the first century B.C

[2] δοῦναι πῦρ καὶ σκώληκας εἰς σάρκας αὐτῶν.

CHAP. VI.

This passage refers obviously to Gehenna, and is valuable in this respect, that it attests a new development in the use of the term Gehenna. Conceived heretofore as the final abode of the apostate Jews, it is now regarded as the final abode of the nations generally, a meaning which it preserves in the next century also (cf. Ass. of Mos. x. 10; 4 Ezra vii. 36).

Only two books more call for consideration, and our survey of the eschatology of this century will be complete. These are a short fragment of the Sibylline Oracles and the Second Book of Maccabees.

Sibylline Oracles III. 1-62 (before 31 B.C.[1])

In these verses God's kingdom is expected, and the advent of a holy king who shall sway the sceptre of every land (ἥξει δ' ἁγνὸς ἄναξ πάσης γῆς σκῆπτρα κρατήσων, iii. 49). This Messianic King is to reign "for all ages" (iii. 50), but these words must not be pressed, for in a few lines later a universal judgment on all men is foretold (iii. 53-56, 60, 61). For a similar limitation of these words, cf. Apoc. Bar. xl. 3, lxxiii. 1 (see *note* on pp. 181, 182).

Messiah to reign for all ages, *i.e.* for a long time.

2 Maccabees (some time between 60 B.C. and the Christian era)

The Messianic kingdom in 2 Maccabees.

In the Second Book of Maccabees there is no direct declaration as to the Messianic kingdom, though we are most probably right in interpreting vii. 37 as referring to it, where the

[1] See *Encyclopædia Biblica*, i. Article on Apoc. Lit. par. 85.

youngest of the seven brethren prays that "God may speedily be gracious to the nation." The hope of this kingdom is implied also in the expectation of the return of the tribes. This expectation appears in the prayer of Jonathan (i. 27):—

> Gather together our dispersed ones,
> Set at liberty them that are in bondage among the heathen,
> Look upon them that are despised and abhorred,
> And let the heathen know that thou art our God.

And in ii. 18:—

> In God have we hope, that he will quickly have mercy upon us, and gather us together out of all the earth into the holy place.

The two last passages indeed do not belong to the original work, but to the two letters which were prefixed to it by the epitomiser of Jason's work or at a later date. It is very difficult to get a clear view of the eschatology of this writer. According to his express statement (ii. 19-23), the main narrative of the book is drawn entirely from a single source, and forms merely an epitome of a work written by one Jason of Cyrene in five books. These five books of Jason, our writer declares that he has "abridged into one work" (ii. 23). They, therefore, if we may reason backwards from the epitome to the original work, dealt with the history of events from 175 B.C. down to the decisive victory of Judas in 161, in all a period of fifteen years, and were written most probably several decades before the close of the second century B.C. Hence if these books of Jason are faithfully epitomised in the Second Book of Maccabees

2 Maccabees an epitome of Jason's five books.

CHAP. VI.

we should have in the latter book the eschatological views of the second century B.C. And in some respects this must be the case; for though this book nowhere enunciates definitely the nature of the future kingdom, we can nevertheless with some degree of certainty infer it from several passages.

Messianic kingdom.

Thus a Messianic or theocratic kingdom of some sort seems to be expected; for God has established Israel for ever (xiv. 15). vii. 37, as we have mentioned above, points to the blessed future which Israel will yet experience, and the same inference might be drawn from vii. 33 also, where the hope is expressed that God will again be reconciled to His servants. But we are left in the dark as to the nature of this kingdom. May we complete the picture from the writer's beliefs on Hades and the resurrection? Immediately after death the righteous and wicked alike depart to Hades (vi. 23). In Hades the departed have a foretaste of their final doom. Thus when bidden to share in the idolatrous sacrifices of Antiochus, Eleazer declares: "Even if for the present time I shall remove from me the punishment of man, yet shall I not escape the hands of the Almighty, either living or dead" (vi. 26). But Hades was only an intermediate state for the righteous (vii. 9, 11, 14, etc.), and likewise for all Israel; for in xii. 44 it is stated that Judas made a certain sacrifice in the belief that those Jews who had fallen in battle would rise again. For the non-Israelite there was no resurrection (vii. 14): "It is good to die at the hands of men and look for the hopes which

Writer's conception of Hades.

CHAP. VI.

are given of God, that we shall be raised up again by him; for as for thee, thou shalt have no resurrection unto life."[1]

The resurrection is to eternal life.

Now as regards the resurrection, its nature was as follows. It was to be to *an eternal life*. Thus the second of the seven brethren addressed Antiochus before he died (vii. 9): "Thou, O miscreant, dost release us out of this present life, but the King of the world shall raise us up, who have died for his laws unto an eternal revival of life" (εἰς αἰώνιον ἀναβίωσιν ζωῆς). And to the same effect the youngest of the seven, addressing Antiochus, declares (vii. 36): "For these our brethren, who have endured a short pain, have now died under God's covenant of everlasting life; but thou, through the judgment of God, shalt receive in just measure the penalties of thy pride."

Thus the heathen enter at death on their eternal doom.

Resurrection of the body.

In the next place, the resurrection is to be one *of the body*. The third of the seven brethren declares (vii. 11): "From heaven I had them (*i.e.* his tongue and hands); and for his laws' sake I contemn them; and from him I hope to receive these back again." And with this thought the mother of the seven encouraged them to endure martyrdom (vii. 22, 23): "I know not how ye came into my womb, neither was it I that bestowed on you your spirit and your life, and it was not I that brought into order the first elements of each one of you. 23. Therefore the Creator of the world, who

[1] The text is σοὶ μὲν γὰρ ἀνάστασις εἰς ζωὴν οὐκ ἔσται.

CHAP. VI.

fashioned the generation of man and devised the generation of all things, will in mercy give back to you again both your spirit and your life, as ye now regard not your own selves for his laws' sake."

Finally, it is said of Razis in xiv. 46 : "He drew forth his bowels through the wound, and taking them in both his hands he shook them at the crowds; and calling upon him who is Lord of the life and spirit to restore him these again, he thus died."

Resurrection to the Messianic kingdom.

Finally, the resurrection was not only to be to an eternal life, and that an eternal life in the body, but also to *a life* to be eternally enjoyed *in the community of the righteous.* This follows from the mother's words in vii. 29: "Fear not this executioner, but proving thyself worthy of thy brethren, accept thy death, that in the mercy of God I may receive thee again with thy brethren."

This last thought of a community of the risen righteous in the body recalls the idea of the Messianic kingdom. Now we found above certain allusions to such a kingdom. If, therefore, we combine the latter with those we have just learnt touching the nature of the expected resurrection, we arrive at a picture of the future that belongs essentially to the second century. The departed righteous are raised to an eternal Messianic kingdom on earth. Thus the writer looked forward to such a kingdom as we find depicted in Eth. En. lxxxiii.-xc., of which the scene is the present earth. This being so, we must regard the writer of this book as having reproduced with

The eschatology of 2 Maccabees belongs to the second century B.C.

some faithfulness, at least in an eschatological aspect, the work of Jason.

Before parting with this interesting book, we should notice the significant rôle played in it by the doctrine of retribution, present no less than future.

Its doctrine of retribution in this life.

Present retribution follows sin alike in the case of Israel and of the Gentiles, but in the case of Israel its purpose is corrective, but in that of the Gentiles it is vindictive (vi. 13-15). Though God punish His people, He does not withdraw His mercy from them (vi. 12-16, xiv. 15). In order to show the certainty of retribution in this life, the writer rewrites history, and makes individual sinners suffer the penalties which he thought, in strict justice, they ought to have suffered. This we may see in the final earthly destinies assigned to the heathen oppressors Epiphanes (vii. 17, ix. 5-12) and Nicanor (xv. 32-35), and to the Hellenising Jews, Jason (v. 7-10) and Menelaus (xiii. 8). Even the martyrs confess their sufferings as due to sin (vii. 18, 33, 37), and pray that God's wrath may be expiated in their sufferings (vii. 38). Immediate retribution is a token of God's goodness (vi. 13). But here we must part with our author, for our present concern is mainly with retribution beyond the grave.

IV. *Development of Special Conceptions*

Syncretism of the two different views in 2 Maccabees.

Soul and Spirit.—Just as in the second, so in this century, the doctrine of the soul and spirit is almost without exception a development of the older Semitic

CHAP. VI.

view. We shall notice the exceptions first. They are to be found in 2 Macc. vii. 22, 23, where we have a syncretism of the two psychologies. Thus in vii. 22 the mother of the seven martyred brethren declares: "It was not I that bestowed upon you your spirit and your life" (τὸ πνεῦμα καὶ τὴν ζωήν[1]). Here the spirit is the life-giving principle of which the life, or living soul, is the product, just as in Gen. ii., iii. These were given by God, and according to the writer's view are taken back by God at death; for in vii. 23 the mother continues: "Therefore the Creator of the world . . . in mercy giveth back to you again both your spirit and your life." Yet the withdrawal of this spirit does not lead to annihilation or unconsciousness in Sheol: for the departed are conscious (vi. 26). Hence the writer possesses no consistent psychology; for the ordinary dichotomy of soul and body is found in vi. 30, vii. 37, xiv. 38, xv. 30. In all the remaining literature of this century there is only a dichotomy—either the spirit[2] and body, or the soul and body. Some writers speak only of the spirit and body, others only of the soul and body, but some also use either indifferently. In none of these cases is spirit conceived as in Gen. ii., iii. Thus in the oldest writing of the century the departed in Sheol are spoken of as spirits (in Eth. En. xcviii. 10, and likewise in ciii. 3, 4, 8): "All goodness and joy and glory are prepared for them, and are

Elsewhere the ordinary dichotomy appears.

Soul and spirit are really identical.

[1] The same phraseology recurs in xiv. 46.

[2] In Eth. En. xv. 4 the antithesis between the spiritual and the fleshly is strongly emphasised, but the contrast is not between two parts of man, but between the nature of angels and of men.

written down for the spirits of those who have died in righteousness, and manifold good will be given to you in recompense for your labours, and your lot is abundantly beyond the lot of the living. 4. And your spirits—(the spirits) of you who die in righteousness, will live and rejoice and be glad, and their spirits will not perish, but their memorial will be before the face of the Great One unto all the generations of the world: wherefore then fear not their contumely. . . . 8. And into darkness and chains, and a burning fire, where there is grievous condemnation, will your spirits enter; and there will be grievous condemnation for the generations of the world. Woe unto you, for ye will have no peace." Again, the departed in Sheol are spoken of as "souls" (cii. 5, 11; ciii. 7): "Know ye that their souls will be made to descend into Sheol, and they will become wretched, and great will be their tribulation." On the other hand, in the nearly contemporaneous books of the Similitudes and Psalms of Solomon the term "spirit" is not used of man at all, but only "soul" (see Eth. En. xlv. 3, lxiii. 10; Pss. Sol. *passim*).

Finally, in the Noachic interpolations only the term "spirit" is used of man (cf. xli. 8; lx. 4; lxvii. 8, 9; lxxi. 1), and likewise in the Essenic appendix to this book, where it speaks of "the spirits of the wicked (cviii. 3, 6) and of the righteous" (cviii. 7, 9, 11).

Final judgment at close of Messianic

Judgment—final on all rational beings, human and angelic, at the close of the Messianic kingdom

CHAP. VI.

kingdom except in Eth. En. xxxvii.-lxx.

except in one author.—Only in Eth. En. xxxvii.-lxx. in the literature of this century is the final judgment regarded as initiating the Messianic kingdom. The scope of this judgment is co-extensive with the human and angelic worlds (see p. 218). This conception of the final judgment, though apparently the same as that which prevailed in the second century, differs, however, from it in this respect, that while the latter ushers in the Messianic kingdom on the present earth, the former ushers in the Messianic kingdom in a new heavens and a new earth.

But—and herein the main difference between the first- and second-century eschatologies under this head is to be observed—all (?) other writers of this century conceived the final judgment as forming the close of the temporary Messianic kingdom. This is clearly so in Eth. En. xci.-civ. and Pss. Sol. i.-xvi., and also in Pss. Sol. xvii., xviii. With the difficulties besetting 2 Maccabees we have already dealt (see pp. 226-231). A preliminary judgment of the sword is found in Eth. En. xci. 12, xcv. 7, xcvi. 1, xcviii. 12, etc., which is executed by the saints, as in Dan. ii. 44. This Messianic judgment is executed in Pss. Sol. xvii., xviii. by the Messiah *forensically*.

Paradise the intermediate abode of the righteous, according to various sections of Ethiopic Enoch.

Places of abode of the departed: (i.) *Paradise.*—Paradise, which in the preceding century had been regarded as the abode of only two men, has come in this to be conceived as the intermediate abode of all the righteous and elect (Eth. En. lxi. 12): "All the holy ones who are in heaven will bless him, and all the elect who dwell in the garden of life."

lxx. 2-4: "And he was carried aloft on the chariots of the spirit, and the name vanished amongst men (lit. 'them'). 3. And from that day I was no longer numbered amongst them, and he set me between the two winds, between the North and the West, where the angels took the cords to measure for me the place for the elect and righteous. 4. And there I saw the first fathers and the righteous who from the beginning dwell in that place." Noachic fragment, lx. 8: "But the male is called Behemoth, who occupies with his breast a waste wilderness named Dêndâin, on the east of the Garden where the elect and the righteous dwell, where my grandfather was taken up, the seventh from Adam, the first man whom the Lord of spirits created." Again in lxxvii. 3 Paradise is called "the garden of righteousness," and in lx. 23 "the garden of the righteous." This Paradise appears to be somewhere in the N.W. From Paradise the righteous pass to the Messianic kingdom in the Similitudes.

Heaven the final abode of the righteous in Eth. En. xc.-civ.; likewise in xxxvii.-lxx.

(ii.) *Heaven.*—For the first time in apocalyptic literature heaven becomes the abode of the spirits of the righteous *after the final* judgment. Thus the portals of heaven will be open to them (Eth. En. civ. 2), and their spirits will live and rejoice (ciii. 4), and "have great joy as the angels in heaven," and "become companions of the heavenly hosts" (civ. 4, 6). Likewise in the Similitudes the new heaven as well as the new earth is to be the abode of the righteous (see xli. 2, li. 4).

CHAP. VI.

Sheol—(*a*) the intermediate abode of the departed.

(iii.) *Sheol.*—During this century Sheol has a variety of meanings, most of which have been attested previously. Thus it = (*a*) Intermediate abode of the departed whence all Israel (?) rises to judgment (Eth. En. li. 1[1]). In 2 Maccabees it appears only in this sense (vi. 23). It is noteworthy that the writer of this book regards a moral change as possible in Sheol, in xii. 42-45. Thus Judas sacrifices on behalf of those who had fallen in battle, and on whose persons idolatrous symbols had been found. "For," the writer adds, "if he had not expected that they that had fallen would rise again, it would have been superfluous and idle to pray for the dead." This is the first trace of a belief in Sheol as a truly moral abode. According to Eth. En. c. 5, the souls of the righteous are preserved in a special part of Sheol (? cf. 4 Ezra iv. 41).

For the first time conceived to be a place where moral transformation becomes possible.

(*b*) Hell or Gehenna the final abode of the wicked.

(*b*) Secondly, Sheol is regarded as the place of final eternal punishment, that is, it has become hell (Eth. En. lvi. 8, lxiii. 10, xcix. 11, ciii. 7). In Sheol the souls are slain (xcix. 11). Yet in Eth. En. xxii. 11-13, which belongs to the preceding century, the souls of the wicked had to be raised out of

[1] Eth. En. li. 1 is difficult. Both Sheol and hell (here Haguel = Abaddon, cf. Job xxvi. 6) are said to give up their inhabitants for judgment. Are we therefore to regard Sheol and hell as mere synonyms here, or Sheol as the temporary abode of the righteous and hell of the wicked? The fact that Paradise is the intermediate abode of the righteous in the Similitudes (see above) favours the former alternative. Thus Sheol would in all cases be a place of punishment intermediate or final in the Similitudes. But Sheol may be regarded as lying in the N.W., and Paradise as a department of Sheol. Paradise in the Similitudes lies in the N.W. and Sheol in the W., according to Eth. En. xxii.

CHAP. VI.

Sheol in order to be slain. The reason is clear. In Eth. En. xxii. Sheol is not an abode of fire. Hence it is the place of final retribution where "souls are slain." In Eth. En. xci.-civ., on the other hand, which belongs to the opening years of the first century, Sheol has become an abode of fire, and therefore synonymous so far with Gehenna. In the Psalms of Solomon Sheol in all cases is a synonym for hell (xiv. 6, xv. 11, xvi. 2). We should observe here how Sheol is associated with fire and darkness. It has thus drawn to itself some of the attributes of Gehenna. In several passages in the Similitudes, and throughout Eth. En. xci.-civ., Sheol and Gehenna are practically identical. In the Similitudes Sheol is the intermediate abode of all (? see footnote) that died before the advent of the Messianic kingdom (li. 1); but after its advent it is henceforth conceived as a final abode of fire (lxiii. 10).

Gehenna. Transformations of this conception.

(iv.) *Gehenna.*—A new development of this idea appears in this century in Eth. En. xlviii. 9; liv. 1, 2; lxii. 12, 13. According to the prevailing view of the second century B.C., Gehenna was to be the final abode of Jewish apostates whose sufferings were to form an *ever-present* spectacle to the righteous; but in the Similitudes (xxxvii.-lxx.) Gehenna is specially designed for the kings and the mighty, and Gehenna and its victims are forthwith to vanish for ever from the sight of the righteous. This latter view appears to be due to the fact that after the judgment in the Similitudes there were to be a new heavens and a

CHAP. VI.

new earth, in which, of course, there was no room for Gehenna. The notable transformation of Gehenna referred to on p. 188 is further attested in Eth. En. xci.-civ., if we may identify Sheol and Gehenna[1] in this book. Elsewhere Gehenna had always been conceived as a place of both *corporal and spiritual* punishment. In the book just mentioned it appears as a place of *spiritual* punishment only. Thus in xcviii. 3 "their spirits will be cast into the furnace of fire" (cf. also ciii. 8). Sheol and Gehenna seem to be equivalent terms in this writer (see xcix. 11, ciii. 7; also c. 9). The old idea of Gehenna as a place of punishment within view of the righteous can no more be admitted in this book than in the Similitudes; for after the destruction of heaven and earth only a new heaven is created. The same conception is found in the Essene writing Eth. En. cviii. 5, 6.

Gehenna a place of spiritual punishment only in Eth. En. xci.-civ.

(v.) *Burning Furnace* = the final abode of the fallen angels (Eth. En. liv. 6; cf. xviii. 11-16, xxi. 1-6).

Burning Furnace = final abode of the fallen angels.

Resurrection.—The doctrine of the resurrection is taught in four books belonging to this century, but the particular form of this doctrine, which appears in 2 Maccabees, belongs, as we have seen above, to the second century B.C., and not to the first. This book puts forward a very definite doctrine of the resurrection of the body. Such a doctrine was

Resurrection. The teaching of 2 Maccabees on this head belongs to second century B.C.

[1] Gehenna is never mentioned by name in this book, but only Sheol. Sheol, however, possesses some of the chief characteristics of Gehenna. It is generally spoken of as "a burning fire," "a furnace of fire," etc.

quite in keeping with the view of the Messianic kingdom which prevailed in the second century B.C. as an eternal kingdom on the present earth. But in the next century, where this specific doctrine of the kingdom is abandoned, and the righteous are regarded as rising either to heaven itself or to the eternal Messianic kingdom in a new heaven and a new earth, the nature of this resurrection is, of necessity, differently conceived. To such spiritual final abodes of the blessed there could not be a mere bodily resurrection. Hence two views arose as to the nature of the resurrection. Whilst some taught, as the writers of Eth. En. xci.-civ. and Pss. Sol., that there would be no resurrection of the body at all but only of the spirit, others, as the writer of the Similitudes, said that there would be a resurrection of the body, but that this body would consist of garments of glory and of light (Eth. En. lxii. 15, 16), and that the risen righteous would be of an angelic nature (li. 4). Thus we find that the doctrine of the resurrection which was current amongst the cultured Pharisees in the century immediately preceding the Christian era was of a truly spiritual nature. And moreover, as regards those who have the right to share in the resurrection, the doctrine is no less high and spiritual. Thus according to the teaching of Eth. En. xci.-civ. and Pss. Sol. i.-xvi. only the righteous are to rise. The testimony of the Similitudes on this head is doubtful. Thus in Eth. En. lxi. 5 it is clearly implied that only the righteous are to share in the resurrection,

Views of first century B.C.

A resurrection (*a*) of the spirit only;

(*b*) Of the spirit clothed in a body of glory and light.

Only the righteous are to attain to the resurrection (Eth. En. xci.-civ. and Pss. of Solomon).

Testimony of Similitudes divided.

CHAP. VI.

but in li. 1, 2 it is just as clearly stated that there is a resurrection both of the just and of the unjust.

Messianic Kingdom.—See general historical development in first century (see pp. 200-203).

Messiah.—In the preceding century the Messianic hope was practically non-existent. So long as Judas and Simon were chiefs of the nation, the need of a Messiah was hardly felt. But in the first half of the next century it was very different. Subject to ruthless oppressions, the righteous were in sore need of help. But inasmuch as the Maccabean princes were themselves the leaders in this oppression, the thoughts of the faithful were forced to look for divine aid. Thus the bold and original thinker to whom we owe the Similitudes conceived the

Supernatural Messiah.

Messiah as the supernatural Son of Man, who should enjoy universal dominion and execute judgment on men and angels. But other religious thinkers returning afresh to the study of the Old

Old Testament conception of the Messiah.

Testament, revived, as in Pss. Sol., the expectation of the prophetic Messiah, sprung from the house and lineage of David (xvii. 23; see above, pp. 220-223). These very divergent conceptions took such a firm hold of the national consciousness that henceforth the Messiah becomes almost universally the central and chief figure in the Messianic kingdom.

No share in a blessed future for the Gentiles.

Gentiles.—The favourable view of the second century as to the future of the Gentiles has in this century all but disappeared. In Eth. En. xxxvii.-lxx. annihilation appears to await them. Only in Pss. Sol. xvii. 32 is it stated that they shall be spared to serve Israel in the temporary Messianic kingdom. This may have been the view of the other writers of this century, who looked forward to a merely temporary Messianic kingdom. In no case does it appear that the Gentiles could attain to a blessed resurrection.

16

CHAPTER VII

(1-60 A.D.)

ESCHATOLOGY OF APOCRYPHAL AND APOCALYPTIC LITERATURE DURING THE FIRST CENTURY A.D.

I. *Authorities for the First Century A.D.*

Book of Jubilees.
Assumption of Moses.
Book of Wisdom.
Philo.
Slavonic Enoch.
4 Maccabees.
Apocalypse of Baruch.
Book of Baruch.[1]
4 Ezra.
Josephus.

II. *General Eschatological Development of the First Century A.D.*

Further effects of growing dualism.

The growth of dualism, which was so vigorous in the preceding century, attains in this its final development. Not only has the thought of an

[1] The earlier part of this work may be as old as the second century B.C.

eternal Messianic kingdom passed absolutely from the minds of men, but also the hope of a temporary Messianic kingdom is at times abandoned in despair (B^2 and B^3 of Apocalypse of Baruch; 4 Ezra, Salathiel Apoc.; 4 Macc.); and in the rest, where it is expected, it is always of temporary duration.

Even the hope of a temporary Messianic kingdom at times given up.

In some books the actual duration of this temporary Messianic kingdom is defined. Thus the Slavonic Enoch ascribes to it a duration of 1000 years, *i.e.* a millennium, and the Ezra Apocalypse (4 Ezra vii. 28, 29) a period of 400 years. According to the latter authority also, some of the saints will rise to share in it. In this way was evolved the doctrine of the first resurrection.

Duration of kingdom defined as 1000 years. Hence the Millennium.

Thus the breach which had set in between the eschatologies of the individual and of the nation in the preceding century has been still further widened in this century, and the differences in the two eschatologies developed to their utmost limits. Either the nation has no blessed future at all, or at best only one of temporary duration. With this the individual has no essential concern. His interest centres round his own lot in the after-life. Thus Judaism has surrendered in despair the thought of the divine kingdom, which was the bequest of the Old Testament prophets.

Extreme individualism in religion follows upon the loss of the Messianic hope.

The transcendent view of the risen righteous which we observed in the preceding century is in this century likewise generally received. Thus it is to be a resurrection of the spirit only (Jubilees, Assumption of Moses, Philo, Book of Wisdom,

Resurrection of spirit only, or of spirit clothed in the glory of God,

CHAP. VII.

or of the earthly body, which was subsequently to be transfigured.

4 Maccabees), or the righteous are to rise vestured with the glory of God (Slavonic Enoch; see also the Pharisaic doctrine in Josephus, *B.J.* II. viii. 14), or with their former earthly body, which is forthwith to be transformed and made like that of the angels (Apocalypse of Baruch; 4 Ezra).

Righteous enter the final abode of happiness after death, according to Hellenistic but not Palestinean Judaism. The latter always taught the doctrine of an intermediate abode for the righteous.

But a new development now takes its rise in regard to the resurrection of the spirit. Heretofore the righteous spirit did not rise from its intermediate abode in Sheol till after the final judgment; but now several writers regard the righteous as entering on a blessed immortality immediately after death. But this view is held only by Alexandrian writers, *i.e.* Book of Wisdom (iii. 1-4; iv. 2, 7, 10, etc.), Philo, 4 Maccabees, or by the Essenes (see Josephus, *B.J.* II. viii. 11). This may possibly be the view of the Book of Jubilees, but it is unlikely. Hence we may conclude that the universal tradition of Palestinean Judaism always taught the doctrine of an intermediate abode for the righteous.

Resurrection extended from Israel to all mankind.

Finally, the scope of the resurrection, which in the past was limited to Israel, is in this century extended in some books to all mankind (Apocalypse of Baruch xlix.-li.; 4 Ezra vii. 32, 37). For the Gentiles, however, this is but a sorry boon. They are raised only to be condemned for ever, and the condemnation that followed such a resurrection was beyond measure severer than had been that which they had endured before its advent.[1]

[1] So Apoc. Bar. xxx. 4, 5, xxxvi. 11; 4 Ezra vii. 87.

III. *Eschatological Systems of the various Writers of the First Century* A.D.

THE BOOK OF JUBILEES (before 10 A.D.)

There is not much eschatological thought in the Book of Jubilees. It is a glorification of legalistic Judaism and of the priesthood. Hence a special blessing is given to Levi by Isaac (xxxi. 13-15): "May the God of all, the very Lord of all ages, bless thee and thy children throughout all ages. 14. And may the Lord give to thee and to thy seed greatness and great glory, and cause thee and thy seed, from among all flesh, to approach him to serve in his sanctuary as the angels of the presence and as the holy ones; (even) as they, will the seed of thy sons be for glory and greatness and holiness, and may he make them great in all the ages. 15. And they will be princes and judges, and chiefs of all the seed of the sons of Jacob; they will speak the word of the Lord in righteousness, and they will judge all his judgments in righteousness, and declare my ways to Jacob and my paths to Israel. The blessing of the Lord will be given in their mouths that they may bless all the seed of the beloved."

A Messiah seems to be expected.

A Messiah of the tribe of Judah seems to be expected by this writer. Thus Isaac blesses Judah: "May the Lord give thee (xxxi. 18, 19) strength and power to tread down all that hate thee; be a prince, thou and *one of thy sons*, over the sons of Jacob; may thy name and the name of thy sons go forth

CHAP. VII.

and traverse the whole earth and the countries; then shall the Gentiles fear thy face, and all the nations shall quake and all the peoples shall quake. 19. In thee may there be the help of Jacob, and in thee may there be found the salvation of Israel." But the words may refer to David.

The Messianic woes.

There is a detailed description of the Messianic woes (xxiii. 13, 14, 18, 19, 22). 13. "For calamity follows on calamity, and wound on wound, and tribulation on tribulation, and evil tidings on evil tidings, and illness on illness, and all evil judgments such as these one with another, illness and overthrow, and snow and frost, and ice and fever and chills, and torpor and famine, and death, and sword, and captivity and all kinds of calamities and pains. 14. And all these will come on an evil generation, which has transgressed on the earth; and their works are uncleanness and fornication, and pollution and abominations. . . . 18. Behold the earth will be destroyed on account of all their works, and there will be no seed of the vine, and no oil; for their works are altogether faithless, and they will all perish together, beasts, and cattle, and birds, and all the fish of the sea, on account of the children of men. 19. And they will strive one with another, the young with the old, and the old with the young, the poor with the rich, and the lowly with the great, and the beggar with the prince, on account of the law and the covenant; for they have forgotten his commandment and the covenant, and the feasts, and the months, and the Sabbaths, and the jubilees, and all the judgments. . . . 22. And a great punishment will befall the deeds of this generation from the Lord, and he will give them over to the sword, and to judgment, and to captivity, and to be plundered and devoured." Thereupon will follow an invasion of Palestine by the heathen nations (xxiii. 23, 24). 23. "And he will wake up against them the sinners of the Gentiles, who will show them no mercy or grace, and who will respect the person of none, neither old nor young, nor any one, for they are wicked and powerful, so that they are more wicked than all the children of men. And they will use violence against Israel and transgression against Jacob, and much blood will be shed upon the earth, and there will be none to gather it and none to bury. 24. In those days they will cry aloud and call and pray that they may be saved from the hand of the sinful Gentiles; but none will be saved."

Invasion of Palestine by the Gentiles.

Then Israel will begin to learn the error of its ways, and repent (xxiii. 16, 26). 16. "And in that generation the sons will convict their fathers and their elders of sin and unrighteousness, and of the words of their mouth and of the great wickedness which they perpetrate, and concerning their forsaking the covenant which the Lord made between them and him, that they should observe and do all his commandments and his ordinances and all his laws, without departing to the right hand or to the left. . . . 26. And in those days the children will begin to study the laws, and to seek the commandments, and to return to the path of righteousness."

Repentance of Israel.

CHAP. VII.

The gradual advent of the Messianic kingdom.

And then as the nation becomes faithful (xxiii. 27-29). 27. "The days of the children of men will begin to grow many, and increase from generation to generation, and day to day, till their days draw nigh to a thousand years, and to a greater number of years than (before) were their days. 28. And there will be no old man, nor one that is not satisfied with his days; for all will be (as) children and youths. 29. And all their days they will complete in peace and in joy, and they will live, and there will be no Satan nor any evil destroyer; for all their days will be days of blessing and healing."

The Messianic period here described is elsewhere (xxv. 20) called "the great day of peace." Though the Gentiles are to be blessed through Israel (xviii. 16, xx. 10, xxvii. 23), it is doubtful if this applies to the Messianic age. Finally, when the righteous die, their spirits will enter into a blessed immortality (xxiii. 31): "And their bones will rest in the earth and their spirits will have much joy, and they will know that it is the Lord who executes judgment, and shows mercy to hundreds and thousands of all that love him." The "day of the great judgment" (xxiii. 11) seems to follow on the close of the Messianic kingdom. At this judgment Mâstêma, the chief of the demons, will be judged (x. 8), and the demons subject to him. We have seen that the writer believes only in a resurrection of the spirit (xxiii. 31). The question now arises: Where do the spirits of the righteous go who die before the final judgment? It cannot be to

No resurrection but a blessed immortality of the righteous.

Judgment on close of Messianic kingdom.

Sheol as this book ordinarily conceives it; for Sheol is "the place of condemnation" to which eaters of blood and idolaters are condemned (vii. 29, xxii. 22). It must either be to an intermediate abode of the righteous, such as Paradise, as in the Similitudes, or else to heaven. All Palestinean Jewish tradition favours the former view.

Assumption of Moses (7-29 A.D.)

The Assumption of Moses is closely allied to the Book of Jubilees in many respects. But whereas Jubilees is a manifesto in favour of the priesthood, the Assumption emanates from a Pharisaic Quietist, and contains a bitter attack on the priesthood in vii. It adds greatly to the interest of this book that it was written during the early life of our Lord, or possibly contemporaneously with His public ministry. As in Jubilees, so here the preparation for the advent of the theocratic or Messianic kingdom will be a period of repentance (i. 18). Seventeen hundred and fifty years after the death of Moses (x. 12) God will intervene on behalf of Israel (x. 7), and the ten tribes brought back from captivity. There is no Messiah: "The eternal God alone . . . will punish the Gentiles" (x. 7). In this respect it may differ from Jubilees. Moreover, the most popular doctrine of the Messiah made Him a man of war. But such a doctrine was offensive to the author of the Assumption. He was a Pharisee of a fast-disappearing type, recalling in all respects the Chasid of the early

The Assumption the work of a Pharisaic Quietist.

Messianic kingdom and restoration of the ten tribes.

CHAP. VII.

Maccabean times, and upholding the old traditions of quietude and resignation. While his party was fast committing itself to political interests and movements, he raised his voice to recall them from the evil ways on which they had entered, and besought them to return to the old paths, but his appeal was made in vain, and so the secularisation of the Pharisaic movement in due course culminated in the fall of Jerusalem.

Israel will be exalted to heaven, and see its enemies in Gehenna.

At the close of this temporary Messianic kingdom Israel will be exalted to heaven, whence it shall see its enemies in Gehenna. The great hymn of the last things is so fine that we shall quote it almost wholly (x. 3-10[1]):—

3. For the Heavenly One will arise from his royal throne,
And he will go forth from his holy habitation,
And his wrath will burn on account of his sons.

4. And the earth will tremble: to its confines will it be shaken:
And the high mountains will be made low,
And the hills will be shaken and fall.

5. And the horns of the sun will be broken, and he will be turned into darkness;
And the moon will not give her light, and be turned wholly into blood.
And the circle of the stars will be disturbed.

6. And the sea will retire into the abyss,
And the fountains of waters will fail,
And the rivers will dry up.

7. For the Most High will arise, the Eternal God alone,
And he will appear to punish the Gentiles,
And he will destroy all their idols.

[1] For the text of this hymn, see the present writer's *Assumption of Moses*, pp. 40-43.

8. Then thou, O Israel, wilt be happy,
And thou wilt mount upon the neck[s and wings] of the eagle,
And (the days of thy mourning) will be ended.

9. And God will exalt thee,
And he will cause thee to approach to the heaven of the stars,
And he will establish thy habitation among them.

10. And thou wilt look from on high and wilt see thy enemies in Ge(henna),
And thou wilt recognise them and rejoice,
And thou wilt give thanks and confess thy Creator.

Gehenna becomes the final abode of the wicked generally.

It is noteworthy that the conception of Gehenna, which was originally the specific place of punishment for apostate Jews, is here extended, as in Judith, so as to become the final abode of the wicked generally. Finally, there seems to be no resurrection of the body, but of the spirit only.

Alexandrian Judaism.

The authorities.

We must now leave Palestinean soil and discuss the hopes which Alexandrian Judaism cherished as to the final condition of the individual and of the nation. The literary representatives of this phase of Judaism are the Book of Wisdom, the writings of Philo, the Book of the Secrets of Enoch, and 4 Maccabees. All these works are more or less leavened by Greek philosophy. But their writers, however saturated with Greek ideas, remain essentially Jews. Their aim is practical, not speculative; is ethical, not metaphysical. They draw their materials from Plato, Aristotle, the Pythagoreans, and Stoics. Of the above four Alexandrian writers, Philo alone can be said to have thought out a definite system. The writers of Wisdom and 4 Maccabees adopt current philosophical expressions

CHAP. VII.

for incidental use: they philosophise, but are not philosophers: while the writer of the Secrets of Enoch is the merest eclectic in this field. In some respects the last work is more nearly related to Palestinean than Alexandrian Judaism.

Points of difference between Alexandrian and Palestinean Judaism. (i.) Eternity and evil nature of matter. Hence no resurrection of the body.

The chief fundamental doctrines of Alexandrian Judaism, as distinct from Palestinean, are three: (i.) The eternity of matter, and its essentially evil nature. From this philosophical dogma it at once follows that there can be no resurrection of the flesh; indeed, three of the above writers deny a resurrection even of the body. Only the Slavonic Enoch teaches that the risen body will be constituted of the divine glory, and therein shows its Palestinean affinities.

(ii.) Pre-existence of soul.

(ii.) In the next place, the doctrine of the soul's pre-existence is taught, not, however, as it appears in the Platonic philosophy,[1] but in such a way as to be consistent with monotheism. According to the Book of Wisdom, a good soul obtains a good body (viii. 20). Are we to infer from this that souls were created originally with a specifically ethical character, some good, some bad? This can hardly be so, since God is conceived as the perfectly good, and as the lover of souls. Thus the ethical character of the soul on its entrance into the mortal body would appear to be the result of its own action in the past.[2] This appears to have been the view of Philo.

Different classes of souls. Why some descend into the body, according to Philo.

According to the latter, the air was the habitation of incorporeal souls. Before the creation of the earth

[1] See above, pp. 147-151.
[2] This was at one time the view of Plato. See p. 148.

these souls had lived in the undisturbed contemplation of God (*De Gigantibus*, 7). By the creation of the earth some souls that were possessed of divine thoughts were wholly unaffected, and always served the Ruler of the Universe, being as it were His lieutenants. Other souls, though less highly endowed, regarding the body as the source of folly and as a prison-house and a tomb, soared aloft to the ether and devoted themselves to sublime speculation. But others, that dwelt nearer to the earth and loved the body, descended to the earth and were united to mortal bodies (*De Somno*, i. 22). Of those who so descended only a few are saved by a spiritual philosophy, "meditating, from beginning to end, on how to die to the life in the body in order to obtain incorporeal and immortal life in the presence of the uncreated and immortal God" (*De Gigantibus*, 3; Mangey, i. 264).

(iii.) At death souls enter immediately on their final award. Hence no intermediate abode of souls and no final judgment.

(iii.) Souls enter immediately after death on their final award, whether of blessedness or torment. Such a doctrine follows naturally from the dogma just enunciated of the soul's pre-existence. Where such a dogma exists, there can be no true solidarity of the race or nation. The soul has no abiding interests in common with the community in which it may chance to be incarnated or born. It pursues, therefore, its own independent destiny, and no concern for others can legitimately retard its own consummation. Since it was held to reach this consummation at death, it ascended, therefore, forthwith to heaven. For it, therefore, there could be no

CHAP. VII.

intermediate abode of partial blessedness where i could grow in wisdom and in knowledge, but i could enter at once on its final perfectionmen independently of its brethren. Accordingly, to this individualistic type of religion there was no Sheol and no final judgment in the ordinary sense This is the teaching of Philo, 4 Maccabees, and most probably of Wisdom. On the other hand, it is just in these two respects that the Slavonic Enoch diverges from Alexandrian Judaism; for under Palestinean influence it teaches the two doctrines of Sheol and the final judgment.

Though these writers conceived the pre-earthly life ethically, they conceived the post-earthly life mechanically.

Thus, apparently, these Alexandrian writers regarded a man's condition in this life as determined by his ethical conduct when a pre-existent soul. It is strange, therefore, that though they conceived the pre-existent life of the soul as essentially ethical and capable of progress upward and downward, they failed to extend this view to the after-life of the soul, and regarded it as mechanically fixed for good or evil unto all eternity.

Book of Wisdom

Writer borrows from Greek philosophy.

The mind of the writer of the Book of Wisdom is of a philosophic cast. He was a student of Greek philosophy, and incorporated many of its conceptions in his book. Thus he adopted from Plato and his successors the doctrine that matter is eternal (xi. 17); that it is essentially evil, and that an ineradicably evil nature attaches therefore to the human body (i. 4); that the soul pre-exists (viii. 20), and finds in the body a temporary prison-house (ix. 15). From Stoic sources he derives the doctrine of the four cardinal virtues—temperance, prudence, justice, and fortitude (viii. 7), and probably his idea of a world-soul (i. 7, vii. 24, xii. 1). The attempted fusion of these and like views with Hebrew thought has led to a great indefiniteness of conception in this writer. And this want of precision of thought must in some measure affect our interpretation. Our author makes no reference to the Messiah. There is, however, to be a Messianic or theocratic kingdom, in which the surviving righteous will judge the nations and have dominion. These events are described in the following terms (iii. 7, 8):—

There is no Messiah, though there is a Messianic kingdom.

And in the time of their visitation they shall shine forth,
And as sparks among stubble they shall run to and fro.

8. They shall judge nations, and have dominion over peoples;
And the Lord shall reign over them for evermore.

Owing to the evil nature of matter, there can of course be no resurrection of the body; the soul is the proper self: the body is a mere burthen taken up by the pre-existent soul, but in due season laid down again. The soul receives a body in keeping so far as possible with its own character. Thus our author writes (viii. 19, 20):—

No resurrection of the body. The soul is the proper self.

I was a child of parts,
And a good soul fell to my lot;

20. Yea, rather being good, I came into a body undefiled.

CHAP. VII.

But even an "undefiled body" is an oppressive weight.

ix. 15. For a corruptible body weigheth down the soul,
And the earthly tabernacle lieth heavy on a mind that museth on many things.

The soul is redeemed through wisdom.

Accordingly, there is only an immortality of the soul. For the soul in such evil straits there is one sovereign remedy, and that is, divine wisdom. Wisdom is the redeemer of the soul, its preserver, and the only spring of its immortality. Thus in viii. 17 he declares:—

When I considered these things in myself,
And took thought in my heart,
How that immortality lieth in kinship to wisdom,

viii. 13. Because of her I shall have immortality.

And again in vi. 18, 19:—

And the love of Wisdom is observance of her laws;
And the giving heed to her laws is an assurance of incorruption;

19. And incorruption bringeth near unto God.

The life of the righteous and their future blessedness.

Thus through the life of divine wisdom man attains to his original destination: "For God created man for incorruption" (ii. 23). The life of the righteous and their future blessedness are set forth in terms remarkable at once for their beauty and vigour (iii. 1-4):—

But the souls of the righteous are in the hand of God,
And there shall no torment touch them.

2. In the sight of the unwise they seemed to die;
And their departure was taken to be their hurt,

CHAP. VII.

3. And their journeying away from us to be their ruin;
But they are in peace.

4. For though they be punished in the sight of men,
Yet is their hope full of immortality;

iv. 2, 7-11. When virtue is present, men imitate it;
And they long after it, when it is departed;
And throughout all time it marcheth crowned in triumph,
Victorious in the strife for the prizes that are undefiled.

7. But a righteous man though he die before his time
Yet shall he be at rest.

8. For honourable old age is not that which standeth in length of time,
Nor is its measure given by number of years:

9. But understanding is grey hairs unto men,
And an unspotted life is ripe old age.

10. Being found well-pleasing unto God, he was beloved of him,
And while living among sinners he was translated;

11. He was caught away, lest wickedness should change his understanding,
Or guile deceive his soul.

v. 2, 3[a], 4, 5, 15. When they see it, they shall be troubled with terrible fear,
And shall be amazed at the marvel of God's salvation. . . .

3. They shall say within themselves repenting, . . .

4. We fools accounted his life madness,
And his end without honour:

5. How was he numbered among the sons of God?
And how his lot among the saints? . . .

15. But the righteous live for ever,
And in the Lord is their reward,
And the care of them with the Most High.

As for the wicked, they will be punished with death (ii. 24); they will be bereft of hope; they will

The wicked and their destiny.

CHAP. VII.

suffer retribution both in this world and in the next (iii. 16, 18):—

But children of adulterers shall not come to maturity,
And the seed of an unlawful bed shall vanish away.

17. For if they live long, they shall be held in no account,
And at the last their old age shall be without honour.

18. And if they die quickly, they shall have no hope,
Nor in the day of decision shall they have consolation.

v. 14. For the hope of the ungodly is as chaff carried by the wind,
And as a thin froth that is driven away with the storm,
And as smoke that is scattered by the wind,
And passeth by as the remembrance of a guest that tarrieth but a day.

xv. 10. His heart is ashes,
And his hope of less value than earth,
And his life of less honour than clay.

The time for repentance is past (v. 3); thick darkness will cover them (xvii. 21); they will be utterly destroyed (iv. 19), yet not annihilated; for they will be subject to pain (iv. 19), and be aware of the blessedness of the righteous (v. 1, 2). The writer gives a dramatic representation of the final judgment in iv. 2–v. 13, but it can hardly be taken literally. The judgment of the individual sets in at death (iv. 10, 14). We have already mentioned the expectation that the righteous in Israel are to judge the nations. This seems to be a later development of the judgment by the sword frequently mentioned in previous literature (cf. Dan. ii. 44; Eth. En. xci. 12, etc.) Thus the judgment of the saints has become a forensic one, as that of the Messiah (cf. 1 Cor. vi. 2).

Final judgment scene in iv. 2–v. 13 not to be taken literally, for the individual is judged immediately after death.

PHILO (25 B.C.–50 A.D.)

In Philo we have the chief exponent of Alexandrian Judaism. We shall only touch, however, on the main points of his eschatology. He looked forward to the return of the tribes from captivity, to the establishment of a Messianic kingdom of temporal prosperity, and even to a Messiah. The *loci classici* on this subject are *De Execrat.* §§ 8, 9 (ed. Mang. ii. 435 *sqq.*), and *De Proem. et Poen.* §§ 15-20 (ed. Mang. ii. 421-428). In the former passage the restoration of a converted Israel to the Holy Land is foretold. Their captivity will be at an end in one day: "If filled with shame they change their ways with all their soul, and avow and confess with cleansed minds all the sins that they have committed against themselves . . . then, though they be at the very ends of the earth, slaves of the foes that took them captive, nevertheless as at a given signal, they shall all be set free in one day, because their sudden change to virtue will strike their masters with amazement; for they will let them go, because ashamed to govern those who are better than themselves. But when this unlooked-for freedom has been bestowed, those, who but a short time before were scattered in Hellas and in barbarous countries, or islands, and continents, will arise with one impulse and hasten from all quarters to the place pointed out to them, led on their way by a divine superhuman appearance, which though unseen by all others, is visible only to the delivered."

Israel on repentance to be set free in one day

and return under the guidance of the Messiah.

CHAP. VII.

In the latter passage there is a description of the Messianic kingdom. The Messiah is mentioned as a man of war—*ἐξελεύσεται γὰρ ἄνθρωπος, φησὶν ὁ χρησμός* (Num. xxiv. 7), *καταστρατάρχῶν καὶ πολεμῶν ἔθνη*. The inclusion of the Messiah in the Messianic kingdom in Philo's eschatology, though really foreign to his system, is strong evidence as to the prevalence of these expectations even in Hellenistic Judaism. Apparently he did not look forward to a general and final judgment. All enter after death into their final abode. The punishment of the wicked was for everlasting (*De Cherub.* § 1, ed. Mang. i. 138): "But he who is cast out by God must endure a never-ending banishment; for though the man who has not yet become the complete captive of wickedness may on repentance return to virtue as to his native country from which he had gone into exile, he, on the other hand, who is in the grip and power of a violent and incurable disease must bear his sufferings for evermore, and be flung into the place of the godless to endure unmixed and unremitting misery." Even the wicked Jews were committed to Tartarus (*De Execrat.* § 6). As matter was incurably evil there could of course be no resurrection of the body. Our present life in the body is death; for the body is the "utterly polluted prison" of the soul (*παμμίαρον δεσμωτήριον*, *De Migr. Abr.* ii.; Mangey, ii. 437): nay, more, it is its sepulchre (*Quod Deus immut.* xxxii.); our *σῶμα* is our *σῆμα*[1] (*Leg. Alleg.* i. 33).

No general judgment.

The everlasting punishment of the wicked.

No resurrection of the body.

[1] This statement goes back to the Orphic mysteries (Plato, *Crat.* 400 C; see above, p. 142).

CHAP. VII.

Slavonic Enoch[1] (1-50 A.D.)

From Philo we pass naturally to the work of another Egyptian Jew, to whom we owe the Book of the Secrets of Enoch. This interesting book, which has only come to light within the last six years, gives a long description of the seven heavens. Its writer deals with many subjects in a thoroughly eclectic spirit. As regards the duration of the world, he reasons that since the earth was created in six days, its history will be accomplished in 6000 years, evidently basing his view on the Old Testament words that "each day with the Lord is as 1000 years"; and as the six days of creation were followed by one of rest, so the 6000 years of the world's history will be followed by a rest of 1000 years. This time of rest and blessedness is the Messianic period. Here for the first time the Messianic kingdom is conceived as lasting for 1000 years, and it is to such an origin that we must trace the later Christian view of the Millennium. On the close of this kingdom, in which there is no Messiah, time will pass into eternity (xxxii. 2–xxxiii. 2). At the termination of the Messianic kingdom the final judgment is held, variously called "the day of judgment" (xxxix. 1, li. 3), "the great day of the Lord" (xviii. 6), "the great judgment" (lviii. 5, lxv. 6, lxvi. 7), "the day of the great judgment" (l. 4, lii. 15), "the eternal judgment" (vii. 1),

The world's history to last 6000 years.

Thereupon should follow the Millennium or temporary Messianic kingdom.

Then the final judgment.

[1] For further details see Morfill and Charles' *editio princeps* of this book. The quotations given from it are drawn from this edition.

CHAP. VII.

Intermediate abodes of souls and fallen angels.

"the great judgment for ever" (lx. 4), "the terrible judgment" (xlviii. 8), "the immeasurable judgment" (xl. 12). But prior to the final judgment the souls of the departed are in intermediate places. Thus the rebellious angels are confined to the second heaven, awaiting in torment the eternal judgment (vii. 1-3). The fallen lustful angels are kept in durance under the earth (xviii. 7); Satan being hurled down from heaven, has the air as his habitation (xxix. 4, 5).

All souls created before the foundation of the world.

As for man, the doctrine of pre-existence is taught. The souls of men, according to our author, were created before the foundation of the world (xxiii. 5), and future places of abode have been prepared for every human soul (xlix. 2, lviii. 5). From the latter context these appear to constitute also the intermediate place for human souls. In xxxii. 1 Adam is sent back to this receptacle of souls on his death, and is transferred from it to Paradise in the third heaven after the great judgment (xlii. 5).

Souls of beasts to be preserved till final judgment.

Even the souls of beasts are preserved till the final judgment in order to testify against the ill-usage of men (lviii. 5, 6).

Description of Paradise in the third heaven—the final abode of the righteous.

The righteous will escape the final judgment, and enter Paradise as their eternal inheritance and final abode (viii.; ix.; xlii. 3, 5; lxi. 3; lxv. 10). The description of Paradise, which is in the third heaven, is naïve and worth quoting: viii. 1. "And these men took me from thence, and brought me to the third heaven, and placed me in the midst of a garden—a place such as has never been known for

CHAP. VII.

the goodliness of its appearance. 2. And I saw all the trees of beautiful colours and their fruits ripe and fragrant and all kinds of food which they produced, springing up with delightful fragrance. 3. And in the midst (there is) the tree of life, in that place, on which God rests when he comes into Paradise. And this tree cannot be described for its excellence and sweet odour. 4. And it is beautiful more than any created thing. And on all sides in appearance it is like gold and crimson and transparent as fire, and it covers every thing. 5. From its root in the garden there go forth four streams which pour honey and milk, oil and wine, and are separated in four directions, and go about with a soft course. 6. And they go down to the Paradise of Eden, between corruptibility and incorruptibility. And thence they go along the earth, and have a revolution in their circle like also the other elements. 7. And there is another tree, an olive tree, always distilling oil. And there is no tree there without fruit, and every tree is blessed. 8. And there are three hundred angels very glorious, who keep the garden, and with never-ceasing voices and blessed singing, they serve the Lord every day. And I said: What a very blessed place is this! And those men spake unto me: ix. This place, O Enoch, is prepared for the righteous who endure every kind of attack in their lives from those who afflict their souls: who turn away their eyes from unrighteousness, and accomplish a righteous judgment, and also give bread to

Its connection with the earthly Paradise, which was on the confines of corruptibility and incorruptibility.

CHAP. VII.

the hungry, and clothe the naked, and raise the fallen, and assist the orphans who are oppressed, and who walk without blame before the face of the Lord, and serve him only. For them this place is prepared as an eternal inheritance." lxv. 10. "And there shall be to them a great wall that cannot be broken down; and bright and incorruptible Paradise shall be their protection, and their eternal habitation. For all corruptible things shall vanish, and there shall be eternal life." xlii. 3. "I went out to the East, to the Paradise of Eden, where rest has been prepared for the just, and it is open to the third heaven, and shut from this world. 5. At the last coming they will lead forth Adam with our forefathers, and conduct them there, that they may rejoice, as a man calls those whom he loves to feast with him; and they having come with joy hold converse, before the dwelling of that man, with joy awaiting his feast, the enjoyment and the immeasurable wealth, and joy and merriment in the light, and eternal life." lxi. 3. "Blessed are those who shall go to the mansions of the blessed; for in the evil ones there is no rest nor any means of return from them."

The heavenly Paradise is incorruptible.

Hell in the third heaven. Enoch's description of it.

The wicked are cast into hell in the third heaven, where their torment will be for everlasting (x. 1): "And the men then led me to the Northern region, and showed me there a very terrible place. 2. And there are all sorts of tortures in that place. Savage darkness and impenetrable gloom; and there is no light there, but a gloomy fire is always burning, and a fiery river goes forth. And all that place has fire on all sides, and on all sides cold and ice, thus it burns and freezes. 3. And the prisoners are very savage. And the angels terrible and without pity, carrying savage weapons, and their torture was unmerciful. 4. And I said: Woe! woe! How terrible is this place! And the men said to me: This place, Enoch, is prepared for those who do not honour God; who commit evil deeds on earth, vitium sodomiticum, witchcraft, enchantments, devilish magic; and who boast of their evil deeds, stealing, lying, calumnies, envy, evil thoughts, fornication, murder. 5. Who steal the souls of wretched men, oppressing the poor and spoiling them of their possessions, and themselves grow rich by the taking of other men's possessions, injuring them. Who when they might feed the hungry, allow them to die of famine; who when they might clothe them, strip them naked. 6. Who do not know their Creator and have worshipped gods without life; who can neither see nor hear, being vain gods, and have fashioned the forms of idols, and bow down to a contemptible thing, made with hands; for all these this place is prepared for an eternal inheritance." xlii. 1. "I saw those who keep the keys, and are the guardians of the gates of hell, standing, like great serpents, and their faces were like quenched lamps, and their eyes were fiery, and their teeth were sharp. And they were stripped to the waist. 2. And I said before their faces, Would that I had not seen you, nor heard of your

CHAP. VII.

The classes for whom it is prepared.

Hell's gate-keepers.

CHAP. VII.

doings, and that those of my race had never come to you! Now they have sinned only a little in this life, and always suffer in the eternal life."[1]

No resurrection of the flesh.

There is no resurrection of the flesh. This would naturally follow where the soul's pre-existence is accepted. But though there is no resurrection of the flesh, the risen righteous are conceived as possessing a heavenly body: for they are clothed with the garments of God's glory. Thus when Enoch was translated, Michael is directed by God to remove Enoch's earthly body and to give him a body composed of the divine glory (xxii. 8-10): "And the Lord said to Michael: Go and take from Enoch his earthly robe, and anoint him with my holy oil, and clothe him with the raiment of my glory. 9. And so Michael did as the Lord spake unto him. He anointed me and clothed me, and the appearance of that oil was more than a great light, and its anointing was like excellent dew; and its fragrance like myrrh, shining like a ray of the sun."[2]

The righteous are to have a heavenly body formed of the glory of God.

The seventh heaven is the final abode of Enoch (lv. 2, lxvii. 2), but this is an exceptional privilege, for the final abode of the righteous is the third heaven.

4 Maccabees (before 70 A.D.)

The last Jewish book of a philosophic character with which we have to deal is that of 4 Maccabees. It is really a discourse or sermon of the Synagogue;

[1] See also xl. 12, xli. 2.

[2] Cf. Eth. En. lxii. 16, cviii. 12.

CHAP. VII.

for it presumes the presence of an audience, and frequently addresses them directly (cf. i. 1, xviii. 1). This discourse constitutes an exposition of Jewish Stoicism. Its theme is announced in i. 13: "The question which we have to determine, therefore, is whether the reason be complete master of the passions." So stated, the writer's fundamental idea seems to be identical with that of Stoicism. But this is not so: for the reason which is to exercise supremacy over the passions is not human reason in itself, but the reason that is inspired by piety—ὁ εὐσεβὴς λογισμός (i. 1, vii. 16, xiii. 1, xv. 20, xvi. 1, xviii. 2). The realisation of the Stoic ideal is possible only in Judaism. For the four cardinal virtues of Stoicism are but forms of true wisdom which can be won only through the Mosaic Law (i. 15-18). The passions, however, are not to be exterminated, as the Stoics taught, but to be ruled (i. 6, iii. 5), for they were implanted by God (ii. 21).

An exposition of Jewish Stoicism.

Stoic ideal can be realised only in Judaism.

Passions not to be exterminated.

Since the means of attaining such piety are furnished by the Jewish religion (v. 21, 23), only the descendants of Abraham, as members of this faith, are capable of true virtue, and are in this respect invincible. Thus the eldest of the seven martyred brothers addresses Antiochus: "By enduring all the tortures I will persuade you that only the children of the Hebrews are invincible in respect of virtue" (ix. 18).

But though descent from Abraham is emphasised repeatedly (xviii. 1, 20, 23), the value of such an ancestry is regarded as only potential in the

CHAP. VII.

individual Israelite, but not actual until the individual has realised the greatness open to him. Hence the children of Abraham are exhorted to die nobly, as became them, on behalf of virtue and godliness (vi. 22, ix. 21, xiii. 12, xiv. 20, xvii. 6). "Inasmuch as they know that these, who have died on behalf of God, live unto God, as Abraham, Isaac, and Jacob, and all the patriarchs" (xvi. 25). There can of course be no resurrection of the body. This is all the more remarkable since this discourse is founded on 2 Maccabees, which takes a very material view of the resurrection. Only a blessed immortality of the soul is taught.

Though this book is founded on 2 Maccabees, it teaches only an immortality of the soul.

The patriarchs, even Abraham, Isaac, and Jacob, will receive the faithful soul on death (xiii. 16,[1] v. 36,[2] xviii. 23). This expression shows us that the phrase "Abraham's bosom" was a current one, but whereas in the Gospels it is an intermediate abode, here it is heaven itself (cf. xvii. 5, 18).

"Abraham's bosom."

The souls of the blessed will enjoy communion with God (ix. 8, xv. 2, xvii. 5). But the wicked will be tormented in fire for ever (x. 11, 15; xii. 12; xiii. 14).

[1] οὕτως γὰρ θανόντας ἡμᾶς Ἀβραὰμ καὶ Ἰσαὰκ καὶ Ἰακὼβ ὑποδέξονται.

[2] ἁγνόν με οἱ πατέρες εἰσδέξονται.

CHAPTER VIII

(60-100 A.D.)

ESCHATOLOGY OF APOCRYPHAL AND APOCALYPTIC LITERATURE DURING THE FIRST CENTURY A.D. —*continued.*

FROM our somewhat long excursion in the last chapter into Hellenistic Judaism we return once more to Judaism on its native soil, and are thereupon confronted with several works of great interest and of no small literary merit. Of these the two chief are the Apocalypse of Baruch and 4 Ezra.

APOCALYPSE OF BARUCH

The Apocalypse of Baruch was written in the latter half of the first century of the Christian era. It is thus contemporaneous with the chief writings of the New Testament. Its authors were orthodox Jews, and it is a good representative of the Judaism against which the Pauline dialectic was directed.

In this apocalypse we have almost the last noble

CHAP. VIII.

utterance of Judaism before it plunged into the dark and oppressive years that followed the destruction of Jerusalem. For ages after that epoch its people seem to have been bereft of their immemorial gifts of song and eloquence, and to have had thought and energy only for the study and expansion of the traditions of the fathers. But when our book was written, that evil and barren era had not yet set in; breathing thought and burning word had still their home in Palestine, and the hand of the Jewish artist was still master of its ancient cunning.

This apocalypse the work of several writers, some before 70 A.D., some after.

This work, as I have shown elsewhere, was written originally in Hebrew, and is very composite.[1] It embraces at least six independent constituents. Of these we shall deal first with the three fragmentary Messiah apocalypses xxvii.–xxx. 1., xxxvi.-xl., liii.-lxxiv., which are differentiated from the remaining portions of the book both in doctrine and time. These three fragmentary works were written prior to the fall of Jerusalem in 70 A.D., and teach the doctrine of a personal Messiah.

First apocalypse, xxvii.-xxx. 1.

In the first of these apocalypses (xxvii.–xxx. 1) there is an account of the final tribulation that is to befall the earth before the advent of the Messiah. This time of tribulation is divided into twelve parts, each of which is marked by some disaster. The duration of this period is to be "two parts weeks of seven weeks," whatever that may mean. At its close the Messiah will be revealed (xxix. 4–xxx. 1):

The Messianic period.

[1] See the present writer's *Apocalypse of Baruch*, 1896, from which the materials that follow are drawn.

"And Behemoth will be revealed from his place and Leviathan will ascend from the sea, those two great monsters which I created on the fifth day of creation, and I kept them until that time; and then they will be for food for all that are left. 5. The earth also will yield its fruits ten thousand fold, and on each vine there will be a thousand branches, and each branch will produce a thousand clusters, and each cluster will produce a thousand grapes, and each grape will produce a cor of wine. 6. And those who have hungered will rejoice: moreover, also, they will behold marvels every day. 7. For winds will go forth from before me to bring every morning the fragrance of aromatic fruits, and at the close of the day clouds distilling the dew of health. 8. And it will come to pass at that selfsame time, that the treasury of manna will again descend from on high, and they will eat of it in those years, because these are they that have come to the consummation of time. xxx. 1. And it will come to pass after these things, when the time of the advent of the Messiah is fulfilled, and he will return in glory, then all who have fallen asleep in hope of him shall rise again."

CHAP. VIII.

The Messiah.

With these words this short apocalypse breaks off. Its view of the temporary Messianic kingdom is very sensuous, and recalls the materialistic prosperity which marked some of the second-century representations of the eternal Messianic kingdom.[1]

The next apocalypse, composed of chaps.

Second apocalypse xxxvi.-xl.

[1] See above, pp. 188, 189.

CHAP. VIII.

xxxvi.-xl., is of greater interest. It recounts a vision which Baruch saw in the night (xxxvi. 2–xxxvii.) On awaking from this vision he prayed to God to make known to him its interpretation. This interpretation we will give in the author's own words (xxxix. 3–xl. 3). xxxix. 3. "Behold! the days come, and this kingdom will be destroyed which once destroyed Zion, and it will be subjected to that which comes after it. 4. Moreover, that also again after a time will be destroyed, and another, a third, will arise, and that also will have dominion for its time, and will be destroyed. 5. And after these things a fourth kingdom will arise, whose power will be harsh and evil far beyond those which were before it, and it will rule many times as the forests on the plain, and it will hold fast the times, and will exalt itself more than the cedars of Lebanon. 6. And by it the truth will be hidden, and all those who are polluted with iniquity will flee to it, as evil beasts flee and creep into the forest. 7. And it will come to pass, when the time of its consummation that it should fall has approached, then the principate of my Messiah will be revealed, which is like the fountain and the vine, and, when it is revealed, it will root out the multitude of its host. 8. And as touching that which thou hast seen, the lofty cedar, which was left of that forest, and the fact, that the vine spoke those words with it which thou didst hear, this is the word."

The fourth empire = Rome.

To be destroyed by the Messiah.

xl. "The last leader of that time will be left alive, when the multitude of his hosts will be put to the sword, and he will be bound, and they will take him up to Mount Zion, and my Messiah will convict him of all his impieties, and will gather and set before him all the works of his hosts. 2. And afterwards he will put him to death, and protect the rest of my people which shall be found in the place which I have chosen. 3. And his principate will stand for the age,[1] until the world of corruption is at an end, and until the times aforesaid are fulfilled."

CHAP. VIII.

Messianic kingdom.

We should observe here that whereas the rôle of the Messiah in the first apocalypse is entirely passive, in this He is conceived as a warrior who slays the enemies of Israel with His own hand. Against Him all the heathen powers are arrayed under a last great leader. This leader represents the Antichrist. The principate of the Messiah is to last until the world of corruption is at an end.

Third apocalypse = liii.-lxxiv.

The third apocalypse, consisting of chaps. liii.-lxxiv., now claims our attention. This work is one of extreme value, as it is the oldest literary evidence for the fusion of early Rabbinism and the popular Messianic expectation. It has come down in tolerable preservation. It was written before the fall of Jerusalem, and not earlier than 50 A.D. The means by which we determine the latter date are interesting. In chap. lix. of this fragment we find that a large number of the revelations and achievements, which earlier times assigned to Enoch, are here attributed to Moses. This robbing of Enoch to benefit Moses is a clear sign of

Written between 50-70 A.D.

Means of fixing the terminus *a quo*.

[1] = εἰς τὸν αἰῶνα (cf. lxxiii. 1).

CHAP. VIII.

Jewish hostility to Christianity. Enoch's acceptance amongst Christians as a Messianic prophet was a ground for his rejection by the Jews. So thoroughgoing, indeed, was this rejection, that, although he was the chief figure next to Daniel in Jewish Apocalyptic prior to 40 A.D., in subsequent Jewish literature his achievements are ascribed sometimes to Moses, as here, at others to Ezra or else to Baruch.

This aggressive attitude of the Synagogue could hardly have arisen before the Pauline controversy. The same hostility is unswervingly pursued in the Talmud, which avoids all reference to this hero of early Judaism. It is noteworthy that the Septuagint experienced somewhat similar fortunes. The fact that the Christians always made their appeal to it led to its disuse by the Jews. It is to the Christian Church that we owe the preservation alike of Jewish apocalypses and of the Septuagint.

We must now, however, return to the contents of this apocalypse. In chap. liii. Baruch receives a vision in which the history of the entire world is depicted. Since this is unintelligible, Baruch prays for its interpretation (liv. 6). In answer to Baruch's prayer the angel Ramiel, "who presides over the visions," was sent to interpret the vision. We are here concerned only with that portion of the interpretation which relates to the future (lxx. 2): "Behold! the days come," we read, "and it will be when the time of the age has ripened and the harvest of its evil and good seeds has come, that the Mighty One will bring upon the earth and upon its

Its account of the future.

CHAP. VIII.

Messianic woes.

rulers perturbation of spirit and stupor of heart." When this last period has arrived, men (lxx. 3, 5) "will hate one another, and provoke one another to fight, and the mean will rule over the honourable, and those of low degree will be extolled above the famous": "And the wise will be silent, and the foolish will speak, neither will the thought of men be then confirmed, nor the counsel of the mighty, nor will the hope of those who hope be confirmed." Thereupon universal war will follow (lxx. 8, 10): "And it will come to pass that whosoever gets safe out of the war will die in the earthquake, and whosoever gets safe out of the earthquake will be burned by the fire, and whosoever gets safe out of the fire will be destroyed by famine. 10. For all the earth will devour its inhabitants." Not so, however, the Holy Land, for it will protect its own (lxxi. 1). Then (lxxii. 2) the Messiah "will summon all the nations, and some of them he will spare and some of them he will slay," and (lxxii. 4) "every nation which knows not Israel, and has not trodden down the seed of Jacob, shall indeed be spared." "But (lxxii. 6–lxxiii. 4) all those who have ruled over you, or have known you, shall be given up to the sword." lxxiii. 1. "And it will come to pass, when he has brought low every thing that is in the world, and has sat down in peace for the age[1] on the throne of his kingdom, that joy will then be revealed, and rest appear. 2. And then healing will descend in dew, and disease will withdraw, and anxiety and anguish

The destruction of all nations who oppressed Israel by the Messiah.

The temporary Messianic period.

[1] As above, in xl. 3 (see p. 273).

CHAP. VIII.

and lamentation will pass from amongst men, and gladness will proceed through the whole earth. 3. And no one shall again die untimely, nor shall any adversity suddenly befall. 4. And judgments, and revilings, and contentions, and revenges and blood, and passions, and envy, and hatred, and whatsoever things are like these, shall go into condemnation when they are removed." lxxiv. 1, 2. "And it will come to pass in those days that the reapers will not grow weary, nor those that build be toilworn; for the works will of themselves speedily advance with those who do them in much tranquility. 2. For that time is the consummation of that which is corruptible, and the beginning of that which is incorruptible."

The Messianic kingdom of temporary duration.

In all these three apocalypses the Messianic kingdom is, as we have seen, of temporary duration, and its felicity of an earthly description. It has of course a severely ethical character. Sin and wickedness have no place therein. But, on the other hand, and this criticism applies to all Jewish representations of the Messianic kingdom, but particularly to the later, there is no adequate account given of the cause of this spiritual transformation. This transformation is brought about catastrophically and in the main mechanically. By the eternal fiat of the Almighty, sin is banished at once and for ever from the hearts of the members of the Messianic kingdom. This catastrophic change is in itself at variance with all the spiritual experience of mankind. Godlike character cannot come from without as an external gift, nor can it be won in a moment, but can only

Entrance into it ethically conditioned,

but the transformation supposed by it is mechanically conceived.

CHAP. VIII.

be the slow result of the spiritual travail of the human heart in communion with the divine.

Other mechanical features in the conception.

Moreover, the hope of a kingdom whence all who fell below a certain conventional standard should be banished is the thought of men whose notions of perfection were mechanical, and whose chief aspiration was not the salvation of mankind at large but that of a few individuals, whose future comfort and blessedness could only be secured through the local separation of the good and the evil. But a goodness which can only maintain itself through local separation from evil cannot be called divine. Moreover, all temporary conditions of existence in the life of moral beings such as that in the temporary Messianic kingdoms here portrayed must in their essence be of the nature of a probation, and if of this nature, then the admixture of good and evil, as in the present world, appears to be not only conceivable, but also to be indispensable for the spiritual education of moral beings.

Three other constituents in this apocalypse—B^1, B^2, B^3.

The remaining constituents of Baruch are three, which for convenience may be named B^1, B^2, B^3. They were all written after the fall of Jerusalem in 70 A.D. B^1 stands by itself, and consists of i.–ix. 1; xliii.–xliv. 7; xlv.–xlvi. 6; lxxvii.-lxxxii.; lxxxvi.; lxxxvii. Its writer is optimistic, and looks forward to the rebuilding of Jerusalem (vi. 9), which has been destroyed by angels lest the enemy should boast (vii. 1), the restoration of the exiles (lxxvii. 6, lxxviii. 7), the Messianic kingdom, but no Messiah (i. 5, xlvi. 6, lxxvii. 12). The future in store for

Outlook of B^1

Restoration of the exiles, the Messianic kingdom, but no Messiah.

CHAP. VIII.

No hope for the Gentiles.

the Gentiles is without hope. This is no doubt due in part to the destruction of Jerusalem (lxxxii. 3, 6, 7): 3. "For lo! we see now the multitude of the prosperity of the Gentiles, though they act impiously, but they will be like a vapour. . . . 6. And we consider the glory of their greatness, though they do not keep the statutes of the Most High, but as smoke will they pass away. 7. And we meditate on the beauty of their gracefulness, though they have to do with pollutions, but as grass that withers will they fade away."

B^2 and B^3 are pessimistic as to this world. No Messiah or Messianic kingdom. The world wholly corrupt: the end at hand.

The two remaining sections, B^2 and B^3,[1] may be treated together. In these all expectations of a Messianic kingdom are absolutely abandoned, and the hopes of the righteous are directed to the immediate advent of the final judgment and to the spiritual world alone. This world is a scene of corruption; its evils are irremediable; it is a never-ceasing toil and strife, but its end is at hand; its youth is past; its strength exhausted; the pitcher is near to the cistern, the ship to the port, the course of the journey to the city, and life to its consummation (lxxxv.) The advent of the times is nigh, the corruptible will pass away, the mortal depart, that that which abides for ever may come, and the new world which does not turn to corruption those who depart to its blessedness (cf. xxi. 19, xliv. 9-15, lxxxv.)

Writer of B^2 mainly concerned with theological problems.

Such being the views of this writer, it is only natural that his main concern is with theological

[1] For the contents of B^2 and B^3, see my *Apocalypse of Baruch*, pp. lxi.-lxiii.

problems and the nature of the incorruptible world that is to be.

CHAP. VIII.

Contrasts between this world and the next.

The world will be renewed (xxxii. 6), and in this renewal, from being transitory and verging to its close (xlviii. 50, lxxxv. 10), it will become undying (li. 3) and everlasting (xlviii. 50); from being a world of corruption (xxi. 19, xxxi. 5; cf. xl. 3, lxxiv. 2), it will become incorruptible and invisible (li. 8, xliv. 12).

In Sheol there are preliminary foretastes of happiness and torment.

Full of world-despair, the writer's regards are fixed on the last day when he shall testify against the Gentile oppressors of Israel (xiii. 3). In the meantime, as men die they enter in some degree on their reward in Sheol, the intermediate abode of the souls of the departed prior to the final judgment (xxiii. 5, xlviii. 16, lii. 2; cf. lvi. 6). This intermediate place is one involving certain degrees of happiness or torment. Thus the wicked in Sheol are said to "recline in anguish and rest in torment," but the pain of Sheol is not to be compared with the torments that are to follow on the final judgment, for then the condemned "know that their torment has come and their perdition has arrived" (xxx. 5).

Of torment.

Of happiness.

As for the righteous, these are preserved in certain "chambers" or "treasuries" which are in Sheol (4 Ezra iv. 41),[1] where they enjoy rest and peace, and are guarded by angels (Eth. En. c. 5; 4 Ezra vii. 15): xxx. 2. "And it will come to pass at that time that the treasuries will be opened,

[1] This statement, which is based on the Latin Version of 4 Ezra, is not supported by the Syriac and Ethiopic Versions. See pp. 294, 302 *note*.

CHAP. VIII.

in which is preserved the number of the souls of the righteous, and they will come forth, and a multitude of souls will be seen together in one assemblage of one thought, and the first will rejoice and the last will not be grieved."

The resurrection.

The teaching of this writer on the resurrection is of great interest and value. Baruch is represented as asking God (xlix. 2, 3): "In what shape will those live who live in thy day? or how will the splendour of those who (are) after that time continue? 3. Will they then resume this form of the present and put on these entrammelling members, which are now involved in evils, and in which evils are consummated, or wilt thou perchance change these things (*i.e.* man's material members) which have been in the world, as also the world?" To these questions God replies: l. 1. "Hear, Baruch, this word, and write in the remembrance of thy heart all that thou shalt learn. 2. For the earth will then assuredly restore the dead, which it now receives, in order to preserve them, making no change in their form, but, as it has received, so will it restore them, and as I delivered them unto it, so also will it raise them. 3. For then it will be necessary to show to the living that the dead have come to life again, and that those who had departed have returned (again). 4. And it will come to pass, when they have severally recognised those whom they now know, then judgment will grow strong, and those things which before were spoken of will come."

"In what body do they come?"

The body will be restored in the same form in which it was committed to the earth, for the sake of common recognition.

We have here, undoubtedly, a very interesting

CHAP. VIII.

view of the resurrection. Thus the dead will rise possessing every defect and deformity they had at the moment of death. This is the earliest appearance of a doctrine which was developed to extravagant lengths in later Judaism and Christianity.[1] Thus, according to the Talmud (Sanhedrin, 90[b]), not only were the dead to be raised exactly as they were when they died, but there was to be a resurrection of the very clothes in which they were buried.

After such recognition the bodies of the righteous are to be transformed.

To return, however. When this recognition by the risen dead of each other is completed, the bodies of the righteous will be transformed, with a view to a spiritual existence of unending duration and glory (li. 3, 7-10, 12): 3. "As for the glory of those who have now been justified in my law, who have had understanding in their life, and who have planted in their heart the root of wisdom, then their splendour will be glorified in changes, and the form of their face will be turned into the light of their beauty, that they may be able to acquire and receive the world which does not die, which is then promised to them. . . . 7. But those who have been saved by their works, and to whom the law has been now a hope, and understanding an expectation, and wisdom a confidence, to them wonders will appear in their time. 8. For they will behold the world which is

[1] Jerome taught that there would be a restoration of the bones, veins, nerves, teeth, and hair, on the ground of his false translation of Job xix. 26. From the *stridor dentium* of the damned he infers the restoration of the teeth, and from the words *capilli capitis vestri numerati sunt* that of the hair. The risen, he writes, *habent dentes, ventrem, genitalia, et tamen nec cibis nec uxoribus indigent.* (*Adv. Errores Joan. Hier.* ad Pammach. *Opp.* t. ii. p. 118 *sqq.* See Hagenbach, *History of Doctrines*, ii. 91 (transl. from the German).

CHAP. VIII. now invisible to them, and they will behold the time which is now hidden from them. 9. And again time will not age them. 10. For in the heights of that world shall they dwell, and they shall be made like unto the angels, and be made equal to the stars, and they shall be changed into every form they desire, from beauty into loveliness, and from light into the splendour of glory. . . . 12. Moreover, there will then be excellency in the righteous surpassing that in the angels."

Thus we see that the Pauline teaching in 1 Cor. xv. 35-50 is in some respects a developed and more spiritual expression of ideas already current in Judaism.

B^3 = lxxxv.

In B^3, *i.e.* lxxxv., there is the same despair of a national restoration as in B^2, and only spiritual blessedness is looked for in the world of incorruption (lxxxv. 4, 5). For this world the writer urges men to prepare themselves; for here alone can such preparation be made (lxxxv. 12, 13): 12. "For lo! when the Most High will bring to pass all these things, there will not there be again an opportunity for returning, nor a limit to the times, nor adjournment to the hours, nor change of ways, nor place for prayer, nor sending of petitions, nor receiving of knowledge, nor giving of love, nor place of repentance, nor supplication for offences, nor intercession of the fathers, nor prayer of the prophets, nor help of the righteous. 13. There there is the sentence of corruption, the way of fire, and the path which bringeth to Gehenna."

CHAP. VIII.

4 *Ezra.*—From the Apocalypse of Baruch we now turn to the sister work of 4 Ezra. Though very closely related, they have nevertheless many points of divergence. Thus, whereas the former work represents faithfully the ordinary Judaism of the first century, the latter holds an isolated position, and is more closely related to Christianity than to Judaism in its teaching on the Law, on Works, Justification, Original Sin, and Freewill.[1] It was no doubt owing to its Christian elements or Christian affinities that it won and preserved a high position in the Christian Church.

4 Ezra more nearly related to Christianity than the Apocalypse of Baruch.

Like the Apocalypse of Baruch, it too is a composite work. As no satisfactory edition has as yet appeared, I will adopt *provisionally* the critical results obtained by Kabisch. Of the five independent writings which he discovers in it, two were written before the fall of Jerusalem in 70 A.D., and three subsequently. The two former he designates respectively as an Ezra Apocalypse and a Son of Man Vision.

A composite work.

(*a*) The Ezra Apocalypse consists of chaps. iv. 52–v. 13[a]; vi. 13-25, 28; vii. 26-44; viii. 63–ix. 12. Its contents are mainly eschatological. The signs of the last times are recorded in great fulness (v. 1-12[2]): "Nevertheless as concerning the tokens, behold, the days shall come, that they which dwell upon earth shall be taken with great amazement,

(*a*) The Ezra Apocalypse.

Signs of the last times.

[1] For full treatment of these questions, see the author's *Apocalypse of Baruch*, pp. lxix.-lxxi., 39, 92, 93.

[2] The following passages are taken from the Revised Version of the Apocrypha. I have introduced some emendations.

CHAP. VIII.

and the way of truth shall be hidden, and the land shall be barren of faith. 2. But iniquity shall be increased above that which now thou seest, or that thou hast heard long ago. 3. And the land, that thou seest now to have rule, shall be waste and untrodden, and men shall see it desolate. 4. But if the Most High grant thee to live, thou shalt see that which is after the third kingdom to be troubled; and the sun shall suddenly shine forth in the night, and the moon in the day: 5. And blood shall drop out of wood, and the stone shall give his voice, and the people shall be troubled; and their goings shall be changed: 6. And he shall rule, whom they that dwell upon the earth look not for, and the fowls shall take their flight away together: 7. And the sea[1] shall cast out fish, and one whom[2] many have not known will make a noise in the night: and all shall hear his voice. 8. And the earth shall be riven over wide regions and fire burst forth for a long period,[3] and the wild beasts shall change their places, and women shall bring forth monsters. 9. And salt waters shall be found in the sweet, and all friends shall destroy one another; then shall wit hide itself, and understanding withdraw itself into

Destruction of Rome foretold.

Rome ≐ the fourth kingdom.

Signs in nature.

Wisdom shall depart from the earth.

[1] Text wrongly adds "of Sodom." But the Sea of Sodom has no fish, as Wellhausen has pointed out (*Skizzen und Vorarbeiten*, vii. 246).

[2] So the text is to be emended with Wellhausen, and *quam* changed into *quem*.

[3] So the Syriac and Armenian, which found χάσμα, instead of χάος, which the Latin implies. The Ethiopic implies ἦχος = sound; the Arabic = θαῦμα, a corruption of χάσμα. It was Wellhausen who first recognised the soundness of the Syriac Version. The additional evidence now advanced of the Armenian, and indirectly of the Arabic, supports his view.

CHAP. VIII.

its chamber. 10. And it shall be sought of many, and shall not be found: and unrighteousness and incontinency shall be multiplied upon earth. 11. One land also shall ask another, and say, Is righteousness, is a man that doeth righteousness, gone through thee? And it shall say, No. 12. And it shall come to pass at that time that men shall hope, but shall not obtain: they shall labour, but their ways shall not prosper." (vi. 21, 22): "And the children of a year old shall speak with their voices, the women with child shall bring forth untimely children at three or four months, and they shall live and dance. 22. And suddenly shall the sown places appear unsown, the full storehouses shall suddenly be found empty." Then all who escape these evils will be saved (vi. 25-28): "And it shall be that whosoever remaineth after all these things that I have told thee of shall be saved, and shall see my salvation, and the end of my world. 26. And they shall see the men that have been taken up, who have not tasted death from their birth: and the heart of the inhabitants shall be changed, and turned into another meaning. 27. For evil shall be blotted out, and deceit shall be quenched. 28. And faith shall flourish, and corruption shall be overcome, and the truth, which hath been so long without fruit, shall be declared."

Further signs.

Enoch and Elijah.

Then the Messiah, the Son of God, shall be revealed, and with Him certain saints (vii. 28; cf. vi. 26). Here we seem to have the idea of a first and

Revelation of the Messiah.

CHAP. VIII.

Kingdom to last 400 years.

At its close the Messiah and all men die.

preliminary resurrection or manifestation of the saints to the temporary Messianic kingdom. This kingdom will last 400 years. The origin of this definite number is in all probability as follows. According to Gen. xv. 13, Israel was to be oppressed 400 years in Egypt. Now in Ps. xc. the writer prays: "Make us glad according to the days wherein thou hast afflicted us, and the years wherein we have seen evil." From the combination of these two passages it was inferred that the Messianic kingdom would last 400 years, as a set-off against the period of oppression in Egypt. We should compare this view with that of the 1000 years broached in the Slavonic Enoch. At the close of this 400 years the Messiah and all men will die. And the earth will return to primeval silence for seven days. Then the judgment will follow (vii. 29-33). To this judgment of the Most High all men will rise. And then the furnace of Gehenna appear, and over against it the Paradise of delight (vii. 36). Of the day of judgment we have the following peculiar account (vii. 39-43): "This is a day that hath neither sun, nor moon, nor stars, 40. Neither cloud, nor thunder, nor lightning, neither wind nor water, nor air, neither darkness, nor evening nor morning, 41. Neither summer, nor spring, nor heat, nor winter, neither frost, nor cold, nor hail, nor rain, nor dew, 42. Neither noon, nor night, nor dawn, neither shining, nor brightness, nor light save only the splendour of the glory of the Most High, whereby all shall see the things

CHAP. VIII.

that are set before them: 43. For it shall endure as it were a week of years.[1]

Son of Man Vision.

(*b*) *A Son of Man Vision.*—The second independent writing embodied in 4 Ezra, and written probably before 70 A.D., is a Son of Man Vision. It consists of chap. xiii. This vision, which is recounted in vers. 2-13, tells of a Son of Man[2] coming in the clouds of heaven and graving for Himself a great mountain and establishing Himself thereon. And against Him there musters a multitude of men without number from the four winds of heaven. And that Son of Man repels their assault, not with spear nor instrument of war, but destroys them as it were with a flood of fire out of His mouth and a flaming breath out of His lips, and thereupon they are reduced to the dust of ashes and the smell of smoke. After the annihilation of this hostile host, there came to Him another multitude, and this multitude was peaceable. And thereupon the dreamer woke and besought of God the interpretation of the vision. And his prayer is answered in the following words (xiii. 29-36): "Behold, the days come, when the Most High will begin to

1 Compare the description of the period of the last judgment in *Oracula Sibyll.* iii. 89-92:—

οὐ νύξ, οὐκ ἠώς, οὐκ ἤματα πολλὰ μερίμνης,
οὐκ ἔαρ, οὐ χειμών, οὔτ' ἂρ θέρος, οὐ μετόπωρον.
καὶ τότε δὴ μεγάλοιο θεοῦ κρίσις ἐς μέσον ἥξει
αἰῶνος μεγάλοιο, ὅτ' ἂν τάδε πάντα γένηται.

2 4 Ezra xiii. 2, 3: "I dreamed a dream by night: and, lo, there arose a wind from the sea, that it moved all the waters thereof. 3. And I beheld and, lo, (this wind made to ascend from the heart of the sea as it were the likeness of a man, and I beheld, and lo,) that man flew with the clouds of heaven." The words in brackets are supplied from the Syriac Version. They were lost in the Latin through *homoeoteleuton.*

CHAP. VIII.

Messianic woes.

deliver them that are upon the earth. 30. And there shall come astonishment of mind upon them that dwell on the earth. 31. And one shall think to war against another, city against city, place against place, people against people, and kingdom against kingdom. 32. And it shall be when these things shall come to pass, and the signs shall happen which I showed thee before, then shall my Son be revealed, whom thou sawest as a man ascending. 33. And it shall be, when all the nations hear his voice, every man shall leave his own land and the battle they have one against another. 34. And an innumerable multitude shall be gathered together, as thou sawest, desiring to come, and to fight against him. 35. But he shall stand upon the top of Mount Zion. 36. And Zion shall come and shall be showed to all men, being prepared and builded, like as thou sawest the mountain graven without hands."

Revelation of the Messiah.

Destruction of the Gentiles and the restoration of the ten tribes.

And thereupon the Messiah will destroy the assailing multitudes. And after this victory He will receive back into Zion the ten tribes who had been taken captive in the time of Hoshea. On the previous history of the ten tribes here given we cannot now touch. The Messiah will be accompanied by certain Old Testament saints (xiii. 52). This is equivalent to a partial resurrection or manifestation.

The first resurrection.

There is no limit assigned as to the duration of this Messianic kingdom, but, since there is no mention of a general resurrection and final judgment, these events were probably regarded as still in the future, and, therefore, as coming at the close of the kingdom.

We must now pass on to the eschatological expectations which appear in the three remaining constituents of this work. These writings belong to various dates between 70 and 96 A.D.

Destruction of Rome, "the fourth beast," by the Messiah.

(*c*) *The Eagle Vision* (x. 60–xii. 35).—And first of these we shall consider the Eagle Vision. Here the destruction of Rome, which is identified (xii. 11, 12) with the fourth beast[1] in Dan. vii. 7, 8, is predicted, through the agency of the Messiah sprung from the house of David (xii. 32)—so Syrian and other versions except the Latin—who will judge that nation and destroy them (xii. 33). He will save the residue of God's people in Palestine, and will fill them with joy to the end, even the day of judgment (xii. 34).

Final judgment.

(*d*) The next constituent is an *Ezra fragment*, *i.e.* xiv. 1-17[a], 18-27, 36-47, which may really be a part of the Ezra Apocalypse (*a*) already discussed. Ezra is to be translated and live with the Messiah till the times are ended (xiv. 9): "For thou shalt be taken away from men, and from henceforth thou shalt remain with my Son, and with such as be like thee, until the times be ended."

Of the twelve times into which the history of the world is divided, ten and a half have already elapsed (xiv. 11). Great woes have already befallen, but the worst are yet to come, as the world through

[1] I have on an earlier page (see p. 173) called attention to this re-interpretation of Daniel's prophecy of the fourth kingdom. The writer of Ezra implies that the interpretation in Dan. vii. 23-25 is wrong.

CHAP. VIII.

age grows weak (xiv. 16, 17). From xiv. 9, which we have quoted above, it follows that when "the times are ended" there will be a Messianic kingdom like that in the Ezra Apocalypse discussed above (*a*).

There is also the same conception of the Messiah at the base of both (cf. xiv. 9 with vii. 28). Hence this fragment may belong to that apocalypse.

Legend on the burning of the Law.

In this chapter we have the strange legend that the Law was burnt on the destruction of Jerusalem (xiv. 21), and that Ezra and five others were commissioned and endowed with spiritual powers by God to rewrite the entire Law in forty days. Thus the writer says (xiv. 42-47): "The Most High gave understanding unto the five men, and they wrote by course the things that were told them, in characters which they knew not, and they sat forty days: now they wrote in the day-time, and at night they eat bread. 43. As for me I spake in the day, and by night I held not my tongue. 44. So in forty days were written fourscore and fourteen books. 45. And it came to pass when the forty days were fulfilled, that the Most High spake unto me, saying, The first that thou hast written publish openly, and let the worthy and unworthy read it: 46. But keep the seventy last, that thou mayst deliver them to such as be wise among thy people: 47. For in them is the spring of understanding, and the fountain of wisdom, and the stream of knowledge." Of the ninety-four books referred to, twenty-four compose the Old Testament, and the remaining seventy are the non-canonical writings.

CHAP. VIII.

Apocalypse of Salathiel (?)

(*e*) The last constituent of 4 Ezra is what Kabisch, rightly or wrongly, calls the Apocalypse of Salathiel, *i.e.* iii. 1-31; iv. 1-51; v. 13[b]–vi. 10; vi. 30–vii. 25; vii. 45–viii. 62; ix. 13–x. 57; xii. 40-48; xiv. 28-35.

Only a few will be saved.

Its writer is thoroughly pessimistic. He has no hesitation in answering the question propounded in the New Testament. Salvation, he holds, is for the few. This is stated in viii. 1-3: "And he answered me, and said: The Most High hath made this world for many, but the world to come for few. 2. I will tell thee now a similitude, Esdras: As when thou askest the earth, it shall say unto thee, that it giveth very much mould whereof earthen vessels are made, and little dust that gold cometh of: even so is the course of the present world. 3. There be many created, but few shall be saved."

And elsewhere Ezra sorrowfully declares (vii. 47, 48): "And now I see, that the world to come shall bring delight to few, but torments unto many. 48. For an evil heart hath grown up in us, which hath led us astray from these statutes, and hath brought us into corruption and into the ways of death, hath showed us the paths of perdition, and removed us far from life; and that, not a few only but well-nigh all that have been created." To this God is represented as saying (vii. 51, 52): "For whereas thou hast said that the just are not many, but few, and the ungodly abound, hear the answer thereto. 52. If thou have choice stones exceeding few, wilt thou set for thee over against them according to their number things of lead and clay?"

CHAP. VIII.

God has, according to this writer, no love for man as man, but only for man as righteous. And since only a few attain to righteousness, God rejoices over these, since they "are hard to get"; but is not concerned over the innumerable hosts that perish (vii. 59-61): "And he answered me and said, Weigh within thyself the things that thou hast thought, for he that hath what is hard to get rejoiceth over him that hath what is plentiful. 60. So also is the judgment which I have promised: for I will rejoice over the few that shall be saved, inasmuch as these are they that have made my glory now to prevail, and of whom my name is now named. 61. And I will not grieve over the multitude of them that perish; for these are they that are now like unto vapour, and are become as flame and smoke; they are set on fire and burn hotly, and are quenched."

But many, according to Apocalypse of Baruch.

How different is this view as compared with that in the Apocalypse of Baruch, where it is distinctly maintained that not a few will be saved (xxi. 11). This very different attitude of these two writers towards this question springs from their respective views on the question of freewill. The latter nobly declares (liv. 15, 19): "For though Adam first sinned and brought untimely death upon all, yet of those who were born from him each one of them has prepared for his own soul torment to come, and again each one of them has chosen for himself glories to come. . . . 19. Adam is therefore not the cause, save only of his own soul, but each one of us has been the Adam of his own soul."

Every man the Adam of his own soul

CHAP. VIII.

Not so, say the Ezra writers. Man is predoomed through original sin.

On the other hand, the Ezra writers hold that man is so very far gone in original sin that his heart is wholly wicked. Adam is the source of all our woe (vii. 118): "O thou Adam, what hast thou done? for though it was thou that sinned, the evil is not fallen on thee alone, but upon all of us that come of thee."

In keeping with our writer's gloomy views of man's future is his declaration as to God's action with regard to that future. Thus he writes (vii. 70): "When the Most High made the world, and Adam and all them that came of him, he first prepared the judgment and the things that pertain unto the judgment." If we combine this statement with the fact that almost all mankind were predoomed to eternal destruction, then the object of God in creation is difficult to determine.

What can the object of creation be?

This subordination of all things to judgment, and that a judgment at once final and all but universally damnatory, makes it, we repeat, difficult to apprehend what this writer conceived God's object to be in making the world. In three different passages, indeed, he declares categorically that the world was created on account of Israel, but, since only a handful even of Israel are saved, we must conclude that, according to this writer, God regards these few as worth a whole eternity of pain on the part of all the rest of humanity.

Just as in the Gospels, so here the question is put: "When shall these things be?" Indeed it is said that the souls of the departed righteous in their chambers inquire as to the time of the coming

CHAP. VIII.

The end will come when the number of the elect is fulfilled.

end: "How long are we here?[1] When cometh the fruit of the harvest of our reward?" (iv. 35). To this the angel replied: "Even when the number is fulfilled of them that are like you." And the sins of the earth cannot delay this consummation: "Hades and (so Syriac and Ethiopic) the chambers of souls are like the womb" (iv. 41): "for like as a woman that travaileth maketh haste to escape the anguish of the travail: even so do these places haste to deliver those things that are committed unto them from the beginning" (iv. 42). But in the meantime retribution sets in immediately after death. Thus Ezra asks (vii. 75): "If I have found grace in thy sight, O Lord, shew this also unto thy servant, whether after death, even now when every one of us giveth up his soul, we shall be kept in rest until those times come, in which thou shalt renew the creation, or whether we shall be tormented forthwith." In vii. 80 it is answered that the spirits of the wicked after death "shall not enter into habitations, but shall wander and be in torments forthwith, ever grieving, and sad in seven ways" (vii. 81-87). 81. "The first way, because they have despised the law of the Most High. 82. The second way, because they cannot now make a good returning that they may live. 83. The third way, they shall see the reward laid up for them that have believed the covenants of the Most High. 84. The fourth way, they shall consider the torment laid up for themselves

Retribution sets in at death in Sheol.

The spirits of the wicked will be tormented in seven ways,

[1] So the Syriac and Ethiopic. The Latin gives: "How long shall I hope in this fashion?"

CHAP. VIII.

in the last days. 85. The fifth way, they shall see the dwelling-places of the others guarded by angels, with great quietness. 86. The sixth way, they shall see the punishment that is prepared for them from henceforth.[1] 87. The seventh way, which is more grievous than all the aforesaid ways, because they shall pine away in confusion and be consumed with shame, and shall be withered up by fears, seeing the glory of the Most High before whom they have sinned whilst living, and before whom they shall be judged in the last times." And after the final judgment they will be tormented more grievously (vii. 84). As for the souls of the righteous, they will be allowed seven days to see what will befall them (vii. 100, 101). They will be guarded by angels in habitations of health and safety (vii. 121; cf. vii. 75, 85, 95), and have joy in seven ways (vii. 91-98): "First of all they shall see with great joy the glory of him who taketh them up, for they shall have rest in seven orders. 92. The first order, because they have striven with great labour to overcome the evil thought which was fashioned together with them, that it might not lead them astray from life into death. 93. The second order, because they see the perplexity in which the souls of the ungodly wander, and the punishment that awaiteth them. 94. The third order, they see the witness which he that fashioned them beareth concerning them, that while they lived they kept the law which was

but more grievously still after the final judgment.

The righteous will have blessedness in seven ways.

[1] I have in this verse followed the Syriac Version, which is supported by the Ethiopic. The Latin is here corrupt.

CHAP. VIII.

given them in trust. 95. The fourth order, they understand the rest which, being gathered in their chambers, they now enjoy with great quietness, guarded by angels, and the glory that awaiteth them in the last days. 96. The fifth order, they rejoice, seeing how they have now escaped from that which is corruptible, and how they shall inherit that which is to come, while they see, moreover, the straightness and the painfulness from which they have been delivered, and the large room which they shall receive with joy and immortality. 97. The sixth order, when it is showed unto them how their face shall shine as the sun, and how they shall be made like unto the light of the stars, being henceforth incorruptible. 98. The seventh order, which is greater than all the aforesaid orders, because they shall rejoice with confidence, and because they shall be bold without confusion, and shall be glad without fear, for they hasten to behold the face of him whom in their lifetime they served, and from whom they shall receive their reward in glory." These chambers of the righteous souls are their intermediate abode: after the final judgment glory and transfiguration await them (vii. 95, 97.)

Intercession not permitted after final judgment.

At this judgment intercession for sinners will not be permitted (vii. 102-105). All things will then be finally determined (vii. 113-115): "The day of judgment shall be the end of this time, and the beginning of the immortality for to come, wherein corruption has passed away. 114. Intemperance is at an end, infidelity is cut off, but righteousness is grown and truth is sprung up. 115. Then shall no man be able to have mercy on him that is cast in judgment, nor to thrust down him that hath gotten the victory." It will be a new creation (vii. 75). With its establishment the righteous enter on their great reward. Then their faces will "shine as the sun," they will be bright as the stars (vii. 97), and beyond them (vii. 125). They will enjoy immortality (vii. 97).

The close affinity of this portion of 4 Ezra to one of the chief constituents in the Apocalypse of Baruch is manifest.

Book of Baruch (from various periods)

The Book of Baruch makes no contribution to our knowledge of Jewish eschatology.

This composite work has very little eschatological interest. i.–iii. 8 is undoubtedly derived from a Hebrew original, and possibly part of iii. 9–iv. 29. It is composed of at least three independent writings. As to their dates nothing satisfactory has yet been arrived at. It is noteworthy that in ii. 17 Hades still possesses its Old Testament connotation. The eschatology of the nation is the chief theme of the last chapters. The enemies of Israel will be destroyed (iv. 25, 33). Jerusalem will be restored (iv. 19-35) and the exiles brought back (iv. 36–v.): v. 5. "Arise, O Jerusalem, and stand upon the height, and look about thee toward the east, and behold thy children gathered from the going down of the sun unto the rising thereof at the word of the Holy One, rejoicing that God hath remembered them."

CHAP. VIII.

JOSEPHUS (37-101 A.D.)

The Messianic kingdom.

Josephus' interpretation of Messianic prophecy as pointing to Vespasian (*B.J.* VI. v. 4) must be set down to the exigencies of his position with regard to the Romans. For it is clear from *Ant.* IV. vi. 5 that he looked forward to a Messianic era. As the troubles predicted by Daniel had fallen to the lot of Israel, so likewise would the prosperity (*Ant.* X. xi. 7). He believed in an intermediate state for the righteous. Thus in *Ant.* XVIII. i. 3 it is said that "souls have an immortal vigour, and that under the earth (ὑπὸ χθονός, cf. *B.J.* II. viii. 14, καθ' ᾅδου) there will be rewards and punishments, according as they have lived virtuously or viciously in this life; and the latter are to be detained in an everlasting prison, but the former will have power to revive and live again." Here the wicked enter at once into everlasting punishment. Sheol is here hell. But the righteous rise from the intermediate place of happiness and enter into other bodies (*B.J.* II. viii. 14). Such was the Pharisaic doctrine according to Josephus. The Essenes believed that a blessed immortality awaited the souls of the righteous (*B.J.* II. viii. 11), but that those of the wicked were destined to a dark, cold region, full of undying torment.

Sheol the intermediate abode of the righteous, but the eternal abode of the wicked.

Only the righteous attain to the resurrection.

The Essene doctrine.

The above account of Pharisaic belief which we derive from Josephus may be regarded as fairly trustworthy; but that which he gives in *B.J.* III. viii. 5 is misleading to a high degree. There he describes the soul as a "particle of Divinity" (θεοῦ μοῖρα) which has taken up its abode in a mortal body. After death the souls of the righteous "receive as their lot the most holy place in heaven, from whence, in the revolution of ages, they are again sent into pure bodies."[1] For the souls of suicides the darkest place in Hades is reserved.

III. *Development of Special Conceptions*

The soul and spirit are regarded as identical in the non-canonical literature of this century.

Soul and Spirit.—There is hardly a trace of the teaching of Gen. ii., iii. on the soul and spirit in the Jewish literature of this century.[2] In Jubilees xxiii. 31 the departed are spoken of as "spirits." So likewise in the Assumption of Moses. See Origen, *In Jos. hom.* ii. 1. On the other hand, the Slavonic Enoch only speaks of "souls" (see xxiii. 5, lviii. 5). Again, whereas the Apocalypse of Baruch uses only the term "soul" in reference to the departed, cf. xxx. 2, 4 (li. 15), the sister work 4 Ezra uses in this reference either "soul" (vii. 75, 93, 99, 100) or "spirit," (vii. 78, 80). The Book of Wisdom, on the other hand, shows clear indications of the diction of Gen. ii., iii. Its psychology, however, is not that of Gen. ii., iii., but more nearly corresponds to the popular

[1] This view is derived from Greek philosophy. See pp. 141, 142, 146, 149.

[2] In the Book of Baruch, chaps. i.–iii. 1-8, which belong in character to the Old Testament, this teaching appears in ii. 17: "The dead that are in Hades, whose spirit is taken from their bodies." Yet in iii. 1 spirit and soul are treated as synonyms according to the popular and older view. This part of Baruch may belong to the second or first century B.C.

Even in 4 Maccabees, which is saturated with Greek philosophy, the familiar dichotomy of soul and body is the normal view of the writer (i. 20, 26, 27, 32; x. 4; xiii. 13, 14; cf. xiv. 6). As he uses also body and spirit to express the same idea, he regarded the soul and spirit as identical. See vii. 14, xii. 20.

CHAP. VIII. dichotomy of man. Thus we have the familiar dichotomy of soul and body in i. 4; viii. 19, 20; ix. 15. The soul in the next life constitutes the entire personality (iii. 1). But the writer uses the term "spirit" also, and this as synonymous with "soul," as appears from a comparison of xv. 8 and xv. 16. This identity is still clearer from xvi. 14:

> ἐξελθὸν δὲ πνεῦμα οὐκ ἀναστρέφει
> οὐδὲ ἀναλύει ψυχὴν παραλημφθεῖσαν.

These conclusions enable us to see that there is no trichotomy in xv. 11. "He was ignorant of him . . . that inspired into him an active soul (ψυχὴν ἐνεργοῦσαν) and breathed into him a vital spirit" (πνεῦμα ζωτικόν). Here, if any difference is to be found, it is in the epithets and not in the substantives. Thus though the phraseology "vital spirit" points back to Gen. ii., iii., yet its teaching is not followed. The soul is here not the result of the inbreathing of the divine breath into the body, but an independent entity synonymous with the spirit. The fact that νοῦς (= mind) is used as equivalent to spirit or soul in ix. 15 is evidence of Greek influence.

Judgment.—This century witnesses but little change in the current beliefs on this head. There is to be a preliminary judgment in all cases where a Messianic kingdom is expected, as in Jubilees, Assumption of Moses, Wisdom, and all the different constituents of the Apocalypse of Baruch and 4 Ezra, save in B^2 and B^3 of the former and the Salathiel Apocalypse of the latter. As for the final judgment,

CHAP. VIII.

The final judgment at the close of the Messianic kingdom: where there was none, at the close of the age.

it is to be executed on men and angels (Jubilees, Slavonic Enoch, and Apocalypse of Baruch). It is to take place at the close of the Messianic kingdom, or, where none is expected, either at the close of the age (Apoc. Bar. B², B³), or when the number of the righteous is completed (4 Ezra, Apocalypse of Salathiel). In Wisdom (?), Philo, 4 Maccabees, however, no such judgment is spoken of. Each soul apparently enters at death on its final destiny (see above, pp. 253, 254). In this last respect only is there a definite divergence from the beliefs of the preceding century, and this development is confined to Alexandrian Judaism.

But none such in Alexandrian Judaism.

Places of Abode of the Departed.—These are many in number, but have for the most part their roots in the past.

Heaven.

Heaven (*or Paradise*).—The final abode of the righteous (Jub. xxiii. 31; Ass. Mos. x. 9; Apoc. Bar. li.)

Paradise.—(*a*) Final abode.

Paradise.—(*a*) The final abode of the righteous (Slav. En. viii., ix., xlii. 3, 5, etc.; 4 Ezra vii. 36, 123; viii. 52.

(*b*) Intermediate abode.

(*b*) The intermediate abode of the righteous (Jubilees? see p. 249).

Hades.—(*a*) Intermediate abode of all men, with two divisions.

Sheol or *Hades*:[1] (*a*) The abode of all departed souls till the final judgment (Apoc. Bar. xxiii. 5, xlviii. 16, lii. 2; 4 Ezra iv. 41; Josephus, see above, p. 298). But Sheol thus conceived had two divisions

[1] Hades is used in its Old Testament sense as the eternal abode of souls in Baruch ii. 17. But the first three chapters of Baruch most probably belong to the second or first century B.C.

CHAP. VIII.

—a place of pain for the wicked (Apoc. Bar. xxx. 5, xxxvi. 11), and a place of rest and blessedness for the righteous (cf. 4 Ezra iv. 41).[1] This latter was called the "treasuries" or "chambers" (cf. Apoc. Bar. xxx. 2; 4 Ezra vii. 75, 85, 95).

(*b*) Final abode of the wicked.

(*b*) *Hell* (Jub. vii. 29, xxii. 22; 4 Ezra viii. 53; Josephus, see above, p. 298).

Gehenna.—This is now generally conceived as the final place of punishment for all the wicked (Ass. Mos. x. 10; 4 Ezra vii. 36). It seems to be referred to in Wisdom (cf. iv. 19) and in Slav. En. xl. 12, and described in this last work in x. and xli. 2.

(i.) Resurrec- of the righteous only.

Resurrection.—(i.) According to all the Jewish literature of this century save the Apocalypse of Baruch and 4 Ezra, there was to be a *resurrection of the righteous* only. But this resurrection was variously conceived. (*a*) The Alexandrian writers, as we might anticipate, taught only a resurrection of the soul or spirit immediately after death, as we find in Wisdom, Philo, and 4 Maccabees. The Palestinean works, Jubilees and the Assumption of Moses, postponed this resurrection of the spirit till after the final judgment. (*b*) On the other hand, the resurrection of the soul or spirit clothed in a body unlike the present (ἕτερον σῶμα) is set forth by Josephus as the doctrine of the Pharisees (*B.J.* II. viii. 14), or, according to the Slavonic Enoch, clothed in the glory of God. (ii.) But besides this spiritual doctrine of the

(*a*) Without a body.

(*b*) In a spiritual body.

(ii.) Resurrection of all mankind.

[1] That is, according to the Latin Version: *in inferno promptuaria.* But the Syriac and Ethiopic = *infernum et promptuaria.*

resurrection, this century attests also that of a general resurrection—not merely a general resurrection, the resurrection of all Israel, as in the preceding two centuries, but a resurrection of all mankind, good and bad, Jew and Gentile alike. This form of the doctrine is first found in B² of the Apocalypse of Baruch xxx. 2-5, l., li.; and the Ezra Apocalypse of Ezra vii. 32-37. (iii.) But the history of the various forms this doctrine assumed is not yet fully enumerated. The consciousness that the resurrection is a privilege of the faithful is not wholly lost, even to those who have made it the common lot of all men. Hence, at all events, in 4 Ezra vii. 28 (cp. xiv. 9), and xiii. 52, in both of which sections a Messiah is expected, the idea of a *first resurrection*—resurrection of special Old Testament heroes—is evolved. These accompany the Messiah when He comes to reign on earth.

(iii.) The First Resurrection.

Messianic Kingdom.—See general historical development in the first century A.D. (see pp. 242-244).

Messiah.—We remarked above that from the middle of the first century B.C. the expectation of the Messiah took such a firm hold of the national consciousness that henceforth the Messiah becomes almost universally the central figure in the Messianic kingdom. This conclusion does not seem capable of justification from the books we have above dealt with, for of these only five express this hope. But the explanation is not far to seek. Against the combination of the Messiah-hope with the national aspirations for an earthly kingdom, advocated, as

CHAP. VIII.

Varying attitude towards the expectation of the Messiah.

we have already seen, by the Psalms of Solomon, a strong body of Pharisees raised an emphatic protest. These, according to the ideal of the ancient Chasids, were Quietists. Their duty was to observe the law; it was for God to intervene and defend them. This standpoint is represented by the Assumption of Moses, and later by the Salathiel Apocalypse in 4 Ezra. Among the Jews of the Dispersion likewise this view naturally gained large acceptance. Hence we find no hint of it in the Slavonic Enoch, the Book of Wisdom, and 4 Maccabees. But this opposition from the severely legal wing of Pharisaism to the Messiah-hope at length gave way, and in Apoc. Bar. liii.-lxxiv., *i.e.* A^3, we have literary evidence of the fusion of early Rabbinism and the popular Messianic expectation.

Expectation all but universal in Palestine.

How widespread was the hope of the Messiah in the first century of the Christian era may be seen not only from Jubilees (?), Philo, Josephus, and the various independent writings in the Apocalypse of Baruch and 4 Ezra, but also from the New Testament and the notice taken of this expectation in Tacitus, *Hist.* v. 13, and Suetonius, *Vesp.* c. 4.

Messiah's reign to be of temporary duration.

Since in all cases only a transitory Messianic kingdom is expected in this century, the Messiah's reign is naturally conceived as likewise transitory.

Messiah to be of the tribe of Judah.

The Messiah is to be of the tribe of Judah (Jub. xxxi. 18, 19; 4 Ezra xii. 32). He is to play a passive part (Apoc. Bar. xxvii.–xxx. 1; 4 Ezra vii. 28, *i.e.* Ezra Apocalypse; see above, p. 285). In the former passage He is to appear at the close of the

Messianic woes; in the latter simultaneously with the first resurrection. But more usually He is regarded as an active warrior who slays His enemies with His own hand (Apoc. Bar. xxxvi.-xl., liii.-lxx.; 4 Ezra x. 60–xii. 35), while others again conceive Him more loftily as one who slays His enemies by the word of His mouth (4 Ezra xiii. 10; cf. Pss. Sol. xvii.).

Sheol or Gehenna the final destination of the Gentiles.

Gentiles.—In most works written before the fall of Jerusalem only the hostile nations are destroyed (cf. Apoc. Bar. xl. 1, 2; lxxii. 4-6), but in later works, as 4 Ezra xiii., all are to be annihilated. In no case have they any hope of a future life. They either descend into Sheol, which thenceforth becomes their eternal abiding-place, or else into Gehenna; but if in any instance they are regarded as having part in the resurrection, it is only that they may be committed to severer and never-ending torment 4 Ezra vii. 36-38).

BIBLIOGRAPHY.—The bulk of the preceding four chapters is mainly based on various books edited by the present writer and referred to in the text. In addition to these and others there cited the reader can consult Lücke, *Einleitung in die Offenbarung des Johannes*, 1852; Hilgenfeld, *Jüdische Apocalyptik*, 1857; Langen, *Das Judenthum in Palästina*, 1866; Drummond, *The Jewish Messiah*, 1877; Hausrath, *NTliche Zeitgeschichte*, 1875-1877; Stanton, *The Jewish and Christian Messiah*, 1886; Baldensperger, *Das Selbstbewusstsein Jesu*, 1888; Deane, *Pseudepigrapha*, 1891; Thomson, *Books that influenced our Lord*, 1891; Schwally, *Das Leben nach dem Tode*, 1892; Briggs, *The Messiah of the Gospels*, pp. 1-40, 1894; *Messiah of the Apostles*, pp. 1-20, 1895; Salmond, *Christian Doctrine of Immortality*, 1896; Marti, *Geschichte der Israelitischen Religion*, pp. 270-310, 1897: Schurer,[3] *Geschichte des Jüdischen Volkes*, vols. ii. and iii., 1898; Art. "Eschatology," by the present writer, in Hastings' *Bible Dictionary*, I. 741-749, 1898; also Art. "Eschatology" in the *Encyclopædia Biblica*.

CHAPTER IX

ESCHATOLOGY OF THE NEW TESTAMENT

General Introduction—The Synoptic Gospels

Incorporation of all the noblest ideas and forces of the past in the spiritual kingdom of Christ, membership of which is constituted by personal relation to its Head.

WHEN we pass from Jewish literature to that of the New Testament, we find ourselves in an absolutely new atmosphere. It is not that we have to do with a wholly new world of ideas and moral forces, for all that was great and inspiring in the past has come over into the present and claimed its part in the formation of the Christian Church. But in the process of incorporation this heritage from the past has been of necessity largely transformed; it no longer constitutes a heterogeneous mass of ideas in constant flux—a flux in which the less worthy, quite as frequently as the more noble, is in the ascendant, and in which each idea in turn makes its individual appeal for acceptance, and generating its little system, enjoys in turn its little day. When received, however, within the sphere of the cosmos of Christian life and thought, all these forces and ideas gradually fall into their due subordination to its centre, and contribute harmoniously to the purpose of the whole. For the Messiah now assumes a position undreamt of in the past, and membership of the kingdom is constituted, firstly and predominatingly, through personal relationship to its divine Head.

Synthesis of the hopes of the individual, and of the race, in Christianity.

In the next place, we have to remember that in the teaching of Christ and of Christianity the synthesis of the eschatologies of the race and of the individual has at last been fully and finally achieved. We saw how Ezekiel, by a doctrine of the individual, partly true, partly false, sought in some fashion to effect a synthesis of the hopes of the individual and of the nation within the sphere of this life, but naturally without success. We saw, further, how the individual, uplifted by the certainty of personal communion with the living God, came at last to formulate as the axiom of his spiritual experience the doctrine of a blessed immortality. God rules, he felt assured, not only in this life, but in the next; and for the man who walks with God here, there can be no unblessed existence in the hereafter. But this great truth was as yet but imperfectly apprehended. It seemed as though it were the reward which the righteous individual won by himself, and for himself, irrespectively of his brethren, and thus in this regard it was a triumph of individualism in the sphere of the highest religion as yet realised on earth. But this imperfect conception could not long maintain itself amongst a people whose hopes were fixed on a national blessedness,

Past attempts at forming this synthesis in Ezekiel.

Rise of the doctrine of an individual immortality.

But the doctrine in this form could not be final, ignoring as it did the national hope of the kingdom.

CHAP. IX.

First synthesis of the two resulting in the doctrine of the resurrection towards close of fourth century.

on that coming kingdom which should embrace all that were fit and worthy in Israel. Hence but a short time elapsed before the hope of the righteous individual and the hope of the righteous nation were combined in one, and thus emerged the doctrine of the resurrection, as we find in the books of Isaiah, Daniel, and Enoch, which taught that the righteous nation of Israel and the righteous individual—alike the quick and the dead—would be recompensed to the full in the *eternal* Messianic kingdom *on earth.* But the synthesis thus established as early as the fourth century B.C. hardly outlived the second, and the expectations of the individual and of the nation again took divergent paths; for the earth had at last come to be regarded as wholly unfit for the manifestation of the *eternal* kingdom of God, and to such a kingdom and none other could the hopes of the righteous individual be directed. The Messianic kingdom was still expected, but one only of temporary duration. Henceforth not the Messianic kingdom, but heaven itself or paradise became the goal of the hopes of the faithful in death. In this severance of the hopes of the individual and the nation true religion suffered, and individualism gained an illegitimate and regulative authority in matters of religion.

Its resolution into its original factors about 100 B.C., when the hope of an eternal Messianic kingdom was abandoned.

Their final synthesis in Christianity.

By the Founder of Christianity, however, the synthesis of the two hopes was established in a universal form finally and for ever. The true Messianic kingdom begins on earth, and will be consummated in heaven; it is not temporary,[1] but eternal; it is not limited to one people, but embraces the righteous of all nations and of all times. It forms a divine society in which the position and significance of each member is determined by his endowments, and his blessedness conditioned by the blessedness of the whole. Thus religious individualism becomes an impossibility. On the one hand, it is true the individual can have no part in the kingdom save through a living relation to its Head;[2] yet, on the other, this relation cannot be maintained and developed save through life in and for the brethren; and so closely is the individual life bound to that of the brethren, that no soul can reach its consummation apart.

Transformation of the past gradual. Presence of Judaistic elements in New Testament.

We have above referred to the incorporation of a large body of Jewish ideas in the system of Christian thought, and their subsequent transformation in the process. It would, however, be a serious error to assume that all ideas that were incorporated from Jewish sources by all the New Testament writers underwent an immediate and complete, or even a partial, transformation.

Parallel phenomena in Old Testament and subsequent Jewish history.

In the course of the preceding chapters we have, I hope, recognised that at all periods of the history of Israel there existed side by side in its religion

[1] It is temporary, according to 1 Cor. xv. 24-28, but not according to the later teaching of St. Paul. St. Paul's earlier epistles imply an eschatology that is in certain respects Judaistic. These Judaistic doctrines are gradually abandoned in his later epistles. See Chapter XI.

[2] This relation need not be a conscious one. All that have done good for the sake of goodness without any ulterior motive have, in reality, shown themselves to be true disciples of Christ, though they may not have known Him (Matt. xxv. 37-40).

CHAP. IX.

incongruous and inconsistent elements. Thus in every period we have, on the one side, the doctrine of God ever advancing in depth and fulness; on the other, we have eschatological and other survivals which, however justifiable in earlier stages, are in unmistakable antagonism with the theistic beliefs of their time. The eschatology of a nation is always the last part of their religion to experience the transforming power of new ideas and new facts.

The recognition of such phenomena in the religion of the past teaches us to expect the occurrence of imilar phenomena in the New Testament.

The recognition of these facts is of primary importance when we deal with New Testament eschatology. In the first place, we shall not be surprised if the eschatology of the latter should, to some extent, present similar incongruous phenomena as the Old Testament and subsequent Jewish literature. And, in the next, we shall be prepared to deal honestly with any such inconsistencies. So far, therefore, from attempting, as in the past, to explain them away or to bring them into harmony with doctrines that in reality make their acceptance impossible, we shall frankly acknowledge their existence, and assign to them their full historical value. That their existence, however, in the New Testament Canon can give them no claim on the acceptance of the Church, follows from their inherent discordance with the Christian fundamental doctrines of God and Christ; for such discordance condemns them as survivals of an earlier and lower stage of religious belief.

Such survivals have no claim on the acceptance of the Church.

That certain Judaistic conceptions of a mechanical

and unethical character have passed into the New Testament must be recognised. But since these possess no organic relation to the fundamental doctrines of Christ, and indeed at times betray a character wholly irreconcilable therewith, they have naturally no true *rationale* in Christianity. In Christianity there is a survival of alien Judaistic elements, just as in the Hebrew religion there were for centuries large survivals of Semitic heathenism. That Judaism should cherish many beliefs of a mechanical or even unethical character ought not to be surprising, seeing that it was false to the fundamental doctrine of monotheism, of which, nevertheless, it claimed to be the true exponent; for if monotheism were true, then Judaistic particularism was false, and God was the God and Saviour of the Gentile also. As an instance of such survivals we may adduce the generally accepted doctrine of Hades, which is truly Judaistic. Just as the Hebrew view of Sheol, which was essentially heathen, gave way to the Judaistic view, which was partially moral, so this in turn must yield to the fully moralised and Christian conception of Hades as a place not of mechanical fixity of character, but of moral movement and progress in the direction either of light or darkness (see pp. 343, 344, 378). The doctrine of eternal damnation also is a Judaistic survival of a still more grossly immoral character. We shall do no more here than point out that this doctrine originated in Judaism when monotheism had become a lifeless

Such a survival is the popular doctrine of Hades,

also that of an eternal hell.

dogma, and Jewish particularism reigned supreme, and when a handful of the pious could not only comfortably believe that God was the God of the Jew alone, and only of a very few of these, but also could imagine that part of their highest bliss in the next world would consist in witnessing the torment of the damned.

Co-existence of various stages of development in the New Testament.

Furthermore, from the history of eschatological thought in the past we shall likewise be prepared to find not only isolated religious survivals of that past in the New Testament, but also the co-existence within it of various stages of development. The New Testament writers have assimilated in various degrees, according to their spiritual intuition, the fundamental teaching of Christ, and in various degrees have applied this to the body of eschatological doctrine which they had brought with them from Judaism. That some ideas morally irreconcilable should exist in the same writer is easily conceivable. For a time the heritage of the past and the revelation of the present could *in some degree* exist side by side. The transformation of the former by the latter in matters of *theoretical* and not of *practical* importance must naturally be a work of time. In the Pauline Epistles we have a very instructive instance of this slow and progressive transformation, during which the great apostle passes from an eschatological standpoint largely Judaistic to one essentially Christian.

We shall now proceed to study the fundamental teaching of Christ as set forth in the Synoptic

Gospels. Seeing that the remaining books of the New Testament present various stages of eschatological development, we shall deal with them in the order which will best bring this fact to light.

Finally, we shall discover in the New Testament the existence of large fragments of Jewish apocalypses wholly unassimilated by Christian thought. These are found for the most part in Revelation. A small Jewish apocalypse is probably also to be recognised in Mark xiii., and another in 2 Thess. ii.

I. Synoptic Gospels.—These give the fundamental teaching of Christ, but leave in doubt some minor points of His eschatological doctrine.

Revelation.—This book presents Judaistic and Christian elements side by side. Its Millenarian doctrine has never been accepted by the Christian Church.

Jude and 2 Peter.

James.

Hebrews.

The Johannine Eschatology.

The Petrine Eschatology.

The Pauline Eschatology.

II. Development of special conceptions.

CHAP. IX.

The Synoptic Gospels

The eschatology of the Synoptic Gospels deals with the consummation of the kingdom of God which is there set forth. This kingdom is likewise called the kingdom of heaven in the first Gospel.[1]

The kingdom of heaven.

This designation fittingly describes its character in opposition to the worldly and political expectations of the Jews. It was essentially *the community in which the divine will was to be realised*[2] on earth as it is already in heaven, and into which the individual could enter only by abjuring all self-seeking individualism. In this aspect the kingdom appears as the common good of man.

Its meaning.

The kingdom = the common good.

Further, the divine will has for its end the salvation of man. Hence the kingdom presents itself as the highest good attainable in the parables of the Hid Treasure and the Goodly Pearl. As such it embraces all goods, and first and chiefly life (Matt. vi. 33 = Luke xii. 31; Mark viii. 36, 37), that is, eternal life (Mark x. 17, 30 = Matt. xix. 16). Eternal life *which cannot be enjoyed apart from the kingdom* is the most comprehensive expression for the blessings of the kingdom. Hence occasionally they seem to be interchangeable terms. Thus "to have life" (Matt. xix. 16), "to inherit life" (Mark x. 17), and "to enter into life" (Mark ix. 43-45 = Matt. xviii. 8, 9) are synonymous with "to inherit the

[1] See Schwartzkopff, *The Prophecies of Jesus Christ*, 210, 211. Sanday, Art. "Jesus Christ" in Hastings' *Bible Dict.* ii. 619. Both expressions are probably original.

[2] See pp. 82, 83 for a discussion of this meaning. See also pp. 129-131.

kingdom" (Matt. xxv. 34), and "to enter into the kingdom" (Mark ix. 47; Luke xviii. 24 = Matt. xviii. 3). There is, however, this distinction that life is the good of the individual, but the kingdom that of the community.[1] By entering into life the individual enters into the kingdom. We have thus the perfect synthesis of the hopes of the individual and of the divine community in Christ's kingdom of God.

Life = the good of the individual.

But the kingdom of God presents two divergent aspects. It is represented now as present, now as future; now as inward and spiritual, now as external and manifest. Since some have sought to controvert the former view of this kingdom, and some the latter as existing in the Gospels, we must here examine the evidence, but as briefly as possible.

This kingdom variously represented.

First, then, as to the actual presence of the kingdom.

Already present.

Christ's conception of the kingdom as already present belongs to the beginning of His ministry. Thus when the Baptist sent his disciples to Christ, and said (Matt. xi. 3), "Art thou he that should come, or are we to look for another?" Jesus answered (Matt. xi. 4-6), "Go your way and tell John the things which ye do hear and see. 5. The blind receive their sight, and the lame walk, the lepers are cleansed, and the deaf hear, and the dead are raised up, and the poor have good tidings

[1] The entrance into life may also be designated a spiritual resurrection. See above, pp. 128-131; see also pp. 78-80. Man can only enter into the kingdom by losing his life, *i.e.* dying to the old life and rising to the new.

CHAP. IX. preached to them. 6. And blessed is he, whosoever shall find none occasion of stumbling in me."

By the works thus enumerated the Baptist is to recognise that the kingdom has come. The same conclusion follows from the text of Christ's sermon in the synagogue of Nazareth, and especially from His comment thereon (Luke iv. 18, 19):—

> The Spirit of the Lord is upon me,
> Because he anointed me to preach good tidings to the poor:
> He hath sent me to proclaim release to the captives,
> And recovering of sight to the blind,
> To set at liberty them that are bruised.
> 19. To proclaim the acceptable year of the Lord.

The comment is given in iv. 21: "To-day hath this scripture been fulfilled in your ears." In other words, the kingdom is already present, and He that fulfils it is already before them. Again, the same truth is attested in the earliest teaching ascribed to Christ by St. Mark (Mark i. 15): "The time is fulfilled, and the kingdom of heaven is at hand; repent ye, and believe the gospel."

As further evidence in the same direction should be cited Matt. xii. 28 (= Luke xi. 20): "But if I by the Spirit of God cast out devils, then is the kingdom of God come upon you." The kingdom, therefore, has already dawned, nay more, as Christ elsewhere declares to the Pharisees, "The kingdom of God is in your midst" (Luke xvii. 21).

Again, the fact that the kingdom is already present is presupposed by many of the parables. Thus in the parables of the Mustard Seed and of the Leaven the kingdom is represented as spreading intensively and extensively. It is thus obviously conceived as present. The same presupposition underlies the parables of the Tares and of the Draught of Fishes; also that of the slowly growing seed in Mark iv. 26-29. "And he said, So is the kingdom of God, as if a man should cast seed upon the earth. 27. And should sleep and rise night and day, and the seed should spring up and grow, he knoweth not how. 28. The earth beareth fruit of herself; first the blade, then the ear, then the full corn in the ear. 29. But when the fruit is ripe, straightway he putteth forth the sickle, because the harvest is come."

The emphasis in the last lies on the gradual growth of the seed, which requires time to mature. The kingdom of God, once planted, gradually but surely will attain to its consummation by its divine indwelling powers. To this question of development we shall return later.

That the kingdom is present in some form follows likewise from Matt. vi. 33: "But seek ye first his kingdom, and his righteousness; and all these things shall be added unto you." vii. 13, 14: "Enter ye in by the narrow gate: for wide is the gate, and broad is the way, that leadeth to destruction, and many be they that enter in thereby. 14. For narrow is the gate, and straitened the way, that leadeth unto life, and few be they that find it." We have already seen that in some aspects "life" and the kingdom are synonymous (Matt. xi. 11, 12):

CHAP. IX.

"Verily I say unto you, Among them that are born of women there hath not arisen a greater than John the Baptist: yet he that is but little in the kingdom of heaven is greater than he. 12. And from the days of John the Baptist until now the kingdom of heaven suffereth violence, and the men of violence take it by force" (= Luke vii. 28, xvi. 16). Thus certain men are said to be already in the kingdom, and this comes out still more clearly in Matt. xxi. 31: "Whether of the twain did the will of his father? They say, The first. Jesus saith unto them, Verily I say unto you, that the publicans and the harlots go into the kingdom of God before you." And in xxiii. 13: "But woe unto you, scribes and Pharisees, hypocrites! because ye shut the kingdom of heaven against men: for ye enter not in yourselves, neither suffer ye them that are entering in to enter."

Elsewhere we remember a certain scribe is declared to be not far from the kingdom of heaven (Mark xii. 34), and that "No man, having put his hand to the plough, and looking back, is fit for the kingdom of God" (Luke ix. 62).

Kingdom already present in its essence.

From the above evidence we may beyond all reasonable doubt conclude that the kingdom of heaven was in some form conceived to be actually present.

Yet still future as regards its realisation.

On the other hand, as the kingdom, according to Jesus' conception of it, could only be truly realised in its completed form, in this sense the kingdom is still conceived as in the future.

But this future may be conceived in two aspects:

either as one brought about in the course of development according to the ordinary laws of spiritual growth. Possibly Matt. vi. 10: "Thy kingdom come. Thy will be done, as in heaven, so on earth," may be interpreted in this way.

This future to be brought about gradually in the course of development.

But the future kingdom is almost universally regarded in the Synoptic Gospels as introduced eschatologically by God Himself. It is to this kingdom that reference is made (Matt. xxvi. 29): "But I say unto you, I will not drink henceforth of this fruit of the vine, until that day when I drink it new with you in my father's kingdom." In Mark ix. 1: "And he said unto them, Verily I say unto you, There be some here of them that stand by, which shall in no wise taste of death, till they see the kingdom of God come with power" (= Luke ix. 27). Likewise in Luke xiii. 28, 29: "There shall be the weeping and gnashing of teeth, when ye shall see Abraham, and Isaac, and Jacob, and all the prophets, in the kingdom of God, and yourselves cast forth without. 29. And they shall come from the east and west, and from the north and south, and shall sit down in the kingdom of God" (= cf. Matt. viii. 11); and in Luke xiv. 15: "And when one of them that sat at meat with him heard these things, he said unto him, Blessed is he that shall eat bread in the kingdom of God." In these passages the kingdom is expressly conceived as future and still to be realised. This future kingdom is contrasted with the present in Mark ix. 1, for its advent is to be "with power."

Or suddenly established by God Himself.

Having now recognised the existence of these

CHAP. IX.

Relations of these two conceptions to each other. Their chronological relation.

two conceptions of the kingdom as already present and as still future in the Synoptics, we have next to inquire their relations, chronological and otherwise. As regards the former there cannot be any reasonable doubt that the conception of the kingdom as already present is the earlier. With the Messiah came simultaneously the Messianic kingdom or the kingdom of God. Such is clearly the teaching of the Gospels, and such, in fact, had been the universal expectation of the Jews in the past. So far, therefore, both expectation and fulfilment were in harmony. The harmony, however, was only superficial. The inward and spiritual character of the kingdom established by Christ was at absolute variance with the outward and materially glorious kingdom hoped for by the Jews.

According to all the past the kingdom comes with the Messiah. This is also the teaching of the Gospels.

Christ preached the kingdom as already present from the outset,

To return, however, to the chronological relations of the present and the future kingdom, we have already seen that Christ spoke of the kingdom as present from the outset. The kingdom of God had essentially in His person already become a present kingdom on earth.

At the outset of His ministry he had, we can hardly doubt, hoped to witness the consummation of this kingdom without passing through the gates of death. But the accomplishment of His task was dependent on the conduct of the people. In the earlier days when His preaching was received with enthusiasm and the nation seemed to be pressing into the kingdom of God, His teaching dwells mainly on the present kingdom of God on earth.

The possibility, therefore, of its consummation through a natural development seemed a natural expectation.

but when His death appeared inevitable, He began to speak of it also as future.

But when the temper of the people changed and His rejection and death appeared as an inexorable necessity, He began to speak of the future kingdom. He never relinquished, indeed, the thought of the present kingdom, but whilst holding it fast, He saw that, if it were ultimately to prevail, it must receive its consummation in the future by the direct intervention of God, or rather by His own return to judge the world.

Organic relation of these two conceptions.

In this way, then, the two conceptions of the kingdom appear to be related chronologically. That they are also organically connected is obvious. Thus both views of the kingdom are put forward in one and the same statement by Christ in Mark x. 15: "Verily I say unto you, Whosoever shall not receive the kingdom of God as a little child, he shall in no wise enter therein" (= Luke xviii. 17; cf. Matt. xviii. 3, 4). These words declare that entrance into the future kingdom of God is dependent on a man's right attitude to the present kingdom of God. In the course of a truly ethical development the latter becomes the parent of the former, and the kingdom of heaven, now founded spiritually in weakness and in secret, will, through the infinite toil of God and man, issue in the completed kingdom of God, which is the perfect expression of the divine goodness and truth, having for its scene a new heaven and a new earth.

CHAP. IX.

We are thus introduced to the eschatological side of Christ's teaching of the kingdom. We have now to deal with the various events which will usher in this kingdom. These are, (*a*) The Parusia, or Second Advent, (*b*) The Final Judgment, (*c*) The Resurrection and the consummation of all things.

Parusia or Second Advent

(*a*) *The Parusia, or Second Advent.*—As the kingdom of God owed its foundation to the divine mission of the Messiah, so also it will owe to Him its consummation. The prophecy of His second coming appears in connection with His first mention of His approaching death. Having foretold His death in Mark viii. 31, He speaks of His return in viii. 38 (Mark viii. 31): "And he began to teach them that the Son of man must suffer many things, and be rejected by the elders, and the chief priests, and the scribes, and be killed, and after three days rise again. . . . 38. For whosoever shall be ashamed of me and of my words in this adulterous and sinful generation, the Son of man also shall be ashamed of him when he cometh in the glory of his Father with the holy angels" (= Matt. xvi. 27 = Luke ix. 26). This coming will take place at the close of the age (*συντέλεια τοῦ αἰῶνος*), (Matt. xiii. 39, 40, 49; xxiv. 3; xxviii. 20).

first foretold in connection with His approaching death.

In regard, however, to the *manner* and *time* of the second Advent the Gospels present us with two somewhat conflicting accounts, which we shall discuss in turn.

Manner of the Advent. Conflicting accounts.

First as regards the *manner*. If the present text of the Gospels is trustworthy, we have two mutually exclusive accounts. On the one hand the Advent will take the world by surprise. This expectation is inculcated in the parable of the Waiting Servants (Mark xiii. 33-36; Matt. xxiv. 42-44; Luke xii. 35-40), which concludes with the words (Mark xiii. 35-37): "Watch therefore: for ye know not when the lord of the house cometh, whether at even, or at midnight, or at cock-crowing, or in the morning; 36. Lest coming suddenly he find you sleeping. 37. And what I say unto you I say unto all, Watch."

(i.) It was to take the world by surprise.

Also in the parable of the Ten Virgins (Matt. xxv. 1-12), which closes with the admonition, "Watch therefore, for ye know not the day nor the hour"; and in the eschatological account of the days of Noah and Lot (Matt. xxiv. 37-41 = Luke xvii. 26-36). This doctrine of His return at an unlooked-for hour goes back undoubtedly to Christ. It belongs to the various contexts in which it occurs, and it forms the motive of several of the undisputed parables.

(ii.) It was to be heralded by unmistakable signs.

This view irreconcilable with the former, and therefore suspicious.

Since this conclusion may be taken as beyond the range of doubt, we must regard with suspicion the conflicting view which is given in Mark xiii. (= Matt. xxiv. = Luke xxi.), according to which the second Advent is to be heralded by a succession of signs which are unmistakable precursors of its appearance, such as wars, and earthquakes, and famines, the destruction of Jerusalem, and the like.

The source of this view (Mark xiii.) suspicious in itself.

And this suspicion is justified when we proceed to examine St. Mark xiii.; for it presents a very composite appearance. Thus (*a*) in ver. 29: "When

CHAP. IX.

ye see these things come to pass, know ye that it is nigh, even at the doors," the expression "these things" can only denote the signs which announce the parusia, and not the parusia itself, whereas its position in the text requires us to refer it to the actual parusia and the events accompanying it, and not to the signs which precede it. In the next verse (ver. 30) the same expression "these things" rightly refers to the parusia, and not to the signs of it. (*b*) In the next place the term "end" has an eschatological meaning in ver. 7, but its ordinary meaning in ver. 13. (*c*) Again, in ver. 30 it is declared with all emphasis that this generation shall not pass away till all these things be fulfilled, whereas two verses later we have an undoubtedly original declaration of Christ in essential contradiction with it: "Of that day or of that hour knoweth no one, not even the angels in heaven, neither the Son, but the Father." (*d*) The words "let him that *readeth* understand" indicate that this prediction appeared first not in a spoken address but in a written form.

Two independent series of sayings worked up in Mark xiii.

But these considerations when followed up only lead to the recognition of still wider divergencies in thought and statement within this chapter. Thus it appears that there are two originally independent series of sayings worked together by the Evangelist in this chapter. Whether both these series of sayings are to be traced back to Christ we shall inquire presently.

Of these two one deals with the persecutions

CHAP. IX.

which will befall the disciples of Christ in reference to their faith at the hands of the Jews. From such persecutions no promise of deliverance is given. They are to endure them unto the end (ver. 13), even unto death (ver. 12); only so can they attain unto salvation.

One series aims at strengthening the faith of the disciples amid persecution, and promises spiritual salvation to the faithful despite bodily death.

But the thoughts and purpose of the other series of sayings in this chapter are absolutely different. The woes predicted here have no relation to the disciples or their faith. They consist of wars and famines and convulsions of nature. The prediction of the chief calamity, namely, the destruction of Jerusalem, has only an indirect reference to the Christians in so far as it secures them from personal participation in its fall. Further, it is declared that on account of the elect God will shorten these days, else should no flesh be saved. Thus whereas in the former source only security against spiritual destruction is promised, in the latter protection against temporal disaster is assured. And whereas faithfulness unto the death of the body is required from the disciples in the one source, in the other they are exhorted to pray that the attack on Jerusalem, which is the beginning of the end, may not be in the winter, lest they should suffer bodily discomfort from the cold!

The other consists of a series of woes having no direct relation to the disciples. In predicting the destruction of Jerusalem it aims at securing men against bodily death.

These and other considerations therefore call for the removal of vers. 7, 8, 14-20, 24-27, 30, 31 from their present context. By this removal harmony is restored to the text, and the passages so removed constitute a very short though complete

The removal of the latter passages restores harmony to the text, which constitute in themselves an

CHAP. IX.

independent apocalypse in three Acts.

apocalypse, with its three essential acts, namely, Act i., consisting of verses 7, 8, which enumerate the woes heralding the parusia :—

Act i. = The travail pains of the Messiah.

7. "And when ye shall hear of wars and rumours of wars,[1] be not troubled: these things must needs come to pass; but the end is not yet. 8. For nation shall rise against nation, and kingdom against kingdom[2]: there shall be earthquakes[3] in divers places; there shall be famines:[4] these things are the beginning of travail." Act ii., verses 14-20, which describe the actual tribulation or θλῖψις: 14. "But when ye see the abomination of desolation standing[5] where it ought not (let him that readeth understand), then let them that are in Judæa flee unto the mountains: 15. And let him that is on the housetop not go down, nor enter in, to take anything out of his house: 16. And let him that is in the field not return back to take his cloke. 17. But woe to them that are with child and to them that give suck in those days! 18. And pray ye

Act ii. = The actual tribulation.

[1] According to Jewish Apocalyptic, wars were to precede the advent of the Messiah or of the kingdom. These were part of the travail pains of the Messiah (חֶבְלֵי הַמָּשִׁיחַ—an expression derived ultimately from Hos. xiii. 13). See Jub. xxiii. 13 *sqq.* (quoted above on p. 247), (Apoc. Bar. xxvii. 2-5; xlviii. 32, 34, 37; lxx. 2, 3, 6, 7; 4 Ezra v. 9; vi. 24).

[2] Universal and civil wars were to be a sign of the end (Apoc. Bar. xlviii. 32; lxx. 2, 3, 8).

[3] Earthquakes, according to the popular expectation, were to precede the end (Apoc. Bar. xxvii. 7; lxx. 8; 4 Ezra ix. 3).

[4] Famines were to be a sign of the last times (Apoc. Bar. xxvii. 6; lxx. 8; cf. 4 Ezra vi. 22.

[5] The phrase "abomination of desolation," owing to its use in Dan. ix. 27, xi. 31, xii. 11, had probably become proverbial. It occurs in 1 Macc. i. 54, and is implied in vi. 7, where it refers to the altar set up by Antiochus to Olympian Zeus in the place of the altar of burnt offering. This phrase in the original apocalypse referred probably to the apprehension of a similar outrage at the hands of the Romans.

CHAP. IX.

that it be not in the winter. 19. For those days shall be tribulation, such as there hath not been the like from the beginning of the creation which God created until now,[1] and never shall be. 20. And except the Lord had shortened the days, no flesh would have been saved: but for the elect's sake, whom he chose, he shortened the days."[2]

Act iii. = The parusia.

Act iii., verses 24-27, describing the actual parusia: "But in those days, after that tribulation, the sun shall be darkened, and the moon shall not give her light, 25. and the stars shall be falling from heaven, and the powers that are in the heavens shall be shaken.[3] 26. And then shall they see the Son of man[4] coming in clouds with great power and glory. 27. And then shall he send forth the angels, and they shall gather together his elect

[1] "Tribulation such as there hath not been," etc. This is a stock eschatological expression. It is first found in Dan. xii. 1; then in 1 Macc. ix. 27; next in Ass. Mos. viii. 1, and subsequently in Rev. xvi. 18.

[2] This idea of the shortening of the days is found in Jewish apocalypses. Thus in Apoc. Bar. lxxxiii. 1-4: "The Most High will assuredly hasten his times, and he will assuredly bring on his hours. And he will assuredly judge those," etc. Cf. xx. 1; liv. 1; 4 Ezra iv. 26. Further, that Mark xiii. 20 reproduces a current tradition has been shown by Bousset (*The Antichrist Legend*, 218, 219). The shortened period is three and a half years (= the half-week of years in Daniel?). Cf. the Pseudo-Johannine Apocalypse, 8, τρία ἔτη ἔσονται οἱ καιροὶ ἐκεῖνοι, καὶ ποιήσω τὰ τρία ἔτη ὡς τρεῖς μῆνας καὶ τοὺς τρεῖς μῆνας ὡς τρεῖς ἑβδομάδας καὶ τὰς τρεῖς ἑβδομάδας ὡς τρεῖς ἡμέρας κτλ.

[3] The expressions in these two verses touching the sun, moon, and stars are familiar from the Old Testament onward. Cf. Is. xiii. 10; Ezek. xxxii. 7; Joel ii. 31, iii. 15; Ass. Mos. x. 5; Rev. vi. 12.

[4] In Matt. xxiv. 30 we have an amplification of this verse: "And then shall appear the sign of the Son of man in heaven, and then shall all the tribes of the earth mourn, and they shall see the Son of man coming in the clouds of heaven." The expression "sign of the Son of man" is unknown in Jewish Apocalyptic and in Early Christian. It may have arisen from a corruption of את into אות (= sign) in יֵרָאֶה אֶת־בֶּן־הָאָדָם. Hence we should read "then shall appear (or be revealed) the Son of man," etc. This apocalypse, like 4 Ezra, Apocalypse of Baruch, etc., was probably composed in Hebrew.

CHAP. IX. from the four winds, from the uttermost part of the earth to the uttermost part of heaven." On this apocalypse follows a short appendix (vers. 30, 31): "Verily I say unto you, This generation shall not pass away, until all these things be accomplished. Heaven and earth shall pass away: but my words shall not pass away."

Now with Colani (*Jésus Christ et les Croyances Messianiques de son Temps*, 1864, pp. 201 *sqq.*), Weiffenbach (*Der Wiederkunftsgedanke*, 90-192), Weizsäcker, Wendt (*Lehre Jesu*, i. 12-21), Baldensperger, H. J. Holtzmann (*NTliche Theol.* i. 327; Hand-Commentar *Synoptiker*, 257-262), Bousset (*The Antichrist Legend*, p. 165), and others, we may very reasonably assume that this apocalypse is not derived from Christ, but is a Christian adaptation of an originally Jewish work, written 67-68 A.D. during the trouble preceding the fall of Jerusalem. In favour of this hypothesis I may call attention to the parallels from Jewish apocalyptic writings which I have given in the footnotes on the preceding pages. Furthermore, its identification of the coming destruction of Jerusalem with the parusia is contrary to the universal practice of Christ elsewhere.[1] Christ often prophesies His parusia in connection with His death and resurrection (Matt. x. 23; Mark ix. 1, xiv. 62), but the destruc-

[1] The combination of the judgment of Jerusalem and the parusia in Matt. xxiii. 35-39 is not original: for the last two verses which speak of the parusia were uttered on another occasion, as is manifest from Luke xiii. 34. Matt. xxii. 7 is an addition of the Evangelist, as appears from the parallel passage in Luke xiv. 21.

tion of Jerusalem invariably by itself (Luke xix. 41-44, xxiii. 28-30; see Schwarzkopff, *Prophecies of Jesus Christ*, p. 254).

Hence this Jewish-Christian apocalypse will not here be cited as an authority.

Hence in our account of the eschatology of the Synoptic Gospels we shall not base our statement on the Jewish-Christian apocalypse as it appears in Mark xiii. or in Matt. xxiv. 6-8, 15-22, 29-31, 34, 35; Luke xxi. 9-11, 20-28, 32, 33. It is probably the oracle (?) referred to by Eusebius (*Hist. Eccl.* III. v. 3). That such oracles were in circulation before the fall of Jerusalem is clear from the statement of Josephus.[1]

The parusia was, whether early or late, to be unexpected.

Thus from the above investigation it appears that as regards the manner of the parusia it was to be sudden and unexpected, whether early or late (Mark xiii. 35; Luke xii. 35-46; Matt. xxv. 1-13).

Certain signs, but not of a definite character, were to precede it.

Certain signs indeed were to precede it, such as persecution of the disciples and their condemnation before Jewish and heathen tribunals (Mark xiii. 9-13). This persecution, moreover, was conceived as lasting continuously from the founding of the Church to the parusia. The experience of Christ was to be likewise that of His disciples (Matt. x. 24, 25; John xv. 20).

Persecution to be always a true mark of the faith.

Persecution, indeed, was to be a true mark of the faith. The preaching of Christ's message would inevitably lead to it (Mark iv. 17 = Matt. xiii. 21; Matt. x. 23): the world which persecuted Him would

[1] *Bell. Jud.* IV. vi. 3: "There was a certain ancient oracle of those men (the Zealots) that the city should then be taken and the sanctuary burnt, by right of war, when a sedition should invade the Jews, and their own hand should pollute the temple of God."

CHAP. IX.

also persecute His servants (Matt. x. 24, 25; John xv. 20). Nevertheless, by enduring such persecutions faithfully unto death, they should testify to Christ throughout Israel in Palestine and the Dispersion, and this testimony would not be completed till their Master's return (Matt. x. 23). But of that day and of that hour knew no man, not even the Son (Mark xiii. 32). Thus we observe that no definite sign of the parusia is given, such as we find abundantly in the Jewish apocalypses and in the small Jewish-Christian apocalypse we have just dealt with.

The time of the Advent.

Having thus shown that the teaching of Christ as to the *manner* of the Advent is that it will be unexpected, we have now to study His declarations as to its *time*. That Christ expected to return during the existing generation is proved beyond question by such statements as Mark ix. 1: "And he said unto them, Verily I say unto you, There be some here of them that stand by, which shall in no wise taste of death till they see the kingdom of God come with power" (= Matt. xvi. 28 = Luke ix. 27[1]). Thus Christ expected to return before all His disciples had passed away, and this expectation is further attested in Matt. x. 23: "But when they persecute you in this city, flee unto the next: for verily I say unto you, Ye shall not have gone through the cities of Israel, till the Son of man be come."

During the existing generation.

Probably the same thought underlies Mark xiv.

[1] Matt. xvi. 28 reads "Son of man" instead of "kingdom of God," but wrongly, since Luke supports Mark.

62: "And Jesus said, I am: and ye shall see the Son of man sitting at the right hand of power, and coming with the clouds of heaven." The circumstance, too, that, whilst the persecution and violent death of the disciples are frequently foreshadowed (Mark viii. 34, 35, xiii. 12, 13; Matt. x. 28, 29) there is hardly a reference to their natural death,[1] is to be explained from this expectation. In view of the quickly approaching parusia natural death came hardly within the purview of practical life. If we go outside the Gospels we find the attestation of this hope universal. For there is not a single writer of the New Testament, as we shall see in the sequel, who does not look forward to the personal return of Christ in his own generation. And what the New Testament taught, all primitive Christendom believed, and fashioned its practical life in accordance with this hope.

We conclude, therefore, that according to the teaching of Christ *the parusia was to be within the current generation.*

This expectation falsified, but the error immaterial.

We must, accordingly, admit that this expectation of Christ was falsified.[2] But the error is not material. It is in reality inseparable from all true prophecy. For the latter, so far as relates to fulfilment, is always conditioned by the course of human development. Herein lies the radical difference between Apocalyptic and Prophecy. The former determines

[1] Only in Luke xii. 15-21, xvi. 19-31.

[2] It is also to some extent neutralised by the recognition of the possibility of a long period of historical development (see below, pp. 333-335).

CHAP. IX.

mechanically the date of consummation of a certain process, irrespective of human conduct, the latter determines only the ultimate certainty of that consummation. Moreover, Old Testament prophecy, and likewise Jewish Apocalyptic, represent the consummation of the kingdom as following immediately on its establishment. Thus all the past gave its suffrage to Christ's expectation. Furthermore, as Christ was convinced that all the prophecies of the Old Testament were fulfilled in Him, and that the age introduced by Him was *final and ultimate* as regards things religious and spiritual, the expectation was in the highest degree natural that this age would be *final* and *ultimate* in a temporal sense also. But whereas the fact that the kingdom should be consummated was a matter of transcendental importance, the time of that consummation had no immediate significance, religious or spiritual. Provided with all knowledge that was needful for His vocation, Christ yet confessed that the knowledge of this date had been expressly withheld (Mark xiii. 32): "But of that day or that hour knoweth no one, not even the angels in heaven, neither the Son, but the Father." By His unique and perfect communion with God He possessed an independent and authoritative judgment in things essentially spiritual and religious, but not in other spheres. In the latter He was dependent on the thought and development of His time.

The time of the consummation of the kingdom of no spiritual significance.

Having now shown that the second Advent was expected to occur within the current generation, and

Though the parusia was expected

also sought to explain the genesis of this misapprehension, we must not fail to observe the fact that account was taken by Christ of the process of human development which must run its course before that advent. Of such a gradual evolution of the kingdom there is hardly a trace in preceding Jewish literature: the consummation of the kingdom was to be *catastrophic, not gradual.*

within the present generation, yet the doctrine of development within that period emphasised,

The kingdom must spread extensively and intensively: extensively till its final expansion is out of all proportion to its original smallness (cf. the parable of the Mustard Seed); intensively till it transforms and regenerates the life of the nation and of the world (cf. the parable of the Leaven, Matt. xiii. 31, 32).

This process has its parallel in the growth of a grain of corn, where there is "first the blade, then the ear, then the full corn in the ear." Then, when the fruit is ripe, cometh the harvest (Mark iv. 26-29).

This representation of the future presupposes a lengthened period of development. It no less than the former goes back to Christ. The contingency that the former view, which is derived from Old Testament prophecy might not be realised, is acknowledged in Matt. xxiv. 48; Luke xii. 45; also in Mark xiii. 35, where the possibilities of an *indefinitely long night of history* preceding the final advent is clearly contemplated.

and likewise the possibility of its continuance beyond that period acknowledged—

The preaching of the Gospel must extend to the Gentiles also. This is the presupposition of the parables above cited. Christ's conception of the

such a continuance presupposed by the mission to the Gentiles implied in the parables,

CHAP. IX.

kingdom of God is essentially a development of the large prophetic doctrine which emanated from Jeremiah and the later prophets of his school, just as the narrow particularism of the Pharisees was the legitimate offspring of Ezekiel's teaching and that of his successors.

In the chapters on the Old Testament we showed the steady trend towards universalism in Jeremiah and his spiritual successors. The movement then inaugurated finds in Christ's conception of the kingdom its highest consummation. For the qualifications for entrance into this kingdom as enumerated in the Sermon on the Mount are purely ethical and spiritual. Thus the difference between Jew and Gentile is implicitly and essentially abolished. The religion of the kingdom cannot be other than the religion of the humanity at large. Thus monotheism attains at last to its full rights in Christianity; for monotheism and universalism are correlative conceptions.

and by the Sermon on the Mount.

Destination of Gospel for the Gentiles belongs to Christ's later teaching.

But it is not improbable that the wide unqualified destination of the Gospel for the Gentiles belongs to Christ's later teaching. At all events, a higher position is assigned to the Jews in the earlier period. The strong words preserved in Matt. xv. 24 point in this direction: "I was not sent but unto the lost sheep of the house of Israel." Also in ver. 26 the Jews are called the children of the kingdom: "And he answered and said, It is not meet to take the children's bread and cast it to the dogs." But, later, after His rejection by the majority of the people, and

His experience of the faith of many non-Israelites, such as that of the Syrophenician woman, the grateful Samaritan, and the Roman Centurion, His attitude towards His countrymen changed. The kingdom, He declared unto them, would be taken from them, and given to others, who would bear appropriate fruits (Mark xii. 9; = Matt. xxi. 40, 41). The invitation of the Gentiles into the kingdom is thus foreshadowed in Matt. xxii. 8, 9, where in the parable of the Wedding Feast the king commands his servants: "The wedding is ready but they that were bidden were not worthy. Go ye therefore into the partings of the highways, and as many as ye shall find, bid to the marriage feast. And those servants went out into the highways and gathered together all as many as they found, both bad and good: and the wedding was filled with guests" (Luke xiv. 22-24). Jerusalem itself, as we learn from other passages, would be destroyed (Mark xiv. 58; Luke xiii. 3-5, xix. 41-44.

No pronouncement as to manner in which Gentiles were to be admitted into the kingdom.

Thus though the destination of the Gospel to the Gentiles is undeniable, yet Christ gave no pronouncement as to the manner in which the Gentile should enter the kingdom, and the mutual relation in which Jew and Gentile should stand within it. In the absence of such a pronouncement, the Apostles naturally inferred that the kingdom could only be realised under the forms of the Jewish Theocracy, and that therefore circumcision was obligatory on all Gentiles that wished to become members of the Christian Church. How this

CHAP. IX.

misconception was removed later, in some degree through the revelation to Peter, but mainly through that to Paul, we have not here to deal.

Christ being the realisation of God's righteousness, man's relation to Christ determines his relation to God. Hence Christ is also the Judge of men.

(*b*) *The Final Judgment.*—Seeing that in Christ the righteousness of God was realised, it follows that a man's relation to Christ's person (Matt. xi. 27) determines likewise his relation to God. Thus Christ, the Saviour of men, becomes, of necessity, the Judge of men. Further, being the Mediator of God's righteousness and love to man, He is necessarily the Mediator of God's judgment on man, which is one of justification or condemnation according to man's attitude to the revelation so mediated.

Christ's judgment in the present.

Christ's judgment, moreover, is both present and future. He is the Mediator of God's continuous and present judgment on the conduct of men. He will be the Mediator of the final judgment of God in the consummation of the world. All things, Christ declares, relating to the kingdom have been delivered into His hands by the Father (Matt. xi. 27 = Luke x. 22). As the Mediator of divine judgment in the present, He forgives sin (Mark ii. 5 = Matt. ix. 2 = Luke v. 20, vii. 48, etc.) He denounces unbelieving cities (Matt. xi. 21-24, xxiii. 37, 38 = Luke x. 13-15, xiii. 34, 35, xix. 41-44), and breaks up the most intimate bonds of social life because founded on a false peace (Matt. x. 34-37).

Final judgment to be at the parusia.

The final judgment is to be executed at the parusia. After the manner of the Old Testament it is called "that day" (Matt. vii. 22): "Many will say to me in that day, Lord, Lord, did we not prophesy in thy name, and by thy name cast out devils, and by thy name do many mighty works?" (Matt. xxiv. 36; Luke vi. 23, x. 12, xxi. 34).

Sometimes it is God who is represented as the Judge of the world. This view appears several times in the Sermon on the Mount, Matt. vi. 4, 6, 14, 15, 18; also in Matt. xviii. 35: "So shall also thy heavenly father," etc. x. 28. "Be not afraid of them which kill the body but are not able to kill the soul; but rather fear him which is able to destroy both soul and body in Gehenna (= Luke xii. 5; see also Luke xviii.) But more usually it is Christ that discharges the duties of Judge.

In some passages Christ appears only as exercising a paramount influence at the judgment,

Just as Christ's judicial action when on earth took various directions, so His part in the final judgment is variously described. In some passages, as Mark viii. 38 = Luke ix. 26, Christ apparently claims no more than a paramount influence in the judgment when He declares that "whosoever shall be ashamed of me and of my words in this adulterous and sinful generation, the Son of man also shall be ashamed of him, when he cometh in the glory of his Father with the holy angels." It is remarkable that in the parallel passage in Matt. xvi. 27 we have a different statement substituted, which represents Christ as the sole Judge: "For the Son of man shall come in the glory of his Father with his angels; and then shall he render unto every man according to his deeds." Elsewhere, in the first

CHAP. IX.

Gospel, x. 32, 33 (= Luke xii. 8, 9), we have a close parallel to the above statement of Mark viii. 38 (Matt. x. 32, 33): "Every one therefore who shall confess me before men, him will I confess before my Father which is in heaven. But whosoever shall deny me before men, him will I also deny before my Father which is in heaven." His office as Judge comes forward strongly in Matt. vii. 22, 23: "I never knew you: depart from me ye that work iniquity." Again in Matt. xxiv. 50, 51: "The Lord of that servant shall come in a day that he expecteth not, and in an hour when he knoweth not, and shall cut him asunder and appoint him his portion with the hypocrites" (cf. xxv. 19). Likewise in Matt. xiii. 30, 41-43, and in the great judgment scene described in Matt. xxv. 31-46, beginning "But when the Son of man shall come in his glory, and all the angels with him, then shall he sit on the throne of his glory: and before him shall be gathered all nations: and he shall separate them one from another as the shepherd separateth the sheep from the goats."

but in others as the sole Judge.

Judgment according to works.

This judgment is universally conceived as a judgment according to works. Thus, according to Matt. xvi. 27, "The Son of man shall come in the glory of his Father with his angels: and then shall he render unto every man according to his deeds." (xiii. 41-43, xxii. 11-14). Every deed of kindness shown to one of His disciples will be duly rewarded (Mark ix. 41; = Matt. x. 42). Nay, more, every disinterested act of goodness will be acknowledged just as much as though it had been rendered personally to Christ Himself (Matt. xxv. 40): "Inasmuch as ye did it unto one of the least of these my brethren ye did it unto me."

Amongst the judged appear His own servants (Luke xix. 22, 23; Matt. xxv. 14-30), the children of Israel (Matt. xix. 28), the heathen (Matt. xxv. 37, 38): not only the contemporaries of Christ, but also all the nations of the past, Nineveh, the Queen of Sheba (Matt. xii. 41, 42; Luke xi. 31, 32), the inhabitants of Tyre and Sidon (Matt. xi. 20-24). The demons probably are judged at the same time (Matt. viii. 29).

Consummation of the kingdom.

(*c*) *Consummation of the Kingdom and the Resurrection.*—The kingdom is consummated, "comes with power" (Mark ix. 1), on the advent of Christ. Into His kingdom, which has been prepared from the foundation of the world, the righteous shall enter (Matt. xxv. 34). Its possession, as we have seen above, means eternal life (Mark x. 17), which is the good of the individual, as the kingdom is the good of the community.

Consummated kingdom of a heavenly character.

The kingdom is not of an earthly but of a heavenly character. The relations of sex are to be abolished (Mark xii. 24, 25 = Matt. xxii. 29, 30; = Luke xx. 34, 35). Certain appetites, however, continue to exist in the kingdom. Thus in Luke xxii. 30 eating and drinking are spoken of: also the drinking of wine in Mark xiv. 25 (= Matt. xxvi. 29 = Luke xxii. 18), and even the eating of the Passover in Luke xxii. 16. In the face of such statements

Certain expressions, as "eating and drinking" in the kingdom of heaven, must be taken in a figurative sense.

CHAP. IX.

two courses are open to us. Either we must take them in a purely figurative sense, or else we must admit that eating and drinking were still conceived as occupations of the heavenly life, and, that thus certain appetites still persisted which modern thought excludes from its conception of that life.

In any case, however, the food in question is not earthly and material; for those also who partake of it are as "angels in heaven" (Matt. xxii. 30 = Mark xii. 25); "are equal unto the angels" (Luke xx. 36). The fact that these very phrases of the Gospels are found in the Ethiopic Enoch (civ. 4, 6; li. 4), and in the Apocalypse of Baruch (li. 10), in passages where the life of the blessed is conceived in the most spiritual manner, makes it clear that in any case the Gospel expressions relating to food must be interpreted in a figurative sense.

Resurrection of the righteous only taught in Matt. xxii. 23-33 = Mark xii. 18-27.

And next as regards the resurrection itself, the teaching of Christ seems clearly to have been that only the righteous attain thereto.[1] Thus in the celebrated passage which recounts the conversation of Jesus with the Sadducees (Matt. xxii. 23-33 = Mark xii. 18-27), it is taught that all who share in the resurrection are "as angels in heaven"; for in the former Gospel we have simply "in the resurrection they . . . are as angels in heaven," and in the latter, "When they shall rise from the dead, they . . . are as angels in heaven." That this is the true teaching of the passage becomes more evident

[1] Observe that, according to the Didache xvi. 6, 7, only the righteous are raised.

as we advance. In the words of God to Moses, "I am the God of Abraham, the God of Isaac, and the God of Jacob," our Lord finds a deeper significance, and this is, that the patriarchs still lived unto God, in other words, that in spite of death they still enjoyed communion with God. He was their God, the God of the spiritually living. It is noteworthy that the right interpretation of the passage is found in 4 Macc. xvi. 25: "Those who die on behalf of God live unto God as Abraham, Isaac, and Jacob."

Life here thus means not the mere shadowy existence in Sheol; for this the Sadducees, from the standpoint of the Old Testament, would not have denied; but a true existence in the enjoyment of the divine fellowship—an existence of which the resurrection is the natural outcome; for this is the question at issue. Such a life, which is in essence the life eternal, the blessed now enjoy, and this life leads of necessity to the resurrection life. In St. Luke xx. 27-40, however, another turn is given to the passage. Instead of saying simply that all who are raised are as the angels in heaven, the writer carefully defines the righteous as "those who are accounted worthy to attain . . . to the resurrection from the dead."[1] The words "accounted worthy" and "attain" are, we should observe, distinctively Lucan and Pauline. In the next place, he gives to the conception of life in this passage the ordinary meaning

But the parallel passage in St. Luke xx. 27-40 so constructed as to teach a general resurrection.

[1] *οἱ καταξιωθέντες . . . τυχεῖν . . . τῆς ἀναστάσεως τῆς ἐκ νεκρῶν.* In Matt. xxii. 31 there is simply *ἡ ἀνάστασις τῶν νεκρῶν* when the same thought has to be expressed.

CHAP. IX.

of existence, whether blessed or unblessed, by adding in xx. 38, after the statement "He is not the God of the dead but of the living," the words "for *all* live unto him." Thus St. Luke interprets the passage to mean that as all men, whether righteous or wicked, live in the after-world unto God, so all men will be raised, and there will be a resurrection of the just and of the unjust. But the parallel passages in St. Matthew and St. Mark are against this interpretation of the passage.

But this is against the sense of the parallel passages in the other two Gospels, and likewise against the terms of the original sources.

It is true that this passage has been interpreted in exactly the opposite sense as teaching only a resurrection of the righteous. But the meaning of the words "all live unto him" seems conclusive against that view. On the other hand, there is not wanting evidence that St. Luke's original sources taught only a resurrection of the righteous; for how else can we reasonably interpret the phrase "sons of God because sons of the resurrection" (xx. 36). The expression "the resurrection of the just," in xiv. 14, is not decisive either way. We hold, therefore, that St. Luke intends this passage to teach a resurrection of the just and of the unjust, similarly as he represents St. Paul as preaching this resurrection of the just and of the unjust in Acts xxiv. 15, though, as we shall find in the next chapter of this book, that St. Paul could not have taught such a doctrine.

Hence we conclude that the Lucan account of our Lord's teaching is not to be followed here, but that of the first two Evangelists.

The doctrine of a final judgment does not necessitate the doctrine of a general resurrection.

In the resurrection the wicked, as we have seen, have no part. It has been said by some scholars that there must be a resurrection of all men in the body at the final judgment. But these two ideas have no necessary connection. In Jubilees there is a final judgment, but no resurrection of the body at all, and in Eth. En. xci.-civ. there is likewise a final judgment, but only a resurrection of the spirits of the righteous (xci. 10, xcii. 3, ciii. 3, 4). The fact, too, that demons and other disembodied spirits (Matt. viii. 29) are conceived as falling under the last judgment is further evidence in the same direction.

As the righteous are raised to the perfected kingdom of God, the wicked, on the other hand, are cast down into Gehenna (Matt. v. 29, 30, x. 28; Mark ix. 43, 45, 47, 48). The fire spoken of in this connection (Matt. v. 22) is not to be conceived sensuously, but as a symbol of the divine wrath, which vividly represents the terrors of this judgment. This place or state of punishment is likewise described as "the outer darkness" (Matt. viii. 12), the place of those who are excluded from the light of the kingdom. The torment appears to be a torment of the soul or disembodied spirit (see pp. 416, 417 on Gehenna).

Christ's recognition of possibility of moral change in Hades.

Though in conformity with Jewish tradition the punishment is generally conceived as everlasting in the Gospels, yet there are not wanting passages which appear to fix a finite and limited punishment for certain offenders, and hence recognise the possibility of moral change in the intermediate state.

CHAP. IX.

Thus some are to be beaten with few, others with many, stripes (Luke xii. 47, 48). It is not possible to conceive eternal torment under the figure of a few stripes (cf. statements as to Sodom and Gomorrah). Again, with regard only to one sin it is said that "neither in this world nor in that which is to come" can it be forgiven (Matt. xii. 32). Now such a statement would not only be meaningless but also misleading in the highest degree, if in the next life forgiveness were a thing impossible. The saying in the Sermon on the Mount (Matt. v. 26), "Thou shalt by no means come out thence till thou have paid the last farthing," admits of a like interpretation. It may not be amiss likewise to find signs of this moral amelioration in the rich man in Hades who appeals to Abraham on behalf of his five brethren still on earth (Luke xvi. 19-31). And if we appeal to the science of ethics, which finds its perfect realisation in Christianity, the idea that forgiveness is impossible in the next life has only to be stated in order to be rejected; for till absolute fixity of character is reached, repentance and forgiveness, being moral acts, must be possible under a perfectly moral Being.

Without such recognition Hades still partially heathen, and God's rule over the next life still in part denied.

Indeed, it is not until we have reached such a conception of the next life that we have banished the last survivals of heathenism that are still inherent in the Judaistic Hades, and made it henceforth part and parcel of the dominion of the Lord and of His Christ. Not until then does God rule in the next world even as in this.

CHAPTER X

ESCHATOLOGY OF THE NEW TESTAMENT—REVELATION, JUDE, 2 PETER, JAMES, HEBREWS, JOHANNINE GOSPEL AND EPISTLES, I PETER.

HAVING dealt with the eschatology of the Synoptic Gospels in the last chapter, and acquainted ourselves so far as possible with the teaching of Christ in this respect, we have now to study in what measure His teaching is reproduced or developed in the other books of the New Testament.

It would seem natural indeed to proceed at once to the fourth Gospel. But since this Gospel presents us in many aspects with a developed phase of Christian doctrine, it is better to adjourn its consideration, and address ourselves first to those books in the New Testament which discover less developed forms of doctrine, and in some cases a greater or lesser admixture of purely Judaistic conceptions.

The fundamental and formative principles of Christianity were necessarily long in operation before they succeeded in transforming the body of inherited Jewish beliefs which the first believers

CHAP. X.

In order to mark the process of transformation and development, both the present order of the New Testament books, as well as their chronological, must be abandoned.

took over with them into Christianity. It is with a view to mark this process of transformation and development that I have decided on abandoning the usual order of these books as they appear in the Bible, and likewise their chronological order.

As regards the former order, nothing could be more misleading, and as regards the latter, or chronological, it would be of no real help to our present purpose to observe it, unless in the case of a collection of works emanating from one and the same writer, as the Pauline Epistles.

The depth and coherence of spiritual or meta-thought does not necessarily grow with the passage of years, and since all the writings which call for examination were written almost within a single generation, it is allowable to take them in the order that best subserves our present object.

At the same time, it is hardly possible to adopt any order that would not be open to weighty objections. Hence the order that will be observed in this and the following chapter does not necessarily and always suppose that each subsequent writer discussed occupies a superior level to those already treated of; for in some cases the degrees of development are hardly distinguishable.

Having so premised, we shall at once address ourselves to the book which contains most Judaistic thought in the New Testament, that is, the Apocalypse.

The Apocalypse

The writer or editor of this book was a Jewish Christian. We cannot here enter on the critical questions affecting this work. It is admittedly a conglomerate of ill-according elements. The ripest products of Christian thought and experience lie side by side with the most unadulterated Judaism.

It is not within our present province to seek to disentangle the Christian sections from the Judaistic.

Although it would be vain to look for a theological system in such a composite production, it is none the less possible to summarise some of its characteristic doctrines in such a way as will not prejudge any of the critical theories which are still at issue. The main object with which the Apocalypse was written was undoubtedly to encourage the persecuted Church to face death with constancy, nay more, with a rapturous joy. It is the glorification of martyrdom. "Blessed are those that die in the Lord."

We shall deal with the teaching of this book under the following heads: (*a*) Parusia and Messianic Judgment. (*b*) First Resurrection and Millennium: the uprising and destruction of Gog and Magog. (*c*) General Resurrection and Judgment. (*d*) Final consummation of the righteous.

Parusia—this thought used in reference to repeated invisible comings for judgment.

(*a*) *Parusia and Messianic Judgment.*—Every visitation of the Churches, every divine judgment upon them, is regarded as a spiritual advent of

CHAP. X.

Christ (ii. 5, 16): "Remember therefore from whence thou art fallen, and repent, and do the first works; or else I come to thee, and will move thy candlestick out of its place, except thou repent." 16. "Repent therefore; or else I come to thee quickly, and I will make war against them with the sword of my mouth" (cf. ii. 22, 23; iii. 3, 20); but this invisible coming ends in a final advent visible to all. Of this visible parusia the date is not revealed (i. 7), yet it is close at hand: iii. 11. "I come quickly: hold fast that which thou hast, that no one take thy crown." xxii. 12, 20. "Behold, I come quickly; and my reward is with me, to render to each man according as his work is. . . . 20. He which testifieth these things saith, Yea: I come quickly, Amen: come Lord Jesus."

Final visible advent.

At His coming all the kindreds of the earth shall wail (i. 7). In chap. xiv. His coming is in the clouds of heaven. The judgment executed by Him appears under various symbolical figures. Thus He reaps the great harvest with a sharp sickle (xiv. 14-16); He treads the winepress of the wrath of God (xiv. 17-20, xix. 15). The judgment of the great day—"the great day of God" (xvi. 14)—is represented under the image of illimitable slaughter, before the beginning of which the birds of prey are summoned to feast on the bodies and blood of men (xix. 17, 18, 21; cf. xiv. 20).

Final judgment.

At Harmageddon, *i.e.* Megiddo (xvi. 16), Antichrist[1] and his allies are annihilated, the Beast and

[1] Observe that, whereas Antichrist in the Johannine Epistles denotes the

the false prophet are cast into the lake of fire (xix. 20), and all their followers slain with the sword (xix. 21).

CHAP. X.

(*b*) *First Resurrection and Millennium: the uprising and destruction of Gog and Magog.*—With the overthrow of the earthly powers, Satan—"the old dragon, the serpent"—is stripped of all his might, and is cast in chains into the abyss, where he is imprisoned for a thousand years (xx. 1-3[1]): "And I saw an angel coming down out of heaven, having the key of the abyss and a great chain in his hand. And he laid hold on the dragon, the old serpent, which is the Devil and Satan, and bound him for a thousand years, and cast him into the abyss, and shut it, and sealed it over him, that he should deceive the nations no more, until the thousand years should be finished: after this he must be loosed for a little time." Thereupon ensues the Millennium, when the martyrs, and the martyrs only, are raised in the first resurrection and become priests of God (cf. Is. lxi. 6) and of Christ, and reign with Christ personally on earth for a thousand years (xx. 4-6), with Jerusalem as the centre of the kingdom. According to an earlier passage (v. 10) they are made unto God "a kingdom and priests; and they reign upon the earth."

On the overthrow of Satan the Millennium sets in.

To this temporary Messianic kingdom the martyrs rise.

false teachers and prophets, in the Apocalypse it designates Rome. In 2 Thessalonians, on the other hand, Rome is a beneficent power which hinders the manifestation of Antichrist.

[1] This idea of the conquest of "the dragon" may be derived from Parsism (?). According to the older Jewish view, this and other sea monsters were overcome in primeval times by God. See prayer of Manasseh 2-4; Gunkel, *Schöpfung und Chaos*, 91-95.

CHAP. X.

Origin of this doctrine in Judaism.

The idea of a temporary Messianic kingdom first emerged, as we have seen in an earlier chapter, at the beginning of the first century B.C. Its limitation, as here, to a thousand years, is first found in Slav. En. xxxii., xxxiii. We have before shown how this number arose.[1] It should be observed that this is the only passage in the New Testament where the doctrine of the Millennium is undoubtedly taught. Some scholars have sought to prove its existence also in 1 Cor. xv. 24-27. But even if their contention were granted, and it would be difficult to do so, it was only a temporary stage in the development of Pauline thought. In all other writers of the New Testament this doctrine is not only ignored, but its acceptance is made impossible in their definite doctrinal systems of the last things, for in these the second advent and the last judgment synchronise. Thus the Millennium, or the reign of Christ for 1000 years on the present earth, or any other form of the temporary Messianic kingdom, cannot be said to belong to the sphere of Christian doctrine.

Here only beyond question in New Testament.

Not admissible in the doctrinal systems of the other New Testament books.

This combination of the temporary Messianic kingdom with the resurrection may have originated in Jewish-Christian circles,

And yet though the Millennium does not belong to Christian theology, it may have been first developed in its present form in a Jewish-Christian atmosphere—in its present form, I repeat, that is, in its combination of the resurrection of the martyrs with a temporary Messianic kingdom under the Christian Messiah. In our earlier chapters we saw that when once the Messianic kingdom came to be regarded as temporary, from that moment—more

[1] See p. 201.

than 150 years before the date of the New Testament Apocalypse—the resurrection was relegated from the beginning of the Messianic kingdom to its close, and the righteous were conceived as rising not to the Messianic kingdom, but to eternal blessedness in a new world or in heaven itself.

but since a kindred doctrine is found on Jewish soil,

The same combination of the temporary Messianic kingdom and the resurrection of a limited number of the righteous is to be found in 4 Ezra. Thus in xiii. 52 and in xiv. 9 the Messiah is represented as dwelling in Paradise or some kindred place with Ezra and other righteous men till the times are ended, that is, probably, till the time of the Messianic kingdom. When this era has arrived, then, according to vii. 28, "The Messiah will be revealed, together with those who are with him." He is to rule over the Messianic kingdom for 400 years, and then die. These sections of 4 Ezra are taken by nearly all scholars to be later than 80 A.D. They are at all events subsequent to the advent of Christianity. But since the doctrine of the temporal reign of the Messiah and of the first resurrection is a favourite theme in the Talmud,[1] it is no doubt to be traced to an exclusively Judaistic source.

both are to be traced to the same Judaistic source.

Satan loosed at the close of the Millennium; uprising of Gog and Magog.

But now to return. At the close of the Messianic kingdom Satan will be loosed from his prison in the abyss, and the nations Gog and Magog—the idea goes back ultimately to Ezek. xxxviii. 2–xxxix. 16—are stirred up to make the last assault on the kingdom of Christ (Rev. xx. 7-9): "And when the

[1] See Weber, *Jüdische Theologie*,[2] 364-371.

CHAP. X.

thousand years are finished, Satan shall be loosed out of his prison, and shall come forth to deceive the nations which are in the four corners of the earth, Gog and Magog, to gather them together to war: the number of whom is as the sand of the sea. And they went up over the breadth of the earth, and compassed the camp of the saints about, and the beloved city." In this attack they are destroyed by God Himself, who sends down fire from heaven (xx. 9). The devil is finally cast into the lake of fire (xx. 10), where are also the Beast and the false prophet.

Their destruction, and the overthrow of Satan.

(*c*) *General Resurrection and Judgment.*—These follow on the close of the Millennium and the destruction of the heathen powers and the final overthrow of Satan. A great white throne is set up, and the Judge takes His seat thereon, and from before His face the present heaven and earth pass away (xx. 11; cf. xxi. 1). God is Judge, and yet in some respects the Messiah also (xxii. 12): "Behold I come quickly; and my reward is with me, to render to each man according as his work is" (cf. also vi. 16, 17). All are judged according to their works, which stand revealed in the heavenly books (xx. 12). The wicked are cast into the lake of fire (xxi. 8; see also xix. 20, xx. 10). So likewise are death and Hades (xx. 14). Hades seems to be conceived in the Apocalypse as the intermediate abode of the wicked only; for it is always combined with death (see i. 18, vi. 8, xx. 13, 14). The souls of the martyrs have as their intermediate abode the place beneath the altar (vi. 9-11). The occupation of the martyred

General resurrection

and judgment

Hades = abode of wicked only.

Souls of the martyrs.

souls in the intermediate state is essentially Judaistic. Their whole prayer is for the destruction of their persecutors. The rest of the righteous were probably conceived as in Paradise or in the treasuries of the righteous (see 4 Ezra). This final award represents the second death (xx. 14, xxi. 8; see also ii. 11, xx. 6).

The second death.

The second death is the death of the soul, as the first is the death of the body. It is not the annihilation, but the endless torment of the wicked that is here meant. The expression is a familiar Rabbinic one (see Jerusalem Targ. on Deut. xxxiii. 6, where for "let Reuben live and not die," we have "let Reuben live and not die the second death"[1]).

Consummation of the righteous in the new heaven and the new earth.

(*d*) *Final Consummation of the Righteous.*—The scene of this consummation is the new world—the new heaven and the new earth (xxi. 1, 5), and the heavenly Jerusalem (xxi. 10-21[2]). Then the ideal kingdom of God becomes actual. This city needs no temple: for God and Christ dwell in it (xxi. 22). The throne of God and of the Lamb is set up therein (xxii. 1, 3). The citizens dwell in perfect fellowship with God (xxii. 4), and are as kings unto God (xxii. 5). The Messiah still exercises His mediatorial functions (see vii. 17, xxi. 22, 23, etc.)

In this book the distinction of Jew and Gentile seems indelible.

It is noteworthy that the distinction of Jew and Gentile seems, according to this writer, to be an

[1] See Wettstein on Rev. ii. 11.

[2] Quite inconsistently with the idea of a new heaven and a new earth (xxi. 1) the writer represents various classes of sinners as dwelling outside the gates of the city of God, the New Jerusalem (xxii. 14, 15). In xxi. 8, on the other hand, these are committed to the lake of fire.

CHAP. X.

indelible one.[1] It persists even through eternity. The firstfruits of the twelve tribes which form the kernel of the New Testament community (vii. 4-8, xiv. 1) are represented in the after-world as a fixed and definite number over against the hosts of the Gentile world (vii. 9). The redeemed of Israel are to dwell in the New Jerusalem, while the Gentiles are to walk in the light thereof (xxi. 24, 26). The former are to eat of the fruit of the tree of life, while the latter are to be healed by its leaves (xxii. 2). The twelve gates of the heavenly city are to be named after the twelve tribes (xxi. 12), and the names of the twelve Apostles are inscribed on the foundation stone of the city. Yet Jew and Gentile form one divine community, and are alike kings and priests unto God (i. 6, v. 10).

From the Apocalypse we shall now proceed to deal with the two closely-related epistles, St. Jude and 2 Peter. The latter is dependent on the former, and the two epistles are probably the latest writings in the New Testament.

St. Jude

St. Jude saturated with Jewish Apocalyptic.

Though St. Jude deals almost wholly with the question of judgment, there is nothing very characteristic in his teaching, save that he is saturated with Jewish apocalyptic literature, and recognises its prophecies as genuine products of the Old Testament saints, and as binding on the Christian con-

[1] See Holtzmann, *NTliche Theol.* i. 474, 475.

science. Thus in this short epistle of twenty-five verses we have in vers. 14^b, 15 a direct quotation from the Book of Enoch i. 9: in ver. 13 the phrase "wandering stars" goes back to Eth. En. xviii. 15; in ver. 14 the words "Enoch the seventh from Adam" to lx. 8; in ver. 6 the statement regarding the angels that kept not their first estate to Eth. En. x. 5, 6, 12, 13.

At least one other such work, *i.e.* the Assumption of Moses, is laid under contribution in ver. 9.[1]

Past judgments types of the final judgment.

As regards its teaching on the last things, the writer finds in the divine judgments of the past types of the final judgment. Such were the destruction of the faithless Israelites that were saved out of Egypt (ver. 5), and the condemnation of Sodom and Gomorrah to the "punishment of eternal fire" (ver. 7). This last is very instructive. It shows how Christians at the close of the first century A.D. read their own ideas into the Old Testament records of the past. Thus the temporal destruction by fire of Sodom and Gomorrah is interpreted as an eternal punishment by fire beyond the grave. With their views of inspiration no other interpretation was possible. Other such judgments were the destruction of Korah and his company (ver. 11), and finally the judgment on the angels, which were guilty of unnatural union with the daughters of men, in accordance with which they are "kept in everlasting

Instance of reading New Testament ideas into the Old Testament.

[1] For a full classification of the coincidences of thought and language between Jude and apocalyptic writers, see Chase's article on Jude in Hastings' *Bible Dictionary*, II. 801, 802.

CHAP. X. bonds under darkness unto the judgment of the great day" (ver. 6). But these judgments are only preliminary to the "judgment of the great day" (ver. 6), when, according to the prophecy of Enoch, "the Lord cometh with ten thousand of his holy ones, to execute judgment upon all, and to convict all the ungodly of all their works of ungodliness which they have ungodly wrought, and of all the hard things which ungodly sinners have spoken against him" (St. Jude 14, 15), and on the fallen angels, who are "kept in everlasting bonds under darkness unto the judgment of the great day" (ver. 6). This extension of the judgment to the angels, which was an accepted dogma of Judaism for at least 300 years previously, is presupposed, as we saw in the Gospels (Matt. viii. 29); it is expressly stated in 1 Cor. vi. 3, and reproduced in 2 Peter ii. 4. At this final judgment with which Jude menaces the godless libertines or, according to many recent critics, the Gnostics of his own day, the faithful will obtain mercy, even eternal life (ver. 21).

Final judgment

on men

and angels.

2 PETER

This epistle is closely related to Jude—in fact, presupposes it. Like Jude, its author recounts various temporal judgments as warnings to the godless of his own day. Thus he adduces the Deluge (ii. 5, iii. 6), the destruction of Sodom and Gomorrah (ii. 6), the condemnation of the fallen angels to Tartarus: "God spared not angels when

Condemnation of fallen angels to Tartarus as

they sinned, but cast them down to hell, and committed them to pits of darkness, to be reserved unto judgment" (ii. 4). This is the only passage where this word "Tartarus" appears. Its use here is not inappropriate in connection with the fallen angels, for it was originally the place of punishment of the Titans. On the other hand, our author has changed it from being a place of eternal punishment into one of temporary and intermediate punishment.

CHAP. X.

an intermediate abode of punishment.

But these were but preliminary acts of judgment. The final "day of judgment" (ii. 9, iii. 7) is impending. In the meantime the unrighteous are kept under punishment (ii. 9): "The Lord knoweth how to deliver the godly out of temptation, and to keep the unrighteous under punishment unto the day of judgment." We observe that no possibility of repentance beyond the grave is here recognised as it is in 1 Peter.

The ultimate doom of the wicked false teachers and their followers will be "destruction," ἀπώλεια (iii. 7); it is coming speedily upon them (ii. 3); the wicked have brought it upon themselves (ii. 1); they shall assuredly be destroyed (ii. 12). At the final judgment the present constitution of the world will perish by fire (iii. 7, 10, 12), as formerly by water (ii. 5, iii. 6), and in their stead there will be a new heavens and a new earth (iii. 12, 13). The destruction of the world by fire is found in the New Testament only in this epistle.

The world to be destroyed by fire.

The day of judgment and the destruction of the world do not take place till Christ's parusia (i. 16;

The final judgment at the parusia.

CHAP. X.

iii. 4, 12). But this parusia is already being denied by evil men, who say (iii. 4), "Where is the promise of his coming?" Now our writer insists that the presence of such mockers is evidence that the last days are already come (iii. 3). Moreover, the parusia is only postponed through the longsuffering of God with a view to the repentance of the faithless and their salvation (iii. 9); it may, indeed, be still far distant, for "one day is with the Lord as a thousand years, and a thousand years as one day" (iii. 8). But the date of the Advent is dependent on human conduct. By holy living and godliness they could prevent its further postponement (iii. 11, 12): "Seeing that these things are thus all to be dissolved, what manner of persons ought ye to be in all holy living and godliness, looking for and hastening the coming of the day of God, by reason of which the heavens being on fire shall be dissolved, and the elements shall melt with fervent heat?"

Date of the parusia dependent on human conduct.

With the parusia the eternal kingdom of Christ begins (i. 11) in the new heavens and the new earth (iii. 12, 13). There the perfect life of righteousness will be realised (iii. 13).

St. James

In this work of primitive Jewish Christianity, in which Christianity is conceived as the fulfilment of the perfect Law, prominence is given to the doctrine of recompense. Hence whilst the fulfilment of the Law under temptation led to a recompense of blessing (i. 12, v. 11), failure for those who are subjects of "the law of liberty" entails an aggravated form of punishment (ii. 12). Greater responsibility leads to severer judgment (iii. 1). None, however, can fulfil the law perfectly (iii. 2), and so claim "the crown of life" (i. 12) as their reward. Men need forgiveness now (v. 15), and must need a merciful Judge hereafter. Only the merciful, by the law of recompense, will find God to be such (ii. 13). Moreover the judgment is close at hand. It is a day of slaughter for the godless rich (v. 5). The advent of the Messiah, who will judge the world, is close at hand (v. 8, 9): "Be ye also patient; stablish your hearts: for the coming of the Lord is at hand. Murmur not, brethren, one against another, that ye be not judged: behold, the judge standeth before the doors." He alone can save or destroy (iv. 12): "One only is the lawgiver and judge, even he who is able to save and to destroy: but who art thou that judgest thy neighbour?"

The judgment at hand.

The Messiah will judge the world.

But as faithful endurance receives life (i. 12), so the outcome of sin is death (i. 15). A fire will consume their bodies (v. 2—? in Gehenna). The death to which the Messianic judgment (iv. 12) will deliver the wicked is not a death of the body only, but also of the soul (v. 20): "Let him know, that he which converteth a sinner from the error of his way shall save a soul from death, and shall cover a multitude of sins."

Finally, the faithful will enter into the promised kingdom (ii. 5).

CHAP. X.

Hebrews

There is a large eschatological element in this epistle. The final judgment—"the day"—is nigh at hand (x. 25). This day appears to be introduced by the final shaking of the heaven and earth (xii. 26, with xii. 25, 29), and the parusia. God is judge (x. 30, 31; xiii. 4); the Judge of all (xii. 23). Though Christ judges not, His second coming is coincident with this judgment (ix. 27, 28; x. 37). Retribution is in some sense reserved unto this judgment (x. 30), which will be terrible (x. 31) and inevitable (xii. 25). Yet as regards the righteous, Christ will come not to judge but to save (ix. 28): "So Christ also, having been once offered to bear the sins of many, shall appear a second time, apart from sin, to them that wait for him, unto salvation." Thus the righteous, it would seem, will in a certain sense escape the final judgment. Their recompense is to be in heaven (vi. 19, 20), where they have an eternal inheritance (ix. 15), a better country (xi. 16), the city which is to come (xiii. 14), even the city which hath the foundations, whose builder and maker is God (xi. 9, 10). Then the present visible world (xi. 3), which is already waxing old (i. 10-12), will be removed, and the kingdom which cannot be shaken will remain (xii. 26-28). Into this new world the righteous will pass through the resurrection. The life of this world is described as a sabbatismos or Sabbath keeping (iv. 9). There is apparently to be a resurrection of the righteous only.

"The day" at hand.

God is Judge.

Recompense of the righteous in heaven,

in the new world.

CHAP. X.

Resurrection of the righteous only.

This follows from xi. 35, "that they might obtain a better resurrection." These words, which refer to the Maccabean martyrs (2 Macc. vii.), set the resurrection in contrast to a merely temporary deliverance from death, and represent it not as the common lot of all, but as a prize to be striven for. The statement in vi. 2 is not conclusive for or against this view. The blessedness of the righteous is described as a participation in the glory of God (ii. 10) and in the divine vision (xii. 14).

Doom of the wicked.

As regards the wicked, their doom is destruction, *ἀπώλεια* (x. 39). It consists not in a mere bodily death (ix. 27), but in something far more terrible. This retribution is represented as a consuming fire (x. 27): "A certain fearful expectation of judgment, and a fierceness of fire which shall devour the adversaries" (cf. vi. 8, xii. 27). Annihilation seems to be the destiny of the wicked.[1]

[1] I have followed in the main the traditional views of scholars in the above. The eschatology of this book might, however, be differently construed. Judgment sets in immediately after death in the case of the individual (ix. 27): "And inasmuch as it is appointed unto men once to die, and after this cometh judgment." The righteous, having undergone this judgment, forthwith reach their consummation, for they are spoken of as "the spirits of just men made perfect" (xii. 23). As such they do not come within the sphere of the final judgment, for the surviving righteous at the Advent are delivered from it (ix. 28): "So Christ also, having been once offered to bear the sins of many, shall appear a second time, apart from sin, to them that wait for him, unto salvation." Hence the resurrection of the spirits of the righteous would thus be conceived as following immediately on death. The Alexandrian origin of the Epistle would favour this view. Likewise the designation of God as "the Father of spirits" (xii. 9). Again, the phrase "spirits of just men made perfect" (xii. 23) points in the same direction. For if moral perfection is meant, these spirits must have already reached their consummation. But if they have reached their consummation as spirits, the writer as an Alexandrian seems to teach only a spiritual resurrection. But the chief obstacle in the way of this interpretation is the meaning of the words "to perfect" and "perfection." See Weiss, *Biblical Theol. of N.T.*, § 123.

CHAP. X.

The Johannine Eschatology

The sources for this eschatology are the fourth Gospel and the Epistles. The Apocalypse springs from a different author, and belongs to a different school of eschatological thought. The salient points of the Johannine eschatology may be summed up under the following heads:—(*a*) The Parusia; (*b*) Judgment; (*c*) The Resurrection and final consummation.

Twofold meaning of parusia in St. John—(*a*) a present spiritual fact.

(*a*) *The Parusia.*—The parusia has a twofold meaning, a spiritual and an historical, in St. John. Thus in John xiv. 18, 19 the coming Advent is resolved into (*a*) an event already present: "I will not leave you desolate: I come unto you. Yet a little while, and the world beholdeth me no more; but ye behold me: because I live, ye shall live also." Thus in a spiritual sense Christ is already present (1 John v. 12): "He that hath the Son hath life." A spiritual and an abiding communion is already established between the exalted Christ and His own (xii. 26): "If any man serve me, let him follow me; and where I am, there shall also my servant be: if any man serve me, him will my Father honour." In this communion as Christ knows and loves His own, so they know and love Him (x. 14, 15): "I know mine own, and mine own know me, even as the Father knoweth me, and I know the Father." By this communion with the Son the communion and love of the Father is assured (xiv. 21): "He that loveth me shall be loved of my Father, and I will love him, and will manifest myself unto him." xiv. 23. "If a man love me, he will keep my word: and my Father will love him, and we will come unto him, and make our abode with him." xiv. 20. "In that day ye shall know that I am in my Father, and ye in me, and I in you." xvii. 23. "I in them, and thou in me, that they may be perfected into one; and that the world may know that thou didst send me, and lovedst them, even as thou lovedst me." xvii. 26. "And I made known unto them thy name, and will make it known; that the love wherewith thou lovedst me may be in them, and I in them."

(*b*) A future event.

(*b*) On the other hand, the parusia is also conceived as a future and historical event. Thus Christ will return from heaven and take His own unto Himself, that they may be with Him in heaven (xiv. 2, 3): "In my Father's house are many mansions; if it were not so, I would have told you; for I go to prepare a place for you. And if I go and prepare a place for you, I will come again, and will receive you unto myself; that where I am, there ye may be also."

That xiv. 2, 3 cannot be interpreted of His coming to receive His disciples individually on death is shown by xxi. 22: "Jesus saith unto him, If I will that he tarry till I come, what is that to thee? follow thou me." According to the New Testament, death translates believers to Christ (2 Cor. v. 8; Phil. i. 23; Acts vii. 59), but nowhere is He said to

CHAP. X.

The parusia at hand.

come and fetch them. This parusia is at hand; for some of His disciples are expected to survive till it appears (xxi. 22), though Peter must first be martyred (xxi. 18, 19). Even in extreme old age the Apostle still hopes to witness it together with his disciples, whom he exhorts to abide in Christ, that they may not be ashamed before Him at His coming (1 John ii. 28).

The Antichrist manifested in false teachers.

In his teaching regarding the Antichrist this evangelist reproduces the teaching of Christ in the Synoptics. This doctrine is referred to as a traditional article of faith, but the conception is Christian and not Judaistic. Just as in the last chapter we saw that Christ foretold the coming of many false Christs and many false prophets (Mark xiii. 6, 21-23 = Matt. xxiv. 5, 23, 24 = Luke xxi. 8, xvii. 23), so St. John declares that the close approach of the parusia is shown by the appearance of false prophets and teachers. These are so many Antichrists, and their advent is a sign of the end (1 John ii. 18): "Little children, it is the last hour: and as ye heard that antichrist cometh, even now have there arisen many antichrists; whereby we know that it is the last hour." An Antichrist is defined in ii. 22 as "he that denieth the Father and the Son," and in iv. 3 as any "spirit that confesseth not Jesus." In these false teachers the Antichrist manifests himself (iv. 3).

How widely different is this doctrine of the Antichrist from that which appears in Revelation.

Judgment, present and subjective,

(*b*) *Judgment.*—Judgment is conceived by this evangelist as present and subjective and as future and objective. Judgment in the former sense is no arbitrary process, but the working out of an absolute law whereby the unbelieving world is self-condemned. For a man is justified or condemned according to the attitude he assumes to the light (John iii. 19-21): "And this is the judgment, that the light is come into the world, and men loved the darkness rather than the light; for their works were evil. For every one that doeth ill hateth the light, and cometh not to the light, lest his works should be reproved. But he that doeth the truth cometh to the light, that his works may be made manifest, that they have been wrought in God." This justification or condemnation follows according to a man's attitude to Christ's person (ix. 39): "And Jesus said, For judgment came I into this world, that they which see not may see; and that they which see may become blind." Hence, from the fact that a man exercises judgment on himself, it is declared that Christ "came not to judge but to save" (iii. 17): "For God sent not the Son into the world to judge the world; but that the world should be saved through him." xii. 47. "And if any man hear my sayings, and keep them not, I judge him not: for I came not to judge the world but to save the world." Indeed, so far removed from judgment is the purpose of His coming that He declares (viii. 15), "I judge no man," though in the next verse the necessity of judging is conceded, for judgment is the inexorable sequel which follows rejection of the proffered salvation. And in this sense elsewhere

proceeds according to a man's attitude to the light,

that is, to Christ's person.

Judgment is self-executed. Christ came not to judge, but to save.

Yet judgment must be the sequel of rejecting His salvation.

CHAP. X.

He declares (ix. 39), "For judgment came I into this world."

Now since it is rejection of the light that brings man within the sphere of judgment or condemnation, acceptance of the light delivers him from it. We read accordingly (iii. 18): "He that believeth on him is not judged: he that believeth not hath been judged already, because he hath not believed on the name of the only begotten Son of God." v. 24. "Verily, verily, I say unto you, He that heareth my word, and believeth him that sent me, hath eternal life, and cometh not into judgment, but hath passed out of death into life." The words "hath passed out of death into life" and "cometh not into judgment" are very definite. They must, however, be interpreted in the sense that so far, and only just so far, as a man is faithful has he passed from death into life and cometh not into judgment. Since this present self-executing judgment is coextensive with the entire human life, it follows that a man's character is the result of all this process in the past, and is, in fact, the verdict of God on man's conduct from first to last. His ultimate destiny has thus already been determined by his spiritual condition. Hence, from this standpoint the final judgment cannot be otherwise conceived than as the recognition and manifestation of judgment already exercised and consummated.

Hence character is the result of this present self-executing judgment.

Final judgment is the recognition of the judgment already consummated.

Contrast of this view to v. 28, 29.

In the face of such a spiritual conception of judgment, what are we to make of John v. 28, 29: "Marvel not at this: for the hour cometh, in which all that are in the tombs shall hear his voice, and shall come forth; they that have done good, unto the resurrection of life; and they that have done ill, unto the resurrection of judgment." We shall return to this question later.

Christ as standard of divine righteousness or mediator is the Judge of man.

Though the object of Christ's coming was not judgment, yet as the unique standard of divine righteousness and the sole mediator between God and man, He is the judge of man. In viii. 50 there is a reference to God as executing judgment, but elsewhere it is definitely stated that God judgeth no man, but has committed all judgment to the Son (v. 22, 27): "For neither doth the Father judge any man, but he hath given all judgment unto the Son." 27. "And he gave him authority to execute judgment, because he is the Son of man." And the justness of the Son's judgment is assured, for it is according to the will of the Father (v. 30): "I can of myself do nothing: as I hear, I judge; and my judgment is righteous; because I seek not mine own will, but the will of him that sent me." viii. 16. "Yea, and if I judge, my judgment is true; for I am not alone, but I and the Father that sent me."

(*c*) *The Resurrection.*—In the Synoptic Gospels "the kingdom of God" and "life" were used to some extent as synonyms. The same usage prevails in the fourth Gospel, only to an indefinitely greater degree. Indeed, the conception of "life," or "eternal life," appears to supersede that of the kingdom. The kingdom is only spoken of three

Conception of "life" almost supersedes that of the kingdom.

CHAP. X.

The kingdom mentioned only in three passages, where it is conceived as spiritual and present.

times—in iii. 3: "Except a man be born from above, he cannot see the kingdom of God"; and in iii. 5: "Except a man be born of water and the Spirit, he cannot enter into the kingdom of God." In these two passages the kingdom is conceived as present and spiritual, and this is no doubt its character in xviii. 36, the only other passage where the phrase occurs: "My kingdom is not of this world: if my kingdom were of this world, then would my servants fight, that I should not be delivered to the Jews: but now is my kingdom not from hence."

But the thought is frequently present.

But though the kingdom is seldom mentioned, the thought is frequently present in the Johannine writings. The divine gift of eternal life, as the good of the individual, can only be realised in so far as it brings the individual into vital union with the divine community, which is none other than the kingdom. The realisation of this life leads to unity with the brethren, such as prevails between the Father and the Son (xvii. 21), and, through this unity consciously apprehended, the individual life attains to its perfection (xvii. 23). Thus eternal life and the kingdom are correlative and complementary thoughts in the fourth Gospel. The indispensable evidence of this life in the individual is his love to the community. He who possesses it not has no divine life as an individual; he neither comes from God nor knows Him (1 John iii. 10, iv. 8), but abides in darkness and death (1 John ii. 10, iii. 14).

Eternal life and the kingdom are correlative thoughts.

But we must discuss more intimately the conception "eternal life," for on the right apprehension of this thought depends our ability to understand the Johannine doctrine of the resurrection.

As death is the evil from which Christ delivers men (viii. 51), so the gift which He brings is life, and that eternal life (iii. 15, 16): "That whosoever believeth may in him have eternal life. For God so loved the world, that he gave his only begotten Son, that whosoever believeth on him should not perish, but have eternal life" (cf. x. 28, xii. 50). This eternal life is already a present possession (vi. 47): "Verily, verily, I say unto you, He that believeth hath eternal life." v. 24. "Verily, verily, I say unto you, He that heareth my word, and believeth him that sent me, hath eternal life, and cometh not into judgment, but hath passed out of death into life." It consists in a growing personal knowledge of God and of His Son (xvii. 3): "And this is life eternal, that they should know thee the only true God, and him whom thou hast sent, even Jesus Christ." And this life is the presupposition and living germ of the resurrection life (vi. 40): "This is the will of my Father, that every one that beholdeth the Son, and believeth on him, should have eternal life; and that I should raise him up." Nay more, this eternal life which the believer at present possesses is already the resurrection life (v. 25): "Verily, verily, I say unto you, The hour cometh, and *now is*, when the dead shall hear the voice of the Son of God; and they that hear shall live." Thus the resurrection, spiritually conceived, is brought into the present, and Christ Himself as the resurrection and the life

This eternal life is a present possession.

The germ of the resurrection life.

Nay more, is the resurrection life,

CHAP. X.

and cannot be affected by death.

is its source (xi. 25): "Jesus said unto her, I am the resurrection, and the life: he that believeth on me, though he die, yet shall he live." This divine resurrection life cannot be affected by death. He that possesses it can never truly die (viii. 51): "Verily, verily, I say unto you, If a man keep my word, he shall never see death." xi. 26. "Whosoever liveth and believeth on me, shall never die."

Eternal life in this sense an ethical and timeless conception.

From the preceding, therefore, we see that the spiritual resurrection life is synonymous with eternal life, and that eternal life in the fourth Gospel is not a time conception, but a purely ethical and timeless one. In only a few passages does it retain a temporal meaning. In these it refers to the future heavenly life (iv. 14, vi. 27, xii. 25). Seeing, therefore, that the resurrection in the fourth Gospel is, spiritually conceived, synonymous with eternal life, and, historically conceived, is the essential fruit of eternal life, two conclusions naturally follow: (1) The believer cannot lose this spiritual resurrection life at death, but must enter rather on a fuller consummation of it. (2) Only the righteous can share in that resurrection life.

Conclusions as to the resurrection.

Are v. 28, 29 genuine?

How, then, are we to deal with such a passage as v. 28, 29: "Marvel not at this: for an hour cometh, in which all that are in the tombs shall hear his voice, and shall come forth; they that have done good, unto the resurrection of life; and they that have done ill, unto the resurrection of judgment." Here the resurrection is adjourned to the last day; both righteous and unrighteous are described as coming forth from the tombs, and the scene is depicted in the most materialistic form—in fact, it would be hard to find a more unspiritual description of the resurrection in the whole literature of the first century A.D. These considerations are of themselves quite sufficient to render these verses questionable in a high degree; for their teaching is in glaring conflict with the fundamental conceptions of this Gospel. Owing to their incompatibility with the rest of the Johannine teaching, a recent writer (Holtzmann, *NTliche Theologie*, ii. 519) has not shrunk from branding them as an accommodation on the part of the Evangelist to current popular views. But the charge is unjustifiable. For, as Wendt has shown, not only is the teaching of these verses at variance with that of the rest of the Gospel, but they are also at variance with their actual context,[1] and their excision restores unity of thought to the passage. The same scholar rightly treats as interpolations from the same hand the words "at the last day" in vi. 39, 40, 44, 54; xii. 48. The popular view of resurrection at the last day is again stated, though not in so gross a form, in xi. 24, where Martha says,

[1] There is an outward resemblance between v. 25 and v. 28, yet an inward antagonism. In the former, "an hour cometh, and now is, when the dead shall hear the voice of the Son of God; and they that hear shall live," the word "hear" is used in the pregnant sense of obedience, whereas the sense is wholly wanting in v. 28: "An hour cometh, in which all that are in the tombs shall hear his voice, and shall come forth," which is obviously, nevertheless, modelled upon v. 25. For the various grounds for the rejection of these verses, see Wendt, *Lehre Jesu*, i. 249-251. It is to be observed that the phrase οἱ ἐν τοῖς μνημείοις in v. 28 is no doubt derived from Isaiah xxvi. 19 (LXX); for it does not appear to occur outside these two passages. In the Old Testament passage this phrase can refer to the righteous only, as the context shows, but its New Testament application relates it to all mankind.

CHAP. X.

touching her brother: "I know that he shall rise again in the resurrection at the last day." But this view of Martha's is not accepted by Christ, but is implicitly corrected in the pregnant words which He utters in reply: "I am the resurrection, and the life: he that believeth on me, though he die, yet shall he live: and whosoever liveth and believeth on me shall never die."

Johannine doctrine of the resurrection.

Thus the Johannine teaching appears to be that in some form the resurrection life follows immediately on death, but that its perfect consummation cannot be attained till the final consummation of all things.

Manifestation of the results of the daily judgment at the consummation of the world.

But the final result of this daily secret judgment must one day become manifest; believers shall have boldness in the day of judgment (1 John ii. 28, iv. 17), for it can only be the recognition and manifestation of judgment already exercised. A man's attitude to Christ determines now, and will determine finally, his relation to God and destiny (iii. 18, 19; ix. 39).

Consummation of the righteous.

(*c*) The final consummation is one of heavenly blessedness. After the final judgment the present world will pass away (1 John ii. 17), and Christ will take His own to heaven—a state rather than a locality[1] (xiv. 2, 3): they are to be with Him where He is (xii. 26, xvii. 24). Eternal life—the resurrection life—is then truly consummated. Begun essentially on earth, it is now realised in its fulness and perfected. The faithful now

[1] See Hort, *The Way, the Truth, the Life*, pp. 13-16.

obtain their "full reward" (2 John 8). As "children of God" they are, through enjoyment of the divine vision, transformed into the divine likeness (1 John iii. 2, 3).

Johannine doctrine of God necessitates a transformation of Judaistic conceptions of Hades and hell.

Though the Apostle does not present us with any fresh teaching touching Hades and hell, he furnishes us with principles which in themselves necessitate a transformation of the Judaistic views regarding these intermediate and final abodes of the departed. Thus, when he teaches that God so loved the world as to give His only Son to redeem it (John iii. 16), that "God is love" (1 John iv. 8), that He is light, and in Him is no darkness at all, then Hades, which is wholly under His sway, must be a place where moral growth is possible; and as for hell, the final eternal abode of the damned, such a conception is impossible in the cosmos ruled by the God of justice and love. Sin, according to the Johannine view, is the destroyer of all life—physical, spiritual, and ontological. Now, to check the ultimate effects of this process of destruction and preserve the sinner in a state of sin, in a state of ever-growing, ever-deepening sin, could in no sense be the work of God so conceived.

The Petrine Eschatology

Earlier form of Petrine eschatology.

The earliest form of this is to be found in Acts iii. 12-26. It is very Jewish in character, and its value in regard to Christian eschatology is historical rather than intrinsic. Thus St. Peter expects that

CHAP. X.

The kingdom to be realised in the forms of the Jewish theocracy.

the kingdom of God will be realised in the forms of the Jewish theocracy (cf. Acts i. 6), and that the Gentiles will participate in its blessings only through conversion to Judaism (iii. 25, 26). At any rate, it required a further revelation (see Acts x.) to teach him that Gentiles as Gentiles should become members of the kingdom. Having thus apprehended the limited scope of the passage before us, we can recognise how idle have been the many discussions that have originated in the familiar phrase "the times of the restoration of all things" (iii. 21).[1] These words, in the mind of the Apostle, relate either to the renewal of the world, or else, and in all likelihood, to the moral regeneration of Israel. This interpretation follows from Mal. iv. 6, which is the ultimate source of the expression, and from the application they receive from our Lord in Matt. xvii. 11. St. Peter urges his hearers to repent that they may be forgiven their sins and so hasten the parusia. He connects the parusia and "the seasons of refreshing." "The times of the restoration of all things" (iii. 21) are preparatory to the parusia, or else they are synonymous with "the seasons of refreshing." In the latter case they would point to a temporary Messianic kingdom which is apparently to be consummated on the earth. In fact, the

Meaning of the phrase "restitution of all things."

[1] Seeing that St. Peter was unacquainted with a fact of immediate and primary importance,—the destination of the Gospel to the Gentiles as Gentiles,—it is unreasonable to wrest his words into a disclosure on a question of merely speculative interest: the ultimate and universal destiny of man. Further, Dalman (*Worte Jesu*, i. 145, 146) shows that this phrase does not refer to the renewal of the word, but to the fulfilment of all that was declared by the prophets.

phrase "seasons of refreshing" is hardly intelligible of any but an earthly Messianic kingdom. The same thought appears in the "rest" (= ἄνεσις) of 2 Thess. i. 7.

Later Petrine eschatology.

1 *St. Peter*.—In this epistle there is a decided advance on the Petrine teaching in Acts iii. It is true that believing Israelites still form, as in Acts iii., the real substance of the Christian Church; but in the Apostle's view this Church embraces all who come to believe in Christ, whether of Israelitish or Gentile origin, in this world or the next (iii. 19, iv. 6). Further, it is not an earthly consummation of the theocracy, but an heavenly one that is looked for. The "inheritance" that awaits the righteous is "incorruptible and undefiled, and reserved in heaven" for them (i. 4). The goal, then, of the Christian hope is this "salvation ready to be revealed at the last time" (i. 5). But this consummation of the heavenly theocracy is initiated by the revelation of Jesus Christ and the judgment of the world.

A heavenly kingdom expected.

Christ the Judge.

Though God is declared in general terms to be the Judge (i. 17, ii. 23), yet this final judgment is expressly assigned to Christ (iv. 5). But the end of all things is at hand (iv. 7): for judgment has already begun with the house of God, *i.e.* with the Church of believing Israel (iv. 17). Persecution is sifting the true from the false members of the Church. But such afflictions will last but "a little while" (i. 6, v. 10). Then Christ will be revealed (i. 7, v. 4), and will execute a universal judgment over

CHAP. X.

the quick and the dead (iv. 5), over the righteous and the wicked (iv. 17, 18 ?). Then the approved disciples will share with their Lord in "eternal glory" (v. 10); they will "receive the crown of life" (v. 4), and live such a life as that of God (iv. 6).

1 Peter iii. 19-21, and iv. 5, 6.

But the question of chief importance in the Petrine eschatology is still to be discussed. It centres in the two difficult passages which describe the preaching to the spirits in prison (iii. 19-21), and the preaching of the Gospel to the dead (iv. 5, 6).

According to iii. 19-21, Christ preached the Gospel to human or angelic spirits in Hades.

The interpretations that have been assigned to these passages[1] are multitudinous, but the majority are simply impossible, attributing, as they do, a false sense to the phrase "the spirits in prison." This phrase can be interpreted *only* in two ways. The spirits in question are either those of men in Sheol, or they are the fallen angels mentioned in 2 Peter ii. 4; Jude 6. In the next place, the words "in prison" denote the local condition of the spirits at the time of preaching. Hence, according to the text, Christ "in the spirit" (*i.e.* between His death and resurrection) preached the Gospel of redemption (for so only can we render ἐκήρυξεν) to

[1] See Dietelmaier, *Historia Dogmatis de Descensu Christi ad Inferos litteraria*, 1741 and 1762; Güder, *Die Lehre von d. Erscheinung Christi unter den Toten*, 1853; Zezschwitz, *De Christi ad Inferos Descensu*, 1857; Usteri, *Hinabgefahren zur Hölle*; Schweitzer, *Hinabgefahren zur Hölle*; Hofmann, *Schriftbeweiss*, ii. 335-341; Salmond,[2] *Christian Doctrine of Immortality*, pp. 450-486, 1896; Spitta, *Christi Predigt an die Geister*; Bruston, *La Descente du Christ aux Enfers*, 1897; Steven's *Theology of the New Testament*, 304-311, 1899; as well as the commentators *in loc.*

human or angelic spirits in the underworld.[1] With the more exact determination of the objects of this mission we are not here concerned. For, however it be decided, we have here a clear apostolic statement that the scope of redemption is not limited to this life in the case of certain individuals, human or angelic. We have now to deal with iv. 5, 6: "Who shall give an account to him that is ready to judge the quick and the dead. For unto this end was the Gospel preached even unto the dead, that they might be judged according to men in the flesh, but live according to God in the spirit." The doctrine we found stated above in iii. 19-21 is here substantiated, as being part of the larger truth now enunciated. Christ is ready to judge the quick and the dead—the latter no less than the former; for even to the dead was the Gospel preached[2] in order that, though they had already been judged in the flesh, they might live the life of God in the spirit. Thus the Apostle teaches that on the advent of the last judgment the Gospel will already have been preached to all. As to how far this preaching of redemption succeeds, there is no hint in the Petrine teaching.

This is only a part of the larger doctrine in iv. 5, 6.

These passages in 1 Peter are of extreme value.

[1] See Gospel of Peter ver. 41. Such may have been St. Paul's belief (Rom. x. 7; Eph. iv. 8-10). This may be the idea at the root of Matt. xxvii. 52, 53. Christ's appearance in Hades was the signal for the release of the saints.

[2] The tense of εὐηγγελίσθη creates no difficulty here. This preaching might be already regarded as a completed act in the past, for in the next verse (iv. 7) the writer declares that the end of all things is at hand. But even if this were not so, the aorist can be used of a continuous practice (cf. 1 Cor. ix. 20; James ii. 6).

CHAP. X.

Here Hades, which had partially been transformed under Judaistic influences, is further transformed under Christian.

They attest the achievement of the all but final stage in the moralisation of Hades. The first stage in this moralisation was taken early in the second century B.C., when it was transformed into a place of moral distinctions, having been originally one of merely social or national distinctions. But this moralisation was very inadequately carried out. According to the Judaistic conception, souls in Sheol were conceived as insusceptible of ethical progress. What they were on entering Sheol, that they continued to be till the final judgment. Thus this conception is mechanical and unethical if judged in the light of Christian theism. It precludes moral change in moral beings who are under the rule of a perfectly moral Being, who wills not that any should perish, but that all should come to repentance.

CHAPTER XI

THE PAULINE ESCHATOLOGY IN ITS FOUR STAGES

In the writings of this Apostle we find no single eschatological system. His ideas in this respect were in a state of development. He began with an expectation of the future that he had inherited largely from Judaism, but under the influence of great formative Christian conceptions he parted gradually from this and entered on a process of development, in the course of which the heterogeneous elements were for the most part silently dropped. We have marked out four stages in this development, but perfect consistency within these stages is not to be looked for. Even in the last the Apostle does not seem to have obtained finality, though he was ever working towards it. It is permissible, therefore, for his readers to develop his thoughts in symmetrical completeness and carry to its conclusion his chain of reasoning. The present writer has not attempted to do so in this volume, but may do so later. The various stages are attested by (i.) 1 and 2 Thessalonians; (ii.)

CHAP. XI.

1 Corinthians; (iii.) 2 Corinthians and Romans; (iv.) Philippians, Colossians, Ephesians.

First Period of Development— 1 and 2 Thessalonians

Earliest form of Pauline eschatology in 1 and 2 Thessalonians.

The two Epistles to the Thessalonians[1] present us with the earliest form of the Pauline teaching and eschatology. They constitute, in fact, the Pauline Apocalypse. In this apocalypse the salient features are (*a*) the great Apostasy and the Antichrist; (*b*) the Parusia and Final Judgment; (*c*) the Resurrection and blessed Consummation of the Faithful. In his teachings on these questions the Apostle appeals to the authority of Christ. What he puts before his readers in 1 Thess. iv. 15-17 is derived from the Lord (see ver. 15). There is, however, a setness and rigidity in the teaching of the Apostle which is not to be found in that of Christ.

The end will come when evil has reached its climax

(*a*) *The Apostasy and the Antichrist.*—St. Paul starts from the fundamental thought of Jewish Apocalyptic that the end of the world will be brought about by the direct intervention of God when evil has reached its climax. The moment for such intervention is thus not arbitrarily determined, but conditioned by the development and final con-

[1] There are undoubted difficulties in the way of reconciling the eschatology of 1 and 2 Thessalonians. The eschatology of the former is closer than that of the second to the Synoptic Gospels. I have with some hesitation used both epistles as depicting the first stage in St. Paul's eschatological views. The conflicting views as to the manner of the Parusia, whether as wholly unexpected (1 Thess.) or as preceded by certains signs (2 Thess.), are not in themselves sufficient grounds for rejecting 2 Thessalonians, since (1) some time elapses between the composition of the epistles, and (2) since some of the eschatological views of the Apostle were in a constant state of flux.

summation of the forces of good and evil at work in the world. In the course of this development the separation of those susceptible of salvation and the unsusceptible is realised gradually but inevitably. The day of the Lord cannot come "except the falling away (ἡ ἀποστασία) come first, and the man of sin be revealed, the son of perdition whose coming is according to the working of Satan—with all deceit of unrighteousness for them that are perishing" (2 Thess. ii. 3, 9, 10). This evil, which already pervades and is leavening the world (2 Thess. ii. 7), must reach its consummation, and this it will do in the son of perdition, the Antichrist. Thus as the revelation of God culminated in Christ, so the manifestation of evil will culminate in Antichrist, whose parusia (2 Thess. ii. 9) is the Satanic counterfeit of the true Messiah. But as the incarnation of evil he appears as the negation not only of Christ but also of God; for, exalting himself above all that is called God, he places his throne in God's temple in Jerusalem, setting himself forth as God (2 Thess. ii. 4). But the climax of evil is the immediate herald of its destruction; for thereupon Christ will descend from heaven and slay him with the breath of His mouth, and consume him with the manifestation of His coming (2 Thess. ii. 8).

and the Antichrist is revealed.

Whence Antichrist was to proceed it is difficult to determine—whether from Judaism or heathenism.[1]

Does the Antichrist proceed from Judaism or heathenism?

[1] Weiss (*Theol. of N.T.*, English transl., i. 305-311) maintains the Jewish origin of Antichrist. He argues that an apostasy, strictly speaking, was impossible in heathenism, and it was only unbelieving Judaism which had as yet shown itself to be the real seat of hostility to Christ. Thus the real obstacle to the spread of the teaching of Christ lay in the fanatical Jews

CHAP. XI.

Not from Rome.

That the Apostle did not conceive him as proceeding from Rome is clear; for the power and person who restrain (2 Thess. ii. 6, 7) the Antichristian revolution are none other than the Roman empire and its imperial head. These, as the representatives of order and justice,[1] repress the outbreak of evil, and delay the coming of Antichrist.[2]

whom the Apostle designates as "unreasonable and evil men" (2 Thess. iii. 2; cf. also 1 Thess. ii. 18). Having for the most part remained unbelieving (Acts xviii. 6; 2 Thess. i. 8), they had always pursued him with persecution and calumny (Acts ix. 23, 24, 29; xiii. 8, 45), had stirred up the heathen against him (xiii. 50; xiv. 2, 5, 19; xvii. 5, 13). Hence the Apostle denounces them as the real foes of Christ. Having slain Christ and the prophets, they were now the relentless persecutors of His Church. Displeasing to God and contrary to all men, the cup of their iniquity was all but full, and wrath was already come upon them to the uttermost (1 Thess. ii. 16-18). When to the above facts we add the further consideration that the false Messiah or Antichrist regards the temple at Jerusalem as the dwelling-place of God (2 Thess. ii. 4), the Jewish origin of the Antichristian principle seems in a very high degree probable. Sabatier (*Apostle Paul*, English transl. 119-121) was originally of this opinion, but now declares that a fresh examination of the passages makes him less confident as to the Jewish character of the Antichrist: "The apostasy in question seems to extend far beyond the limits of Judaism, and to be the outcome of a general and hopeless revolt of the whole world against God and the order established by Him." The Apostle "leaves the personality of Antichrist indefinite, precisely because this personality did not as yet present a distinct form to the eyes." Beyschlag (*N. T. Theology*, English transl. ii. 257, 258) takes somewhat the same view. That the Antichrist is a personification of God-opposing heathenism is the view of Baur, Hilgenfeld, Döllinger, Schmiedel, and Julicher. Bousset (*The Antichrist Legend*), on the other hand, supports with great learning and force the Jewish origin of the Antichrist. Holtzmann (*NTliche Theol.* ii. 192) is of opinion that, notwithstanding Bousset's work, it is impossible to maintain the Jewish origin. The attempt to establish such a view must, he holds, be hopelessly wrecked on the fact that the Antichrist, who claimed to be God (2 Thess. ii. 4), could never have been regarded as the Messiah by the Jews. If we regard the Antichrist as proceeding from heathenism, the thought in its ultimate derivation springs from the Gog and Magog assault of the Gentiles on Jerusalem in Ezek. xxxviii., xxxix. Thus we should have an excellent parallel to Rev. xx. 7-10.

[1] The power of Rome had repeatedly protected the Apostle from the attacks of the Jews (Acts xviii. 12-16, xix. 35-41, xxii. 22-29). In Rom. xiii. 1 its magistrates are declared by him to be God's ministers. Later, this distinction between the Roman Emperor and Antichrist disappeared. Thus the Emperor is the Beast and Rome the mystery of iniquity in Rev. xiii., xvii.

[2] We should observe that the figure of Antichrist, which belongs to the earliest type of Paulinism, does not reappear in his later teaching.

CHAP. XI.

(*b*) *Parusia and Final Judgment.*—The Apostle expects the parusia of Christ in his own lifetime (1 Thess. ii. 19): "For what is our hope, or joy, or crown of rejoicing? Are not even ye before our Lord Jesus at his coming?" iii. 13. "To the end that he may establish your hearts unblameable in holiness before our God and Father at the coming of our Lord Jesus with his saints." iv. 15. "For this we say unto you by the word of the Lord, that we which are alive and are left unto the coming of the Lord, shall in no wise precede them that are fallen asleep." v. 23. "And the God of peace himself sanctify you wholly; and may your spirit and soul and body be preserved entire, without blame at the coming of our Lord Jesus Christ." The parusia follows immediately on the culmination of evil (2 Thess. ii. 1-4): "Now we beseech you brethren, touching the coming of our Lord Jesus Christ, and our gathering together unto him; to the end that ye be not quickly shaken from your mind, nor yet be troubled, either by spirit, or by word, or by epistle as from us, as that the day of the Lord is now present; let no man beguile you in any wise: for it will not be, except the falling away come first, and the man of sin[1] be

Parusia n the Apostle's life-time.

It will be preceded by certain signs, according to 2 Thess. ii.

[1] There is a very close affinity between the conception of Antichrist in the above passage and in the Apocalypse. In both he is clearly conceived as the Satanic counterfeit of Christ. Thus the Antichrist has his parusia (2 Thess. ii. 9=Rev. xvii. 8): he is an instrument of Satan, who enables him to perform lying signs and wonders (2 Thess. ii. 9=Rev. xiii. 2, 4, 13, 15), whereby he deceives the faithless (2 Thess. ii. 10=Rev. xiii. 14). He blasphemes God and claims the worship of men (2 Thess. ii. 4=Rev. xiii. 4, 5, 6, 8, 12). Finally he will be destroyed (2 Thess. ii. 3=Rev. xvii. 8, 11): Christ will destroy him with the breath of His mouth (2 Thess. ii. 8=Rev. xix. 15, 21).

CHAP. XI.

revealed, the son of perdition, he that opposeth and exalteth himself against all that is called God or that is worshipped; so that he sitteth in the temple of God, setting himself forth as God." Yet the day of the final catastrophe is uncertain; for it comes as a thief in the night (1 Thess. v. 1-3): "But concerning the times and the seasons, brethren, ye have no need that aught be written unto you. For yourselves know perfectly that the day of the Lord so cometh as a thief in the night. When they are saying, Peace and safety, then sudden destruction cometh upon them, as travail upon a woman with child; and they shall in no wise escape" (cf. Matt. xxiv. 43). With what vividness and emphasis the Apostle must have preached the impending advent of Christ is clear from 1 Thess. v. 1-3, as well as from the second epistle, where he seeks to quiet their excitement, almost bordering on fanaticism. In His second advent Christ will descend from heaven (1 Thess. i. 10), with the voice of the archangel and the trump of God (cf. 1 Cor. xv. 52) (1 Thess. iv. 16; 2 Thess. i. 7), and His glory will then be revealed (2 Thess. i. 7) (ἀποκάλυψις). Angels will accompany Him as the executors of His decrees (2 Thess. i. 7).

Yet come as a thief in the night (1 Thess.)

Parusia is also the day of judgment.

But the parusia is likewise the *day of judgment*. For the Old Testament designation of the day of judgment is used of the parusia. Thus the latter is spoken of as "the day of the Lord" (1 Thess. v. 2), "the day" (1 Thess. v. 4), "that day" (2 Thess. i. 10). This judgment deals with Antichrist and all the wicked and godless. First of all, Antichrist is annihilated (2 Thess. ii. 8); "with flaming fire" vengeance will be taken on the godless amongst the Gentiles and Jews (1 Thess. iv. 6; 2 Thess. i. 8), alike on the careless (1 Thess. v. 3) and the actively hostile (2 Thess. i. 6). The doom of the wicked is "eternal destruction," ὄλεθρος αἰώνιος (2 Thess. i. 9; cf. 1 Thess. v. 3), described likewise as ἀπώλεια (2 Thess. ii. 3, 10). In this harsh forecast of the future the Apostle has hardly outgrown the narrow intolerance of Jewish eschatology. We shall see that later it is not the consummation of evil and the unbelief of mankind, but rather the triumph of Christianity in the conversion of the world that ushers in the fulness of the times and the advent of Christ. To the Apostle's maturer mind God so shapes the varying destinies of Jew and Gentile "that he may extend his mercy unto all" (Rom. xi. 32).

This forecast of the future abandoned later in favour of a more Christian one.

(*c*) *The Resurrection and the blessed Consummation of the Faithful.*—The Apostle's disclosure on the resurrection is occasioned by an apprehension in the young Church which he had founded that those who died before the parusia would fail to share in its blessedness. Hence he refers them to a special statement of Christ on this subject (1 Thess. iv. 15; cf. Matt. xxiv. 31). The dead in Christ, who are said "to sleep,"[1] shall rise first (1 Thess. iv. 16), but the teaching on this point is not quite clear.[2] The

[1] That this does not imply a latent existence, as Holtzmann asserts (*NTliche Theol.* ii. 196), Schmiedel, Hand-commentar *Thessalonians*, p. 28, we have already shown (see pp. 127 *note*, 187, 196).

[2] According to 1 Thess. iii. 13, these are to accompany Christ at His

CHAP. XI.

Resurrection only of the righteous.

word "first" is not intended here to contrast this resurrection with a second resurrection, but rather to denote the two classes of the righteous who share in the resurrection. The first are those who have died before the parusia; the second are those who survive to meet it. Both are caught up to meet the Lord in the air. The scene of their blessedness is, probably, a transformed heaven and earth (cf. 1 Cor. vii. 31). Since the resurrection and the final judgment take place at the parusia, it is not a temporary Messianic kingdom but the eternal abode of the blessed into the possession of which the risen and surviving righteous enter. The elect are gathered together unto Christ (2 Thess. ii. 1; cf. Matt. xxiv. 31). There is no reference to a resurrection of the wicked in these two epistles.[1] It is to be inferred that after the resurrection the world from

parusia—that is if, according to the usage of the New Testament, we take the ἅγιοι here as "the faithful," and not as "the angels." It is true that in 2 Thess. i. 7 the angels are spoken of, but purely as agents of the divine judgment. That we are to understand 1 Thess. iii. 13 of men, and not of angels, follows also from 1 Thess. iv. 14. Hence the resurrection of the faithful dead, according to iii. 13, iv. 14, is coincident with the Advent, since they accompany Christ at His advent, but according to iv. 16 this resurrection is subsequent to the Advent. This vagueness of language need not necessarily imply a corresponding vagueness of thought.

[1] Indeed, as we shall discover later, there could be no resurrection of the wicked according to St. Paul's views. Hence we cannot regard the statement attributed to St. Paul in Acts xxiv. 15, that "there shall be a resurrection both of the just and of the unjust," as an accurate report. To share in the resurrection, according to the all but universal teaching of the New Testament, is the privilege only of those who are spiritually one with Christ and quickened by the Holy Spirit. Only two passages—John v. 28, 29, and Rev. xx. 12, 13—attest the opposite view. But the latter passage occurs in a Judaistic source of that book, and the former stands in clear contradiction to the entire drift of the fourth Gospel in this respect (see pp. 370, 371). In all Jewish books which teach a resurrection of the wicked the resurrection is not conceived as a result of spiritual oneness with God, but merely as an eschatological arrangement for the furtherance of divine justice or some other divine end.

which the righteous have been removed is given over to destruction. After the resurrection follows the blessed consummation of everlasting fellowship with the Lord (1 Thess. iv. 17). Owing to the organic connection between Christ and His people, they will be raised even as He (1 Thess. iv. 14), and therefore not to an earthly but to a heavenly life, in which they share in the glory of God and of Christ (1 Thess. ii. 12; 2 Thess. ii. 14), in the completed kingdom of God (1 Thess. ii. 12; 2 Thess. i. 5). The kingdom is here conceived as in the future.

Second Period of Development—1 *Corinthians*

The second stage in the development of the Pauline eschatology is to be found in the 1st Epistle to the Corinthians. In many respects the teaching of this epistle is in harmony with that of the Epistles to the Thessalonians, but it is marked off from them by the omission of all reference to the Antichrist when dealing with the enemies of the Messianic kingdom. Other divergencies will appear in the sequel. We shall now sketch shortly the teaching of this epistle under the following heads: (*a*) The Parusia and the Final Judgment. (*b*) The Resurrection. (*c*) The Consummation of the Blessed.

The parusia in the Apostle's lifetime.

(*a*) *The Parusia and Final Judgment.*—The Apostle looks forward to the parusia of Christ[1] (1 Cor. iv. 5): "Wherefore judge nothing before the

[1] So also in Phil. iii. 20, 21: yet he had always the possibility of meeting death before him. This is possibly the case in 1 Cor. xv. 31, 32.

CHAP. XI.

time, until the Lord come, who will both bring to light the hidden things of darkness, and make manifest the counsels of the hearts; and then shall each man have his praise from God." xi. 26. "For as often as ye eat this bread, and drink the cup, ye proclaim the Lord's death till he come." xv. 51, 52. "Behold I tell you a mystery: We shall not all sleep, but we shall all be changed, in a moment, in the twinkling of an eye, at the last trump: for the trumpet shall sound, and the dead shall be raised incorruptible, and we shall be changed." xvi. 22. "If any man loveth not the Lord, let him be Anathema Maranatha." It will be preceded by severe trials[1] (vii. 26, 28): "I think, therefore, that this is good by reason of the present distress, namely that it is good for a man to be as he is. . . . But and if thou marry, thou hast not sinned; and if a virgin marry she hath not sinned. Yet such shall have tribulation in the flesh: and I would spare you." The interval preceding the parusia will be short: hence the faithful should not give themselves up even to the legitimate joys of this life (vii. 29). This second coming will be one which will manifest His glory (i. 7): "So that ye come behind in no gift; waiting for the revelation of our Lord Jesus Christ," and likewise bring the world to a close (i. 8): "Who shall also confirm you unto the end, that ye be unreproveable in the day of our Lord Jesus Christ" (cf. 2 Cor. i. 13, 14). With the

It will be preceded by severe trials,

but of short duration.

[1] These are the nearest approach to the terrible picture of the future troubles in 2 Thess. ii. They represent the travail pains of the Messiah.

CHAP. XI.

The judgment follows immediately upon the parusia. Christ is Judge.

parusia is immediately connected the final judgment, at which the Judge will be Christ (iv. 4, 5): "For I know nothing against myself; yet am I not hereby justified: but he that judgeth me is the Lord. Wherefore judge nothing before the time, until the Lord come, who will both bring to light the hidden things of darkness, and make manifest the counsels of the hearts; and then shall each man have his praise from God."[1] That this second coming is conceived as one of judgment is seen also in the designation elsewhere applied to it, *i.e.* "the day of the Lord Jesus Christ" (i. 8), "the day" (iii. 13), "the day of the Lord" (v. 5). Observe that the judgment is according to works (1 Cor. iv. 4; iii. 17; vi. 9, 10)—that is, when the life is looked at from without and in its final consummation. On the other hand, in the subsequent epistles, performance and reward are treated in their inner organic relation. Wages of sin = death. Whatsoever a man soweth that shall he also reap (Gal. vi. 7).

From the above facts it follows that the Apostle did not expect the intervention of a temporary Messianic or millennial period *between* the parusia and the final judgment, as some have inferred from 1 Cor. xv. 22-24. According to this passage, every power hostile to God in the world is stripped of its influence by the time of the parusia. With the resurrection which ensues

[1] As in the Thessalonians (see above). This doctrine appears also in 2 Cor. v. 10, "the judgment seat of Christ." The judgment is also spoken of as the judgment of God (Rom. xiv. 10); "the judgment seat of God." Cf. also Rom. ii. 5, 6, iii. 6, xiv. 12; 2 Cor. vii. 1. In Rom. ii. 16 the two views are reconciled: God will judge the world through Jesus Christ.

CHAP. XI.

thereupon is involved the destruction of the last enemy, even death (xv. 26). Thus the parusia, accompanied by the final judgment and the resurrection, marks the end of the present age and the beginning of the new. The angels are to be judged—but their judges are the righteous (1 Cor. vi. 3; see on Book of Wisdom above, p. 258). Some scholars[1] have indeed attempted to interpret 1 Cor. xv. 22-24 of the Millennium. But this interpretation is untenable; for in the passage cited the period of Christ's domination *precedes* the parusia. The character, moreover, of Christ's kingdom therein portrayed is wholly at variance with that of the temporary Messianic kingdom of Apocalyptic and the Millennium of the Apocalypse; for the Messianic reign is here one of unintermitting strife, whereas in the literature above referred to it is always one of peaceful dominion and blessedness. What the Apostle speaks of here is a Messianic reign of temporary duration from Christ's exaltation to the final judgment. In his later epistles the Apostle conceives this reign as unending.

No Millennium taught in 1 Cor. xv. 22-24.

(*b*) *The Resurrection.*—The resurrection of man is connected organically with that of Christ. As God has raised up Christ, so also He will raise us up (1 Cor. vi. 14): "God both raised the Lord and will raise us up through his power"; cf. 2 Cor. iv. 14). The doctrine of man's resurrection had been denied by certain members of the Church of Corinth, who did not question the resurrection of Christ. To these the Apostle rejoined that

Resurrection of Christ and that of man organically connected.

[1] See Schmiedel, Hand-commentar 1 *Corinther*, p. 196.

CHAP. XI.

both were indissolubly united, and stood or fell together. The ground of man's resurrection hope was based on his living fellowship with Christ: "As in Adam all die, so also in Christ shall all be made alive" (xv. 22). The relation manifestly in each case is the same. Now as this relation cannot be a natural and genealogical one, it must of necessity be an ethical and spiritual one. Furthermore, from the position of the words ἐν τῷ Ἀδὰμ πάντες ἀποθνήσκουσιν, the "in Adam" must be connected with "all." Hence it is equivalent "all who are in Adam." Similarly "all in Christ" = "all who are in Christ."[1] Thus the verse means: "as all who are ethically or spiritually in fellowship with Adam die, so all who are spiritually in fellowship with Christ shall be made alive." This being made alive = being spiritually quickened[2] (ζωοποιεῖσθαι), involves the "being raised" (cf. Rom. viii. 11). There can be no resurrection but in Christ. That the righteous only are raised we shall be forced to conclude also from the Apostle's teaching on *the origin of the resurrection body* in xv. 35-49. In answer to the question, How are the dead raised? the Apostle rejoins: "Thou fool, that which thou sowest is not quickened except it die" (xv. 36). That is, a man's own experience should instruct him herein; for it overturns the objection that is raised.

As spiritual fellowship with Adam leads to death, so spiritual fellowship with Christ leads to life.

That only the righteous attain to the resurrection follows also from the Apostle's teaching on the resurrection body.

[1] For similar constructions, see xv. 18; 1 Thess. iv. 16; Col. i. 4; Rom. ix. 3.

[2] That this is the meaning of ζωοποιεῖσθαι appears to follow from its use in xv. 36: "that which thou sowest is not *quickened* except it die." Here, as in xv. 22, the fresh inward quickening of life is referred to, not its outer manifestation.

CHAP. XI.

The death of the seed consists in the decomposition of its material wrapping. By this process the living principle within it is set free, and seizes hold of the matter around it, wherewith it forms for itself a new body.[1] In like manner the resurrection is affected through death itself. What appears as the obstacle is actually the means. The spirit of man must free itself from the body which contains it before it fashions for itself an incorruptible body. We are next instructed as to the nature of the resurrection body in xv. 42-44: "It is sown in corruption, it is raised in incorruption: it is sown in dishonour, it is raised in glory: it is sown in weakness, it is raised in power; it is sown a psychical body, it is raised a spiritual body." The sowing here cannot mean the *mere burying* of the body in the grave: such a meaning of σπείρειν is wholly unattested: it is rather the placing the vital principle or spirit in its material environment here on earth, where, even as a seed gathers to itself a body from the matter around it, so the spirit of man fashions for itself a body out of the materials around it. Thus the entire life of man in this world, from its first appearance to the obsequies that attest its departure, corresponds to the sowing of the seed in the earth.[2] That this is

1 Cor. xv. 42-44.

Man's life on earth corresponds to the life of the seed germ under ground.

[1] The Pauline way of stating this formation of the new body is noteworthy: "God gives it a body." We moderns say: The new body is the result of the vital principle in the grain acting on its environment in conformity with God's law in the natural world. St. Paul says in such a case: "God gives it a body" (xv. 38). This is important to remember in connection with 2 Cor. v.

[2] Such is to a large extent the view advocated by Reuss (quoted by Heinrici, 1 *Corinther*, p. 529), that in the first term, "sowing," the Apostle embraces the entire earthly life until the act which determines its close, and in the second term, "raising," the entire future existence from its earliest

the Apostle's meaning will become clearer if we consider the opposing members in the various contrasts drawn in xv. 42-44. Thus it is sown "in corruption" (xv. 42). This description is no doubt applicable to the interment of the body; but still more, it characterises human life as a whole. The phrase "in corruption" (= ἐν φθορᾷ) is especially Pauline in reference to the present life of man. For this life is in "the bondage of corruption," δουλεία τῆς φθορᾶς (Rom. viii. 21); and the living body is at present undergoing corruption, διαφθείρεται (2 Cor. iv. 16). Furthermore, "flesh and blood," the constituents of the present living body, are declared in ver. 50 of the present chapter to be "corruption" (φθορά). This interpretation is, further, supported by the current definition of this life in apocalyptic literature as the sphere of the corruptible. Thus, according to the Apocalypse of Baruch, the whole present world belongs to this sphere. Even the Messianic kingdom falls within it (xl. 3, lxxiv. 2). All, that is, is doomed to corruption (xxxi. 5). In 4 Ezra also this age is spoken of as the age of corruption (iv. 11; see also vii. 111, 113[1]).

Characteristics of the present or psychical body.

"In dishonour" denotes the miseries of this earthly life, which we experience in "this body of our humiliation" (Phil. iii. 21). "Weakness" is another fitting description of the body as an agent

beginning. Heinrici writes: "The two members of the antithesis designate the two conditions of existence, and include a reference to the facts of life and death which are decisive as regards the essence of each." Calvin was practically of the same view: "Praesentis vitae tempus metaphorice sationi comparat, resurrectionem vero messi."

[1] See the present writer's *Apocalypse of Baruch*, pp. 40, 41.

2 Cor. 13.4 He was crucified through weakness, yet he liveth through the power of God. For we also are weak with him, & we shall live with him through the power of God

CHAP. XI.

of the spirit—"the spirit is willing but the flesh is weak." In 1 Cor. ii. 3, 4; 2 Cor. xii. 9, 10 we find the same contrast, "weakness" and "power," as here. To apply such a term as "weakness" to the dead body would be absurd, but such a term rightly describes the inherent weakness of the body, issuing ultimately in death. Finally, this present body is psychical as an organ of the psyche or soul, whereas the risen or spiritual body is an organ of the spirit.

Contrasts between the psychical and spiritual bodies.

Thus as the psychical body is *corruptible*, and *clothed with humiliation* and *weakness*, the pneumatical or spiritual body will enjoy *incorruptibility*, *honour*, and *power*.

Yet connected in that they are successive expressions of the same personality.

Hence between the bodies there is no exact continuity. The existence of the one depends on the death of the other. Nevertheless some essential likeness exists between them. This essential likeness proceeds from the fact that they are successive expressions of the same personality, though in different spheres. It is the same individual vital principle that organises both. From this description of the resurrection body it is obvious that only the righteous can share in the resurrection.

Further, it follows that, since the faithless lose their psychical body at death, and can never, *so long as they are such*, possess a spiritual body, they are necessarily conceived as "naked," that is, disembodied beings.

When does the resurrection take place? At the parusia, according to xv. 51, 52.

We have now dealt with the characteristics of the risen body and its relation to the present body. The question now arises: *When does this resurrection of the body take place?* In conformity with the universal Jewish tradition, the Apostle makes it to follow on the parusia (xv. 51, 52): "We shall not all sleep, but we shall all be changed . . . at the last trump; for the trumpet shall sound, and the dead shall be raised incorruptible." But such a time determination, while fully conformable to the mechanical systems of Judaism, fails to establish an organic connection with the doctrine of the risen body stated above. Hence, unless our interpretation of this doctrine is wholly wrong, its entire trend points not to a period externally determined and at some possibly remote age, but to the hour of departure of the individual believer. The analogy of the seed points in this direction. Seeing that with the corruption of the material husk the vital principle is set free to form a new body or expression of itself, the analogy urged by the Apostle leads to the inference that with the death of the present body the energies of the human spirit are set free to organise from its new environment a spiritual body—a body adapted to that environment. Thus in a certain sense the resurrection of the faithful would follow immediately on death, and not be adjourned to the parusia. Of this variance between his living and growing thought and his inherited Jewish views the Apostle does not seem conscious in 1 Corinthians. In the 2nd Epistle to the Corinthians we shall find that the Apostle has become conscious of the inherent inconsistencies of his former view, which was the traditional one, and abandoned it in favour of the doctrine of a resurrection of the righteous following immediately on death.

On the death of the believer, according to his doctrine of the risen body.

Thus his growing thought conflicts with his inherited.

CHAP. XI.

(*c*) *The Final Consummation.*—With the resurrection of the righteous dead, "each in his own company" (1 Cor. xv. 23), and the transfiguration of the righteous living, death is finally overcome (1 Cor. xv. 26, 51-54). But, death being the last of all enemies, the end has come (xv. 24, i. 8), when the Son will deliver up to God, even the Father, the kingdom which He had ruled since His exaltation. The resurrection[1] of the righteous dead will take place in a moment, at the last trump (xv. 52). Then will follow the transfiguration of the righteous living, when the corruptible will put on incorruption and the mortal immortality (xv. 53). Thereupon begins the perfected kingdom of God[2] in a new and glorious world, which has taken the place of the present, which is already passing away (1 Cor. vii. 31). That which is perfect has then come (xiii. 10), and the blessed in immediate communion see God face to face (xiii. 12).

Kingdom of Christ terminates with the end of this world.

The resurrection synchronises therewith, and thereupon begins the kingdom of God.

In this perfected kingdom God has become "all in all" (xv. 28). This statement is limited to the blessed. It does not apply to the powers in xv. 25, 28. These have been reduced to unwilling obedience.

[1] Seeing that the resurrection is only possible through living fellowship with Christ, there can be no resurrection of the wicked.

[2] The phrase "kingdom of God" is used in St. Paul to denote the kingdom of the consummation, and so as future (1 Cor. vi. 9, 10, xv. 50; Gal. v. 21). In a few cases, however, he applies it to the kingdom as it is at present being realised on earth (1 Cor. iv. 20; Rom. xiv. 17). Yet even here Weiss argues that the passages refer, not to the kingdom of God in its realisation, but in its essence. In Col. i. 13 the present kingdom is called "the kingdom of his dear Son."

Third Period of Development—2 Corinthians and Romans

In these epistles we arrive at the third stage in the development of the Pauline eschatology. This development will be mainly apparent in the Apostle's conscious change of view as to the time of the resurrection, and in his enlarged conceptions as to the universal spread and comprehensiveness of Christ's kingdom on earth. We shall give the chief features of the eschatological teaching of these epistles under the following heads: (*a*) Universal Spread of Christ's kingdom on earth; (*b*) The Parusia and Judgment; (*c*) The Resurrection—the immediate sequel of departure from this life.

This period marked by the Apostle's conscious change of view as to the time of the resurrection and the comprehensiveness of the kingdom.

(*a*) *Universal Spread of Christ's Kingdom on Earth.*—In the interval between the writing of the Epistles to the Thessalonians and that of the Romans we are obliged to assume an essential change in the Apostle's views of the future. In the earlier epistles, as we have seen, the Apostle, under the influence of Jewish inherited beliefs, looked forward to a great apostasy and the revelation of the man of sin as the immediate precursor of the parusia. Thus the history of the world was to close in the culmination of evil and the final impenitence of the bulk of mankind. In Rom. xi., on the other hand, the Apostle proclaims the inner and progressive transformation of mankind through the Gospel, culminating in the conversion of the entire Gentile and

The history of the world to culminate in the conversion of all mankind.

CHAP. XI.

Jewish worlds as the immediate prelude of the advent of Christ. The present generation of unbelieving Jews were indeed as "vessels of wrath" (ix. 22) hastening to destruction. But this temporary rejection of the Jews has become the cause of the fulness of the Gentiles, and when the Gentile world has entered Christ's kingdom then "all Israel shall be saved" (xi. 25). God has thus shaped the history of both Jew and Gentile "in order that he might have mercy upon all" (Rom. xi. 32).

The judgment follows on the parusia.

(*b*) *Parusia and Judgment.*—The parusia is "the day of our Lord Jesus Christ" (2 Cor. i. 14; cf. Phil. i. 6, 10; ii. 16); it is close at hand (Rom. xiii. 11, 12[1]). At this judgment the Judge will be Christ (2 Cor. v. 10)—likewise God (Rom. xiv. 10; see *note*, p. 389). All men must appear before the judgment seat (Rom. xiv. 10), and each render an account of himself to God (xiv. 12). The judgment will proceed according to works (Rom. ii. 6); for, if faith is operative, it can only be in the sphere of works. Moreover, the purpose of the mission of Christ is "that the righteous demands of the law might be fulfilled in us who walk not after the flesh but after the spirit (Rom. viii. 4). We are what we make ourselves. Destiny is related to character as harvest to seed-time (Gal. vi. 7, 8). Every man bears in his character his own reward and his own punishment (2 Cor. v. 10). Hence, since character is the creation of will, arises the all-importance of the principle that rules the will—whether faith or

Judgment according to works, for these determine the real value of the faith.

[1] The hope of surviving is found also in Phil. iii. 21.

unbelief, life to God or life to ourselves. Retribution present and future follows in the line of a man's works (2 Cor. xi. 15[1]).

Special pleading?

No conflict between the doctrine of an immediate resurrection after death and of the final judgment.

The idea of the final judgment is not really at variance with the doctrine of the resurrection following immediately after death, as certain scholars allege. It is a perfectly philosophical idea. It teaches that at the consummation of the universe all rational beings will receive *their due unto the full.* We have above shown that according to the doctrine of the kingdom the individual member cannot reach his consummation apart from the consummation of the blessedness of all. Hence, though the righteous attain to the resurrection immediately after death, they have therein only partially achieved their consummation, which will be realised finally when alike the community and the individual have reached their perfectionment.

(*c*) *The Resurrection—the immediate sequel of departure from this life.*—In the earlier epistles we have sought to show that certain inconsistencies in regard to the time of the resurrection are discoverable, and that, although the Apostle formally adjourns this event to the parusia, in accordance with Jewish eschatology, his teaching with regard to the resurrection body is implicitly at variance with it. During these earlier years the Apostle was still unconscious that he had

[1] The retributive character of the judgment is expressed in still sharper terms in the later epistles. Thus: "he that doeth wrong shall receive again the wrong that he hath done" (Col. iii. 25); "whatsoever good thing each one doeth, the same shall he receive from the Lord" (Eph. vi. 8).

CHAP. XI.

in spirit broken with the traditional belief. In the interval, however, that elapsed between the first and second epistles, he came to a conscious breach with the older view, and henceforth taught the resurrection to be the immediate sequel of departure from this life. The main evidence for this later doctrine of the Apostle is found in 2 Cor. v. 1-8: "We know that if the earthly house of our tabernacle be dissolved, we *have* a building from God, a house not made with hands, eternal, in the heavens. 2. For verily in this we groan, longing to be clothed upon with our habitation which is from heaven: 3. If so be that we shall be found also clothed, not naked. 4. For indeed we that are in this tabernacle do groan, being burdened; not that we would be unclothed, but that we would be clothed upon, that that which is mortal may be swallowed up of life. . . . 6. Knowing that whilst we are at home in the body, we are absent from the Lord. . . . 8. We are willing rather to be absent from the body, and to be at home with the Lord." In ver. 4 the Apostle declares his wish to live to the parusia in order to escape the dissolution of the earthly body and be transformed alive. But in other verses he faces the possibility of death, and comforts himself and his readers with the prospect before them. *When* we die—observe the determination of the point of time —we have (ἔχομεν), we come into possession of, an immortal body in heaven. That this is a *real* and not an *ideal* possession to be realised at the parusia follows from the date assigned for our becoming

New form of doctrine taught in 2 Cor. v. 1-5.

Resurrection of righteous follows at death.

possessed of it. *Ideally*, the faithful receive their immortal bodies from the time of their election,[1] and *actually*, as our text declares, at death.[2] Now this idea of the future body being a divine gift in no way contradicts the teaching in 1 Cor. xv. 35-49, but forms its complement and completion. We have already seen (p. 392, *note* 1) that whereas we should describe the new embodiment of the vital principle in the grain as the result of the action of this principle on its environment, in accordance with divine law, the Apostle describes this process and result wholly in the words "God gives it a body" (1 Cor. xv. 38). Thus, regarded from one standpoint, the new body is the result of a secret vital process; from another, it is a divine gift. Similarly with regard to the glorified body. In one aspect it is the result of the action of the human spirit when quickened by God, in another it is a divine gift. This twofold way of regarding one and the same fact may be exemplified from Gal. vi. 8 and Rom. vi. 23. According to the former passage, eternal life is the harvest of a man's sowing to the Spirit; but according to the latter, it is the gift of God.

The new body is, from one standpoint, the result of the action of the individual spirit; from another, it is a divine gift.

Analogous ways of regarding eternal life.

Thus as 1 Cor. xv. 35-49 implied that the resurrection followed immediately on the death of the faithful, so in 2 Cor. v. 1-8 we have this fact stated categorically. But read on to v. 10: For we must all be made manifest before the judgement seat of Christ that each one may receive the things done in the body

[1] Rom. viii. 29: "whom he foreknew, he also pre-ordained to be conformed to the image of his Son."

[2] St. Paul's doctrine "of the Spirit" (τὸ πνεῦμα) must have contributed in some degree to this change of view; for according to St. Paul's psychology the πνεῦμα is the real bearer of the personality as opposed to the soul.

CHAP. XI.

Further signs of this change of view.

cf 2 Cor 5 10

The resurrection of the righteous at the parusia no longer spoken of, but their revelation.

The views of the Apostle having thus changed in this respect, we should naturally expect to find further evidence of this change in his references to the faithful at the parusia. And such surely we find in Rom. viii. 19: "The earnest longing of the creation waiteth for the revelation of the sons of God." Just as at His second coming there will be a revelation of Christ (1 Cor. i. 7; 2 Thess. i. 7), that is, a manifestation of the glory He already possesses, so likewise there will be a manifestation of the glory *already possessed* by the faithful. Thus the Apostle no longer speaks of a resurrection of the faithful to glory at the parusia,[1] but a manifestation of the glory they already possessed. Glory (δόξα) is to be the clothing of the faithful. This manifestation of Christ and His people at His parusia are expressly connected in Col. iii. 4: "When Christ who is our life shall be revealed, then shall ye also be revealed with him in glory."

The spiritual resurrection of the faithful dwelt upon.

It is, further, noteworthy that, though the Apostle does not speak of the resurrection of the faithful at the parusia, but rather of a revelation of the glory already possessed by them, he speaks in these later epistles of the *spiritual resurrection* of the faithful, an idea, indeed, which is not absent from the earlier.

1 In Rom. viii. 11 it is not a quickening of the dead body that is spoken of, but of the body *which is subject to death* (τὰ θνητὰ σώματα), but not actually dead. In the latter case we should have τὰ νεκρὰ σώματα. Hence we interpret the words of those who shall be alive at the coming of Christ. The parusia is close at hand (Rom. xiii. 11, 12). By the quickening of the "mortal body" (Rom. viii. 11) it becomes immortal. Compare 1 Cor. xv. 54: "when this mortal shall have put on immortality." The hope of being alive at the parusia had not deserted St. Paul when he wrote the Philippians (see iii. 20).

Thus they are already "alive from the dead" (Rom. vi. 13), already "raised with Christ through faith" (Col. ii. 12, iii. 1); yea, "quickened together and raised up," and "made to sit with him in heavenly places" (Eph. ii. 6).

Fourth Period of Development—Philippians, Colossians, Ephesians

In these epistles we have the final stage in the development of the Pauline eschatology, which deals with the cosmic significance of Christ. In the earlier epistles, while the creation of the world was effected through the Son (1 Cor. viii. 6), its consummation was to be realised in the Father, when the Son had resigned His mediatorial kingdom to the Father (1 Cor. xv. 24-28). But in these epistles not only is the Son the creative agent in the universe—"in him were all things created" (Col. i. 17)—not only is He the principle of cohesion and unity whereby it is a cosmos and not a chaos —"in him all things hold together," *συνέστηκεν* (Col. i. 17)—but He is also the end to which they move—"all things were created . . . unto him" *εἰς αὐτόν* (Col. i. 16). He is thus at once the starting-point and the goal of the universe, its creative principle and its final cause, and as such all things are to be summed up in Him as their centre (Eph. i. 10).

Christ not only the creative agent of the universe but also its goal.

From the above Christology follow two conclusions: (*a*) the everlasting duration of the kingdom

CHAP. XI.

of Christ; (*b*) the extension of Christ's redemption to the world of spiritual beings.

Hence (*a*) Christ's kingdom is no longer temporary, but one and the same with the eternal kingdom of God;

(*a*) *The everlasting duration of the kingdom of Christ.*—Whereas God alone is "all in all" in the final consummation, according to 1 Cor. xv. 28, in the present epistles Christ too is conceived as "all in all" (Eph. i. 23; Col. iii. 11), and so the goal of the universe is no longer the completed kingdom of God, in which God is "all in all" in contrast to the mediatorial kingdom of Christ (1 Cor. xv. 24-28), but the end towards which the entire universe is advancing is the "kingdom of Christ and God" (Eph. v. 5[1]).

(*b*) and Christ's atonement is extended from mankind to the spiritual world.

(*b*) *The extension of Christ's redemption to the world of spiritual beings.*— Since all things, in heaven and earth, visible and invisible, whether thrones or dominions or principalities or powers, were created by Christ (Col. i. 16), and, according to the same passage, were to find their consummation in Him (ἔκτισται εἰς αὐτόν), they must therefore come within the sphere of His mediatorial activity; they must ultimately be summed up in Christ as their Head, ἀνακεφαλαιώσασθαι τὰ πάντα ἐν τῷ Χριστῷ (Eph. i. 10). Hence, since in the world of spiritual beings some have sinned or apostatised, they too must share in the Atonement of the Cross of Christ, and so obtain reconciliation[2] (Col. i. 19, 20):

[1] In 2 Tim. iv. 1 this kingdom is called the kingdom of Jesus Christ. It is a kingdom, not of this world but a heavenly one (2 Tim. iv. 18). The final judgment is referred to as "that day" (2 Tim. i. 12, 18; iv. 8), or generally as "judgment" (1 Tim. v. 24). Christ is Judge (2 Tim. iv. 1, 8).

[2] It is absurd to say that it is the good angels who are spoken of here.

"For it was the good pleasure (of the Father) that in him should all the fulness dwell; and through him to reconcile all things unto himself, having made peace through the blood of his cross; through him (I say), whether things upon the earth or things in the heavens"; these having been reconciled, should join in the universal worship of the Son (Phil. ii. 10). How successful this ministry of reconciliation in the spiritual world is, the Apostle does not inform us, nor yet whether it will embrace this entire world, *i.e.* the angels of Satan. Since, however, all things must be reconciled and summed up in Christ, there can be no room finally in the universe for a wicked being, whether human or angelic. Thus the Pauline eschatology points[1] obviously, in its ultimate issues, either to the final redemption of all created personal beings[2] or—and this seems the true alternative—to the destruction of the finally impenitent. But this destruction would not be of the nature of an external punishment, but subjective and self-executed.

Since all things must finally be summed up in Christ, either all created personal beings must be redeemed or the finally impenitent destroyed through subjective and self-executed judgment.

The text can only refer to rebellious or fallen angels; for the word "reconciliation" necessarily presupposes previous enmity (see Eph. ii. 16), and no less so does the phrase in the text, "having made peace through the blood of the cross." (See Sanday on Rom. viii. 38.) On St. Paul's belief in the seven heavens and the presence of evil in them, see Morfill and Charles's *Book of the Secrets of Enoch*, pp. xl.-xlii.

[1] The Apostle appears, in these later epistles no less than in the former, not to have arrived at final and consistent views on these questions. For though he speaks of the reconciliation of hostile spirits, he does not seem to have included Satan's angels amongst them, but his leading principles involve this.

[2] It is generally agreed that the doctrine of Christ's preaching to the spirits in Sheol is referred to in Eph. iv. 9, 10.

CHAP. XI.

Development of Special Conceptions

Soul and Spirit.—We shall treat these conceptions under two heads: (*a*) as found in the Gospels and the other books of the New Testament save the Pauline Epistles; (*b*) as found in the Pauline Epistles.

(*a*) The meaning attached to these conceptions by all the books of the New Testament, save the Pauline Epistles, is in the main that which prevailed among the people.

The soul = the bearer of the sensuous life.

The Soul.—The soul is conceived as the bearer of the bodily-sensuous life, and also of the emotions and of the higher spiritual life. As the former, it is sustained by food (Matt. vi. 25), is capable of sensuous impressions (Mark xiv. 34). If the blood is shed the soul departs. Thus ἐκψύχειν = to die (Acts v. 5, 10; xii. 23). Further, the soul is identified with the personality, as in the Old Testament. Thus so many souls = so many persons (Acts ii. 41, vii. 14, xxvii. 37; 1 Peter iii. 20). But in the New Testament, just as in the Judaism of that and the preceding generations, the soul is the seat of the emotions and of the higher spiritual life also. Thus it is the subject of fear (Acts ii. 43), of grief (Matt. xxvi. 38; Mark xiv. 34; Luke ii. 35), of trouble (John xii. 27), of rest (Matt. xi. 29), of pleasure (Matt. xii. 18; Heb. x. 38), of love (Matt. xxii. 37), of hate (Acts xiv. 2). In a spiritual sense it can become stronger (Acts

Soul = person.

The soul = the seat of the emotions,

xiv. 22) or weaker (Heb. xii. 3); it can be subverted by heresy (Acts xv. 24), or entrapped into sensuality (1 Peter ii. 11; 2 Peter ii. 14). It is probably from this conception of the soul that the adjective ψυχικός derives its bad signification in James iii. 15; Jude 19). Again, the soul, in the higher conception of the word, can be cleansed (1 Peter i. 22), and preserved from evil (1 Peter iv. 19; Heb. xiii. 17). By the sacrifice of its lower and sensual life it can attain to the higher and eternal life (Matt. x. 39, xvi. 25 (= Mark viii. 35 = Luke ix. 24), John xii. 25). Thus it is capable of eternal salvation (Heb. x. 39; James i. 21, v. 20; 1 Peter i. 9, ii. 11, 25; Luke xxi. 19). Surviving death (Matt. x. 28), it passes first to an intermediate abode of the departed. This abode is in either the blessed department of Hades (Acts ii. 27), called Abraham's bosom (Luke xvi. 23), or in the unblest part of Hades (Luke xvi. 23). According to Rev. vi. 9, the souls of martyrs are beneath the altar in heaven. In the next life the departed are designated "souls" (Rev. vi. 9, xx. 4). As the bearer of the entire spiritual personality after death, the soul is in this sense *identical with the spirit*, as we shall see from the next section.

and of the spiritual life.

The bearer of the entire spiritual personality before and after death, and herein identical with the spirit.

The Spirit.—In the case of the spirit, as in that of the soul, we find—with possibly two or three exceptions—no fresh developments, but only the acknowledged and popular conceptions of Judaism. The spirit is the higher side of the soul. Like the soul, it is the subject of grief (Mark viii. 12), of trouble (John xiii. 21), of joy (Luke i. 47, x. 21), of

The spirit = the seat of the emotions,

CHAP. XI.

indignation (John xi. 33; Acts xvii. 16), of zeal (Acts xviii. 25), of meekness (1 Peter iii. 4). It is the seat of purpose and volition (Acts xix. 21, xx. 22). Again, as with the soul, if the spirit departs, death ensues (Matt. xxvii. 50; Luke xxiii. 46; Acts vii. 59); the body apart from it is dead (James ii. 26); but if it returns, so does life (Luke viii. 55). Thus ἐκπνέειν (Mark xv. 37, 39; Luke xxiii. 46) is synonymous with ἐκψύχειν.

also of volition.

Spirit = bearer of personality after death.

But the spirit, like the soul, exists independently after death as the bearer of the personality. Though the same or similar diction is found in the Old Testament and in a few of the later books, the idea conveyed in either case is absolutely different. The New Testament usage is that of the current Judaism.[1] In the next life the departed are called "spirits" (1 Peter iii. 19, iv. 6; Heb. xii. 23), as elsewhere they are called "souls." Thus in this respect *the terms "soul" and "spirit" are identical.*

Spirit and soul identical terms in all books of New Testament save Pauline Epistles.

But the spirit is the seat also of the higher spiritual life. Man is described as a synthesis of the spirit, so conceived, and of the flesh (Mark xiv. 38). Since in Matt. x. 28 he is regarded as a synthesis of the soul and body, it is clear that here also spirit and soul are interchangeable terms. Growth in the spirit is set over against growth in the body (Luke i. 80, ii. 40). The spirit which God has placed in man longeth for man's salvation

[1] According to Gen. ii., iii., the spirit is a breath of life from God, which on death returns to God, the Fount of Life (Eccl. xii. 7). As such it has no individual or personal existence. In Rev. xi. 11, xiii. 15 the diction of Gen. ii., iii. is reproduced.

(James iv. 5). It discerneth that which is not manifest to the senses (Mark ii. 8). In these cases we have approaches to the Pauline use.

No trichotomy in these books.

There is no trichotomy in the New Testament outside the Pauline Epistles. The only doubtful passage is Heb. iv. 12.

Pauline use of terms "soul" and "spirit" different from that of rest of New Testament.

In the Pauline Epistles St. Paul breaks with the entire traditional use of the terms "soul" and "body," and gives them a new connotation, and yet not wholly new, as we shall discover presently. His views take their origin in a fresh study of Gen. ii., iii., and his doctrines of the soul and spirit are developed more or less directly from the psychology of these chapters. His doctrine of the soul may be said to be directly founded on Gen. ii., iii., that of the spirit indirectly. Now first as to the soul, we discover that the teaching has been adopted almost without change. He appeals to Gen. ii. 7 as the foundation of his argument on the nature of the soulish body in 1 Cor. xv. 45. According to Gen. ii., iii., the soul is regarded as the supreme function of the body quickened by the spirit.[1] So conceived it naturally perishes on the withdrawal of the latter. It has, therefore, no existence in the next life. And such, in fact, appears to be the view of the Apostle. The soul, he holds, is the vital principle of the flesh (σάρξ). Hence the epithets "fleshly" and "soulish" (σαρκικός and ψυχικός) over against "spiritual" (πνευματικός) are taken

Doctrine of soul—based on Gen. ii., iii.

Soul—is a function of the body, and perishes with it.

[1] As the supreme function of the body it would, logically conceived, embrace all the intellectual powers, like the ψυχή of the Greek philosophers. But St. Paul does not so accept it. To him it is essentially the transitory element in man.

CHAP. XI.

to be synonymous (1 Cor. xv. 44, 46). The soulish or natural man (ψυχικὸς ἄνθρωπος) is incapable of receiving the things of the spirit. The soul is never conceived *as the bearer of a higher spiritual life* by St. Paul. Further, he never speaks, as almost all the other writers of the New Testament do, of *the salvation of the soul* save in one instance in his first epistle (1 Thess. v. 23), which scholars are agreed in regarding only as a popular statement, and not as an expression of the Apostle's own psychology.

The spirit—not the soul—is to be saved.

It is true, indeed, that the all but universal usage is to connect the term "salvation" not with any one part of man, but with man in his essence. In one passage, however, he speaks of the saving of the spirit (1 Cor. v. 5), no doubt as forming the essential element in man. Now in such a passage the Apostle could not have spoken of the saving of the soul; for though according to the current view he describes man as a synthesis of "spirit and flesh" (Col. ii. 5) and "spirit and body" (1 Cor. v. 3), he never uses the still more popular expression "soul and body." Again, that according to St. Paul the soul belongs wholly to the sphere of this life follows also from his teaching on the soulish body and the spiritual body. The whole after-life of the faithful belongs to the spiritual sphere. They are spirits clothed in spiritual bodies.

The existence of the soul appears, therefore, to be confined to this life. The soul is the bearer of the bodily life in the Pauline epistles as in the rest of the New Testament (cf. Rom. xvi. 4; 2 Cor. xii.

15; Phil. ii. 30). It is menaced when a man's life is sought (Rom. xi. 3). It is the bearer of the personality in a general sense (Rom. xiii. 1, ii. 9).

Doctrine of spirit starts from Gen. ii., iii.—not, however, of the human spirit as such, but of the Holy Spirit infused into the faithful.

The Pauline doctrine of the spirit is beset with difficulties. Since, however, we know that the Apostle had Gen. ii., iii. continually in his thoughts, it will be best to start from the doctrine of the spirit in these chapters in our attempt to learn the Pauline doctrine. Now in Gen. ii., iii. the spirit which quickens the material body is the breath of God. Thereby all *physical* life is derived from God. Similarly St. Paul teaches that all *spiritual* life is likewise sprung immediately from God—in each case a new creation—a spiritual one (2 Cor. v. 17; Gal. vi. 15), as opposed to the soulish or psychical creation in Gen. ii. 7 (1 Cor. xv. 45).

This new creation is due to the entrance of God's Spirit into man, which henceforth becomes a divine immanent principle within man, dwelling in him (1 Cor. iii. 16; Rom. viii. 9, 11), and making thereby the individual man a temple of God (1 Cor. iii. 16, 17). In these passages, as well as Rom. viii. 14; 1 Cor. vi. 11, vii. 40, xii. 3, the spirit is regarded as God's Spirit dwelling in and influencing the faithful, and is not identified with the human spirit. The presence of the Spirit is essential to man's *spiritual* life, just as the "breath of life" is to the *psychical* existence. But since this Spirit may finally withdraw from man if he is unfaithful, and since the unfaithful man survives death, we have still to inquire wherein consists the immaterial part

CHAP. XI.

of man. It cannot be in the soul, as we have seen above.

Part of the Pauline psychology drawn from Palestinean and part from Hellenistic Judaism.

Thus far the analogy of the spiritual creation to the psychical in Gen. ii. 7 is perfect, but does not admit of further development. Gen. ii., iii. has helped the Apostle to formulate the doctrine of the spiritual creation of man by the infusion and indwelling of the Holy Spirit, but, if he would set forth the complex internal nature of man, he must perforce resort to popular Palestinean Judaism, or else to Hellenistic, for his conceptions and terminology. In actual fact he has recourse to both. The conceptions and terminology in question deal with (1) the higher nature of man as an intellectual and moral being, and (2) the immaterial personality of man as surviving death. For the former the Apostle has recourse to the world of Hellenistic Judaism. Hence he borrows the phrase "the inner man" (ὁ ἔσω ἄνθρωπος). This phrase goes back to Plato, *Rep.* ix. 589 A (ὁ ἐντὸς ἄνθρωπος), and appears in various forms in Philo; ἄνθρωπος ἐν ἀνθρώπῳ (Mangey, p. 533) and ἄνθρωπος ὁ ἐν ἑκάστῳ ἡμῶν τίς ἂν εἴη πλὴν ὁ νοῦς (*De Agric.* § 2). Its equivalent is found in 1 Peter iii. 4 (ὁ κρυπτὸς τῆς καρδίας ἄνθρωπος). The Pauline phrase has no reference to man as created anew or otherwise, but denotes him simply as an intellectual and moral personality. From the same source St. Paul adopts the term "mind" (νοῦς), which belongs to "the inner man" and signifies *the higher nature of man as man.* In this sense the Apostle employs also the term

Higher nature of man as man expressed according to Hellenistic Judaism as "the inner man" and the "mind," "spirit," after a current usage of Palestinean Judaism. Accordingly, we find the ordinary synthesis of "spirit and body" (1 Cor. v. 3) and of "spirit and flesh" (Col. ii. 5), just as in Rom. vii. 25 the synthesis of "mind" and "flesh" is presupposed. In this sense also St. Paul writes: "His spirit hath been refreshed by you all" (2 Cor. vii. 13), and again in 1 Cor. ii. 11: "Who among men knoweth the things of a man save the spirit of the man, which is in him?" Since this spirit is human and finite, it is capable of suffering. Hence we find in 2 Cor. ii. 13, "I had no relief for my spirit" (*οὐκ ἔσχηκα ἄνησιν τῷ πνεύματί μου*), just as elsewhere in vii. 5, "Our flesh had no relief" (*οὐδεμίαν ἔσχηκεν ἄνεσιν ἡ σὰρξ ἡμῶν*).

as "the spirit" according to Palestinean Judaism.

In this sense "the mind" or "spirit" can receive refreshment, knowledge; can suffer, become reprobate, and defiled.

But the higher side of man's nature, whether we term it "mind"[1] or "spirit," may fall under the power of the "flesh." Thus "the mind" can become vain (Eph. iv. 17) or "corrupt" (Rom. i. 28), or the slave of the flesh (Col. ii. 18), and "the spirit" can become defiled (*μολυσμοῦ . . . πνεύματος*), 2 Cor. vii. 1.

(2) Next in order to denote man as an immaterial personality surviving death the Apostle is obliged to have recourse to Palestinean psychology. In this sense he adopts the term "spirit," as we see in 1 Cor. v. 5, where he directs the Corinthian Church to deliver the incestuous person "unto

The human personality which survives death expressed by the term "spirit."

[1] By the mind the natural man can know God through creation (Rom. i. 20), and feels the obligation of obedience to His will (Rom. vii. 25), but without divine renewal cannot gain the mastery over the flesh.

CHAP. XI.

Satan for the destruction of the flesh, that *the spirit* may be saved in the day of the Lord Jesus."

Third meaning of term "spirit"—essentially Pauline = human faculty for divine communion created anew by God.

(3) We have only to notice one more sense of the term "spirit" as employed by St. Paul. In the two preceding uses he has simply followed the psychology of the time. But this third sense of the word is distinctly his own.

The spirit so conceived is *that part of man's immaterial nature which is capable of direct communion with the Spirit* (Rom. viii. 16), *but not this faculty as it exists by itself, but as it is recreated by God.* In this sense the spirit is no longer synonymous with the mind, but is the suzerain of the latter. Unless the mind is obedient to the spirit so conceived, it becomes corrupt (see above). The difference of the mind and of the spirit in this third sense is brought out in 1 Cor. xiv. 14, 15: "For if I pray in a tongue, my spirit prayeth, but my mind is unfruitful. What is it then? I will pray with the spirit, and I will pray with the mind also." The mind still exists in the spiritual man as he deals with matters of human judgment.

The spirit in this sense to be distinguished from the mind.

The renewed spirit is "our spirit," and lives in communion with the Spirit of God (Rom. viii. 16). By virtue of it man becomes spiritual (1 Cor. ii. 15, iii. 1).

Points of agreement and disagreement between the Pauline and Philonic psychologies.

Since the psychology of Paul has certain external resemblances to that of Philo, we shall notice some of the points wherein they agree and wherein they differ. Philo presents the usual Hellenistic dualism of soul (ψυχή, called also νοῦς) and body (σῶμα and σάρξ). Man's nature has two sides. Each has its own distinct faculty—an animal soul and a rational soul. The animal soul has its seat in the blood, and, subsequently to its first creation, is due to human generation, but the rational soul comes direct from God to all men as the πνεῦμα (*Quod deterius*, §§ 22-24). The rational soul (called νοῦς or διάνοια, ψυχή or πνεῦμα) possesses intellect and freedom of will, and can fulfil the law, if it will. St. Paul differs herein from Philo in teaching that man is incapable of fulfilling the divine law since, though he has νοῦς, he has not the *divinely renewed* πνεῦμα. The enmity of the mind and of the flesh comes to consciousness at the age of seven according to Philo, but according to St. Paul, as soon as we come to the knowledge of law.

Since the body is only the tomb of the soul according to Philo, it—no less than the flesh—is the foe of the soul. But from this foe the soul of the righteous is delivered by death. According to the Apostle, on the other hand, though the flesh is in antagonism with the spirit, there is no such antagonism between the body and the spirit. Nay, rather the body is indispensable to the completed well-being of the latter. A bodiless human spirit is "naked," is in a state of weakness and deprivation.

Places of Abode of the Departed

Paradise.—(i.) The abode of the blessed *in Hades* (Luke xxiii. 43; Acts ii. 31). (ii.) A division of *the*

Paradise (i.) and (ii.) an intermediate

CHAP. XI.

abode, (iii.) a final abode.

third heaven, being likewise an intermediate abode of the righteous (2 Cor. xii. 4). (iii.) Apparently a final abode of the righteous (Rev. ii. 7).

Hades = intermediate abode (i.) of departed, (ii.) of wicked only, (iii.) a place of further probation.

Hades.—(i.) Intermediate abode of the departed, with two divisions for the righteous (= Abraham's bosom) and the wicked respectively (Luke xvi. 23). (ii.) Intermediate abode of the wicked only (?) (Rev. i. 18; xx. 13, 14). (iii.) Intermediate abode of further moral probation (1 Peter iii. 19, iv. 6), (see p. 378).

Tartarus.—The intermediate place of punishment for the fallen angels (2 Peter ii. 4).

Gehenna—the final place of punishment for the souls of the wicked.

Gehenna.—Final place of punishment for the wicked, and apparently a place of spiritual punishment only.[1] In Luke xii. 5 it is clearly only a punishment of the soul that is referred to, and not of the body; for the body is first destroyed on earth: "Fear him which after he hath killed hath power to cast into Gehenna." This passage is found also in Matt. x. 28, but in a different form. "Fear him which is able to destroy both soul and body in Gehenna." The more original form of the statement seems to be given in Luke xii. 5. Otherwise we may explain the destruction of the soul and body with Weiss in connection with the impending judgment which would take effect on the current generation. Again in Matt. v. 29, 30, we cannot necessarily conclude to a punishment of the body; for since in these verses "eye" and "hand"

[1] I herewith withdraw the interpretation of Gehenna given in Hastings' *Bible Dictionary*, ii. 120, as a final place of corporal punishment.

are used only symbolically of certain desires, the most natural interpretation is to take the phrase "the whole body" likewise symbolically. From the above considerations Gehenna appears to be a place not of corporal but of spiritual punishment.

Called also "the furnace of fire," "the outer darkness,"

Gehenna is a region of fire (Matt. v. 22, xviii. 9), of unquenchable fire (Mark ix. 43), a furnace of fire (Matt. xiii. 42, 50). It is probably to be identified also with "the outer darkness" (Matt. viii. 12, xxii. 13, xxv. 30). It appears as "the lake of fire" in Rev. xix. 20; xx. 14, 15, "the lake of fire and brimstone" (Rev. xx. 10), into which are cast the beast and the false prophets (Rev. xix. 20); the devil, (xx. 10), death and Hades (xx. 14), and all whose names were not written in the book of life.

"the lake of fire."

Some Recent Bibliography.—Wendt, *The Teaching of Jesus* (transl. from the German), 1893; Weiss, *Lehrbuch d. bibl. Theologie des N.T.*,[6] 1895 (there is an English translation of the third edition); Beyschlag, *New Testament Theology* (transl. from the German), 1896; Holtzmann, *NTliche Theologie*, 1897; Stevens, *Theology of the New Testament*, 1899; also Farrar, *Eternal Hope* (3rd ed.), 1879; *Mercy and Judgment*, 1881; Pusey, *What is of Faith as to Everlasting Punishment*, 1881; Davidson, *Doctrine of Last Things*, 1882; Plumptre, *The Spirits in Prison*, 1884; Russell, *The Parusia* (new ed.), 1887; White, *The Life of Christ;* Petavel-Olliff, *Problems of Immortality* (transl. from the French), 1892; Kabisch, *Eschatologie des Paulus*, 1893; Haupt, *Aussagen Jesus in d. synopt. Evangelien*, 1894; Chambers, *Our Life after Death*, 1894; Briggs, *The Messiah of the Gospels*, 1894; *The Messiah of the Apostles*, 1895; Teichmann, *Die Paulinischen Vorstellungen von Auferstehung und Gericht*, 1896; Salmond, *Christian Doctrine of Immortality*,[2] 1896; Beet, *The Last Things*, 1897; Schmidt, *Die Lehre des Apostels Paulus*, 1897; Dalman, *Die Worte Jesu*, 1898; Art. "Eschatology," by the present writer, in *Encyclopædia Biblica*.

INDEX

THE END

Printed by R. & R. Clark, Limited, *Edinburgh.*

WORKS BY REV. R. H. CHARLES.

THE APOCALYPSE OF BARUCH.

TRANSLATED FROM THE SYRIAC.

Crown 8vo. Cloth. Price 7s. 6d. net.

"Mr. Charles's last work will have a hearty welcome from students of Syriac whose interest is linguistic, and from theological students who have learned the value of Jewish and Christian pseudepigraphy; and the educated general reader will find much of high interest in it, regard being had to its date and its theological standpoint."—*Record.*

"Mr. Charles has in this work followed up the admirable editions of other pieces of apocalyptic literature with an edition equally admirable. Some of the notes on theological or other points of special interest are very full and instructive. The whole work is an honour to English scholarship. . . . The work before us is one that no future student of the apocalyptic literature will be able to neglect, and students of the New Testament or the contemporary Jewish thought will find much to interest them in it."—*Primitive Methodist Quarterly Review.*

"As is intimated in the title-page, the Syriac text, based on ten MSS., from which the Epistle of Baruch is translated, is included in the volume. The learned footnotes which accompany the translation throughout will be found most helpful to the reader. Indeed, nothing seems to have been left undone which could make this ancient writing intelligible to the student."—*Scotsman.*

"To say that this is *the* edition of the Apocalypse of Baruch is to say nothing. Let us say that it is an edition which alone would give an editor a name to live."—*Expository Times.*

THE ASSUMPTION OF MOSES.

Translated from the Latin Sixth Century MS., the unemended Text of which is published herewith, together with the Text in its restored and critically emended form.

WITH INTRODUCTION, NOTES, AND INDICES.

Crown 8vo. Cloth. Price 7s. 6d.

"In this admirable little book the Rev. R. H. Charles has added another to the excellent series of editions by which he has earned the gratitude of all students of early Christian literature."—*Times.*

"Nothing has been left undone by the author which could contribute to the settling of the text, the elucidation of the general purpose of the book, and the interpretation of particular passages. In short, it is worthy to rank with his edition of the 'Apocalypse of Baruch,' and higher praise than that could hardly be given."—*Primitive Methodist Quarterly Review.*

"If ever man found his vocation in life, it is Mr. Charles. He is at home and happy among these unknown apocryphal authors, as you or I might be with Isaiah or St. Paul, and he sees to it that the edition of their works he publishes is better than any edition that has gone before. There have been editions of the Assumption of Moses before; there is no edition that one would dream of buying now but this."—*Expository Times.*

"The Rev. R. H. Charles's edition of 'The Assumption of Moses' adds another to the number of valuable books which he has given to students of the non-canonical scriptures of the Jews."—*Scotsman.*

A. & C. BLACK, SOHO SQUARE, LONDON.